IMMATERIALITY AND EARLY MODERN
ENGLISH LITERATURE

EDINBURGH CRITICAL STUDIES IN SHAKESPEARE AND PHILOSOPHY
Series Editor: Kevin Curran

Edinburgh Critical Studies in Shakespeare and Philosophy takes seriously the speculative and world-making properties of Shakespeare's art. Maintaining a broad view of 'philosophy' that accommodates first-order questions of metaphysics, ethics, politics and aesthetics, the series also expands our understanding of philosophy to include the unique kinds of theoretical work carried out by performance and poetry itself. These scholarly monographs will reinvigorate Shakespeare studies by opening new interdisciplinary conversations among scholars, artists and students.

Published Titles
Rethinking Shakespeare's Political Philosophy: From Lear to Leviathan
Alex Schulman
Shakespeare in Hindsight: Counterfactual Thinking and Shakespearean Tragedy
Amir Khan
Second Death: Theatricalities of the Soul in Shakespeare's Drama
Donovan Sherman
Shakespeare's Fugitive Politics
Thomas P. Anderson
Is Shylock Jewish?: Citing Scripture and the Moral Agency of Shakespeare's Jews
Sara Coodin
Chaste Value: Economic Crisis, Female Chastity and the Production of Social Difference on Shakespeare's Stage
Katherine Gillen
Shakespearean Melancholy: Philosophy, Form and the Transformation of Comedy
J. F. Bernard
Shakespeare's Moral Compass
Neema Parvini
Shakespeare and the Fall of the Roman Republic: Selfhood, Stoicism and Civil War
Patrick Gray
Revenge Tragedy and Classical Philosophy on the Early Modern Stage
Christopher Crosbie
Shakespeare and the Truth-Teller: Confronting the Cynic Ideal
David Hershinow
Derrida Reads Shakespeare
Chiara Alfano
Conceiving Desire: Metaphor, Cognition and Eros in Lyly and Shakespeare
Gillian Knoll
Immateriality and Early Modern English Literature: Shakespeare, Donne, Herbert
James A. Knapp

Forthcoming Titles
Making Publics in Shakespeare's Playhouse
Paul Yachnin
The Play and the Thing: A Phenomenology of Shakespearean Theatre
Matthew Wagner
Shakespeare's Staging of the Self: The Reformation and Protestant Hermenuetics
Roberta Kwan

For further information please visit our website at: edinburghuniversitypress.com/series/ecsst

IMMATERIALITY AND EARLY MODERN ENGLISH LITERATURE

Shakespeare, Donne, Herbert

◆ ◆ ◆

JAMES A. KNAPP

EDINBURGH
University Press

Edinburgh University Press is one of the leading university presses in the UK. We publish academic books and journals in our selected subject areas across the humanities and social sciences, combining cutting-edge scholarship with high editorial and production values to produce academic works of lasting importance. For more information visit our website: edinburghuniversitypress.com

Edinburgh University Press Ltd
The Tun – Holyrood Road
12(2f) Jackson's Entry
Edinburgh EH8 8PJ

First published in hardback by Edinburgh University Press 2020

Typeset in 12/15 Adobe Sabon by
IDSUK (DataConnection) Ltd

A CIP record for this book is available from the British Library

ISBN 978 1 4744 5710 1 (hardback)
ISBN 978 1 4744 5711 8 (paperback)
ISBN 978 1 4744 5712 5 (webready PDF)
ISBN 978 1 4744 5713 2 (epub)

CONTENTS

PART III: THINKING

8. Cognition and Its Objects, or Ideas and the Substance
   of Spirit(s)   287

9. 'Thinking makes it so': Mind, Body and Spirit in
   The Rape of Lucrece, Hamlet and *Much Ado
   About Nothing*   320

10. 'Neither Fish nor Flesh, nor Good Red Herring':
    Phenomenality, Representation and Experience in
    The Tempest   358

Coda   391

Bibliography   394
Index   417

ACKNOWLEDGEMENTS

Writing this book required the support, knowledge and wisdom of a great many people. In the years since I began thinking about immateriality I have had conversations that shaped the project in ways I never could have envisioned on my own. I am especially indebted to those who read and commented on individual chapters of the manuscript, including Andrew Cutrofello, Joe Csicsila, Hanne Jacobs, Tim Harrison and Richard Strier. Gary Kuchar read a significant portion of the book, always offering invaluable guidance, and Scott Trudell heroically read through the complete manuscript while I was in the final stage of the project. These acts of intellectual kindness undoubtedly saved me from missteps and inaccuracies, helped me to focus my argument, and confirmed my faith in the collaborative spirit of the scholarly community.

The members of the SAA (Shakespeare Association of America) seminar I led on the topic of 'The Shakespearean Immaterial' in 2010 contributed to my thinking in important ways, as did those in the seminar entitled 'Shakespeare and the Power of the Face' in 2012. I have had many fruitful conversations about the project with scholars at SAA and RSA (Renaissance Society of America) while working on the book. In particular I would like to thank Sibylle Baumbach, Joe Campana, Chris Crosbie, Michelle Dowd, Patricia Fumerton, David Goldstein, Wendy Hyman, Jim Kearney, Julia Lupton,

Arthur Marotti, Steve Mentz, Richard Preiss, Alfred Thomas, Henry Turner, Jen Waldron and Will West.

I am also grateful to have had the opportunity to present a version of Chapter 3 to the Chicago Area Renaissance Seminar and to the members of that group for their helpful comments. The fruits of conversations there with David Bevington, Gina Buccola, Bradin Cormack, Lara Crowley, Tim Crowley, Paul Hecht, Megan Heffernan, Ada Palmer, David Simon and Michael Murrin surely made their way into the book. Jim Kearney was kind enough to invite me to present an earlier version of the book's final chapter at the Annual Conference of the Early Modern Center at the University of California Santa Barbara. The feedback I received there as well as the many contributions of collaborators on conference panels and essay collections over the years have been invaluable to the project. I owe a particular thanks to Jennifer Bates, Paul Cefalu, Carla Della Gatta, Mary Floyd-Wilson, David Hawkes, Ken Jackson, Laurie Johnson, Sean Lawrence, Kent Lenhoff, Carla Mazzio, Simon Palfrey, Jan Purnis, Mike Witmore, Karen Raber, Kellie Robertson, Michael Schoenfeldt, Bruce Smith, Matt Smith, John Sutton, Adam Rzepka, Evelyn Tribble and Jessica Wolfe.

The generous support of my colleagues at Loyola University Chicago has enriched the project from its start. I would especially like to thank David Chinitz, Jeff Glover, Suzanne Gossett, Steve Jones, Chris Kendrick, Jack Kerkering, Michael Shapiro, Virginia Strain, Joyce Wexler and Edward Wheatley. The Edward L. Surtz Professorship at Loyola supported early stages of my research at the Folger Shakespeare Library, and a Faculty Research Fellowship from the Hank Center for the Catholic Heritage at Loyola allowed me to continue my work at the British Library. Support from Loyola also came in the form of a Faculty Leave in the fall of 2017 that was crucial as I was completing the manuscript.

Throughout the project graduate students in a series of seminars helped me see the project in new light, most memorably Stephanie Kuscera, Devon Maddon, Mark Owen and Anna Ullman. As a research assistant, David Macey uncovered a surprising range of oddities from the archive that bolstered my argument about the period's interest in the immaterial.

Versions of some of this material appeared in early forms in several edited collections. An early version of Chapter 3 was published in *Shakespeare and Continental Philosophy*, edited by Jennifer Bates and Richard Wilson (Edinburgh University Press, 2014); Chapter 4 is a revised version of an essay first published as '"'Tis insensible then?": Language and Action in *1 Henry IV*', in *The Return to Theory in Early Modern English Literature, Volume 2*, edited by Paul Cefalu, Gary Kuchar and Bryan Reynolds (Palgrave Macmillan, 2014), reproduced with permission of Palgrave Macmillan; and an earlier version of the material on *Much Ado* in Chapter 9 appeared as 'Mental Bodies in *Much Ado About Nothing*', in *Embodied Cognition and Shakespeare's Theater: The Early Modern Body-Mind*, edited by Laurie Johnson, John Sutton and Evelyn Tribble (Routledge, 2014).

I am grateful to Kevin Curran, Michelle Huston and the anonymous readers at Edinburgh University Press for their support and guidance in bringing the project to print. In addition to developing this important series, Kevin was supportive at all stages of the process. Michelle's careful stewardship and flexibility were always on display and took all mystery out of the process. And Ersev Ersoy made navigating the many stages of the publication process as smooth as could be imagined.

My greatest debt is to my family. My parents, James F. and Peggy Ann Knapp, read the entire manuscript and offered criticism and support in equal measure. My children, Celia,

Eli and Riley, understood the project and humoured me when I found resonances of the immaterial in every Shakespeare production we attended. I could not have written the book without the support of my wife Kate. This book is dedicated her, without whom it would have come to nothing.

SERIES EDITOR'S PREFACE

Picture Macbeth alone on stage, staring intently into empty space. 'Is this a dagger which I see before me?' he asks, grasping decisively at the air. On one hand, this is a quintessentially theatrical question. At once an object and a vector, the dagger describes the possibility of knowledge ('Is this a dagger') in specifically visual and spatial terms ('which I see before me'). At the same time, Macbeth is posing a quintessentially philosophical question, one that assumes knowledge to be both conditional and experiential, and that probes the relationship between certainty and perception as well as intention and action. It is from this shared ground of art and enquiry, of theatre and theory, that this series advances its basic premise: Shakespeare is philosophical.

It seems like a simple enough claim. But what does it mean exactly, beyond the parameters of this specific moment in *Macbeth*? Does it mean that Shakespeare had something we could think of as his own philosophy? Does it mean that he was influenced by particular philosophical schools, texts and thinkers? Does it mean, conversely, that modern philosophers have been influenced by him, that Shakespeare's plays and poems have been, and continue to be, resources for philosophical thought and speculation?

The answer is 'yes' all around. These are all useful ways of conceiving a philosophical Shakespeare and all point to lines of enquiry that this series welcomes. But Shakespeare is philosophical in a much more fundamental way as well. Shakespeare is philosophical because the plays and poems actively create new worlds of knowledge and new scenes of ethical encounter. They ask big questions, make bold arguments and develop new vocabularies in order to think what might otherwise be unthinkable. Through both their scenarios and their imagery, the plays and poems engage the qualities of consciousness, the consequences of human action, the phenomenology of motive and attention, the conditions of personhood and the relationship among different orders of reality and experience. This is writing and dramaturgy, moreover, that consistently experiments with a broad range of conceptual crossings, between love and subjectivity, nature and politics, and temporality and form.

Edinburgh Critical Studies in Shakespeare and Philosophy takes seriously these speculative and world-making dimensions of Shakespeare's work. The series proceeds from a core conviction that art's capacity to think – to formulate, not just reflect, ideas – is what makes it urgent and valuable. Art matters because unlike other human activities it establishes its own frame of reference, reminding us that all acts of creation – biological, political, intellectual and amorous – are grounded in imagination. This is a far cry from business-as-usual in Shakespeare studies. Because historicism remains the methodological gold standard of the field, far more energy has been invested in exploring what Shakespeare once meant than in thinking rigorously about what Shakespeare continues to make possible. In response, Edinburgh Critical Studies in Shakespeare and Philosophy pushes back against the critical orthodoxies of historicism and cultural studies to clear a space for scholarship that confronts aspects of literature that can neither be reduced to nor adequately explained by particular historical contexts.

Shakespeare's creations are not just inheritances of a past culture, frozen artefacts whose original settings must be expertly reconstructed in order to be understood. The plays and poems are also living art, vital thought-worlds that struggle, across time, with foundational questions of metaphysics, ethics, politics and aesthetics. With this orientation in mind, Edinburgh Critical Studies in Shakespeare and Philosophy offers a series of scholarly monographs that will reinvigorate Shakespeare studies by opening new interdisciplinary conversations among scholars, artists and students.

Kevin Curran

For Kate

INTRODUCTION: SHAKESPEARE'S NAUGHT

To be or not to be, I there's the point.

The Tragical History of Hamlet [Q1][1]

But no obiect of what nature or force so euer it bee can
make the least alteration or impression into the will of
GOD, whose nature is immutable, yea impassible. For hee
is not materiall as are the creatures, yea euen the Angels
themselues who must needs be granted to consist of, and
in some matter, which may suffer and bee altered, whereof
it commeth that not onely men, but euen the spirituall
Angels, are subiect to affection, passion and perturbation:
but God is a pure and mere forme, and therefore altogither
actuall, hee is immateriall, and therefore impassible.

Thomas Morton of Berwick, *A Treatise of
the Nature of God*[2]

Mannes minde . . . standeth . . . in contemplation of immortall,
and perdurable thinges: therto, in suche as fade, and fall, it
teacheth, ordayneth, appointeth, commaundeth . . . Yet is the
selfsame minde by the felouship, and companie of the senses,
and desires, many a time called away from that principall
office, to consider these unstable, and mutable thinges: and
sometime to cast in conceite fourmes disseuered from the
mater, mathematically: and sometime to view things sensible,
that can in no wise bee sondered from the materiall substance:

> as Elementes, Beastes, Herbes, Trees, Metalls, Stones, and
> such like: all that which must needes be sensed . . .
>> Nicholas Grimald, 'To the Reader', *Marcus Tullius*
>> *Cicero, his three books of duties*[3]

Being, believing, thinking. In early modern England, discourse concerning the 'big questions' turned on the distinction between the material and immaterial. While much recent scholarship has focused on material culture, the present study is concerned with its immaterial complement. In particular, the following pages explore the metaphysical status of immateriality and its figurative power in England from the last decades of the sixteenth century through the first half of the seventeenth. What occurred during these turbulent and eventful years amounts to a sea change in the way immateriality and materiality were conceived and represented, providing writers with an opportunity to capitalise on shifts in the shared understanding of the nature of things and thus produce some of the most celebrated literature in English.

Throughout the Christian Middle Ages, theologians and philosophers relied on a conception of reality necessarily comprised of both material and immaterial things. Though the distinction between the two realms was counted among the mysteries of God's creation, philosophers and theologians developed a range of theories to explain the nature of material and immaterial entities and the manner in which the two did and did not interact. Over the course of the long Middle Ages, St Augustine's Neoplatonist metaphysics eventually gave way to Aristotelian scholasticism as the accepted metaphysical authority, even as fierce debates over the compatibility of Aristotelian and Platonic metaphysics with Christian doctrine and dogma raged. The nature of the triune God and the relationship of body and soul animated scholastic debate on ancient philosophical problems in the high Middle Ages.

Schoolmen devoted a great deal of attention to the metaphysical status of abstraction (ideas) – seeking to explain how immaterial universals (apparently not available to sensuous perception) were related to the world of perceptible material things. Unlike those ancient philosophers willing to rule out the existence of immaterial entities – often in an attempt to avoid the logical contradiction of positing the existence of nothing – medieval philosophers could not afford to doubt the existence of immaterial things without risking the loss of basic tenets of Christianity (most importantly, the immortality of the soul and the incorporeal nature of God the Father). Mystical and scholastic theologians alike viewed sensuous experience with the natural world as a conduit to the spiritual and incorruptible realm beyond mortal comprehension. God was in all things and all things led to God.

After the works of Islamic philosophers such as Avicenna (Ibn Sīnā) and Averroës (Ibn Rushd) enabled the reintroduction of central aspects of Aristotelian thought to the European universities in the thirteenth century, Aristotle's hylomorphic metaphysics increasingly grounded the basic understanding of the nature of things material and immaterial. Combining the Greek terms for matter, 'hyle', (ὕλη) and form, 'morphe', (μορφή), hylomorphism refers to Aristotle's theory of reality in which all things exist as compounds of matter and form, expressing essence. Unlike Platonic particulars that imperfectly express a separable, immaterial and perfect form – the proper object of philosophical attention – in Aristotle's system reality, and thus the truth of things, is to be found in the analysis of enformed matter. As I will discuss in more detail in the next chapter, the Aristotelian concept of matter, as well as that developed by his intellectual heirs, is complex and unfamiliar.

The first significant early modern challenge to the Aristotelian ascendency would come in the fourteenth and fifteenth centuries, when Italian humanists began to contemplate the

impact of newly available ancient texts. Humanist translations of Plato's works into Latin led to new efforts to reconcile
Platonic and Neoplatonic metaphysics with Christian theology, revivifying Augustinian Neoplatonism as an alternative
to scholastic Aristotelianism. Marsilio Ficino announces this
aim explicitly in the proem to his *Platonic Theology*: 'Augustine chose Plato out of the ranks of the philosophers to be his
model, as being closest of all to the Christian truth. With just
a few changes, he maintained, the Platonists would be Christians.'[4] This move opened the door for natural philosophers
to disentangle the material and immaterial realms, undoing
the Aristotelian hylomorphic synthesis by reintroducing a
realm of ideal Forms, distinct from the material things in
which they were available to sensuous experience. This was
nothing new for Christian metaphysics, as Augustinian Neoplatonism had never disappeared, coexisting in the thought
of medieval mystics like St Bonaventure and evident in even
the more overtly Aristotelian thought of schoolmen like St
Thomas Aquinas. Nevertheless, the Aristotelian position
had dominated accounts of human cognition and the soul –
two areas in which the interaction between materiality and
immateriality is crucial – and the introduction of Latin translations of and commentaries on ancient texts by Ficino, Pico
della Mirandola, and others reignited metaphysical debates
about the constitution of the natural and spiritual worlds
that would have profound implications for the conception
of immateriality in early modern England. Consonant with
a Christian metaphysics of transcendence, the Neoplatonic
re-emphasis of immaterial Forms prompted renewed speculation and reflection on the nature of the material/immaterial
relation itself.[5]

By the end of the sixteenth century, seismic changes in
the European intellectual landscape had complicated conventional accounts of the relationship between immaterial
and material things. In addition to the humanist revival of

Platonic metaphysics, challenges came from two additional, seemingly opposite directions, as the Protestant Reformation fostered suspicion of outward appearance at the same time that the emergence of the new science encouraged close observation of the natural world. The apparent conflict between a reformed view of the material world and the growing interest of natural philosophers in divining that world's secrets is more accurately viewed as a shifting of perspective.[6] Doctrinal controversies over everything from idolatry and vestments to the nature of the soul and the Eucharist focused attention on accounts of the relationship between the material and immaterial that had been tentatively settled by traditional authorities. Where the presence of the immaterial God in all things was assumed in the conversations of the schoolmen, reformers now questioned whether an inanimate material statue could lead to spiritual edification. In the 1571 'Homily against Peril of Idolatry', the theological objection to Roman Catholic practice is articulated in explicitly metaphysical terms:

> For how can God, a most pure spirit, whom man never saw, be expressed by a gross, bodily, and visible similitude? How can the infinite majesty and greatness of God, incomprehensible to man's mind, much more not able to be compassed with the sense, be expressed in a small and little image? How can a dead and dumb image express the living God?[7]

In other words, the homilist asks: How can two distinct substances subsist in one thing? This was, in fact, a question asked and answered by the scholastics, but the disruption of the Reformation placed new pressure on the contorted logic provided by the schoolmen to resolve apparent conflicts between Christian doctrine and philosophical argument. The impact of revisiting such questions was widely felt in works ranging from literature to natural philosophy and theology.

Just as the fragile medieval reconciliation of ancient philosophy and Christian theology was shaken with the onset of the Reformation, the emergence of an empiricism grounded in experimentation and observation in natural philosophy contributed to a re-evaluation of accepted propositions concerning both physics and metaphysics. In the mid-sixteenth century, Copernicus, Vesalius and Fracastoro challenged the established accounts of important authorities in natural philosophy, including Ptolemy, Galen and Aristotle, setting the stage for the rapid expansion of experimental science in the seventeenth century. Spearheaded by Francis Bacon and later William Harvey, Robert Boyle and others in England, and culminating in the establishment of the Royal Society in 1660, the new methods would soon be extended to all areas of enquiry into the natural world. One important result of seventeenth-century developments in natural philosophy was an increase in efforts to remove immaterial things from conversations about the natural world. Invisible forces, long considered supernatural, were brought under the power of empirical science, aided by new methodologies and innovative apparatuses: microscopes and air-pumps would make visible that which had been previously invisible, and the analysis of the data they provided would be ordered and re-examined to derive more accurate theoretical knowledge from nature. For most this meant relegating immaterial things to theology, though others denied their existence altogether, both moves which appear to us now as evidence of the onset of modernity. Yet throughout the period all such enquiry was carried out under the rubric of natural philosophy, and it is important to remember that the philosophical aspect of this work remained central to its methods and rhetoric. Some important figures in the scientific revolution are still identified primarily as philosophers – Descartes, Bacon, Hobbes – despite making significant contributions to both natural science and metaphysics, and bemoaning the continued reliance on suspect authority. Most important for the present study is that, like all historical change, changes in the understanding of material and immaterial interaction were slow to take hold. While the relegation of immaterial things to theology or superstition would eventually define the Enlightenment, they remained an important part of the conversation even as experimental science gained ground in the first half of the seventeenth century. Even if one accepts that modern science was essentially born in the sixteenth and seventeenth centuries, to describe its emergence as a revolution is problematic. As John L. Heilbron writes of even the best accounts of the scientific revolution, 'The wine is new, the bottle old, the label misleading.'[8]

As Heilbron's description indicates, old ideas and methods mixed with new ones throughout the period, even as experimental science gained ground in the second half of the seventeenth century. By the Restoration in Britain, debates over the existence of 'immaterial substances' were raging on two fronts: one the one hand, materialist philosophers like Thomas Hobbes and Margaret Cavendish challenged the substance dualism championed by Cartesians and Neoplatonists. The Cambridge Platonist Henry More, for example, went so far as to make 'immaterial substance' a centrepiece of his philosophical system. On the other hand, theologians and churchmen insisted that the soul was an immaterial substance in an attempt to stem the tide of what they believed was a form of rationalism that denied sprit and thus led to atheism. By the early eighteenth century, the rational view would become dominant. In defending 'the doctrine of immateriality' in his 'Essay on Nothing', Henry Fielding would 'point at the stupidity of those, who instead of immaterial *essence*, which would convey a rational meaning, have substituted immaterial *substance*, which is a contradiction in terms'.[9] Fielding's firm distinction between essence and substance was the product of a century of philosophical debate

originating with Descartes and his materialist interlocutors
(especially Pierre Gassendi in France and Hobbes and Cavendish in England). The backdrop to the rise of science and
reason was thus a significant metaphysical debate about the
nature of things, the reality of the natural and supernatural world. Fielding's confidence in the distinction between
essence and substance was not shared by those writing at the
turn of the seventeenth century, at a moment when medieval
Latin translations of Aristotle still informed early modern
natural philosophy and theology, and in which the crucial
concept of *ousia* was variously translated as essence and
substance.[10]

Immateriality and Early Modern English Literature focuses
on the messy period of transition between these two poles
– from an era in which the intertwining of the natural and
spiritual worlds was taken for granted to one in which the
two worlds represented distinct objects for reflection. In this
in-between period, and especially the years that are the subject
of this book, roughly the 1590s to the 1630s, the focus was
as much on the interaction between the material and immaterial as it was on establishing their existence or distinct nature.
For the philosophers, theologians, natural philosophers, physicians and poets discussed below, the material and immaterial
realms interpenetrated one another in productive and surprising ways. While early modernists, seeking to correct a long
tradition of scholarship focused on the history of ideas, have
shifted critical attention to materiality and material culture,
such studies tell only part of the story. The 'material turn' in
early modern studies has rightly redirected scholarly attention
to the intersection between material (often termed 'embodied') experience and cultural production in the period. But at
times an over-investment in materiality has led to the dismissal
of the role that immateriality and immaterial things played
in that same culture.[11] Francis Bacon, the putative founder
of modern science in England, includes divinity in his 'small

Globe of the Intellectual World' as essentially settled truth: 'I can report no deficience concerning them: for I can find no space or ground that lieth vacant and unsown in the matter of divinity.'[12] Thomas Hobbes, perhaps the most trenchant English advocate for a materialist metaphysics in the seventeenth century, similarly reserved a space for the spiritual outside of the realm of his materialist philosophy, a view he repeatedly voiced despite charges of atheism. Though this may have been a feint aimed at avoiding serious charges of heresy, his willingness to affirm a real but incomprehensible theological realm suggests how difficult it was to be a thoroughgoing materialist in the seventeenth century.[13]

This is not to say that early modern accounts of the natural and supernatural worlds do not reflect profound changes in the intellectual landscape, including an increased interest in Lucretian atomism, humanist Neoplatonism and the emerging emphasis on experimental observation. My argument is that competing metaphysical systems vied for authority as the ground for understanding the natural world and its relationship to theological truth. Aristotelianism was especially slow to disappear; the rejection of scholastic Aristotelianism by humanist scholars failed to blunt its continued popularity in a range of discourses from psychology to theology.[14] The authority of Thomist Aristotelianism actually grew in the sixteenth century. Paul Oskar Kristeller makes the point that,

> beginning with the sixteenth century it often happened –
> as it never did during the Middle Ages – that the ordinary
> reader who was not a theologian, and even the reader
> who was not a Catholic nor a philosopher, considered
> St. Thomas to be the sole representative of medieval phi-
> losophy and theology who deserved to be excluded from
> the general contempt for that tradition.[15]

The metaphysical debate broadly associated with Aristotelian and Platonist positions still dominated the intellectual landscape, even as confessional identity altered the stakes involved in taking one side or the other.[16]

The humanist translation and dissemination of important works of classical philosophy that had been lost to medieval Europe fostered renewed interest in metaphysical speculation. The most well known and important is the Neoplatonism ushered in by Ficino and other Italian humanists, but Lucretian atomism and the hermetic tradition were equally disruptive to authoritative accounts of material and immaterial interaction. It was arguably the Reformation, however, that created the most turbulence in early modern natural philosophy and metaphysics, the two areas in which ideas about the nature of materiality and immateriality had to be directly reconciled with religious belief and doctrine. As acrimonious as medieval debates on these subjects had been, the tenor of Reformation polemic reached a whole new level. Theological debates over the Eucharist, to take an obvious example, had long drawn on what we would consider today to be contradictory philosophical systems. When medieval scholastics wrestled with an ancient metaphysical inheritance that was in many ways incompatible with their theological convictions, they did so in the shadow of a unified Church. Reformers and counter-reformers appealed to different theological authorities. An important result of all of this philosophical and theological uncertainty was that conventional accounts of the human relationship to both the natural and supernatural worlds were increasingly revealed to be contradictory, and sometimes simply incoherent. This created, I argue, a unique opportunity for literary innovation, but not because it ushered in the dawn of the modern era, and with it modern subjectivity. Rather, on this particular set of issues, the early modern was decidedly pre-modern, looking back as much as forward in the hope of stabilising uncertainties about both the earthly world and the eternal realm beyond its limits.

An important premise of this book is that it is necessary to understand the important role ideas about immaterial things played in the lives of the writers under consideration here, accepting that a dynamic interplay between immateriality and materiality saturated the period's language and thought. This is not as easy to do as it sounds, for today, outside of overtly religious, theological discourse, immateriality is viewed with suspicion. Important recent scholarship on early modern astrology, alchemy and the occult has begun to make strides in understanding a past that was saturated with anxiety and belief about the nature of immaterial things ranging from spirits and demons to thoughts and invisible forces.[17] Yet even in such excellent recent work, belief in the immateriality of souls and spirits, among other things, is often characterised as naive, such theories about the world deemed absurd or silly. When signs of proto-modern scientific sensibility are found alongside clearly pre-modern fallacies about the functioning of the natural world, the tendency has been to trace a route from nascent scientific intuition to the present assumptions of modern science. The fact that early modern atomists could conceive of a world made up of tiny particles – however unlike the actual atomic structure recognised by modern physics – is evidence of proto-modern, forward thinking.[18] What we lose when we search for clues to the development of the modern sensibility is a clear picture of the way unfamiliar early modern ways of experiencing and thinking about the world informed its religion, politics and culture. While not advocating for a re-evaluation of debunked theories long since abandoned by science, I suggest that a focus on early modern belief in things immaterial can illuminate the literature of the period by offering a corrective to some of the more familiar accounts of the period's cultural development, including the so-called secularisation thesis. In this sense, my project is basically historicist, though, as I will explain below, my approach is indebted to philosophical phenomenology and thus more akin to the historical phenomenology proposed by Bruce Smith and other early modernists working in the phenomenological tradition, including Julia Lupton, James Kearney and Jennifer Waldron.

In this book, I ask a question similar to the one Gail Kern Paster asks in her influential study, *Humoring the Body*: that we imagine a way of thinking about the world that seems utterly different from our own.[19] Paster asks readers to consider that emotion was, for the early moderns, an entirely material phenomenon, a position that enables an 'ecology' of early modern emotion focused on an understanding of the physical features of the internal body. Early modern passions, in Paster's account, 'have an elemental character more literal than metaphoric in force'.[20] This view goes against the modern (still largely Cartesian) distinction between extended body and non-extended thought. This distinction, which defined the 'mind–body problem' in philosophy from Descartes through much of the twentieth century, has recently broken down in the wake of research into cognitive neuroscience linking specific physical activity in the brain and related somatic responses to particular emotions long considered immaterial. Antonio Damasio sums up the recent rejection of Cartesian dualism in his book *Descartes' Error*, describing the 'error' of his title as follows:

> . . . the abyssal separation between body and mind, between the sizable, dimensioned, mechanically operated, infinitely divisible body stuff, on the one hand, and the unsizable, undimensioned, un-pushpullable, nondivisible mind stuff; the suggestion that reasoning, and moral judgement, and the suffering that comes from physical pain or emotional upheaval might exist separately from the body. Specifically: the separation of the most refined operations of the mind from the structure and operation of a biological organism.[21]

In early modern studies, Paster, Mary Crane and others who have drawn on this research use the current model of neuroscience to reconsider the way emotion was experienced in the early modern period; humoral theory and cognitive neuroscience use different terms but describe embodied emotion in strikingly similar ways. This helps bring a seemingly alien understanding of human emotion (humoral theory) into focus, but it does so at the risk of imposing a contemporary perspective on our description of early modern experience. We might ask how much of this revisionist sense of early modern cognitive experience is a reflection of our own moment and its re-evaluation of the connection between the material body, thought and emotion. In other words, is a materialist theory like Galenic humoralism starting to make sense to us because our own understanding of emotion is increasingly materialist?

The consequences of the so-called material turn in early modern studies – bolstered, perhaps, by a reverence for experimental science as the engine of an increasingly complex technological culture – has had the unfortunate side effect of demoting the immaterial as a category for serious enquiry.[22] The recent explosion of interest in the 'Lucretian Renaissance', to borrow a phrase from Gerard Passannante, rests, in part, on the belief that modern physics is more like Lucretian atomism than either of the Aristotelian or Neoplatonic alternatives available in the early modern period. Such studies suggest that a re-evaluation of the impact of Lucretius in the Renaissance will help clarify the 'modern' in 'early modern'.[23] Yet, as Ada Palmer has noted, most of those reading Lucretius in the Renaissance were not atomists, and in fact, many dismissed or even condemned his overall metaphysics.[24] This is in part due to the fact that the very idea that everything that exists is material was anathema to most, though certainly not all, early modern writers who weighed in on the topic. For most people in early modern England, the objects of contemplation that were thought to be immaterial were every bit as, if not more, important than material ones, even if the process of revealing them involved embodied experience. *Immateriality and Early Modern English Literature* asks what we might learn by taking seriously this early modern belief in things immaterial. To do so, we would have to entertain a way of thinking about the world as unfamiliar as the one described by Paster on the question of emotion. Where Paster's work helped us see materiality where we had assumed immateriality, my aim is to foreground belief in the immaterial as an active component in early modern material life. And, just as current shifts in thinking about cognition and emotion have guided some of the important work on materiality in early modern studies, the increased influence of religion in contemporary politics and culture has refocused scholarly attention on early modern belief, potentially pushing immateriality back to the fore.[25] But rather than urge a pendulum swing back to the history of ideas and away from the emphasis on materiality that has dominated the last two decades of early modern scholarship, I propose a way forward that more rigorously examines the dynamic interplay between material and immaterial metaphysics in the early modern period.

To this end the current study builds on the work of scholars focused on early modern materiality by offering a complementary analysis of the role immateriality played in early modern thought. Sarah Wall-Randell has recently undertaken a similar project in the area of Renaissance book history. In *The Immaterial Book*, she urges 'practitioners [of Renaissance literary studies] to attend to materiality's inverse, its shadow, the *immaterial*, to investigate what immateriality might mean in the period and investigate its effects'.[26] Her work focuses on the books represented in literary texts from the period and their role in the early modern imagination, complementing my own examination of the philosophical, theological and medical discourses informing the representation of materiality and immateriality in early modern poetics. In *Dark Matter*, Andrew Sofer explores the importance of the unseen in the theatre, 'the invisible dimension of theater that escapes visual detection, even though its effects are felt everywhere in performance'.[27] The role of the immaterial is often the implied other to the material conditions and objects under consideration.

Katherine Eggert has recently argued eloquently that the early modern confusion over evolving science – sparked by the shift from humanism to modern empiricism – led writers to deploy knowledge they knew to be false.[28] It is a compelling argument, and Eggert's position is beautifully articulated in readings of some of the same authors under consideration in the present study. Eggert is clearly right that, for some, the collapse of faith in medieval physics led to a lack of confidence in the traditional theories of matter that had underwritten much of late medieval natural philosophy and theology. Even more important is her related point that no coherent theory of matter filled the void left by the collapse of tradition at the turn of the seventeenth century. But I'm not convinced that the seeming incoherence of the theories circulating at the turn of the seventeenth century means that the people who deployed these theories knew them to be false; instead, it seems more accurate to say that they believed some things that appear to be simply incoherent to us in the twenty-first century. That incoherent belief was belief nonetheless.

The destabilisation of long-held, if often inconsistent, accounts of the material and immaterial in early modern natural philosophy is the rich reserve from which the poets and dramatists of the age drew some of their most memorable figures. Eggert's focus on alchemy adds weight to her conclusion, as many early modern writers expressed their scepticism of this particular form of what we now consider junk science, and certainly some drew on outmoded theories in order to get at elusive problems figuratively. John Donne's reference to the intertwining of 'eye beams' in *The Ecstasy* is a likely example of a poet deploying a theory known to be false.[29] But a wide range of equally alien beliefs about the world were clearly held in earnest – aspects of humoral theory, for example, but also many of the ideas underlying alchemy itself. My own argument is that early modern English habits of mind were shaped by an intellectual culture in which the immaterial was a category as vibrant and necessary as the material. Only in retrospect can we locate the beginning of the scientific revolution in England at the turn of the seventeenth century. From our vantage, we may be able to identify the 'new science' as an already nascent form of our own modern science. And of course, in very important ways, it was. But the aspects of these emerging modes of enquiry that we identify as modern were often tangential to those older and less familiar views that guided enquiry into nature and faith during the period.

Focus on the development of the modern sometimes makes it difficult to accept that early modern intellectual giants – thinkers like Shakespeare, Bacon and Donne – were not always able to tell where Galen and Aristotle went wrong. When we consider Shakespeare 'our contemporary', we make a choice to highlight the familiar at the expense of the outmoded.[30] Advocates of 'presentism' offer a compelling defence of the relevance of Shakespeare and early modern literature for our current moment, but they do so at the risk of overstating the continuity between a distant past and our own moment.[31] Of course, the opposite is a danger if we accept the position that historical alterity is so absolute as to be impossible to recover even provisionally; this idea is often proposed in relation to early modern dramatic performance, as both the historical conditions of spectatorship and the details of dramatic practice are lost to time. This component of historicist approaches, maintaining the inaccessibility of the past except that which can be recovered provisionally through a survey of the now silent voices available in extant texts and material artefacts, effectively places any enquiry into past *experience* off limits. In response to this critical problem, I turn to historical phenomenology. As a critical practice, phenomenology may offer a middle ground between the poles of presentism and historicism, especially when its own methods are made historical.

The way early modern writers engaged with the variety of theoretical explanations concerning the nature of material and immaterial things suggests a complex and deeply felt anxiety about human knowledge and experience of the natural and supernatural world. We might hear this anxiety in Othello's frustration at the height of the temptation scene when his experience fails to yield a coherent understanding of his predicament: 'I think my wife be honest and think she's not . . . I'll have some proof!'[32] Othello's problem is that the proof he seeks is not forthcoming – or even possible – at least not in material form.[33] The idea that Desdemona's fidelity can be proven or disproven on the grounds of 'ocular proof' drives the tragedy, as does a similar lack of empirical proof of Old Hamlet's murder in *Hamlet* – 'there are more things in heaven and earth than are dreamt of in your philosophy' (1.5.168–9), decries a flummoxed Hamlet to a pragmatic Horatio.[34] In both cases, the protagonists are forced to grapple with alternatives to both tradition and empirical, material evidence – they are forced to engage with the immaterial. Similarly, when John Donne implores God to 'batter [his] heart', or George Herbert questions how man, 'a crazy, brittle glass', can convey God's word, they express a larger cultural anxiety that is played out along the fault line separating the material and immaterial.

This anxiety has sometimes been taken as a primarily epistemological problem. Advocates of Shakespeare's scepticism, most notably Stanley Cavell, point to the distrust of proof in Shakespeare as evidence of the playwright's espousal of a properly philosophical scepticism.[35] Such a position centres the debate on epistemological questions rather than onto-logical ones. The theatre invites epistemological speculation because it offers its truths through deceptive appearances. In the cases of poets like Donne and Herbert, however, to focus on epistemological questions would be to suggest that their affliction is a result of their inability to know rather than feel, evacuating an aspect of the religious content from their devotional verse. And while textual evidence for a sceptical Shakespeare can be compelling, true philosophical scepti-cism is a position unlikely to have actually been held in early modern England. For most, early modern epistemology was predicated on an ontological belief: that eternal, immaterial things (God, but also, in certain modes, souls and angels) both exist and are beyond the comprehension of materially embodied humans. Epistemological doubt was almost always accompanied by an investment in this ontological certainty. There was a truth, even if it was in some aspects inaccessible. The nature of existence was more important than the human capacity to have knowledge of that nature. Put slightly differ-ently, doubt about the truth value of almost anything in the sublunary world was subordinated to a belief in the ontolog-ical fact of God's existence: immaterial, imperceptible things were thus as real and in fact more important than the things found in the material sensorium. Accepting this as a basic aspect of early modern thought helps explain Descartes' sur-prising leap to the existence of God in his third meditation, after proposing what appears to be a convincing, modern philosophical scepticism. In fact, of course, Descartes' proof of God was always primary, his scepticism a rhetorically powerful method to get to the more important argument. For most early modern Christians the fallibility of sense per-ception served to accentuate the transitory and insignificant nature of earthly, mortal existence. In its ability to produce epistemological doubt, sensation provided evidence of the theological truth of postlapsarian human corruption. The material world nevertheless provided the only access to the incomprehensible truths of the immaterial realm, and thus the material/immaterial dyad can be found at the heart of early modern philosophical and theological accounts of both the nature of the world and the place of humans in it.

One of the aims of the present study is to try to provide a description of how it felt to live at a time when this complex and now quite unfamiliar understanding of material and immaterial interactivity pervaded the intellectual scene. Rather than try to identify the philosophical school into which the literary writers under consideration may be classified (Shakespeare the Neoplatonist, for example), my goal is to explore how the conflicts over metaphysics and theology were felt by those living through the change. Poetry and drama is precisely where we should look for this kind of representation of experience, for poets and dramatists primarily seek to convey experience, even when that experience is informed by ideas or theories. This is the difference between literature and history or philosophy in Sir Philip Sidney's account – the requirement of literature to move or 'delight' is about replicating experience. It is for this reason that overtly didactic literature almost always fails in comparison to literature that presents rather than dictates (hence the advice to creative writers to show rather than tell). This is, however, not to say that the poets and dramatists of the period were not concerned with the ideas themselves, or with a kind of aesthetic didacticism that was explicitly intended to persuade. My point is, rather, that the demands of aesthetic production open a window onto the way serious philosophical, ethical and theological debates were experienced in the social and cultural world of the time.[36]

In both philosophy and literary theory, the method focused most squarely on experience as a category has been phenomenology. As a philosophical movement, phenomenology turned to the category of experience as a way of interrogating consciousness of the world in contrast to naturalism's emphasis on material reality, and it has remained consistent in its focus even as shifting ideas about the nature of experience have changed the course of phenomenological enquiry since it first appeared at the turn of the twentieth century.[37] Though literary critics have drawn on the work of phenomenologists since at least the 1960s, only in the last two decades or so have we seen a considerable revival of interest in phenomenological approaches to early modern studies. The most prominent advocate for such an approach has been Bruce R. Smith.[38] In *Phenomenal Shakespeare* Smith offers a manifesto-style defence of what he calls 'historical phenomenology', arguing that phenomenology is an attractive alternative to literary criticism that approaches literary and cultural materials with an agenda underwritten by the assumptions (axioms) of a particular theoretical system (Marxist, psychoanalytic, ecocritical etc.).[39] Such axiom-driven studies, Smith argues, produce analyses that force the texts under consideration to conform to the presupposed axioms of the method. Smith compares such readings to the demonstration (Q.E.D.) in mathematical problem solving. The demonstration proves the theory rather than the theory offering proof of its conclusions. Smith advocates phenomenology because it abandons the kind of critical axioms that interpretive schools favour, reducing method to a single axiomatic position: 'you cannot know anything apart from the way that you come to know it'.[40] This characterisation has special relevance for the present examination of materiality and immateriality in early modern culture. Smith explicitly compares the phenomenological method to that proposed by Bacon in *The Advancement of Learning* (1605) and *The New Organon* (1620). As Smith points out, phenomenology's insistence on analysing the *experience* of the phenomenal world shares with Bacon a desire to begin at the bottom and work up towards axioms rather than proceeding from the other direction. As we will see, this concern with directionality – from sense experience to thought rather than thought to sense experience – is at the heart of debates over the material and immaterial in the English Renaissance.

Smith has been joined by other early modernists who have recognised phenomenology's potential to open up early modern experience to analysis.[41] Smith is clear that to get at such experience requires some historical reconstruction, and he admits that this process will always fail to reach its subject entirely. But the advantage of reorienting critical attention towards the history of lived experience is to recover an important component of the early modern literary lifeworld that is obscured by programmatic criticism guided by theoretical agendas. As his previous phenomenologically oriented studies have shown, the approach offers insight into aspects of early modern culture that scholars and historians have otherwise deemed inaccessible. In *The Acoustic World of Early Modern England*, for example, Smith asks if early modern people experienced sound differently than we do today. He then sets out to answer the question by analysing both the ways writers discussed sound in surviving texts and the ways in which the cultural meanings of their works were shaped by the acoustic conditions in which they were experienced. His project in *The Key of Green* provides a similar journey through the visual experience of a single colour in the period, reading the language of green against its appearance in texts, objects and designs from the period as a starting point for reconstructing a history of sensuous response. Smith's approach is especially well suited to the 'material turn' in early modern studies, due to its attention to material things beyond the linguistic, textual record, as well as its emphasis on embodied experience.

But phenomenology's relationship to materialism is a complicated one. Julia Reinhard Lupton, another practitioner of the phenomenological approach in Shakespeare studies, follows Michael Lewis and Tanja Staehler in describing phenomenology as 'the science of appearances'.[42] Lupton's association of phenomenology with both 'science' and 'appearance', like Smith's emphasis on sensuous experience, may suggest to some that phenomenology's focus is on materiality, or perhaps the affordances any material environment may offer.[43] At the same time, however, it is helpful to consider what is meant by 'appearance', for the term can indicate the sensuous coming to visibility of a natural (material) object, or the presentation of an immaterial object in the mind.[44] A key conclusion in the early development of phenomenology was Edmund Husserl's claim that 'there is no duality between being and appearance'.[45] This claim was directly aimed at breaking down the Kantian distinction between noumena and phenomena (things-in-themselves and appearances, respectively), but also the psychological account of mental activity as distinct from physical sensation as described by Descartes. Husserl developed two of the most important concepts of phenomenological analysis – intention and intuition – in order to clarify his position on the unity of appearance and being. And though Husserl was ostensibly working to overcome Kantian and Cartesian dualities that had created an unbridgeable gap between appearance and existence, it is important for the present study that part of the solution was to return philosophy to a state prior to their influential contributions.[46]

Contemporary phenomenology has its origins in Franz Brentano's nineteenth-century attempt to develop a rigorous science of psychic activity. Brentano drew on both Aristotle and Thomist scholasticism in developing his theory of mental activity, hoping to provide a solution to the problem of distinguishing between objects in the world and mental objects. His conclusion that 'psychical phenomena' are 'intentional' provided the jumping-off point for Husserl's development of the theory of intentionality.[47] Brentano makes his debt to the scholastics clear:

> Every psychical phenomenon is characterized by what the Scholastics of the Middle Ages called the intentional (or sometimes the mental) inexistence of an object, and what we should like to call, although not quite unambiguously, the reference (*Beziehung*) to a content, the directedness (*Richtung*) towards an object (which in this context is not to be understood as something real) or the immanent-object-quality (*immanente Gegenstandlichkeit*). Each contains something as its object, though not each in the same manner. In the representation (*Vorstellung*) something is represented, in the judgment something is acknowledged or rejected, in the desiring it is desired, etc. This intentional inexistence is peculiar alone to psychical phenomena. No physical phenomenon shows anything like it. And thus we can define psychical phenomena by saying that they are such phenomena as contain objects in themselves by way of intention (*intentional*).[48]

Brentano was explicitly interested in the distinction between material objects in the natural world and mental objects, which appear to have no material existence. These two kinds of objects, he thought, are clearly related, but also clearly different in kind. The concept of intention would subsequently become central to phenomenology, as a way to avoid speculation about metaphysical questions that were not grounded in experience, for, as Husserl would demonstrate, all objects about which something could be truthfully predicated (both natural and mental) are intentional objects. In Husserl's hands, the concept of intentionality would be refined to indicate that all experience of phenomena involves being conscious of an object of intention, that all consciousness is consciousness of something.

While all phenomenal experience involves intention towards an object, according to Husserl, not all intentional objects are of the same kind. Perceptual appearance (that which appears to sight, for example) is never complete, despite our experience of the object being given to consciousness as a whole. As Steven Crowell explains,

> If, for instance, I reflect on my perception of this apple, I note that the apple is given as a whole but that only one side of it appears while the others are occluded. Further, the apple is given as the same even as other sides of it come into view. But reflection also shows that the order and connection that defines the object of such experience necessarily makes reference to the subject whose experience it is. This side of the apple is currently appearing because *I* am seeing it from here; these other sides come to appear because *I* am now seeing it from another angle, and so on.[49]

In recognising that the apple is given as whole, one also recognises that something beyond empirical observation of the world 'as it is' must be caught up in the act of perception. This recognition is the product of philosophical reflection. In what Husserl calls the 'natural attitude', we assume the existence of the world and the manner of its constitution based on preconceptions and prior experience. We have seen a lot of apples, for example, and we do not pause to consider how it is that we experience three-dimensional objects with facets that we cannot see. This naive view is crucial to living in the world (we would never open doors without the implicit awareness that the room on the other side was indeed going to be there to welcome us). Similarly, we don't launch into reflections on consciousness every time we see an apple. Yet, as Smith notes regarding Bacon's method, preconceptions complicate the effort to seek knowledge on a pure rather than practical level. The knowledge sought in reflection on and description of phenomenal experience is the revelation of both the essential structure of our experiences as well as what appears. For the phenomenologist, in order to reach these scientific truths about the world one must inhibit oneself from the natural attitude.

This deliberate resistance to the natural attitude is called the 'phenomenological reduction'. Associated with Husserl's term *epoché* or 'bracketing', the reduction is not a scepticism of knowledge (as in Descartes' *Meditations*), but a setting aside of all knowledge, withholding it while undertaking the act of philosophical reflection.[50] The result is an intuitive opening onto another mode of being. If intentionality identifies the condition of perceptual experience as oriented towards an object (either material or mental), philosophical intuition focuses on the immediate givenness of that object to consciousness. Philosophical reflection reveals the structure of this relation between object and consciousness. The role of phenomenological intuition and description when perceiving with the senses – what Husserl called 'external intention' – is to highlight the inadequacy of sense perception to the object, to recognise that what appears to the senses is not all that appears in the phenomenal experience of the object. On the other hand, 'internal intuition' reveals the object under consideration to be an object 'of consciousness', apprehended as a whole.[51] Moreover, the appearance of a non-material object before consciousness is, for Husserl, real in the same way as the appearance of an extramental object: the proper focus for the science of phenomenology is phenomenal appearance in consciousness.

Thus, despite one strand of phenomenology that emphasises the material things of experience (the 'appearance of objects' in the first sense), another important strand is explicitly focused on the fact that the experience of phenomena involves both visible and invisible objects of analysis. This is where the second key phenomenological term becomes important: intuition. If intention (directedness towards an object) is the condition of phenomenal perception, intuition allows for its facilitation. Here again, phenomenology's inheritance from scholastic thought provides an important historical parallel. In developing the concept of intuition, Husserl invoked the long history of the term *intuito*, which was central to medieval scholastic thought – used variously by Aquinas, Duns Scotus and Ockham. For the scholastics, *intuito* was a broad term for something like immediate knowledge. The term was a matter of much scholastic refinement and debate, often associated with Augustinian divine illumination to distinguish it from the more limited faculty of human reason. In developing a modern phenomenological theory of intuition, Husserl hoped to create a more scientific account of intuition's functioning by tying it to the same methods of phenomenological analysis outlined for the world of sense experience, that is, in Herbert Spiegelberg's description, to move from the 'careful consideration of representative examples, which are to serve as stepping stones, as it were, for any generalizing "ideation"'.[52] While this shares with induction a movement from the particular to the general, it exceeds the inductive method by intertwining the facts gleaned from concrete examples of experience with the descriptive analysis of the essential structure of those experiences, a product of the phenomenological method known as eidetic reduction.

In the context of medieval scholasticism, 'intuition' was a broad term referring to something like 'direct perception' of reality; it identified the ways in which things were known to be true or real, despite the limits of human reason, the obvious case being the knowledge of God. It was not, Jaakko Hintikka points out, concerned with 'an internal or introspective source of knowledge',[53] the way the term is generally used today. Hintikka's account of the shift from the medieval to the modern sense of intuition reveals much about the way this development has been historicised:

> It seems to me that the main historical reasons why the broad scholastic concept of intuition was not long-lived are obvious. The geometrical and mechanical vision of the

world of early modern science showed that what looks like a direct perception is in reality a complex process involving all sorts of inferences, albeit often unspoken and even unconscious ones. Such ideas as the Copernican explanation of the apparent movements of the sun in terms of the earth's unperceived motion or Berkeley's analysis of depth vision through stereoscopic seeing showed how many potential slips there are between the cup and the lip – or, rather, between the cup and the eye. A perceiver's relation to the objects of perception could no longer be thought of as an immediate, i.e. intuitive, one. The only area left where we seem to have truly direct knowledge is our inner world the world of our ideas and mental acts.[54]

Hintikka's two examples, Copernicus and Berkeley, writing in the early decades of the sixteenth century and the first half of the eighteenth respectively, suggest that scientists and philosophers alike recognised the inadequacy of the scholastic concept of direct perception. What is interesting for the present study is that scholastic intuition was specifically formulated as an answer to the problem of experience with the immaterial as real. Hintikka's early modern mechanists, with their geometry and mechanical vision, shifted the immaterial to the realm of ideation exclusively, thus creating a chasm between the material and immaterial (as in Cartesian substance dualism). It is a familiar story, but one that is belied by the actual habits of thought that pervaded the early modern period from the fifteenth to the eighteenth centuries. Though attitudes to the capacity for sensuous perception to yield truths about the natural world evolved dramatically over the course of these centuries, the persistence of belief in the other side of perception – the access to intuitive knowledge of the invisible – is evidence of how incomplete the scientific revolution was throughout the early modern period.

Phenomenology's twofold emphasis on the science of appearance thus provides a compelling methodology for examining the early modern experience of a world comprised of both heaven and earth. By focusing on phenomena, that which appears to consciousness, phenomenology, especially in the hands of the French practitioners I draw on in this book, is open to the full field of experience that captivated the early modern poets and dramatists under consideration here. Another way to describe phenomenological 'appearing' is 'givenness'. Today the primary practitioner of this formula for phenomenological analysis is the Catholic philosopher Jean-Luc Marion. While appearance suggests or demands that there is a material phenomenon available to experience, givenness expands the realm of experience to the invisible and immaterial. If, as some have argued, Brentano's penchant for science was driven in part by his rejection of Catholicism, the return to the immaterial in French phenomenology could be seen as a radical break with the original phenomenological project. But Marion's phenomenology is not simply an attempt to co-opt phenomenology for religious ends, though he is upfront about his religious convictions. Rather, it takes up an important strand in phenomenology that had been there from the start. Part of the impetus for bringing human experience under the power of science (arguably the goal of the first practitioners) was to explain what seem to be non-material aspects of human experience in material terms. As the French version of phenomenology developed, especially in the hands of two very different philosophers responding to Heidegger's existential phenomenology – Maurice Merleau-Ponty and Emmanuel Levinas – the emphasis on what does not appear became more pronounced.

For Levinas, the focus of philosophy must be the ethical demand of the other person, both as embodied individual and impossible idea. This position calls into question any attempt at a science of phenomenal experience that begins with sensuous, material perception, even if that perception is ultimately submitted to the eidetic reduction, for the essence of the other person is in Levinas's view irreducibly other.

One could say that Levinas's entire effort to reorient metaphysics or 'first philosophy' from ontology to ethics resulted in a call to turn from what appears to what is withheld in the process of appearing. Heidegger's concern with what he called the 'unhiddenness' of truths also reflects the early phenomenological interest in the other side of the appearing phenomenal thing. But while Heidegger acknowledges the hidden or invisible in defining ontological truth as a matter of the 'unhiddenness of beings', he fails to submit the hidden to ethical analysis in Levinasian terms.[55] In his repudiation of Heideggerian ontology, Levinas prioritises precisely what always remains hidden in human intersubjective experience: the otherness of the other person. He thus draws on phenomenological methods in order to place ethics and intersubjectivity before ontology and the egocentric as the proper goals of philosophy.

In Merleau-Ponty's work we find a different but comparable trajectory, beginning with his scientific exploration of experience in *The Phenomenology of Perception*, which evolved into a speculative and searching analysis of the relationship between the visible and the invisible in experience. For Merleau-Ponty, philosophy's problem, and thus the main challenge for phenomenology, was its reliance on foundational philosophical language that posited the conscious (mental) subject – a product of the Cartesian *cogito* – prior to embodied experience in the phenomenal world. For the present study, the most important development of these later turns in phenomenological thought is the increasing emphasis by the French phenomenologists on the other side of 'appearing', that which doesn't appear, perhaps even in consciousness: the invisible. Merleau-Ponty's last, unfinished work is a striking attempt to go back to foundational philosophical questions to address the intertwining of the visible and invisible, the sensuous and ideational.[56] Merleau-Ponty, like Bacon, was concerned that conventional philosophical language had contaminated the search for truth, and that looking anew was the only way to salvage the endeavour.[57]

This attempt to return to questions about the invisible in phenomenology receives its fullest development in the work of Michel Henry and Jean-Luc Marion. Henry, whose work has had less impact outside of France than either Levinas or Merleau-Ponty, worked to develop a 'material phenomenology' that returned philosophical analysis to the examination of 'life' as experienced – a focus that Henry felt Husserl departed from in his late turn to idealism. Though focused on the concrete, and highlighting the material, Henry's phenomenology is concerned with the 'life that gives birth and growth to consciousness'.[58] In the characterisation of Henry's English translator, Henry sought to reveal a 'radical immanence' through phenomenological analysis that would include those aspects of lived experience that exceed conventional descriptions of the perceptible.[59]

The influence of Henry's material phenomenology can be felt in Marion's work on givenness, and specifically his interest in what he calls 'saturated phenomena', experiences that exceed and overwhelm but simultaneously constitute comprehension and consciousness. Merold Westphal describes Marion's saturated phenomena as follows:

> a saturated phenomenon is one in which what is given to intuition exceeds the intentionality that becomes aware of it. My transcendental ego cannot anticipate it, nor can my concept contain or comprehend it. My horizons are overwhelmed and submerged by it. I am more the subject constituted by its givenness than it is the object constituted by my subjectivity.[60]

Not surprisingly, significant challenges to both Levinas and Marion have come in the form of accusations that they confuse philosophy and theology. Levinas has been accused of substituting the philosophical concept of the absolute Other for God, a case supported by the fact that he was also an accomplished Talmudic scholar.[61] Marion's overt Catholicism and willingness to consider religious subject matter in his philosophical works have opened him to charges of theological obfuscation – that phenomenology is simply a cover for a project of Catholic apology. The earlier close association of phenomenology with religion, from its origins with Brentano and his vexed relationship to Catholicism and the close connection between Heidegger and theology in the mid-twentieth century, also led to suspicion of phenomenology's project, especially from politically oriented critics.[62]

In the secular climate of late twentieth-century criticism such suspicion was understandable, and even after the 'turn to religion' in early modern studies one can see how theology masquerading as philosophy might trouble those who have accepted the idea that modernity was ultimately a secular development. Yet recent political events have placed God in the same company as Mark Twain: *pace* Nietzsche, rumours of the death of God appear to be greatly exaggerated. And while this has led to renewed interest in religion on the part of scholars, including at times a full-throated rejection of the secularisation thesis, such interest still threatens to reduce religious belief to political ideology, draining religious experience of its peculiar form of feeling, along with any meaning or access to truth.[63] Any attempt to understand early modern religious feeling must resist the temptation to reduce religion to political control. While those aspects of religion-as-political-coercion relied on an investment in religious experience as a means of the ideological consolidation of power, other forms of religious belief less clearly support the hegemonic structure and deserve to be examined on their own terms.[64] It is for this reason that phenomenology, even with, or perhaps because of, its theological baggage, is precisely the approach to take. An attention to the lived, concrete experience of the early modern world ought to include experience of the invisible, immaterial, in addition to the material conditions of the day.

In order to explain further the ways in which a complex interaction of material and immaterial things pervaded early modern thought, my first chapter provides an overview of the role immateriality plays in three key discursive fields – metaphysics, theology and psychology. The chapter reviews how the period's language reflects an intense interest in defining the categories of the material and immaterial as well as a fascination with their interaction. This discussion lays out the larger organisation of the book into three parts, corresponding to the three primary areas where questions surrounding the relation of materiality and immateriality are most acutely felt in the period: being, believing and thinking. In addition to the literary works that are the primary subject of this study, texts ranging from religious polemic to natural philosophy and medicine grapple with the immaterial and thus provide a sense of how pervasive interest in the realm was in the early modern period.

Having laid the groundwork for the project in an overview of the range of discourses surrounding early modern immateriality, I turn in Part I to the role of immateriality in addressing ontological and metaphysical questions in the period. Chapter 2 considers the fact that immateriality posed a set of ontological problems. The discussion revolves around a range of writers' reflections on the existence of 'things', as well as the periods's playful interest in 'nothing' and the possibility of such an entity as 'nothingness'. The paradox arising from the concept of nothing – nothing as an object of thought that has, by definition, no being – provides an introduction to the themes explored in the following chapter on Shakespeare's *Richard II*. In this chapter I examine the concept of nothingness in *Richard II* by looking at the ways in which Shakespeare gradually empties Richard of his sense of self, revealing it to have been a fiction, and culminating in his final (and only) soliloquy, in which he comes to the conclusion that 'whate'er I be, / Nor I, nor any man that but man is, / With nothing shall be pleased till he be eased / With being nothing'. While Richard's conclusion has been described as anticipating a Nietzschean nihilism or Cartesian scepticism, I read this moment as an affirmation of the inescapability of the immaterial as an object of thought. My argument draws on Jean-Luc Marion's concept of saturated phenomena, and the medieval Islamic philosopher Avicenna's (Ibn Sīnā) theory of internal sensation. The following chapter examines ontology from another angle, focusing on the relationship between immaterial judgements and material action in *1 Henry IV*, and arguing that Shakespeare exploits the lack of consensus over the ontological basis for personal character in generating a central tension in the play: Hal's conflicted identity as either honourable hero or Machiavellian shape-shifter. Falstaff articulates his scepticism of the concept of honour by privileging the concrete evidence of embodied materiality over the immateriality of the concept. Hal, on the other hand, defends his honour as immanent within himself, its manifestation only available through the language of materiality and enacted on the battlefield. Paul Ricoeur's phenomenology of time and narrative, derived from Aristotle's *Poetics* and Augustine's *Confessions*, offers a theoretical framework for the discussion.

In the second part of the book, on believing, I turn to the theological context for understanding the immaterial in the period. An attempt to offer granular detail of the theological debates on this subject would be well beyond the scope of this project. My aim here is to argue that debates over the nature of matter and spirit that lay at the heart of theological divisions wrought by the Reformation necessarily led to renewed interest in established doctrine concerning the nature and interaction of material and immaterial entities. These issues receive further treatment in the two case studies that follow. Chapter 6 focuses on Donne's *Anniversary* poems published at the moment he transitioned from a private secular poet circulating verse among friends at the early modern Inns of Court (law schools) to the public Protestant preacher who would become Dean of St Paul's Cathedral and the author of devotional poems and sermons. In the *First Anniversary*, published as *An Anatomy of the World*, Donne's interest in novel scientific thought rests uncomfortably alongside his consideration of the nature of the soul's substance. The scholastic and phenomenological concepts of intention and intuition help make sense of Donne's approach in this otherwise difficult poem. In Chapter 7 I turn to George Herbert's collection of devotional poetry, *The Temple*, examining his approach to inaccessible devotional truths through the language of material experience. Herbert consistently resists prioritising either material presence or spiritual immateriality in his poetic choices, despite always staying focused on the immaterial objects of his devotion. The material conditions of his own life – marked by a combination of affliction through bodily illness and a sensuous joy in nature, music and art – inform Herbert's reflections on his spiritual fate, always withheld, but always guiding him in his poetic devotions.

The third and final part of the book is addressed to thinking, an action implicated in both metaphysical reflection and belief, and one in which the interaction between the material and immaterial is perhaps most complex. I begin, in Chapter 8, by briefly surveying theories of cognition available in an early modern period that was still primarily shaped by the scholastic synthesis of ancient Aristotelian, Neoplatonic and Galenic philosophy and physiology. The chapter focuses on how early modern cognitive theories attempted to account for the interaction of immaterial ideas and material sensuous experience. Returning to Shakespeare in Chapter 9, I extend the discussion begun in the previous chapter by addressing the concept of immateriality in *Much Ado About Nothing*. Reading the play alongside early modern medical literature, especially as it had been shaped by the medieval reception of Galenic and Aristotelian conceptions of mind, soul and bodily 'spirits', the chapter traces the relation between cognitive knowledge/error and material perception/misperception. In the final case study, I argue that Shakespeare addresses the problematic distinction between mind and body, immateriality and materiality, in *The Tempest*, ultimately creating a world in which the distinction becomes meaningless. I demonstrate how the play consistently blurs the line between thought and sensation, breaking down the distinction, and offering in its place an account of embodied experience that is more akin to what the modern phenomenologist Maurice Merleau-Ponty called the *chiasm*, or 'intertwining' of the visible and the invisible.

Notes

1. Shakespeare, *Tragical History of Hamlet*, D4v.
2. Thomas Morton of Berwick, *Treatise of the Nature of God*, K5v–K6r.
3. Cicero, A3r–A3v. Grimald's translation was first published in 1556 by Richard Tottel, and went through eight more editions between then and 1605, all including Grimald's prefatory matter.
4. Ficino, *Platonic Theology*, vol. 1, p. 11.
5. The popularity of a work like Baldassare Castiglione's *Book of the Courtier*, with its long Neoplatonic account of the ladder of love in Book 4, is evidence of the popular circulation of Neoplatonic ideas during the second half of the sixteenth century in England. How seriously English poets took the metaphysics is another question.
6. See Harrison, *The Territories of Science and Religion*.
7. Jewel, *The Homily Against Peril of Idolatry*, p. 50.
8. Heilbron, 'Scientific Revolution?', p. 8.

9. Fielding, *Miscellanies*, vol. 1, pp. 235–6.
10. Aristotle does distinguish between essence and substance, but the distinction was obscured by medieval translations that were influential in debates in the Renaissance. I discuss this further in the next two chapters.
11. For a broad overview of this critical shift, see my 'Beyond Materialism in Shakespeare Studies'. See also Stanley Stewart, 'Author Esquire: The Writer and "Immaterial Culture" in Caroline and Jacobean England'.
12. Bacon, *Philosophical Works*, p. 175.
13. Hobbes wrote in 1655: 'Thus philosophy excludes from itself theology, as I call the doctrine about the nature and attributes of the eternal, ungenerable, and incomprehensible God, and in whom no composition and no division can be established and no generation can be understood' (Hobbes, *De Corpore*, 1.8).
14. The work of Charles B. Schmitt is indispensable here. See especially his *Aristotle and the Renaissance* and *John Case and Aristotelianism in Renaissance England*.
15. Kristeller, *Medieval Aspects of Renaissance Learning*, p. 42.
16. I explore the dual influence of Aristotelian and Platonic philosophy in detail in the following chapter. For an excellent discussion of both the friction between and agreement among medieval followers of Aristotelian and Platonic thought, see Kellie Robertson, *Nature Speaks*, esp. Part 1.
17. See, for example, Mary Floyd-Wilson, *Occult Knowledge, Science, and Gender on the Shakespearean Stage*; Suparna Roy-choudhury, *Phantasmatic Shakespeare: Imagination in the Age of Early Modern Science*; Katherine Eggert, *Disknowledge: Literature, Alchemy, and the End of Humanism in Renaissance England*; Glyn Parry, *The Arch Conjurer of England: John Dee*; and Anthony Grafton, *Cardano's Cosmos: The Worlds and Works of a Renaissance Astrologer*.
18. An obvious example here is Stephen Greenblatt's *The Swerve: How the World Became Modern*. His thesis has received considerable pushback from early modernists, especially those working in the history of science. But even a much more

measured approach to Lucretian thought in the period like Ada Palmer's *Reading Lucretius in the Renaissance* makes a similar case.

19. Paster, *Humoring the Body*, p. 5.

20. Ibid., p. 19.

21. Damasio, *Descartes' Error*, pp. 249–50.

22. See David Hawkes, 'Against Materialism in Early Modern Studies'. Responses to this essay were critical. See the special issue 'A New Idealism?' *Early Modern Culture: An Electronic Seminar*, 9 (2012). https://web.archive.org/web/20121225174854/emc. eserver.org/ (last accessed 25 December 2012).

23. Passannante's study, *The Lucretian Renaissance*, is an exception, as his thesis is more about the way Lucretius' poem informed poetic language prior to the moment when atomism began to receive serious attention from natural philosophers.

24. Palmer, *Reading Lucretius in the Renaissance*, pp. 4–5. Palmer cites the influence of Lucretius on Giordano Bruno and Fracastoro, but notes that neither could be called an atomist. It was not until the seventeenth century that the atomist position was seriously felt in science. Palmer nevertheless suggests that it was the influence of Lucretius that ultimately pushed Western thought towards modern science.

25. The 'material turn' in early modern studies has occurred alongside what Arthur Marotti and Ken Jackson dubbed 'the turn to religion in early modern studies' in their article of that name in the journal *Criticism*. While these have generally developed independently, the two may be more connected than they at first appear. Interest in the immaterial is, of course, more germane to those associated with the religious turn.

26. Wall-Randell, *The Immaterial Book*, p. 3.

27. Sofer, *Dark Matter*, p. 3.

28. Eggert defines her neologism 'disknowledge' as 'the conscious and deliberate setting aside of one compelling mode of understanding the world – one discipline, one theory – in favor of another' (*Disknowledge*, p. 3).

29. For an account of the development of theories of vision, see, for example, Stuart Clark, *Vanities of the Eye* and David C. Lindberg, *Theories of Vision*.

30. The phrase is Jan Kott's from his celebrated book of the same name.

31. On presentism see Terence Hawkes, *Shakespeare in the Present*; Hugh Grady and Terence Hawkes, *Presentist Shakespeares*; Hugh Grady, *Shakespeare's Universal Wolf*; and, more recently, Ewan Fernie, *Shakespeare for Freedom: Why the Plays Matter*.

32. *Othello*, 3.3.400, 402 in *The Norton Shakespeare*, 3rd edn, ed. Stephen Greenblatt et al. (New York: Norton, 2015). Unless otherwise indicated, all references to Shakespeare will be to this edition and cited in the text.

33. See Frank Kermode's introduction to the play in the Riverside edition, in which he follows J. C. Maxwell in suggesting that the ocular proof Othello demands is impossible.

34. The Folio version of this line, 'our philosophy' rather than 'your philosophy', makes the point even more clearly.

35. See, for example, Cavell's *Disowning Knowledge*.

36. On this point see Gary Kuchar's discussion of Herbert's didacticism in 'Distraction and Ethics of Poetic Form in *The Temple*'.

37. Some identify G. W. F. Hegel with phenomenology, though he is more often identified with German Idealism. In early modern studies, see particularly the work of Paul Kottman. My focus is on the form of phenomenology that began with Edmund Husserl, building on the work of Franz Brentano, in an effort to respond to the German Idealism of Hegel and Immanuel Kant. Though Hegel and Kant had a profound effect on phenomenology, the practice and focus of phenomenological enquiry that interests me is associated primarily with the French offshoot identified with Maurice Merleau-Ponty, Emmanuel Levinas, Michel Henry and Jean-Luc Marion. All of these philosophers are in one way or another responding to Martin Heidegger's existential phenomenology through a return to phenomenality. I discuss these developments in more detail below.

38. See Smith, *The Acoustic World of Early Modern England* and *The Key of Green*.

39. Smith, *Phenomenal Shakespeare*, p. 178.

40. Ibid., p. 180.

41. On the variety of phenomenological approaches to Shakespeare, see the special issue on 'Shakespeare and Phenomenology', *Criticism*, 54.3 (2012), ed. Kevin Curran and James Kearney. Paster's work on humoral theory and early modern emotions is also important here, as are the essays in two important collections on early modern sensation: Elizabeth Harvey's collection *Sensible Flesh* and Gail Kern Paster, Katherine Rowe and Mary Floyd Wilson, *Reading the Early Modern Passions: Essays in the Cultural History of Emotion*.

42. Lupton, 'Macbeth's Martlets', p. 365. Lupton is following Michael Lewis and Tanja Staehler, *Phenomenology: An Introduction*.

43. The concept of 'affordances' has received considerable attention recently. In Komarine Romdenh-Romluc's description of the term as defined by James Gibson, 'an affordance is a possibility for action offered by an environment of a certain sort to a particular kind of creature. The possibilities for action that an environment affords a creature depends on the physical structure of that creature, its motor capacities, the nature of the environment, and how the creature is situated with respect to that environment'; 'Thought in Action', p. 199.

44. See *OED*, 'appearance', 14. a. concr. 'That which appears; an object meeting the view; esp. a natural occurrence presenting itself to observation; a phenomenon', and 14.b. 'That which appears without being material; a phantom or apparition.'

45. Husserl, *Ideas I*, § 42, pp. 120–2.

46. Heidegger would go even further, to the Presocratics, in order to avoid Platonic dualism.

47. On this development, see Spiegelberg, *Phenomenological Movement*, vol. 1.

48. Brentano, qtd in Spiegelberg, *Phenomenological Movement*, vol. 1, pp. 39–40.

49. Crowell, 'Transcendental Phenomenology', p. 29, emphasis original.

50. Crowell identifies three stages of the reduction that have been identified, though not without considerable debate. The *epoché* is the first, followed by the transcendental-phenomenological reduction, and the 'eidetic reduction' proper, which is where Husserl located knowledge of essences; 'Transcendental Phenomenology', p. 28.

51. See Husserl, *Ideas I* and Emmanuel Levinas, *The Theory of Intuition in Husserl's Phenomenology*.

52. Spiegelberg, *Phenomenological Movement*, vol. 1, p. 118. Considering these roots of phenomenological analysis in medieval and early modern thought helps to recover something of the early modern cultural experience that has been obscured by an acceptance of two now highly questionable critical assumptions about the period's historical development: (1) that Renaissance humanism, and its concomitant Neoplatonism, led to an utter rejection of scholastic Aristotelianism, and (2) that around the same time, the rise of empirical science and the revival of atomism undermined Aristotelian natural philosophy, making way for the modern scientific era. Both claims have been used to explain how early modern English intellectual culture shifted from one in which textual authority and reason-based logic guided the pursuit of knowledge to one in which empirical observation and demonstration displaced tradition, placing the human capacity for experimental demonstration at the centre of the knowledge-making process.

53. Hintikka, 'The Notion of Intuition in Husserl', p. 169.

54. Ibid., p. 170.

55. See Heidegger, *The Essence of Truth: On Plato's Cave Allegory and Theaeteus*, pp. 1–84.

56. Merleau-Ponty, *The Visible and the Invisible*.

57. See Merleau-Ponty, 'Indirect Language and the Voices of Silence'.

58. Scott Davidson, 'Translator's Preface', p. viii.

59. See Dan Zahavi, 'Michel Henry and the Phenomenology of the Invisible'.

60. Westphal, 'Transfiguration as Saturated Phenomenon', p. 26.

61. See for example, Alain Badiou, *Ethics: An Essay on the Understanding of Evil*. Badiou claims that Levinas's concept of the 'Altogether-Other' is 'quite obviously the ethical name for God' (p. 22).

62. See Bruce R. Smith, 'Phenomophobia, or Who's Afraid of Merleau-Ponty?', p. 481.

63. This is the point made by Arthur Marotti and Ken Jackson in their article 'The Turn to Religion in Early Modern Studies'.

64. Louis Althusser's powerful examination of the church as an example of an 'ideological state apparatus' along with Marx's characterisation of religion as an ideologically mystifying cultural institution have led to the commonplace conflation of religion and ideology. See Althusser's influential essay 'Ideology and Ideological State Apparatuses: Notes Toward an Investigation'.

CHAPTER 1

IMMATERIALITY AND THE LANGUAGE OF THINGS

First of all, and before that any creature was, God made heaven and earth of nothing.

> Marginal gloss to Genesis 1: 1, Geneva Version

At a pivotal moment in the middle of *Othello*'s temptation scene, Emilia offers Iago an object he has long desired. The exchange is evocative:

> IAGO   How now? What do you do here alone?
> EMILIA Do not you chide: I have a thing for you.
> IAGO   You have a thing for me? It is a common thing –
> EMILIA   Ha?
> IAGO   – To have a foolish wife.
> EMILIA Oh, is that all? What will you give me now
>   For that same handkerchief? (3.3.298–305)

The 'thing' Emilia has for Iago is arguably the most important thing in the play: the storied handkerchief, Othello's symbolically freighted first token of love for Desdemona. Iago, thinking Emilia refers to the one thing she has in the relationship that gives her power – her sexuality – attempts to get the upper hand by humiliating her with a bawdy joke.

The only 'thing' she has is common to all women and therefore not particularly valuable to him; Emilia's 'thing' is, in
the misogynist lingo of the day, 'nothing'. Anticipating the
joke that will come at her expense, and the expense of all
women, Emilia interrupts him with 'ha?' only to allow Iago
to change course and suggest that the 'common thing' to
which he refers is that it is common for a man to have a
'foolish wife'. The joke is still on Emilia, but without the
demeaning reference to female anatomy. Emilia's surprise 'is
that all?' confirms that she had a clear idea of where Iago's
jab was originally headed, and it would not have been lost on
early modern audiences that the interplay between thing and
nothing lay at the heart of the joke.[1]

The play on the relationship between thing and nothing
in the banter between Iago and Emilia reflects the period's
fascination with the difference between material and immaterial things. The elusive concept of immateriality functions
in early modern literature in a way similar to how 'nothing' does in Emilia and Iago's exchange, for just as 'nothing'
has no meaning without things, immateriality always operates semantically in relation to materiality. The first sense in
the OED for the English term 'immaterial' makes this clear:
'Not formed or consisting of matter; incorporeal; intangible;
not material'.[2] This use of the term dates from John Walton's
verse translation of Boethius' Consolation of Philosophy
(c. 1410), and is current into the early modern period and
still in use today. In 1598, John Florio included the Italian
term immateriale in his A vvorlde of wordes, or Most copious, and exact dictionarie in Italian and English, defining
it simply: 'without matter'.[3] Meaning is constituted through
classic structural opposition in this case, and the categories to
which the related terms refer are mutually exclusive: just as a
thing cannot be nothing, and nothing cannot be a thing, the
immaterial cannot be material, and the material cannot be
immaterial. As I have already discussed in the Introduction,

the distinction between material and immaterial grounded some of the early modern period's most foundational categories – body and soul, earthly and spiritual, visible and invisible, brain and mind, extended and non-extended, sense and thought, and so on. Attitudes towards the immaterial and material structured the way early modern writers represented the nature of things and the claims they made about reality. Whether something was material or immaterial determined where it was to be placed in the overall taxonomy of things, and consequently, how it was to be analysed and understood. Earthly, visible things like bodies existed in the natural world, and were placed under the purview of natural philosophers and physicians, while invisible, spiritual things like souls were the subject of theology and left to divines. Yet the materiality and immateriality of these categories was complicated by their supposed interaction. Immaterial minds were thought to be 'seated' in the material brain, bodies were the 'prisons' of souls, sensation led to thought, material affliction was a path to God. This interplay between the material and immaterial realms is reflected most clearly in the language used by metaphysicians, theologians and natural philosophers to describe the natural and spiritual worlds. My discussion here begins with a survey of the language of materiality and immateriality in those discursive fields.

'Thing', the key term in the exchange between Emilia and Iago, operated on both sides of the material/immaterial divide in early modern usage, as it still does today. The *OED* reminds us that 'thing' can refer to both 'That which is thought; a thought, an idea, a notion, an opinion, a belief' and 'A material object, an article, an item; a being or entity consisting of matter, or occupying space'.[4] Two Latin–English dictionaries from the period emphasise the second sense in their definitions of the Latin *materia*. Thomas Cooper cites Quintilian on the meaning of *materia*: 'Matter whereof any *thing* is made: timber: woode: the body of the tree vnder the barke'.⁵ This sense appears at first to be closely related to the one Aristotle proposes in *Physics*:

> Things which come to be without qualification, come to be in different ways: by changing of shape, as a statue; by addition, as things which grow; by taking away, as the Hermes from the stone; by putting together, as a house; by alteration, as things which turn in respect of their matter.
>
> It is plain that these are all cases of coming to be from some underlying thing.⁶

As simply an 'underlying thing', matter would be the stuff from which something is made (wooden things are made of wood, metal things, metal, etc.). But Aristotle refines the definition of matter specifically in relation to his 'hylomorphic' theory of substance:

> The underlying nature can be known by analogy. For as the bronze is to the statue, the wood to the bed, or the matter and the formless before receiving form to anything which has form, so is the underlying nature to substance, i.e. the 'this' or existent.⁷

Aristotle's concern is with ontology here, the nature of existence, an enquiry that leads him to the more important category of 'substance'. The word 'substance', like the word 'thing', can refer to both material and immaterial entities. Both mark existing entities without specifying their material or immaterial nature. The Aristotelian tradition informing Cooper's definition of '*materia*' via Quintilian is the largely *theoretical* Aristotelian proposition that matter is a formless substrate ('that which underlies'). But though it is *like* the bronze that underlies the statue, it differs in that it cannot be identified on its own as bronze can be; it is stuffness, not specific stuff. This is theoretical because the necessity of matter is a logical proposition: for example, there must be some matter that underlies in order for there to be a material thing.

Here, another early modern translation of *materia* complicates the distinction between material and immaterial. In his *Dictionarium linguae Latinae et Anglicanae* (1587), Thomas Thomas includes the same reference to Quintilian, but adds 'also, the argument of a booke, oration, or poesie'.[8] Matter here is substrate not only of material things but also immaterial ideas; it can be taken physically as in the 'body of the tree under the bark' or figuratively, as in the 'argument' underlying the linguistic work: Gertrude's 'More matter with less art' (2.2.95). Thomas's second sense of matter appears to be more Platonic than Aristotelian. Rather than the formless substrate that will take on the form, ideational matter for Thomas is the form in the Platonic sense: the immaterial 'argument' that informs the sensible 'book, oration, or poesie'.[9]

The language of 'things' is further complicated in the theological context. For his entry on 'thing' in his *Christian dictionarie* (1612), Thomas Wilson derives both the material and immaterial senses of the term from scripture:

1. Some reall substance or quality, eyther good or euill. Ephe. 1, 11. *Which worketh all thinges after the counsell of his will.*

2. Some word spoken of God, touching that which was after to be done. Luke 1, 37. *With God shall nothing be vnpossible.* In the Greeke Text it is read (no word shall be impossible.)

3. The doctrine of the Gospell. Actes 17, 32. *We will heare thee againe of this Thing.*[10]

Again we find the trace of Aristotle in the reference to substance, but the shift to the theological register places an additional rhetorical emphasis on the immaterial over the material. This is clear in the second two senses, which identify 'word' and 'doctrine' as the 'things' to which one should attend. But Wilson's first definition also points to the inter-mingling of material and immaterial things. 'Some reall sub-stance or quality' could refer equally to a 'reall' (existing) but immaterial thing, like God, or a 'reall' (existing) material thing in the earthly world. Indeed, in the verse just before the one Wilson quotes, St Paul refers to 'all things in Christ, both which are in heaven and which are on earth' (Eph. 1: 10; KJV). 'Thing' is thus a catch-all term referring to what Aristotle calls 'existents': 'substances' of varying material and immaterial nature.

The same play between things material and immaterial obtains in the scene from *Othello* with which I began this chapter. When Emilia tells Iago she has 'a thing' for him, we know from context that the thing she has is a material object, the handkerchief she opportunistically picked up when it fell from Othello's hand. Nevertheless, Iago initially imagines that Emilia refers to her sexuality – that the thing she has *for him* is the ability to please him with her anatomical 'lack'. Her 'nothing' here ironically draws on the meaning of 'thing' as something material (a part of her physical anatomy misog-ynistically and paradoxically figured as absence).[11] Iago's pivot, that the 'thing' is the 'common' knowledge that men have 'foolish wives', shifts from the material to the immate-rial sense of the term (that men have foolish wives is an *idea*, albeit a misogynist one). Intriguingly, the *pleasure* Emilia intended to offer Iago all along is less clearly on one or the other side of the material/immaterial divide. Upon picking up the handkerchief in the first place, she says that only 'heaven knows' what Iago wants with it, her own intention is 'noth-ing, but to please his fantasy' (3.3.297). Her phrasing here leads us from things to the thoughts we have about them, raising an important early modern question about the meta-physical status of the objects of thought – whether knowl-edge, ideas, illusions, desires and so on exist materially or immaterially (or in some combination).

What kind of things are thoughts? What exactly is Iago's 'fantasy'? Emilia indicates that it is hidden to all but God (only 'heaven knows' his thought), and yet it is apparently a thing of some sort, something that could presumably be 'pleased'. The peculiar status of thought is also apparent when Othello demands of Iago: 'Show me thy thought' (3.3.115). On the one hand, Iago's 'fantasy' could be considered material, or at least a direct product of material sensation. Following scholastic, primarily Aristotelian, faculty psychology, ideas were understood to be images (*phantasms*) impressed on the mind by the faculty of the imagination (*phantasie*), in a process that can be compared to the material impression of a seal in wax.[12] Belief in the materiality of sense impressions is apparent in such moments as the opening of *A Midsummer Night's Dream*, when Egeus claims that Lysander has 'stolen the impression of [Hermia's] fantasy' (1.1.32). His language is derived from the world of material things, in which impressions are made and things are stolen. Whether the materiality of the mental impression is of the same kind as a physical impression like that of metal on wax was a matter of some debate in the period; Egeus could be intending a figurative use, for example. But accepting for the moment that such language points to the material status of imagination – or at least the imagination's grounding in material sensation as Aristotle would have it – the pleasure Emilia offers, though not sexual, could be considered sensuous. In pleasing Iago's fantasy, Emilia implies that she will affect him somatically – she will move him – at the same time that she will fulfil an intellectual desire (his thought).

On the other hand, however, 'fantasy' was also associated with mental images divorced from any material support, including perhaps most problematically, illusions – pure fabrications of the mind.[13] Consider the immateriality of

Theseus's 'airy nothing' to which imagination gives 'a local habitation and a name', or the 'baseless fabric' that underwrites Prospero's spectacular masque. Poetically speaking, both of these examples identify powerful illusions with a mental power, the ability to produce 'conceits', the things of poets, what the sonneteers would call 'ideas'.[14] And, unlike the phantasm of Aristotelian faculty psychology, the poetic notion of the conceit is more readily accommodated by a Platonist than an Aristotelian articulation of the form/instance relation. The Neoplatonic model is signalled, for example, in Sir Philip Sidney's formulation of 'Idea' as 'fore-conceit'. The conceit precedes and exists apart from the poem in which it is imperfectly represented.[15] Prospero's description of his masque as an 'insubstantial pageant' – the earliest use of the term 'insubstantial' cited in *OED* – suggests that the idea and the vehicle of perception are distinct in kind and different in fact.[16] If the pageant is insubstantial, 'illusory', 'lacking in reality', the experience we and the two young lovers have just had must exist in another realm. The dismissal of the pageant's material substance underscores the fundamental immateriality of the idea behind it without denying its ideational power – we have no trouble understanding the masque's point, its 'conceit'. Prospero's language appears to be explicitly Neoplatonic and Christian. For the Platonist, the form has priority over the particular – apart from any material instantiation – and when reconciled with Christian theology, Neoplatonism supports the transcendental hierarchy in which spiritual (immaterial) things have real substance while material, mutable things are insubstantial. Prospero's identification of his 'insubstantial pageant' with the natural world, 'the great globe itself', puts both of them on the side of the corruptible materiality that will ultimately fade into nothing, and 'leave not a rack behind'. The idea (or form) of perfect, fecund marital union, however, remains.

In his preface to Euclid's *Geometry*, the polymath John Dee offers a taxonomy of things that reflects the period's interest in making such distinctions along material and immaterial lines:

> All thinges which are, & haue beyng, are found vnder a triple diuersitie generall. For, either, they are demed Supernaturall, Naturall, or, of a third being. Thinges Supernaturall, are immateriall, simple, indiuisible, incorruptible, & vnchangeable. Things Naturall, are materiall, compounded, diuisible, corruptible, and chaungeable. Thinges Supernaturall, are, of the minde onely, comprehended: Things Naturall, of the sense exterior, are hable to be perceiued. In thinges Naturall, probabilitie and coniecture hath place: But in things Supernaturall, chief demonstration, & most sure Science is to be had. By which properties & comparasons of these two, more easily may be described, the state, condition, nature and property of those thinges, which, we before termed of a third being: which, by a peculier name also, are called *Thynges Mathematicall*. For, these, beyng (in a maner) middle, betwene thinges supernaturall and naturall: are not so absolute and excellent, as thinges supernatural: Nor yet so base and grosse, as things naturall: But are thinges immateriall: and neuerthelesse, by materiall things hable somewhat to be signified.[17]

As Dee's Neoplatonic account indicates, the pressing question that lay behind the desire for a metaphysical taxonomy of things concerned the commerce between what appeared to be two distinct ontological realms.[18] The ontological distinction raises an epistemological problem. How can immaterial things comprehended 'of the mind onely' be compared to material things 'hable to be perceived'? What, in other words, is the relationship between thought and perception, idea and sensation, truth and experience? Dee's distinction between the methods required for the comprehension of natural and supernatural things reveals his belief that the latter is the more valuable; 'probabilitie and conjecture' are suitable for gleaning knowledge of the natural, material world, but 'chief demonstration and most sure Science' are required for an understanding of immaterial, supernatural things. The term 'science' here is potentially confusing, as Dee uses it in the medieval sense of 'wisdom, knowledge'.[19] In the hierarchy of knowledge, the highest is the most pure, the least touched by materiality. Elsewhere Dee outlines the method even more explicitly, thanking God for giving him the ability 'incessantly to seek' after divine truth:

> by the true philosophical method ... proceeding and ascending (as it were) *gradatim* from things visible, to consider of things spiritual: from things bodily, to conceiue of things spirituall: from things transiorie, and & momentanie, to meditation of things permanent: by things mortall (*visible and invisible*) to have some perceiverance of immortality.[20]

Dee's hierarchy of things relies on commonly accepted qualities marking the distinction between natural (material) and supernatural (immaterial) realms: bodily, transitory and mortal are opposed to spiritual, permanent and immortal.[21] The material nature of human corruption, the vulnerability of the body to death, for example, and the immaterial nature of God, an incorruptible perfect being, were unquestioned truths at the end of the sixteenth century. Yet the clarity of this ontological distinction only placed more pressure on the question of how the material and immaterial were related, a question that was often expressed in epistemological terms. Following Plotinus, Dee's third category of things, 'being (in a manner) middle', is thus in many ways the most important. This middle category is where Dee places mathematical things – for example, numbers and, in the case of Euclid, geometric shapes. These, though unchanging like supernatural immaterial things, can be 'somewhat signified' by material things. Mathematics is a special case of abstraction that is very closely tied to the distinction between immaterial and material.[22] Numbers are special because, while abstract, they are never misleading, always potentially grounded. The material signification of immaterial mathematical propositions or concepts seems to suggest a direct connection between the immaterial and the material that is elsewhere withheld. The number two always aligns with two material things. Other abstractions, however, are not so reliable. Non-mathematical abstractions, ideas about anything from colours to human intentions or desires, could be illusory or the result of cognitive error.

Immaterial illusions (ideational errors about reality) had to be accounted for in material terms, as error is by nature imperfect, and thereby earthly. Despite the fact that thoughts seemed to be immaterial – or at least very close, 'trifles, light as air' – they could not be placed in the same category with eternal truths, unchanging laws. This is the basis of the distinction between Ideas (known in the intellect) and thoughts (part of the process of cognition), although both remain tethered to the material. The proposition that immaterial ideas (free from material corruption) could effectively govern human action became one of the touch points in religious debates over the efficacy of faith versus ceremony, and word versus deed. To one extent or another, reformers held that the corruption of the Roman church was a result of an over-investment in its material components; reform meant purging the church of ornament and ceremony in excess of God's word and the believer's faith.

For the Roman Catholic authorities, on the other hand, the removal of the material elements of devotion was a dangerous path to conceptual error. The desire to account for thought in material terms was in part a way of protecting the purity of the immaterial realm as separate and spiritual. In 1633, the

English Jesuit Lawrence Anderton used precisely this argument in his polemic against the validity of the Protestant Church, and Calvinism in particular:

> Calvin defineth the true Church (and therefore in his owne judgement the Protestant Church) to *consist only of the number of the faythfull & Elect, and only to be knowne to God.* Now, what other thing is this Church, then a bare Intention (as the Philosophers speake) or phantasme wrought in the shop of his owne brayne?[23]

In his title, Anderton specifically refers to the Protestant church as 'a Platonical Idea', 'a mere nothing'. The insulting charge of Platonism reflects Anderton's metaphysical commitment to the Aristotelian tradition, limiting knowledge to that which is first available to the senses, only later to ascend to the contemplation of God. But it also highlights an anxiety about the inaccessibility of the divine to thought; if only God knows who is faithful, how can one even talk about the faith of others or one's own faith? There must be something experiential that connects imperfect nature with perfect spirit.

Identifying his fantastical masque with a 'harmless', 'insubstantial pageant' – a mere illusion – Prospero walks a fine line. On the one hand, he seeks to calm the agitated Ferdinand by stressing the illusion's lack of material substance; these 'spirits' who melted into 'thin air' cannot harm precisely because they are not material things. But, in another way, they are like material things in that they are transitory and corruptible as opposed to eternal and unchanging like the concepts they portray. The interaction between these two kinds of things is highlighted further in Prospero's concern over Ferdinand's fragile mental state, a concern based on a material change in his appearance: he 'look[s] ... in a moved sort, / As if [he] were dismayed' (4.1.146–7). Prospero worries that the visions have physically moved, perhaps even undone, poor Ferdinand. Importantly, the visible change in Ferdinand is also a response to a physical change in Prospero, his stated agitation over the Caliban plot. Prospero mingles the material and immaterial here, first citing his 'weakness' as a result of his vexation, his 'troubled brain', only to suggest the cure will be physical movement, 'a turn or two, I'll walk / To still my beating mind' (4.1.162–3). One would expect to hear of a mind 'troubled' and a brain 'beating' (throbbing), but the terms are reversed, suggesting a movement from brain to mind. Shakespeare's poetic inversion of brain and mind – the material organ and the immaterial faculty respectively – reflects the period's concern with the commerce between sensation and cognition. In the still dominant Aristotelian account, thoughts were always derived from sense experience, the materiality of their origin in sense grounding them in a process that moved incrementally from perception to abstraction. In Prospero we find the commingling of the Aristotelian and Platonic traditions seen in Dee's method. Though Dee advocates a methodical attention to things, in which one moves 'gradatum' from material to immaterial (in Aristotelian fashion), his taxonomy of things is ultimately hierarchical and Neoplatonic in its favouring of the immaterial as the goal of science, knowledge. Prospero's concern that the uncertain materiality of the 'insubstantial' spectacle had dismayed Ferdinand masks his ulterior motive to use a conceit to achieve his goal of driving home the lesson about ideal generative marriage to the man who will be his daughter's husband. The move suggests his confidence that immaterial fictions had the power to guide human action in the material world. This possibility is also, of course, the basis for Iago's entire plan in *Othello*. He will undo the General with *ideas*, 'Dangerous conceits [which] are, in their natures, poisons' (3.3.323). When Iago's immaterial poison begins to work, Othello will be moved to an act of material destruction.

The 'thing' Emilia has for Iago is the hinge between the reason-bound Othello of the first acts – one who muses in the abstract that he would not 'make a life of jealousy', but rather 'see before I doubt; when I doubt, prove' – and the murderer of the later scenes who will 'tear' Desdemona 'to pieces' on the authority of a reported dream (3.3.175, 188, 427). These two Othellos correspond roughly to two different directions for ideation: the first, Aristotelian, in which sense perception leads to conceptualisation, and the second, Platonist, in which an idea (Desdemona's infidelity) informs the play's physical action. The handkerchief manages to cross the threshold of the material and immaterial, being at once thing and nothing: the material, 'ocular proof' on which Othello condemns Desdemona, and one of the immaterial 'trifles, light as air' that Iago knows to be 'strong as holy writ'.[24]

That the handkerchief, explicitly identified as a 'thing', lies at the centre of the play's exploration of the dynamic interplay between the material and immaterial is suggestive for another linguistic reason. In addition to the term's denotations as both immaterial thought and material object, it can also refer to the meeting place between them. As has been noted by practitioners of 'thing theory', the term has an ancient association with the Scandinavian political assembly or meeting, and the earliest English sense of the term in *OED* is: 'A meeting, or the matter or business considered by it'.[25] This is evidently the sense Iago intends when speaking to Othello just prior to his exchange with Emilia. Iago urges Othello to 'Scan this thing no further' (3.3.244). 'Thing' here could refer to either the 'matter' that just came up or the momentous meeting between the ensign and his commander. The play's engagement with the language of the law similarly links the term to judicial proceedings, as a reference to a court or cause, echoed later in the murder scene.[26] By extension, the meeting between Othello and Iago in 3.3 can be read as a meeting of the material and immaterial: practical, material Othello, meets the immaterial, rhetorically virtuosic Iago. The opposition is set up in the play's opening act, when the overtly racist Brabantio describes Othello as a 'thing', and Iago's opaque, self-description, 'I am not what I am' (1.1.63), suggests he is nothing.[27]

Even a brief review of the early modern language of things reveals how central the interrelation of materiality and immateriality was in the three particular discursive fields surveyed here: metaphysics, theology and psychology. As I indicated in the Introduction, these fields correspond to three areas of human experience – being, believing and thinking – around which I have chosen to organise this book. The purpose of this chapter has been to stress that these discursive fields were hopelessly intertwined in the period. Natural philosophers mused over metaphysical questions as well as psychological and theological ones, as did theologians and metaphysicians (commonly called 'philosophers'). Physicians ostensibly focused on the nature of the body and thus the brain, and yet the mind and the thoughts it produced affected the body and were fair game in their accounts. And though the soul was the ostensible purview of theologians, philosophers and natural philosophers routinely opined on its nature and physicians mused over its relation to the body. Dividing this book into three parts corresponding to being, believing and thinking is thus a purely strategic way to organise material in which these categories continually interpenetrate one another. And, as the present project seeks to explore early modern attitudes towards the nature of things, there is no better place to start than with the topic of being to which I now turn.

Notes

1. Iago's association of Emilia's 'common thing' with 'nothing' depends on a lack perceivable only when the female anatomy is figured as the negation of its male counterpart: one is a thing, the other nothing.

2. *OED* A.adj.1a. The entry ends with 'Also: spiritual, ethereal'. I will address this important addendum below.

3. Florio, *A vvorlde of wordes*, p. 167.

4. *OED* n1.I.5b, n1.II.11a.

5. Cooper, *Thesaurus linguæ Romanæ & Britannicæ*, EEee3r, emphasis added. Aristotle's term 'hyle' also means 'wood'.

6. Aristotle, *Complete Works*, vol. 1, p. 325 (*Physics*, 190b 5–10).

7. Ibid., p. 326 (191a 9–12).

8. Thomas, *Dictionarium linguae Latinae et Anglicanae*. Thomas also includes an entry on 'Materialis' (materiality) attributed to Macrobius: 'that is of some matter'.

9. That an essentially Aristotelian account of matter can exist alongside a Platonic one is not surprising, as the two philosophical positions had been commingled since late antiquity. After centuries of transmission and interpretation through the Christian Middle Ages, early modern Neoplatonists held Aristotelian positions and Aristotelians regularly drew on Platonic formulae. But the two metaphysical positions are really not compatible, and the uneasy alliance that held through the medieval period became increasingly unstable in the Renaissance. See Will West, 'What's the Matter with Shakespeare: Physics, Identity, Playing'.

10. Wilson, *A Christian dictionarie*, Ii3r, emphasis original.

11. Much excellent scholarship has detailed the early modern identification of the female anatomy with lack. Hamlet's bawdy banter with Ophelia during The Mousetrap is often a point of departure. In addition to the play on the word 'nothing', the letter 'o' is consistently associated with both an iconic representation of the vagina and a signifier for symbolic absence. See, for example, Amy Cook, 'Staging Nothing: Hamlet and Cognitive Science'. As Cook points out: 'Hamlet manipulates "nothing" into something, calling Ophelia's nothing "a fair thought to lie between maids' legs." In Hamlet's dexterous use of words, nothing is suddenly the genital space, and Ophelia's nothing must be viewed through the mental space of the penis's thingness. Compared to Hamlet's thing, Ophelia's is absent;

but both are made mentally visible through Hamlet's language'
(p. 87).

12. See *OED* 'Fantasy / Phantasy, n': 'Mental apprehension of an
object of perception; the faculty by which this is performed'
(1a). And 'The image impressed on the mind by an object of
sense' (1b). The comparison appears in Plato's *Theaetetus*.
The impression of the seal in wax is among Shakespeare's
favourite tropes. I address cognition and imagination in more
detail in the third part of this book.

13. Recall Leontes' affection speech in which 'Affection' is
'coactive' with 'what's unreal', and as a result can 'fellow'st
nothing' (1.1.141–2).

14. For example, Sir Philip Sidney's definition of conceit in his
Defence of Poesy and Samuel Daniel's sonnet sequence *Idea's
Mirror*.

15. It is possible to explain this using Aristotelian potentiality
and actuality (the fore-conceit representing potentiality), but
considering the humanist origins of the Sidnean conception
of the poetic 'Idea', Neoplatonism is the more likely source.
It is not surprising, however, that Sidney himself was alternatively influenced by Neoplatonism and Aristotelianism in the
Defence.

16. *OED* 'Insubstantial: Not existing in substance or reality; not
real; imaginary; illusive; non-substantial' (adj. 1).

17. Euclid, *The elements of geometrie*, *4v.

18. See Aristotle, *Metaphysics*, trans. Hugh Lawson-Tancred,
p. 24 (987b): 'Again, in addition to sensible objects and Forms,
they said that mathematical objects existed between them, differing from the sensibles in that they were eternal and unchanging and from the forms in that there were many similar ones
but only one Form of any kind.'

19. *OED*, 'science', 1.a., 'The state or fact of knowing. Knowledge or cognizance of something'. A comparison can be found
in the development of phenomenology as a 'science' in the
hands of Husserl and other early practitioners. Though they
claimed to seek a pure science of experience, their philosophical methods diverged from what we currently associate with

modern science (most notably, repeatable experimentation). Merleau-Ponty and Henry both continue to consider the goal of phenomenology to be scientific in this older sense.

20. Dee, *A Letter*, A2v, emphasis original.

21. Dee does not include the visible and invisible in the first opposition, opening the possibility of grouping things both visible and invisible under the rubric of 'things mortall'. This is important, and I will return to it below.

22. The distinction of mathematics as a special case is commonplace in the period. Typical is the seventeenth-century *Physiologie, or a Treatise of Naturall Philosophy* found in BL MS Sloane 2521, which begins by equating natural philosophy with physics and then goes on to make the distinction between natural things ('things subject to generation and corruption') and those that concern metaphysics, which 'treat[s] of things supernatural such as God and Angels', but also mathematics, 'for though they treat of natural things, yet soe as they are abstract from all matter. But physics treat of things concreat and adhering or adjoyning to matter' (f. 2r).

23. Anderton, *Non-Entity of Protestancy*, H6v–H7r, emphasis original.

24. Iago's reference to 'holy writ' invokes the complex theological concept of the 'Word', or Logos, Christ as intermediary between earth and heaven. On the phenomenology of vision and the dual role of the handkerchief, see my *Image Ethics in Shakespeare and Spenser*, ch. 6.

25. *OED*, 'thing', I. See Bill Brown, 'Thing Theory', and Martin Heidegger, 'The Thing' in *Poetry, Language, Thought*.

26. See Patricia Parker, 'Othello and Hamlet: Dilation, Spying, and the "Secret Place" of Woman', p. 68.

27. Brabantio charges that Desdemona would never 'Run from her guardage to the sooty bosom / Of such a thing as thou, to fear, not to delight' (1.1.70–1). Iago's statement would have been recognised immediately as an inversion of God's 'I am that I am' (Ex. 3: 14). Othello's recounting of being sold into slavery and his 'redemption thence' further establishes the play's thematic association of Othello with materiality.

While Othello seemingly succumbs to Brabantio's racist suggestion in the end, describing himself as a 'dog' just before committing suicide in the final scene, his ability to recognise his own inhumanity ironically confirms that he possesses the intellect that separates the human from the beast. In contrast, Iago disappears with a vow of silence: 'From this time forth I never will speak word' (5.2.297), only to become subject to the material power of the state, 'the censure' described in explicitly material terms: 'The time, the place, the torture – oh, enforce it' (5.2.361).

PART I

BEING

'THERE ARE MORE THINGS IN HEAVEN AND EARTH': MATERIAL AND IMMATERIAL SUBSTANCE AND EARLY MODERN ONTOLOGY

Iago's claim, 'I am not what I am' (1.1.63), can be read as his assurance to Roderigo that he is playing Othello by appearing to be what he is not ('I am not what I appear to be'). On one level, of course, this has to be what he means.[1] But what he actually says invokes metaphysical questions related to the material/immaterial distinction that is the subject of this book. As an explicit inversion of the divine enunciation 'I am that I am' (Ex. 3: 14), Iago at the very least gestures at his own non-being.[2] God's being is self-evidently reflected in the form of the scriptural statement, which amounts to 'I exist, I am.' Iago's inversion of the positive statement appears to result in an equally self-evident statement of non-existence: 'I am not.' But as an utterance, the statement is impossible, a paradox: if the 'I' does not exist, there can be no statement of its non-existence. This was essentially Descartes' insight with the *cogito*: even in thinking one's non-existence, one confirms that existence. Despite the categorical sweep of Iago's statement, something remains after the negation. If Iago means to say 'I am not that General's lackey', he suggests that he is something else, though he is silent on what exactly that is.

'I am not' is opposed to 'I am' in the same way that 'immaterial' is opposed to 'material'. As we saw in the last chapter, the primary sense of 'immaterial' is 'not material'. But related senses of the word are also instructive: the legal sense, 'irrelevant', for example, labels a thing as *nothing worth considering*, despite the fact that the irrelevant thing clearly exists. This sense is found in everyday language, as in the common phrase 'It is nothing', often uttered in response to the question 'What is it?' or 'What is the matter?' Most of the time when people say 'it is nothing' they do not mean that 'it' lacks existence; more likely they mean that 'it' lacks the quality of relevance, that it doesn't *matter*. Nevertheless, the distinction between something and nothing, like that between the material and immaterial, carries ontological freight, especially in logic. Logic (reason) defines the categories as opposites, the distinction making them comprehensible: x, by virtue of being x, cannot be not-x.[3] Something cannot be both material and immaterial (not material). If something is both x and not-x, we have a paradox. It is in this context that the material/immaterial relation comes closest to the thing/nothing distinction I discussed in the last chapter. The term 'nothing' refers to the absence of some thing (or any thing) in the same way that the immaterial refers to the absence of the material. But just as we have seen that the absence of the material does not necessarily indicate non-existence (it is possible to conceive of the existence of immaterial things), nothing, despite its name, is routinely a very real object of contemplation.

On Nothing

A wide body of excellent scholarship has detailed the ways in which the term 'nothing' and the concept of nothingness captured the early modern English literary imagination. Some of the period's most popular poets and dramatists, including

Shakespeare and Donne, made 'nothing' a thematic focus, while minor poets and essayists mused over the paradox of nothing in numerous mock encomia and other works.⁴ As Paul Jorgensen, Rosalie Colie and others have noted, playful explorations of the notoriously paradoxical concept rest uneasily alongside quite serious theological and metaphysically searching passages in a wide range of early modern English texts.⁵ 'Nothing' is particularly interesting for poets and dramatists precisely because it paradoxically refers to something that is not. Lear's fool can joke that he is 'better' than his master: 'I am a fool; / thou art nothing'. Earlier in the play Cordelia's 'nothing' is no joke, generating as it does the catastrophic tragedy that follows. In both cases 'nothing' refers to 'something'. The referential character of the term 'nothing' was well understood and exploited by Shakespeare, as when Edmund's claim that he conceals 'nothing' leads as planned to increased scrutiny from Gloucester: 'The quality of nothing hath not such need to hide itself' (1.2.33–4). Gloucester's concern is with the very material letter Edmund has deliberately rushed into his pocket before his Father's eyes. Nothing is interesting at such moments primarily because it is impossible. In the literary examples I discuss in this study, nothing is almost always something. Sometimes that something is material (like Edmund's letter) and sometimes it is immaterial (as with Cordelia's love). Only rarely do we find examples of 'nothing' signifying what we might think of as nothingness rather than negation.⁶

A notable exception in the period is theological, and it makes an appearance, interestingly enough, in the opening scene of *King Lear*. When Cordelia responds to Lear's request that she articulate her love for him with a simple 'nothing', his famous response is that 'Nothing will come of nothing' (1.1.76). Though modern readers often take Lear's retort to be axiomatic, Paul Jorgensen has pointed out that Shakespeare's audience would have immediately recognised the statement to be heretical.[7] Despite the ancient dictum *ex nihilo nihil fit*, in the sixteenth century Christians across the Protestant/Roman Catholic divide accepted God's creation of the world *ex nihilo* as settled doctrine. Not only can something come of nothing, everything first came of nothing. *Creatio ex nihilo* was at the heart of the many popular and playful poems on the paradox of nothing that circulated in the English Renaissance.[8] A good example appears in the Folger Shakespeare Library copy of William Cornwallis's *Essayes on Certaine Paradoxes* (London, 1616), which includes his translation of the Latin poem 'Nihil' by the French poet Jean Passerat, under the title 'In Prayse of Nothing'. The Folger copy includes the following handwritten riddle, with an attribution to Cornwallis (W.C.) at the end of the printed text:

> Riddle
> Though I am not the Deity
> Tis known, I am as great as He:
> For I am able to withstand
> Th' Omnipotence of his right hand;
> Or I can hide me from his face,
> Though I'm extended more than Space.
> But I was visible ev'n here
> Before the Earth or Heavens were;
> And, if the Heavens and Earth should pass
> I should be where and what I was.
> W. C.

Cornwallis' trick, like others who wrote in this tradition, was to make nothing into something through personification.

The nothing out of which God created everything is nevertheless precisely the pure nothingness that had been ruled out by metaphysical philosophers since Thales.[9] Presocratic materialist accounts of the nature of the world – that everything is composed of water, air, fire and so forth – all rested uncomfortably alongside conceptions of the Gods or God.

Polydore Vergil's sixteenth-century account of the ancient understanding of the nature of God reflects the tension as understood by Renaissance humanists:

> As *Thales Milesius*, which fyrst serched suche maters, sayd that God was an vnderstandyng, that made and fashioned all thynges of the water as matter preiacent. *Pythagoras* called him a liuely mynde, that pearsed and passed through al thynges, of whom all liuyng creatures receyued theyr lyfe: and *Cleanthes* defined God to be the ayre. *Anaxagoras* estemed him to be an infinite mynde, whiche did moue it self, *Chrysippus* thought he was a natural power endued with godly reason, Some were of the opinion that there was no goddes. As *Diagoras* and *Theodorus* affirmed plaine that there was no God at al. *Protagoras* reported that he knew no certaintie of the Goddes, wherefore the Atheniens banished him out of their empire. *Epicurus* graunted there was a god, but suche one as was neither liberal, bounteful, nor that had any regarde of thinges: that is to say, God is no God, but a cruel & vnkynde monster. *Anaximander* supposed the Goddes to be borne and not to dye tyll after many ages.[10]

The specific metaphysical problem was that all of these accounts of God were derived from material experience: either through comparisons of God to the understanding or the mind, or the denial of God due to lack of material proof. All such approaches were wrongheaded, as Vergil points out:

> But in suche varietee of opinions it is a thyng difficile too determine the first ofspryng of the goddes both bycause they be but vayne, and also sprong out of mortal humanitie. And againe to speake of God as he is in his supernatural essence is a thing daungerous, bycause we can neither behold the resplendent brightnesse of his maiestie with oure corporal eyes, nor with any quickenesse of wit comprehende his infinite might.[11]

The Christian God had to be distinct from such material contamination, and it was Plato and Aristotle who offered later Christian theologians two possible ways to do this. Vergil characterises the Platonic solution as equating God with goodness (as creator and source):

> AND *Plato* saieth there is but one God, and affirmeth that this worlde was created by him: and was called God, bycause he geueth frely to men all thynges good & profitable, and is of all goodnesse in this worlde the cause principal, fountain and spryng.[12]

Christian Aristotelians would concentrate similarly on God as cause, focusing on the infinite nature of God's causal power, and emphasising Aristotle's account of the prime mover and first causes over his earlier theory of material causality and the primacy of particulars.[13]

Nothingness was thus a logical necessity for theologians seeking to define the divine essence in this way. In order for God's causal power to be infinite (perfect), He must be able to create something from nothing. In his *Treatise of the Nature of God* (1599), Thomas Morton of Berwick provides the standard explanation:

> For (by the confession of all men) the first creation of the world, requireth a power not limited, but infinit, for that it is impossible to any finite power, to create: that is, to make something of nothing: & if the power be infinit, the subiect wherein it is, must be of the same nature.[14]

The very idea that God could *not* create something out of nothing contradicts the definition of God as omnipotent.

The reference to God's creation of the world out of nothing leads to another aspect of paradox often articulated in the period: the *contemptus mundi* tradition which portrayed the material world as nothing – all is vanity – the very position articulated by Prospero in his revels speech. Consider the closing remark in the mid-sixteenth-century prose tract *The Prayse of Nothing*:

> . . . as the excellent substance of the heauens and earth were at the first created: so shall they within few reuolutions of yeares returne, as vnto their first matter: from that time forth shal iniquitye be vnhorsed, that now ouerruneth the godly with many tiranies, and then shall the good people of God tryumph wyth the Lambe for euer.[15]

In another context, the reference to 'first matter' might lead one to believe that the author is an advocate for *creatio ex materia* (the view that there was a pre-existing material chaos from which God created the world), but as the entire tract is in praise of nothing, it is clear that the anticipated return is not to chaos or unformed primal matter, but to eternal perfection, presumably the state of God's creation prior to the Fall. The point of the tract is that everything material is nothing insofar as it is the opposite of the eternal and immaterial existence that is yet to come upon salvation.

This paradox – that mortal, material existence is nothing compared to the immaterial existence to come – is, of course, a good thing because it portends a future in which 'the good people of God' will 'triumph with the Lambe forever'. The proposition that the world is vanity – derived directly from scripture – is as far from nihilism as one might get.[16] In all of this musing on nothing, it is clear that immaterial things are not nothing, non-things, but often the things most desirable to the devout believer. The crucial questions had to do with the relation of the material to the immaterial, for the real problem with ancient matter theories that failed to account for creation *ex nihilo* was that they prioritised the material over the immaterial. This hierarchy is reversed for Christian writers of all persuasions, for whom material, earthly existence is inferior to immaterial, everlasting salvation. As Donne writes in Holy Sonnet X, 'One short sleep past, we wake eternally, / And death shall be no more, Death thou shalt die'.[17] The immaterial is not nothingness, it is materiality's other; the negation of the material – its non-materiality – is positive not negative.[18] Despite this positive valence, the immaterial is nevertheless always withheld from sense. The familiar refrain 'all flesh is grass' refers to the things of the material world, all that which is subject to generation and corruption. That sensuous world's opposite is eternal, unchanging, unified, perfect. Far from being nothing, immaterial things are thus given a special ontological status. They are, in a sense, more real than material reality. But if they are always withheld from material experience, how can they be known? The fact that material things are never actually negated – that things do not become nothing, even when they cease to be what they had been – is one place to look for an answer to this question.

Substance and Change

Change from one thing to another complicates any metaphysical project. After painstakingly defining the basic substances of the world in the *Categories*, Aristotle had to address the question of how such basic substances could be one thing at one moment and another at the next. The analysis of change involves an analysis of states, and this turns out to be another important way to understand the relationship between the material and immaterial. One explanation that Aristotle develops in the *Physics* is the concept of privation, as opposed to negation. Early modern poets had a range of rhetorical strategies at their disposal that could be more properly conceived of as privation than as Iago-style negation. Upon disguising himself to avoid the notice of his father, Edgar makes the jarring, but less existential statement

'Edgar I nothing am' (2.3.21). Whereas Iago's formula is an example of pure negation, a direct contradiction (x = not x), Edgar's designates a change from one state to another: 'I am not Edgar', or more accurately, 'I am no longer Edgar', 'I have become something else'. Nevertheless, 'I am' subsists. If we take Edgar seriously, his transformation is a function of privation in the Aristotelian sense. In the *Physics*, Aristotle writes: 'we maintain that a thing may come to be from what is not in a qualified sense, i.e. accidentally. For a thing comes to be from the privation, which in its own nature is some-thing which is not'.[19] Poor Tom does not exist until Edgar ceases to be himself. Yet Edgar does not cease to exist in this formula; he ceases to be Edgar when he becomes Poor Tom.[20] Edgar's transformation into Poor Tom is an object lesson in theatre, a paradigmatic moment of Shakespearean metathe-atricality, and like other such moments, this one invites con-templation on larger questions concerning identity, essence and persistence. We know Edgar is still Edgar, just as we know that the actor playing Edgar and Poor Tom is still the same actor throughout the play and in the world beyond the play. But how do we know this? And, more to the point, what is it exactly that we know to persist? What is the thing that subsists?

All metaphysical systems must account for the relation of persistence and change. Such an attempt prompted the Presocratics to propose various monist ontologies, and it led Plato to the theory of Forms and Aristotle to hylomorphism. For materialist monists, the material substrate of the world persisted while its states appeared to change. For Plato, the transcendental realm included the persistent Forms, echoed imperfectly in the changeable material world. And in the most complicated formulation, Aristotle accounted for change through a theory of composites of matter and immanent form. Each explanation has its advantages and shortcomings. It is not surprising, then, that the problem remained an obsession in the Middle Ages and Renaissance, both periods dominated by a religion based on a remarkable event in which the immaterial became material: the word was made flesh.[21]

For the present purpose, I want to highlight how important immateriality was in the early modern exploration of being, stasis and change. As we saw in the previous chapter, the key term in the discourse surrounding this exploration is *substance*. The first philosophical definition of substance listed in the *OED* is: 'A being that subsists by itself; a distinct individual entity; (also gen.) a thing, being'.[22] The term is also used to designate that which makes a thing a particular thing, despite change over time: for example, how devout John Donne, the Dean of St Paul's, is the same as saucy John Donne, author of 'The Flea' (an example of accidental change), as well as the more difficult problem of what persists when an egg becomes a bird (a substantial change). Thus the subsequent definition: 'The essential element underlying phenomena, which is subject to modifications; the permanent substratum of things; that in which properties or attributes inhere.'[23] In the first definition one can see the persistence of the Platonic theory of transcendental Forms, something like pure existence, subsistence 'by itself', 'distinct'. Here the nature of substance, and thus of being, reality, and so forth, is static. But experience of the world teaches that change is inevitable, thus requiring some explanation. For Platonists, the answer is that reality, being, true substance transcends human experience, which is bound to the illusory, mutable world. Aristotle was not satisfied with this account of substance, and rather than posit a static ideal world beyond the one to which we have sensuous access, he developed a theory of substance that could accommodate change. While, for the Platonist, separable Forms were the 'permanent substratum of things', for Aristotelians, the important part of the second

definition was in how 'the essential element underlying phenomena' is 'subject to change', how 'properties or attributes
inhere' in substances – 'the permanent substratum of things'.
The second definition should recall the earlier discussion
of 'matter' as it relates to form, especially in the sense that
Aristotle uses the Greek term ὕλη (Latin *hyle*) to indicate the
material of composite enformed particulars explained by the
theory of hylomorphism. Both senses of 'substance' concern
the nature of what philosophers call an 'existent' and what
makes that existent thing the particular thing that it is despite
the capacity for change.

In the *Metaphysics*, Aristotle argues that there are 'two
ways of giving an account of substance, as the ultimate subject, which is never predicated of something else, and as
something which is a this-something and is also separable'.[24]
In his discussion in Book Delta, he further breaks down these
two ways of defining substance. First, in terms of predication,
things can be said to be substances 'because, far from being
predicated of some subject, the other things are predicated
of them'. This first explanation of substance, as that which
is the subject of predication, is fairly clear: Tom can be poor
and still be Tom, but poor cannot be a substance because it
is always the predicate of some subject – for example, Tom.
Alternatively, Aristotle notes that a substance can also be
'something which, being intrinsic to one of the sort of things
that are not predicated of another, is the cause of being for
it, as the soul is for the animal'.[25] This second way of understanding substance is more complicated because it begins to
sound like a distinction between matter and form: the soul
of the animal is what makes it that animal and not another;
Tom's soul sounds a lot like 'Tomness'. This more difficult
causal sense of substance is particularly important in the special case of ensouled animals and humans, to which I will
turn in a moment. For now, suffice to say that the distinction
allows Aristotle to imagine, for the purposes of argument,

two kinds of substance, one material and one formal. He will subsequently add a third, the composite of matter and form, the key to his hylomorphism. In each case a negotiation of the material and immaterial is central.

Before moving on to the question of the soul, it is worth pausing over the second half of Aristotle's definition of substance in the *Metaphysics*, which approaches substance as essence according to divisibility: substances can be seen to be 'The intrinsic parts of such things, which delimit them and indicate their thisness, parts on the elimination of which the whole is eliminated.'[26] This is in some ways the most straightforward statement of substance in the sense identified in the *OED* definition above, 'a being that subsists in itself', for if the substance is removed the thing is no longer the thing. Aristotle then puts this idea in slightly different terms to include particulars in the category of substances: 'The what-it-was-to-be-that-thing, whose account is a definition, is also said to be the substance of the particular.'[27] Substance here is equivalent to 'essence', which would seem to bring Aristotle close to Plato, whose Forms could be described as the unchanging essences of things (only poorly copied in the material world). But Aristotle retains the requirement of matter in his definition of substance – albeit a kind of matter that is not itself a substance that is discernible in its particularity or is otherwise separable. The account is summarised in an anonymous seventeenth-century treatise on natural philosophy as follows:

> Substances cannot proceed from, or be made out of that which is no substance itself; But the materia prima [first matter] is noe substance therefore no principle . . . The first matter void or deprived of all form is noe reall substance, yet it is the beginning of every substance, for by uniting of it and the forme together, it is made a perfect substance, and body: wherefore it may be called a substance though incompleat, and imperfect without the assistance of a forme.[28]

In Aristotle's fully developed system, the components of composite substances, form and matter, will correspond in their pure states to actuality (without matter) and potentiality (without form) respectively. Thus, while Aristotelian substance appears to describe that which 'underlies' discernible things, making them what they are, Aristotle largely avoids the temptation to think about essential substances apart from their iteration in things, which are always composites of form and matter in time. Aristotelian substances do not underlie as much as they simply are: the what-it-is-to-be-that-thing is immanent in the thing that is that thing.

The fact that Aristotle's Greek ousia (οὐσία) was translated in medieval Latin as both substance (*substantia*) and essence (*essentia*) confuses the matter, especially when a distinction is to be made between the two, as Aristotle seeks to do in his critique of Platonic Forms.[29] As I have already discussed, Aristotle makes an important distinction between matter and substance: the matter is the unformed 'stuff' that underlies particular substances, while the substance is (usually) the form/matter composite in which things are the things that they are. Immateriality is yet again key to the disagreement, since Plato has no problem conceiving of the Forms (what might be called substances) in immaterial terms, while Aristotle is particularly concerned with the question of whether non-sensible (immaterial) things can be considered substances. His entire system, beginning in the *Categories* and further developed in the *Physics*, is based on the idea that knowledge of substance begins with natural bodies, which are explained in the *Physics* to be the composites of matter and form. In the *Metaphysics*, he extends the category of substance to matter and form, as well as the hylomorphic matter/form composite, but he does so by qualifying the substance status of matter and form as potentiality and actuality respectively. In this more mature formulation, real particular substances are still always enformed matter, but matter that has yet to be enformed is substance potentially, while form is substance actually, though only realisable when enformed in matter. The theory is summarised at the opening of Book II of *De anima*:

> One kind, then, of the things that there are we call substance, and part of this group we say to be so as matter, that which is not in itself a particular thing, a second part we say to be so as shape and form, in accordance with which, when it applies, a thing is called a particular, and a third as that which comes from the two together. Now matter is potentiality, and form is actuality, and this in two ways, one that in which knowledge, the other that in which contemplation, is actuality.[30]

The elaborate way that Aristotle allows for the existence of substances that are immaterial is by starting with material sensible objects, a product of his belief that there is simply no reasonable way to posit the existence of separable forms untethered to experience. He repeatedly states that 'bodies are the most believed to be substances', and his entire philosophy builds from there.[31] This feature of his thought gives material things priority, at least initially, while retaining a crucial place for form: all substances are formed of matter, but matter itself has no form, and cannot thus be a substance. The difficulty of Aristotle's metaphysics derives directly from the lengths he is willing to go to reject Platonic Forms, as the separable substances that comprise existing reality. For the present purpose, it is important to note that of the three kinds of substance (matter, form and composite), only the composite is found in the phenomenal world of material things. The other two are only available theoretically: there must be matter, if everything consists of enformed matter, and there must be form, if matter is to be enformed. Those both must exist (be real), but they are only substances when experienced through things that exist hylomorphically.[32]

The philosophical disagreement I have been revisiting is well known, but my hope is to draw attention to the central role played by the categories of the material and immaterial in the development of the two positions broadly speaking. It would be a mistake to put too much pressure on fine distinctions between Platonic and Aristotelian metaphysics, since the period with which we are concerned received its ancient philosophy through intermediaries, like Plotinus, who set out intentionally to synthesise the two systems. The subsequent scholastic synthesis is especially important, perhaps most clearly in the way Aristotle's *De anima* was incorporated into a Christian theology not entirely suited to its conclusions. In the second part of this book I will turn directly to the ways in which theologians took up some of the metaphysical questions raised here concerning the nature of the soul. But first, it is important to consider how Aristotle's concept of soul is incorporated into his metaphysics of substance.

The attraction of accommodating Aristotle's treatise on the animating force of life to a theological context is initially clear. Is not the subject of *De anima* essentially what a medieval or early modern person would call the soul? The answer is at once yes and no. While medieval and early modern commentators would assume the subject of the book to be the Christian soul, Aristotle's ostensible subject (*psyche*) would more accurately be termed the 'vital principle of living things', the 'principle of life' or the 'principle of animation'.[33] As the subject of *De anima* is a 'principle' – a force or cause – as much as it is an entity, the question with which Aristotle begins his own exploration is whether the soul is a substance in the way that form is a substance (as the actuality of a thing when it is a particular thing). Aristotle's answer is an emphatic yes, but the nature of this soul-substance is complicated. In the simplest terms, the soul is the substance of the living body: 'the first actuality of a natural body with organs'.[34] This holds for living things that possess souls on a hierarchy that begins with the nutritive, and ascends through the perceptive, appetitive and locomotive, reaching its heights in the intellective, reserved only for humans. The first four faculties of the soul are relatively easy to explain in hylomorphic terms and can be accommodated to the logic that Aristotle gives to his metaphysical rejection of separable Platonic Forms. Intellect is the most complex, and the one faculty that makes the human soul exceptional.

Among the most disputed chapters in Aristotle's corpus is *De anima* 3.5, where the philosopher offers a theory of the 'active intellect' in which he attempts to retain a hylomorphic theory of substance, while also allowing for an intellective faculty that is somehow separable from the enformed matter that constitutes the realm of experientially available substance. The special case derives from the philosopher's attempt to account for the substance of the ensouled human subject. The individual substance of the human subject is only itself when it is ensouled, yet Aristotle appears to suggest that the intellective (or rational) soul can be separated from the body and still be intelligible as itself.[35] The chapter is worth quoting in its entirety:

> Since in every class of objects, just as in the whole of nature there is something which is their matter, i.e. which is potentially all the individuals, and something else which is their cause or agent in that it makes them all – the two being related as an art to its material – these distinct elements must be present in the soul also. Mind in the passive sense is such because it becomes all things, but mind has another aspect in that it makes all things; this is a kind of positive state like light; for in a sense light makes potential into actual colours. *Mind in this sense is separable, impassive and unmixed, since it is essentially an activity*; for the agent is always superior to the patient, and the originating cause to the matter. Actual knowledge is identical with its object.

Potential is prior in time to actual knowledge in the individual, but in general it is not prior in time. Mind does not
think intermittently. When isolated it is its true self and
nothing more, and this alone is immortal and everlasting
(we do not remember because, while the mind in this sense
cannot be acted upon, mind in the passive sense is perishable), and without this nothing thinks.[36]

While this could be a purely analytical position – that is,
Aristotle is suggesting that only if one abstracts the active
intellect in its pure state ('when isolated') is it possible to
comprehend its separability – some scholastic theologians
drew on this passage to explain how the soul could be
both substantial and separable from the body, that it could
subsist after the death of the body. This interpretation is
found in Aquinas's commentaries on *De anima*. The argument, according to Aquinas, is that the 'passive intellect',
that which could be acted on in the same manner as material things act on the sensitive soul, must be inferior to
the 'active' or 'agent' intellect, which is mind in the pure
sense. The schoolman focuses on the idea of the soul as
separable:

[Aristotle] says, first, that only separated intellect is that
which truly is. This claim, of course, must be understood,
not as regards agent intellect or possible intellect alone, but
as regards both; for it was in regard to each of them that he
said earlier that 'it is separated' [III.7.429b5; cf. 430a17].
And so it is clear that he is speaking here of the whole intellective part, which is called separated, of course, because
it has its operation without a corporeal organ. Now at the
beginning of this work [I.2.403a10–11] he said that if any
operation of soul is special (*propria*) to it, then it can be
the case that soul is separated. And thus he concludes that
that part of the soul alone, the intellective part, is imperish-
able and everlasting. This is what he presupposed earlier

in Book II [4.413b25–7]: that this sort of soul is separated from the others 'as the everlasting from the perishable'. It is called everlasting, however, not because it always was but because it always will be. Thus the Philosopher says in Metaphyisics XII [1070a21–6] that a form never exists before its matter, but soul remains after its matter – 'not all of it, but intellect'.[37]

The interpretation was bolstered by Aristotle's discussion of the Prime Mover in Book Lambda of the *Metaphysics*, where his explanation hinges, like that of the active intellect, on the concept of pure actuality. In both cases, for the scholastics, the existence of an immaterial substance was clearly possible.[38]

Despite the scholastic finesse of the problem of the existence of the substantial rational soul, substance continued to be thought of in material terms. As J. B. Bamborough notes of Elizabethan cosmology, 'although they spoke of the non-corporeal nature of the Soul, many Elizabethans had difficulty in thinking of an immaterial substance. Often they seem to have in mind some extremely rarified matter . . .'[39] To discern true substances, even those beyond sensuous apprehension, one had to begin with material things. It is only through reflection on the nature of the ensouled human subject that one can discern the immortal soul. And the distinction between matter and substance raised another potential problem. Though Aristotle is quite clear that matter is not a substance because it has no form, matter is nonetheless necessary to all substances that have actuality, which would suggest that an immaterial substance is a contradiction for Aristotle. This crux in Aristotelian thought helps to explain why it was so difficult for the early moderns to think of immaterial substances, even when they were fully committed to belief in a wide range of seemingly immaterial entities.

Substance and Shadow

An example from Shakespeare's *1 Henry VI* demonstrates the complex way in which the material and immaterial were intertwined in the concept of substance. When the opportunistic Countess of Auvergne entices the legendary Lord Talbot to her castle with the intention of imprisoning him, she is at first unable to match the man she sees before her with the image she has gleaned from 'rare reports' of his achievements:

> I thought I should have seen some Hercules,
> A second Hector for his grim aspect
> And large proportion of his strong-knit limbs.
> Alas, this is a child, a silly dwarf.
> It cannot be this weak and writhled shrimp
> Should strike such terror to his enemies. (2.3.18–23)

Upon taking him prisoner, the Countess inverts the representational logic she just used to insult him, arguing that his painted portrait is less substantial than his living image:

> Long time thy shadow hath been thrall to me,
> For in my gallery thy picture hangs:
> But now the substance shall endure the like,
> And I will chain these legs and arms of thine,
> That hast by tyranny these many years
> Wasted our country, slain our citizens
> And sent our sons and husbands captivate. (2.3.35–41)

The Countess draws on conventional mimetic logic in both cases. First the man is a poor copy of his heroic image, and then the portrait image she has in her gallery is a shadow (a poor copy) of the real substance, Talbot, the man, the subject of the portrait.[40]

Yet Talbot rejects the Countess's logic, laughing at what she perceives to be her cleverness:

TALBOT	I laugh to see your ladyship so fond
	To think that you have aught but Talbot's shadow
	Whereon to practice your severity.
COUNTESS	Why, art not thou the man?
TALBOT	I am indeed.
COUNTESS	Then have I substance too.
TALBOT	No, no, I am but shadow of myself:
	You are deceived, my substance is not here;
	For what you see is but the smallest part
	And least proportion of humanity:
	I tell you, madam, were the whole frame here,
	It is of such a spacious lofty pitch,
	Your roof were not sufficient to contain't.
	(2.3.44–55)

The Countess's initial slight draws on a Neoplatonic conception of substance, one in which substance is separable from its material copy; the image in each case is an imperfect copy of Talbot's real substance (ironically, in the first instance, and literally in the second). Talbot takes the shadow–substance relation to another level. Against the Countess's assertion that she has 'substance too', to accompany her portrait, Talbot draws on the deeper notion of substance I have been discussing: his physical presence, his body is 'but the smallest part / And least proportion of [his] humanity'. Though Talbot's rhetorical playfulness is his dramatic way of introducing the soldiers he has waiting in the wings to thwart the Countess's plan to imprison him, the language he uses here reflects how popular discourse about the nature of representation and reality was highly influenced by the ongoing metaphysical debates over the nature of substance, essence and matter that I have been discussing in this chapter.

An important premise of my argument is that these philosophical debates made their way into the popular imagination through the language and literature of the period. Linguistic changes and literary licence reflect changes in beliefs about the relationship between appearance and reality. Poets in particular often figured in the vexed relationship between the invisible and the visible (the love behind the lover's glance, for example), prompted by anxieties about material experience as a path to the immaterial (salvation, knowledge, etc.).[41] Talbot's witty one-upmanship may seem a far cry from such serious theological concerns as those associated with creation *ex nihilo* discussed above, but the Countess explicitly identifies his approach with philosophical paradox:

> COUNTESS   This is a riddling merchant for the nonce;
> He will be here, and yet he is not here:
> How can these contrarieties agree? (2.3.56–8)

In explicitly pointing out the paradox – that Talbot cannot both be 'here' and 'not here' – the Countess highlights the problem as a philosophical, ontological problem. Talbot's response comes in the form of a material demonstration:

> TALBOT   That will I show you presently.

> *Winds his horn. Drums strike up: a peal of ordnance. Enter soldiers*

> How say you, madam? Are you now persuaded
> That Talbot is but shadow of himself?
> These are his substance, sinews, arms and strength,
> With which he yoketh your rebellious necks,
> Razeth your cities and subverts your towns
> And in a moment makes them desolate. (2.3.59–65)

Though the scene ends in a seemingly light-hearted reconciliation, with the Countess admitting defeat and begging

Talbot's pardon for her 'abuse', the exploration of 'substance' here reveals its status as a complex and unstable metaphysical concept. Even as he essentially confirms that substance requires a materiality that shadows lack (the material presence of his soldiers 'are his substance'), Talbot evokes the more complicated notion of substance as essence, at least analytically distinct from matter. The material appearance of his soldiers completes Talbot's substance in the scene as the events embody the essence of Talbot, the fearless and fearsome warrior the Countess hoped to capture. The scene is consistent with the later depiction of Talbot as an emblem of Aristotelian substance in the scenes of his fall (4.5–4.7), where he and his son each seek to convince the other to flee to seek revenge another day. Flight is not in Talbot's essence, and John Talbot knows this, claiming: 'No more can I be severed from your side / Than can yourself yourself in twain divide' (4.5.48–9).

1 Henry VI anticipates an even more overtly philosophical exploration of substance in the deposition scene in *Richard II*. When Shakespeare returns to the idea of substance in *Richard II*, he treats it explicitly in terms of Richard's personhood, specifically articulated as a composite of his physical 'external' presence and his soul, that which 'lies within'. Richard's complex negotiation of his own substance is the subject of the next chapter, in which I explore Richard's attempt to distinguish between interiority and exteriority. Richard's grief is difficult to account for in purely material terms – as the product of a humoral theory of affect, for example – suggesting that the period's account of material feeling was complicated by an understanding of immaterial affect. As we will see, the instability of the substance of Richard's grief points to an ongoing cultural anxiety over the status of the unseen entity as an example of an immaterial substance.

Notes

1. The line comes at the end of a speech in which Iago details how he serves Othello only to take his revenge on him.

2. The gloss to the Geneva version of this verse is to Revelations 1: 8: 'The God which ever have been, am, and shall be: the God almighty, by whom all things have their being, and the God of mercy, mindful of my promise.'

3. This is the law of non-contradiction, and in metaphysics it is importantly related to Parmenides' ontological assertion that something cannot both be and not be, a position that ostensibly led to Democritus' atomistic proposition that all is matter and void.

4. Shakespeare and Donne's interest in the term 'nothing' is discussed in detail in Chapters 3, 4 and 6, below. Examples of mock encomia include E.D. (Edward Dyer or Edward Dyce), *The Prayse of Nothing* (London, 1585) and William Cornwallis's translation of Jean Passerat's 'Nihil' (1567), 'The Praise Nothing', in *Essayes of Certaine Paradoxes* (London, 1616).

5. Paul Jorgensen, *Redeeming Shakespeare's Words* and Rosalie Colie, *Paradoxia Epidemica: The Renaissance Tradition of Paradox*.

6. Macbeth's lament that 'Life's but a walking shadow, a poor player / That struts and frets his hour upon the stage / And then is heard no more: it is a tale / Told by an idiot, full of sound and fury, / Signifying nothing' (5.5.24–8), is a common example of the *contemptus mundi* topos, thus negating the value of the earthly world without claiming its non-existence. The persistence of the view that nature abhors a vacuum is an example of how unlikely belief in nothing was in the period.

7. Jorgensen, *Shakespeare's Words*, p. 25.

8. For discussions of Renaissance paradox, see Colie, *Paradoxia Epidemica*, Peter G. Platt, *Shakespeare and the Culture of Paradox*, Henry Knight Miller, 'The Paradoxical Encomium with Special Reference to Its Vogue in England 1600–1800', and A. E. Malloch, 'The Techniques and Functions of the Renaissance Paradox'.

9. This idea is often associated with Parmenides, though it likely dates back as far as Thales. See Frank Close, *Nothing: A Very Short History*, p. 5.

10. Vergil, *An abridgeme[n]t of the notable worke of Polidore Vergile*, a2r–a2v.

11. Ibid, a3r.

12. Ibid., a3v–a4r.

13. The development of Aristotle's metaphysics begins in the *Categories*, which prioritises composite particulars over universal concepts or classes as the most basic building blocks of existence (reality). The theory is modified in the *Physics* to accommodate change and movement, and is then complicated once more in the *Metaphysics*, in which Aristotle provides at least two, perhaps conflicting metaphysical systems. I discuss this development below.

14. Morton (of Berwick), *Treatise of the nature of God*, G2r. See also the examples collected by Jorgensen, *Shakespeare's Words*, p. 25.

15. E.D., *The Prayse of Nothing. By E. D.*, H1v.

16. Isaiah 40: 6; 1 Peter 1: 24. The Geneva gloss to the Isaiah verse is 'Meaning, all man's wisdom and natural powers'. Geneva references James 1: 10: 'Again, he that is rich, in that he is made low: for as the flower of the grass, shall he vanish away.' The gloss here is 'An argument taken of the very nature of the things themselves, for that they are most vain and uncertain.'

17. Donne, *Complete English Poems*, p. 313.

18. For a recent overview of the theological arguments on this subject see Paul Cefalu, *The Johannine Renaissance*, ch. 1.

19. Aristotle, *Complete Works*, vol. 1, p. 327 (191b, 14–17).

20. For a discussion of the complexity of this transformation, see Simon Palfrey, *Poor Tom: Living 'King Lear'*.

21. The extraordinary popularity of Ovid's *Metamorphoses* is the most obvious literary evidence of the persistence of this obsession.

22. *OED*, 'substance', I.2.

23. *OED*, 'substance', I.4.a. The definition notes that this sense is often contrasted with 'accident'.

24. Aristotle, *Metaphysics*, p. 127 (1017b).

25. Ibid., pp. 126–7 (1017b).

26. Ibid., p. 127 (1017b).

27. Ibid., p. 127 (1017b). Lawson-Tancred, the translator, notes that Aristotle's phrase here 'what-it-is-to-be-that-thing' is often translated as 'essence'.

28. *Physiology, or A Treatise of Naturall Philosophy*, MS BL Sloane 2521, f. 6r. The anonymous author notes that the matter in question 'hath no peculiar form, though capable of all form' (f. 5r).

29. The distinction is subtle, as Aristotle does allow that substance and essence are identical; the two terms still refer to different modes of being, actual and potential respectively. See *Metaphysics*, Zeta, pp. 6–7.

30. Aristotle, *De Anima (On the Soul)*, trans. Hugh Lawson-Tancred, p. 156 (412a). In what follows, I will also refer to the Loeb Classic Library edition, Aristotle, *On the Soul, Parva Naturalia, On the Breath*, trans. H. S. Hett. Aristotle's reference to substance as 'one kind . . . of the things that there are' refers to his accounting of existing things in the *Categories*. Substance is there defined as the primary existent: 'A Substance – that which is called a substance most strictly, primarily, and most of all – is that which is neither said of a subject nor in a subject' (*Complete Works*, vol. 1, p. 4 [2a]).

31. *De Anima*, trans. Lawson-Tancred, p. 156 (412a).

32. As Lawson-Trancred notes, Aristotle does not necessarily believe in 'non-physical substances' because 'Substance (*ousia*) is not a category that can subsist in actuality wholly denuded of the concomitant material cause for whatever it is that it composes' (*De Anima*, p. 247n112).

33. Aristotle's term is *psyche*. Though commonly translated 'soul', Aristotle's translators note that this is misleading. 'Vital principle' is H. S. Hett's phrase, while the latter two are Lawson-Tancred's.

34. *De Anima*, trans. Lawson-Tancred, p. 157 (412b).

35. Soul as life-giving force is further differentiated by Aristotle. The rational soul is unique to humans, whereas all animals have a sensitive soul and plants have a nutritive soul.

36. *On the Soul*, trans. Hett, p. 171 (430a10–25), emphasis added. Lawson-Tancred translates the italicised as follows: 'Now this latter intellect is separate, unaffected and unmixed, being in substance activity' (p. 205). Hett's 'mind' (νοός) is Lawson-Tancred's 'intellect' and J. A. Smith's 'thought' (*Complete Works*, vol. 1, p. 684).

37. Aquinas, *Commentary on Aristotle's De anima [Sentencia libri De Anima]*, p. 369. The passage is a commentary on *De Anima* 3.5 (430a22–3). Aquinas's commentaries addressed a corrupt Latin translation of Aristotle's text that removed some of the passage's ambiguity. Other scholastics – Duns Scotus, for example – did not agree with this interpretation.

38. Duns Scotus also explored the idea of an immaterial substance by parsing Aristotle's use of the term 'immaterial' (*immateriale*). See Stephen Priest, 'Duns Scotus on the Immaterial'.

39. Bamborough, *The Little World of Man*, p. 30.

40. The same convention is employed by Bassanio in *The Merchant of Venice*, praising Portia's portrait after having successfully chosen in the casket challenge: 'Yet look – how far / The substance of my praise doth wrong this shadow / In underprizing it, so far this shadow / Doth limp behind the substance' (3.2.126–9).

41. The fact that Thomas Nashe collaborated on *1 Henry VI* suggests that its composition included university-educated as well as professional writers, and there is no question that Nashe would have been exposed to metaphysics at St John's College, Cambridge, where he earned his BA.

CHAPTER 3

'FOR I MUST NOTHING BE': *RICHARD II* AND THE IMMATERIALITY OF SELF

Just after his deposition in *Richard II*, Shakespeare's 'poet king' famously calls for a mirror in perhaps his most performative gesture of the play. When Bolingbroke humours him by having an attendant produce the glass, Richard laments that the image offered in the mirror fails to reflect the depth of his sorrow:

> Hath sorrow struck
> So many blows upon this face of mine
> And made no deeper wounds? (4.1.270-2)

In apparent disgust at its failure to register his grief, Richard casts the mirror down, dramatically re-enacting the deposition itself – his divine authority represented in the majestic image, 'the pompous body' of the king 'cracked in an hundred shivers' (4.1.243, 282). Unfazed, the usurping Bolingbroke belittles the 'moral' of Richard's high drama – 'see how quickly my sorrow hath destroyed my face' – with his observation that in breaking the glass Richard has only played with appearances: 'The shadow of your sorrow hath destroyed / The shadow of your face' (4.1.285-6).[1]

In Richard's response, Shakespeare offers what appears to be a characteristic gesture towards interiority, inward self-reflection. The newly deposed king – the simply mortal Richard – agrees with Henry, 'the silent king', that the face reflected in the mirror

> And these external manner of laments
> Are merely shadows to the unseen grief
> That swells with silence in the tortured soul. (4.1.289–91)

The use of analogy – 'shadows to' – rather than empirical description – 'shadows of' – emphasises the immaterial nature of Richard's 'unseen' grief.[2] But Richard's insistence that his 'grief lies all within' confuses the use of analogy with a material metaphor, begging the question: within *where?* It is tempting to identify in Richard's lines evidence of a modern form of subjectivity, one that anticipates a Cartesian dualism in which the extended body and non-extended mind have different modes of existence. But the form of his analogy makes things more complicated: his external laments are to his 'unseen grief' as shadows are to material things. The analogy places special pressure on the material: material things block light to cause shadows, and though shadows have no substance, they indicate an unseen material substance presumably accessible to sense from another perspective (e.g. when not looking at the shadow but at the object producing it). We have the same kind of dynamic interplay of material and immaterial that produced the tension in the scene between Talbot and the Countess discussed in the previous chapter. Richard's 'unseen grief / That swells with silence in the tortured soul' is 'the substance' that creates the 'external manner of laments' available to the senses, the insubstantial shadows of his grief, though the only access to that substance is through the 'insubstantial' materiality of those very external laments.[3] When Shakespeare returned to this idea at the beginning of *Hamlet*, he severed the connection between the prince's interior grief 'which passeth show' and the 'trappings and the suits of woe', that are mere 'actions that a man might play' (1.2.84–6). For Richard, the distinction is muddled, as he envisions his 'unseen grief' in explicitly sensuous terms. The grief that 'swells with silence in [Richard's] tortured soul' points less to the emergent interiority of modern subjectivity some find in *Hamlet* than to a difficult immateriality, the no*thing* that will finally release his suffering body at the end of the play, captured in his later lament that he, and indeed all men, 'with nothing shall be pleased till he be eased / with being nothing' (5.5.40–1).

In this chapter, I examine how Shakespeare stages Richard's struggle with reality as a function of his attempt (and ultimate failure) to read in his experience with the material world its immaterial other: the absent, divine and conceptual, but also the *self*. Taking as a starting point Nietzsche's account of art arising from the productive opposition of Apollinian and Dionysian forces in *The Birth of Tragedy*, I then turn to the work of Jean-Luc Marion to explore how Shakespeare establishes the relationship between the material and immaterial in phenomenological terms. In particular, I draw on Marion's phenomenology of givenness, especially as it relates to what he calls 'saturated phenomena', that which exceeds conventional experience and offers access to the 'irregardable'. Attending to Richard's engagement with the world through the lens of phenomenology, and focusing explicitly on the status of the immaterial in the play, reveals Richard's tragedy to be a consequence of his confrontation with the impossibility of self-knowledge rather than a result of his political failures as they relate to the historical concerns of the sixteenth century.

History or Tragedy?

Due to the historical subject matter it treats – the ostensible origin of the devastating Wars of the Roses – scholars have often considered the play as an Elizabethan answer to the question: 'What caused Richard's fall?' In the past century, the range of critical explanations for Richard's fall include E. M. W. Tillyard's 'Tudor myth' of history, Ernst Kantorowicz's influential discussion of the medieval doctrine of the king's two bodies and, more recently, the new historicist readings of Stephen Greenblatt, Phyllis Rackin and others that depict Shakespeare's Richard as an emblem of Elizabethan national trauma, recovery and nostalgia. Such readings make it possible to view all of Shakespeare's historical plays as stemming from the ideological collapse of a medieval form of political theology based on divine right, and the desire for either the system's rehabilitation – Hal's willingness to 'pay the debt [he] never promised' (*1 Henry IV*, 1.2.184) – or an alternative. In an important sense, then, Shakespeare's histories are *about* political theology, and in particular they are about the Elizabethan need to shore up the coherence of divine right monarchy in relation to the facts of a national history that would seem to call that concept into question.[4]

In addition to historical concerns, the question 'What caused Richard's fall?' also raises the issue of the play's genre.[5] Though early commentators recognised tragic elements in the play, they largely rejected that it succeeded in producing a genuinely tragic effect due in large part to its reliance on historical events. Samuel Johnson would conclude that the play fails 'to affect the passions, or enlarge the understanding'.[6] Such early critical assessments of the play, as John Halverson notes, did not prevent a great many critics from arguing that we find in Richard something like the 'psychological complexity and development and . . . deep awareness of the human condition' that we find in *Lear*.[7] The argument for this version of Richard reaches its height in Jan Kott's claim that, 'Just before being hurled into the abyss, the deposed king reaches the greatness of Lear.'[8] To accept that Richard is a tragic hero in the mould of Lear and Hamlet requires that we take Richard's self-indulgent poetics of suffering seriously, as the pathos of a man truly coming into an awareness of his reality before our eyes. Halverson takes considerable care to point out that such a reading would need the support of evidence for Richard's psychological complexity and awareness of the human condition that is difficult to find in the text of the play. Richard's tragedy may be a tragedy of history, but it is not, according to this view, a human tragedy.

Convinced that the play does allow for a reading of Richard's fall as a human tragedy, I will suggest an alternative reading that emphasises Shakespeare's exploration of Richard's material expression and immaterial experience of grief. Beginning with Nietzsche's conception of lyric and choric understanding in *The Birth of Tragedy*, I will offer a reading of *Richard II* as a meditation on the difficulties attending the medieval scholastic (largely Arabic and Aristotelian) account of identity and embodiment. Though inward self-reflection is thematically potent in the play, looking forward to something like modern subjectivity, Richard's experience with his own embodiment ultimately suggests that this knowledge is inaccessible to the title character – at least, until it is too late.

Richard II *and* The Birth of Tragedy

As early as Walter Pater's reflections on the play's powerful lyricism, critics have noted the poetic nature of Shakespeare's title character. In this section, I explore the philosophical implications of the distinction between the play's subject matter – its political, historical or ideological content – and its aesthetic power, specifically Shakespeare's ability to catalyse an experience with the phenomenal world and onto-theology that exceeds conventional explanation. Nietzsche's theory of tragedy rests on a distinction between drama as a guide to understanding and drama as a guide to living. I find the distinction useful, as attempts to account for the play's elaboration of political theology tend to focus on Shakespeare's ability to make both the promise and the liability of divine right monarchy manifest to the understanding – to render the whole system of early modern political theology an object for contemplation and critique. Similarly, to find in Richard the tragic hero awakened to an understanding of the human condition is to bring the play in line with a conventional story of tragic self-awareness. Both readings bring a sense of order to the play's action and render it a guide to understanding. In contrast, focusing on the play's aesthetic power as tragedy in Nietzsche's sense emphasises the play's portrayal of the individual's experience of that system as it relates to one's sense of being. The combination of intelligible experience and aesthesis is peculiar to representational art, and is perhaps most forceful in the case of drama; its effect is to highlight the way in which our experience of the play is a mode of experience that has the potential to draw attention to the way perception exceeds the merely perceptible.

Nietzsche opens *The Birth of Tragedy* with the sweeping statement that 'the continuous development of art is bound up with the Apollonian and Dionysian duality'.[9] He then elaborates by tracing that development to its roots in Greek tragedy, locating the power of Attic tragedy in the productive tension between these two impulses: the Apollonian towards the form of sculpture and dream as coherent vision, and ultimately abstraction; the Dionysian towards music, the incoherence of drunkenness and ultimately the ecstatic physicality of nature, of human being embodied. In the context of the present study, the distinction can be understood as that between the immaterial and the material respectively. The impulse towards the Apollonian is at its heart the impulse to make sense of the world, to make it conform to the understanding; the Dionysian always haunts this fragile truce with experience, as it beckons to the meaningless and absurd reality of existence always kept at bay by the order offered in the coherence of the Apollonian dream. The opposition is captured early on in Nietzsche's distinction between the Dionysian folk wisdom of Silenus in response to King Midas's question of what is best in the world for man: 'What is best of all is utterly beyond your reach: not to be born, not to *be*, to be *nothing*. But the second best for you is – to die soon.'[10] Nietzsche contrasts this impossible Dionysian wisdom to the Apollonian alternative offered in the figure of the Homeric hero: 'to die soon is worst of all for them, the next worst – to die at all'.[11] While the Dionysian truth is incomprehensible on its own terms, the Apollonian dream relies on a naive fiction; the Apollonian triumphs over 'an abysmal and terrifying view of the world and the keenest susceptibility to suffering through recourse to the most forceful and pleasurable illusions'.[12] The miracle of Attic tragedy for Nietzsche is its ability to bring the real power of Dionysian recognition before our conscious apprehension through the Apollonian 'genius' of coherence, structure and calm. The crucial point is that this can be achieved only as a result of the productive tension that exists between the two forces.

When we first meet Richard, we meet a king firmly immersed in the comforting illusion of divine right monarchy. In assuring Mowbray that he will be an impartial judge, Richard stresses his divinity in the language of materiality:

> Now by my sceptre's awe I make a vow
> Such neighbor-nearness to our sacred blood
> Should nothing privilege him, nor partialize
> The unstooping firmness of my upright soul. (1.1.118–21)

Richard's authority here relies on a fine balance of the immaterial and the material – his 'sceptre's awe', 'sacred blood' and 'upright soul'. The power of the divine illusion – 'the unstooping firmness of [Richard's] upright soul' – effectively abnegates Richard of responsibility in the situation. He will not be partial to Bolingbroke because his character is fixed, defined by his soul's 'unstooping firmness', which resides in an immaterial realm untouched by material mutability, and yet his 'vow' is guaranteed by the awe wrought by his sceptre rather than his personal integrity.

It is precisely this freedom from personal responsibility, underwritten by his providential view of history, that allows Richard to leave the precarious political situation to a higher power: 'Since we cannot atone you, we shall see / Justice design the victor's chivalry' (1.1.202–3). Richard's confidence in his divinity here appears to coincide with that of the more practical members of the ruling class depicted in the play. For example, Gaunt defends his refusal to revenge Gloucester's death by referring to the conceptual logic of divine right monarchy:

> Heaven's is the quarrel, for heaven's substitute,
> His deputy anointed in His sight,
> Hath caused his death, the which, if wrongfully
> Let heaven revenge, for I may never lift
> An angry arm against His minister (1.2.37–41)

Gaunt's impulse is to follow the rules – his obedience is to the system. This is true of Bolingbroke and Mowbray as well, as we find each willing to place their fate in God's hands according to the logic of trial by combat. Yet Richard's unwillingness to accept the outcome of the trial is only our first clue that his belief in divine justice, and by extension his own divinely anointed position on earth, is not what it appears to be.

In preventing the combat, Richard rejects the providential outcome and opts instead for the politically expedient path. He acts on the knowledge that either outcome would reflect poorly on his political authority. This detail makes it difficult to argue that Richard's tragedy is a result of his eventual recognition that his sacred and mortal bodies are dissoluble.[13] It also ironises his bombastic speeches about the inviolable

nature of his divine right, thus making him a poor representative of medieval political theology against the encroaching
Machiavellianism of Bolingbroke. The Richard who returns
from Ireland is famous for what appears to be an audacious,
but sincerely felt, fantasy of divine right monarchy. The king
himself recognises that his invocation to the earth to rise up
against the rebel forces in defence of his divine authority will
be met with disbelief: 'Mock not my senseless conjuration,
lords / This earth shall have a feeling, and these stones / Prove
armed soldiers, ere her native king / Shall falter under foul
rebellion's arms' (3.2.23–6). His subsequent defence of his
passivity takes the form of an extended metaphor comparing
himself to the sun, a conventional use of the sun symbol that
leads up to what appears to be a self-assured defence of his
divine authority:

> Not all the water in the rough rude sea
> Can wash the balm from an anointed king.
> The breath of worldly men cannot depose
> The deputy elected by the Lord.
> For every man that Bolingbroke hath pressed
> To lift shrewd steel against our golden crown,
> Heaven for His Richard hath in heavenly pay
> A glorious angel. Then, if angels fight,
> Weak men must fall, for heaven still guards the right.
> (3.2.49–57)

As memorable as this rallying cry for divine right monarchy
is, Richard can't possibly believe what he is saying here.[14] Like
his call for the earth to rise up in his defence, Richard's appeal
to heaven is performative and self-consciously ironic. Immediately after this speech the king learns of further defections
to the rebel side, prompting him to additional poetic musings:
'But now the blood of twenty thousand men / Did triumph in
my face, and they are fled' (3.2.71–2). When Aumerle urges

him to lead – 'Comfort my liege. Remember who you are' –
Richard's response is comic:

> I had forgot myself. Am I not king?
> Awake, thou sluggard majesty, thou sleep'st!
> Is not the king's name forty thousand names?
> Arm, arm, my name! A puny subject strikes
> At thy great glory. (3.2.78–82)

Can we really imagine that this is an introspective speech,
that Richard has 'forgot' *himself* and then suddenly remem-
bered *who he really was*? We might recall the successful use
of the battle cry 'A Talbot!' from *1 Henry VI*, an externali-
sation of an idea of Talbot that had surprisingly powerful
force, as one soldier remarks, 'The cry of Talbot serves me
for a sword, / For I have loaden me with many spoils / Using
no other weapon but his name' (2.1.80–2). Richard's reference to 'myself' is certainly not the 'self' that we identify with
the modern subject. Rather, we stand witness to Richard's
poetic performances, his lyric attempts to capture the proper
response a king might have to the news of his impending
loss – to approximate his lyric conception to the experience at
hand. First believing that his favourites have joined the rebels,
Richard responds with rage – 'O villains, vipers damned without redemption!' (3.2.124) – only to turn melancholy at the
clarification that they had been executed: 'Of comfort no man
speak!' (3.2.140). This second slip into despair introduces his
wonderful speech on the mortality of kings, a moment that
appears to mark in Richard a growing awareness of the distinction between his mortal and sacred body:

> Throw away respect,
> Tradition, form, and ceremonious duty,
> For you have but mistook me all this while.
> I live with bread, like you, feel want,
> Taste grief, need friends. Subjected thus,
> How can you say to me I am a king? (3.2.167–72)

The temptation to identify this passage with Richard's sudden realisation of his mortality is understandable.[15] Richard's nod to his common humanity calls to mind the great speeches on the subject that Shakespeare would later write for Shylock and Lear. We might imagine that, like Lear, his recognition of the monarchical illusion renders him a common man.[16] But this would be to impose on the play a reading of Richard's development from confident monarch to humble everyman that the text does not support.

Rather, what Richard seems to be doing at such moments is avoiding the kind of self-reflection that would put him face to face with the terrifying reality of existence that Nietzsche identifies with Dionysian wisdom. Instead of reflecting on his inward soul or the reality of the political threat, Richard opts to hide behind the 'forceful and pleasurable illusions' of his lyric imagination: the anointed king defeating a rebel army first with the aid of the animated earth itself, then an army of angels, and finally – in the most abstracted fantasy – the power of his own name. These fantasies are all powerfully realised in Richard's performative language. Richard, as the poet king, tries on different linguistic masks in the process of keeping the more absurd reality of his existence at bay. For the knowledge that haunts Richard's self-understanding is not only that he is a man, like any other, clothed in the majesty of a king. What seems to worry Richard more is that his only escape from his particular tragic life is beyond his reach – what is best for man according to Silenus's Dionysian wisdom: to not have been born, to not be, to be *nothing*. This is an impossibility that haunts Richard's speeches to the end of the play. His resignation that he will 'pine away' at Flint Castle (3.2.203) and weak request that Bolingbroke 'give [him] leave to go' 'so I were from your sights' (4.1.306, 308) pale in comparison to his continued, and emotionally charged, exploration of his own non-existence. If Richard does not gain knowledge of himself as a subject, he does seem to try; his many efforts to create for himself another self in language nevertheless lead him to the unfortunate conclusion that that his temporal existence is irreversible:

> O God, O God, that e'er this tongue of mine,
> That laid the sentence of dread banishment
> On yon proud man, should take it off again
> With words of sooth! Oh, that I were as great
> As my grief, or lesser than my name,
> Or that I could forget what I have been,
> Or not remember what I must be now. (3.3.133–9)

Deposition as (anti-) Reversal

The impossibility of reversal is especially important to what follows, as critics have long viewed the deposition scene as an inverted ritual.[17] To find Richard's inner self by heeding the king's plea, in act 3, to 'throw away respect, / Tradition, form and ceremonious duty' – thus revealing the mortal man who lives 'with bread' – would be to simply substitute one of Richard's poetic illusions for another: the divinely anointed monarch for the common mortal man. Richard is aware that this divestment of monarchical ornament cannot change the fact that he is the king, just as he knows that Bolingbroke must reject his request to 'Give Richard leave to live till Richard die' (3.3.174).[18]

Considering Richard's awareness of the situation he faces, it is difficult to view the deposition scene as anything but political theatre for all involved. As many critics have noted, the highly ceremonial character of the scene recalls the opening scenes of the play in which Richard presides over the dispute between Mowbray and Bolingbroke. But the event of the deposition is of a different magnitude. Gary Kuchar highlights the theological implications of the scene as part of a process of desacrilisation at work in the play: 'the dividing asunder of divine narrative from lived history'.[19] In the early scenes, Richard's understanding of events does not penetrate any deeper than the level of signification: Bolingbroke's banishment signifies his transgression of monarchical authority; it has no reality for Richard, who is willing to reduce the sentence by four years with a word, 'such is the breath of kings' (1.3.209). That Richard's word, 'the breath of kings', makes the world, suggests that the substance of things proceeds from Richard to the world, rather than the other way around.[20] The deposition represents the utter failure of this system of representation and, by extension, Richard's entire world. One would imagine that this would mark the moment of tragic recognition – that, having lost everything, Richard will finally recognise his existential condition, and despair. But at this point in the play, Richard can only see such a failure through the language of his former illusions, as a negation of his monarchical fantasy. While his repeated claim that in losing his crown he becomes 'nothing' might otherwise indicate an existential crisis, an encounter with the abyss, Richard's use of 'nothing' is not radical but contingent, a matter of negation rather than non-existence: he is 'not king' rather than 'no thing'. Though he claims to fear his coming fate, which he figures poetically as his descent into nothingness, what he actually says betrays his increasing awareness that no matter how often he lays linguistic claim to nothingness, he is able to come no closer to an understanding of what that could possibly mean. This is the awful truth of Silenus: that it is already too late.

For Nietzsche, the truly Dionysian man resembles Hamlet: 'both have once looked truly into the essence of things, they have gained knowledge, and nausea inhibits action; for their action could not change anything in the eternal nature of things ... Knowledge kills action; action requires the veils of illusion'.[21] Following Nietzsche, it would seem that Shakespeare's characterisation of Richard does look forward to *Hamlet*, but not because both characters experience a tragic reflection on their emerging awareness of an inner self, of a modern form of subjectivity. While Richard's passivity does seem to be a result of a recognition of powerlessness – that his fall and Bolingbroke's rise are inevitable, 'What must the king do now? Must he submit?' (3.3.143) – his return to action in the deposition scene highlights his unwillingness to abandon the most absurd 'veils of illusion'. Richard's command, 'Give me the crown', forcefully introduces the following display of ceremony and ritual throughout which Richard is in complete control. His command of the power of ceremonial speech eclipses Bolingbroke's weak attempts to legitimate the proceedings by eliciting Richard's consent: 'I thought you had been willing to resign', and then more directly, 'Are you contented to resign the crown?' (4.1.183, 193). We know by this point that Bolingbroke understands the importance of ceremony, as he has revealed his intentions earlier to York and Northumberland: 'Fetch hither Richard, that in common view / He may surrender. So we shall proceed / Without suspicion' (4.1.149–51). But his is a concern for the utility of ceremony for political purposes – the appearance of legitimacy – whereas Richard's insistence on unmasking ritual power as illusion at first appears to derive from a desire to reveal the underlying unchangeable reality governing the political system itself.

Richard's emphasis on grief throughout the scene might be taken as a sign of remorse or regret, as the first evidence of contrition on the part of the failed monarch. It soon becomes clear, however, that he grieves more for himself than the monarchy. The scene is dominated by the language of sorrow: Richard's tears first filling his bucket in the image of the well, then washing away the balm of the anointed king, and finally, obscuring his ability to see the articles of treason he is meant to read aloud before the assembly. Importantly, his expression of his grief is saturated with the language of material experience, betraying his obsession with the idea that it is tangible in some way. His earlier claim that he had, like other men, 'taste[d] grief' informs the deposition scene, in which he seeks to locate his grief and include it in the sensuous world. If it is accessible, then it might provide him with hope of the existence of something other than his own soaring rhetoric, which has been revealed to have little relation to material reality. Until this point, of course, he hadn't tasted grief, or felt much of anything apparently, despite being surrounded with characters expressing their own experiences with grief: Bolingbroke's on being banished, Gaunt's at the decay of England's greatness, York's at Richard's transgression of the rule of inheritance, and so on. In each case the grief of others is unintelligible to him.[22]

Before turning to Richard's experience with grief in the deposition and prison scenes, it is helpful to look at the play's earlier meditation on the subject in the remarkable exchange between the Queen and Bushy in 2.2:

> BUSHY   Madam, your majesty is too much sad.
> You promised when you parted with the King
> To lay aside life-harming heaviness
> And entertain a cheerful disposition.
>
> QUEEN   To please the King I did; to please myself
> I cannot do it. Yet I know no cause
> Why I should welcome such a guest as grief,
> Save bidding farewell to so sweet a guest
> As my sweet Richard. Yet again methinks
> Some unborn sorrow, ripe in fortune's womb,
> Is coming towards me, and my inward soul
> With nothing trembles. At something it grieves,
> More than with parting from my lord the King.
> (2.2.1–13)

As theatrical foreshadowing, the Queen's experience of 'some unborn sorrow' anticipates the news of Bolingbroke's increasing power and the inevitability of Richard's fall. But the terms in which she considers her experience of grief provide a striking contrast to Richard's later meditations on his own experience. Scott McMillin identifies 2.2 as the first indication of the play's 'strange meditation on "nothing,"' a meditation which surfaces in patches of difficult writing about the "eye" or the "I"'.[23] He goes on to suggest that the passage emphasises something like feminine intuition: 'the weeping Queen's intuition about the approach of disaster [is right]. Through her tears she sees the truth'.[24]

Focusing on the relationship between material sensation and immaterial perception in the Queen's description of her phenomenal experience reveals that a different form of intuition is at work in the scene. She locates her grief in her 'inward soul' and identifies its source as both 'nothing' and 'something', evoking early modern accounts of perception, and specifically the 'inner sense' (or 'common sense') inherited from Islamic and scholastic natural philosophy and metaphysics in the Aristotelian tradition. Daniel Heller-Roazen identifies Augustine as the first to bring the Aristotelian concept of the 'common sense' together with the language of inwardness.[25] The Queen's description points to just such an 'inward sense', especially as it was further developed by the medieval Islamic philosopher Avicenna (Ibn Sīnā), whose account had a significant influence on medieval scholastic thought and Aquinas in particular.[26] As Marina Paola Banchetti-Robino explains,

> perception, for Ibn Sīnā, occurs when common sense receives sensible forms, that is, form without matter. This account of perception is directly inherited from Aristotle, for whom the reception of form without matter was interpreted by the Scholastics as 'intentional in-existence'. Once the form without matter has been received by common sense, the imaginative faculty retains these sensible forms. Thus, the estimative faculty receives intentions on the basis of the sensible forms,

or form without matter, that are received by common sense and that are retained by the imagination. This, then, establishes the dependence of the faculty of estimation, or of intentionality, on sense perception.[27]

This remarkable conception of the inward sense helps explain the paradox of how the Queen's palpable experience could be focused on nothing – that the Queen's inward soul 'trembles with' nothing. The implication is that a real, but immaterial, entity is the source of the Queen's trepidation.

In his attempt to placate the Queen, Bushy fails to understand what she is saying about the relationship between her inward and external sense. For Bushy, all grief has an essential substance, which can be misperceived by an imaginative faculty corrupted by strong emotion. He employs optical comparisons in his attempt to convince her that what she perceives is not real:

> Each substance of a grief hath twenty shadows,
> Which shows like grief itself, but is not so;
> For sorrow's eye, glazed with blinding tears,
> Divides one thing entire to many objects;
> . . .
> 　　　　　　　　　　　　　Then, thrice-gracious Queen,
> More than your lord's departure weep not: more's not seen;
> Or if it be, 'tis with false sorrow's eye,
> Which for things true weeps things imaginary. (2.2.14–27)

In the context of the scene's immediate action, the unsuspecting Bushy can only see Richard's departure from the Queen for what it is, a temporary spatial separation. Though the ominous reality of the Irish war as prelude to Bolingbroke's usurpation would have been on the minds of everyone in the audience, having not yet seen any external threat, Bushy attributes the Queen's trepidation to her compromised power of imagination. But the Queen's acceptance of the intuition of her inward soul relies in part on the physical change in her body that she is unable to ignore:

> It may be so, but yet my inward soul
> Persuades me it is otherwise. Howe'er it be,
> I cannot but be sad; so heavy sad
> As though on thinking on no thought I think,
> Makes me with heavy nothing faint and shrink. (2.2.28–32)

Avicenna's account of the inward sense in perception sheds light on the Queen's puzzling experience by highlighting the concept of intentional objects:

> There are some faculties of internal perception which perceive the form of the sensed things, and others which perceive the 'intention' thereof . . . The distinction between the perception of the form and that of the intention is that the form is what is perceived both by the inner soul and the external sense; but the external sense perceives it first and then transmits it to the soul, as for example, when the sheep perceives the form of the wolf, i.e., its shape, form, and colour . . . As for the intention, it is a thing which the soul perceives from the sensed object without its previously having been perceived by the external sense . . . Now, what is first perceived by the sense and then by the internal faculties is the form, while what only the internal faculties perceive without the external sense is the intention.[28]

Following this account of inward sensation, the Queen's 'heavy nothing' can be understood to be an *immaterial substance*: 'no thing' that the external senses can perceive (a sense object), but 'some thing at which [her soul quite reasonably] grieves' (an intentional object). But this doesn't explain her knowledge of this grief, however circumscribed it is by her inability to name it. One might say that she knows her grief before she understands it. Avicenna's account of 'intuition' offers an explanation:

The acquisition of knowledge, whether from someone else or from within oneself, is of various degrees. Some people who acquire knowledge come very near to immediate perception, since their potential intellect which precedes the capacity we have mentioned is the most powerful. If a person can acquire knowledge from within himself, this strong capacity is called 'intuition'.[29]

The flatterer, Bushy, serves as the Queen's foil in the scene, arguing that her elaborate explanation of grief born of nothing is 'nothing but conceit' (2.2.33). Her grief is a product of her imagination making something of nothing. In her response, ''Tis nothing less: conceit is still derived / From some forefather grief' (2.2.34), the Queen qualifies Bushy's dismissal of her experience by an appeal to Aristotelian faculty psychology which holds that all ideas require a phantasm (or mental image) – that all conceits are based on something. The question that haunts her concerns the nature of her current grief, which has seemingly arisen from an inner faculty that is in turn made sensuously available to the outward senses: 'with heavy nothing I faint and shrink'. Bushy's account is the reverse: he seeks to give a name to her sadness by drawing on the plausible explanations gleaned from past experience. The Queen laments the lack of precedent; unlike Bushy's conceit, 'derived from some forefather grief', the Queen's:

> is not so,
> For nothing hath begot my something grief,
> Or something hath the nothing that I grieve;
> 'Tis in reversion that I do possess,
> But what it is, that is not yet known what,
> I cannot name. 'Tis nameless woe, I wot. (2.2.35–40)

The object of the Queen's understanding is potential rather than actual at this point, though as McMillin and others have noted, the Queen's woe does not remain nameless for long. The external guarantee comes in the form of Green's entrance with the news of Bolingbroke's landing at Ravenspurgh, which immediately follows this speech. Yet before Green enters, the Queen's inward sense impresses upon her inward soul a perception of the world not yet available to the outward senses.[30]

Returning to the deposition scene, we find Richard faced with a similar recognition of a foreboding future that Bolingbroke attempts to paper over with a pretty illusion: the absurd fiction that Richard is content to resign the crown. Just before the inverted ritual of the deposition, Richard responds to Bolingbroke's question, 'Are you contented to resign the crown?', with the iconic existential pun: 'Ay, no; no, ay; for I must nothing be' (4.1.194). Yet, unlike the Queen, Richard is not responding to an intuitive understanding of his experience; he is voicing his reluctance to participate in Bolingbroke and Northumberland's political theatre and, specifically, the demand that he give up the externally visible trappings of kingship. This becomes clear in the inverted ritual that follows: 'I give this heavy weight from off my head / And this unwieldy sceptre from my hand', and so on. Richard 'unkings' himself through a series of linguistic acts of negation, poetic flourishes that accompany his abdication of the material signs of his kingship. Intermingling the material objects – sceptre, crown – with what they represent – 'pride of kingly sway', Richard's 'sacred state' – Richard dematerialises all through the power of language, his monologue culminating in an utterance fully dependent on the materiality of language itself: '"God save King Henry," unkinged Richard says' (4.1.213).[31]

The politically meaningful ritual of the deposition, in which Richard is in fact divested of his monarchical authority, leads up to the mirror scene, a theatrical echo that Richard orchestrates as a substitute for the official 'paperwork' that

would legitimise the transfer of power. Despite Northumberland's repeated insistence that Richard 'Read o'er this paper'
to 'satisfy the Commons', the fallen King claims he can read
truth elsewhere: 'They shall be satisfied. I'll read enough /
When they do see the very book indeed / Where all my sins
are writ, and that's myself' (4.1.262, 266–8). Richard ostensibly offers to go much further than simply admitting his guilt
here: he promises to display his inward soul to all present.[32]
Taking Richard at his word, what we are about to witness is
the material manifestation of his contrite soul in the reflection
of his face. He will reveal before all present 'a traitor with the
rest' brought low by his own 'soul's consent'. No longer able
to entertain the fiction of his earlier majesty, of the 'unstooping firmness of his upright soul', he will now face reality. The
mirror scene that follows is thus all the more surprising for
its utter failure as both political drama and tragic catharsis.
The glass in which he hopes to see his soul's sorrow reflected
yields no such satisfaction. Where the Queen 'faints' under
the weight of her 'nothing' grief, Richard has no material
access to the immaterial change he has just undergone; he
is frustrated that he cannot see his sorrow reflected in his
face: 'O flattering glass, / Like to my followers in prosperity, /
Thou dost beguile me' (4.1.272–4). Unavailable to sense, the
'substance' of Richard's grief must be learned indirectly: it is
only through a recognition of the inadequacy of the material,
'external manner of laments' that he can consider the unseen,
but ultimately more real grief which 'remains silent'.

Though he comes close, this Richard does not appear
to have changed in anything but the register of his poetic
expression. The supposedly assured Richard of the play's
early scenes grounded his sense of self in discursive fictions
of divine providence that the king himself was unwilling to
trust in practice. Having exhausted the language of divine
right marked by external references to balm, crowns and
the pompous body of the king, Richard now tries on the

language of inwardness introduced by the Queen in 2.2. If Richard is to learn anything about his substantial *self*, if we are to witness any form of tragic recognition, we must look to the final scene in the prison and his remarkable extended soliloquy on materiality, thought and time.

Music as Saturated Phenomena

Finally alone, Richard tries to make sense of his embodied, temporal experience, turning once again to the figurative, and analogy in particular: 'I have been studying how I may compare / This prison where I live unto the world' (5.5.1–2). Evoking the conventional comparison of the body to a prison of the soul, Richard reflects on his immediate experience in prison in the hopes of coming closer to an understanding of his place in the world beyond the prison walls. But try as he might to make the comparison, he 'cannot do it' (5.5.5). His failure is not surprising considering his earlier inability to correlate experience and expression, routinely substituting lyric illusions for a world collapsing around him. Though vowing to 'hammer it out', Richard reveals that he may have finally reached the limits of his lyric sensibility. And yet he remains in thrall to the powerful illusions of his own language:

> Sometimes am I king;
> Then treason makes me wish myself a beggar,
> And so I am. Then crushing penury
> Persuades me I was better when a king;
> Then am I kinged again, and by and by
> Think that I am unkinged by Bolingbroke,
> And straight am nothing. (5.5.32–8)

As he recounts the events of his fall, he continues to see them as the products of his own creative power, as if he brought the conditions of the world into being through proclamation. It is this self-focused recapitulation of the play's central events that brings Richard to his darkest observation, and what appears to be the tragic moral of the play:

> But whate'er I be,
> Nor I, nor any man that but man is,
> With nothing shall be pleased till he be eased
> With being nothing. (5.5.38–41)

Richard's stark conclusion represents the King at his most overtly existential, even nihilist.[33] Yet at the very moment when he contemplates non-being as the solitary truth, when he comes closest to affirming Silenus's wisdom, he is interrupted by music.[34]

The music is an intrusion of the phenomenal world into Richard's prison of linguistic reflection. Up to this point in the soliloquy, Richard struggles to understand his experience without attending to the phenomenal world. Hearing the music intertwines him with his world. The music throws him back into that world, and back into time:

> And here I have the daintiness of ear
> To hear time broke in a disordered string,
> But for the concord of my state and time
> Had not an ear to hear my true time broke (5.5.45–8)

While music could refer conceptually to the harmony of the spheres – celestial concord, for example – the music Richard hears is phenomenal, calling to him somatically with a force that he cannot resist, despite his efforts to disregard it.[35]

Jean-Luc Marion's theory of givenness and his related concept of the saturated phenomenon speak directly to such moments. Marion's philosophy is an attempt to account for the experience of Revelation in phenomenological terms that stress the interrelatedness of concrete experience and understanding.[36] In *Being Given* he writes that 'the very concept of Revelation belongs by right to phenomenality'.[37] His project is a radical development in phenomenology considering that his work seeks both a return to a grounding of phenomenological enquiry in appearance itself and a call to move beyond a Husserlian conception of the limits of phenomenological engagement with the objects of consciousness. Although, as a Catholic phenomenologist, Marion's interest in Revelation is explicitly theological, in his philosophical work he seeks to extend the special case of Revelation to the whole of phenomenality and the phenomenal experience of revelation in general.[38] In particular, Marion's philosophical interest is in returning to the relationship between intuition and intention in classical phenomenology (and especially Husserl) as a way of elucidating a theory of 'givenness' that moves beyond Heidegger's turn to Being and Levinas's emphasis on the Other.[39] Thinking givenness itself, Marion argues, allows phenomenological analysis to consider experience that falls outside certain limitations evident in Husserl's initial formulation of phenomenology, specifically the limitations imposed by intention on intuition. For Husserl, phenomenological intuition cannot exceed intention; the intention of the subject towards the object marks the limit to which the subject's intuition – or apprehension of the given – is confined.

Marion is particularly interested in questioning why phenomenology cannot accommodate an experience in which intuition exceeds intention. The role of intuition in the scholastic philosophical tradition sheds important light on Marion's project and, as I discussed in the introduction, the concept is especially relevant to early modern thought. As Jaakko Hintikka explains,

> the primary sense of intuition in Husserl is basically the pre-Kantian one. Intuition is not a special capacity of the human mind. Intuitiveness is simply a label for immediate knowledge

of any sort. This immediately (intuitively?) explains the central role of *Anschauungen* in Husserl's overall phenomenological enterprise. This enterprise involved tracing back our conceptual world to its sources in immediate experience . . . The identification of the intuitive with what is immediately given to me means that intuition is simply a generic term for the stopping-points of the [phenomenological] reductions. It is the medium in which things are given to me. It is a collective term for the given.[40]

Hintikka highlights two aspects of Husserl's notion of intuition that are relevant to the present discussion. First, Husserl's use of the term *Anschauung* (usually translated 'intuition' or 'sense intuition') to designate 'immediate knowledge of any sort . . . a collective term for the given' helps trace the origins of phenomenology to its medieval scholastic roots, and specifically to the scholastic concept of intuition as intelligibility without mediation discussed above in the Queen's experience of her foreboding grief. Second, Hintikka's account draws attention to the centrality of 'the given' in Husserlian phenomenology, the feature that most interests Marion.

It is important here to contrast the Queen's meditation on grief with Richard's. Whereas the Queen identifies her experience of grief as originating in her 'inward soul', in the deposition scene Richard has to be reminded by Bolingbroke that this is where he should be looking. In prison, rather than heeding Bolingbroke's lesson on 'how to lament the cause' and looking into the recesses of his 'inward soul' to find his 'unseen grief', Richard begins with his 'brain': 'My brain I'll prove the female to my soul, / My soul the father' (5.5.6–7). Unlike the Queen, whose 'inward soul' trembles in contemplation of nothing, Richard cannot think in immaterial terms. Even as he tries to imagine his immaterial soul providing a new understanding of his self, he turns to the most material of images: his soul as 'father' to his 'female' brain.

Inverting the conventional gender of feminine soul, this conceit leads him to imagine something like a forcible assault of soul on body – his male soul fathering 'breeding thoughts' in his female brain.

Richard's elaborate final image of himself transformed into a mechanical time-piece marks his reification as a material thing, symbolic of his failure to recognise in himself anything like an internal, immaterial soul. The clock image figures him as a material substance fixed in an inevitable temporal trajectory, an unavoidable descent from monarch to dust. Importantly, the music plays throughout the second half of the soliloquy. The music is the one thing that exceeds Richard's lyric expression, shaking him back to the gaol cell from his fantastic metaphysical conceit as Bolingbroke's 'jack of the clock': 'This music mads me,' he exclaims, 'let it sound no more' (5.5.61). But he cannot will the music away; its effect on him is confusing:

> Yet blessing on his heart that gives it me
> For 'tis a sign of love, and love to Richard
> Is a strange brooch in this all hating world. (5.5.64–6)[41]

Up to this point, Richard has been able to insulate himself with language capable of maintaining his illusion of control. He has not experienced the kind of unmeditated knowledge that the Queen has of her grief; intuition has not posed a threat to his intentionality. But this moment is different.

Richard's confusion here reflects Nietzsche's claim that 'Language can never adequately render the cosmic symbolism of music, because music stands in symbolic relation to the primordial contradiction and primordial pain in the heart of the primal unity, and thereby symbolises a sphere which is beyond and prior to all phenomena.'[42] For Nietzsche, the 'primordial contradiction' is too much to experience; it leads to nausea, to fainting, which can only be held off by the imagination, by a return to illusion. But for Marion such an event marked by excess is 'saturated', overflowing intuition, and leading to revelation: 'Determining the saturated phenomenon as irregardable amounts to imagining the possibility that it imposes itself on sight with such an excess of intuition that it can no longer be reduced to the conditions of experience (objecthood), therefore to the I that sets them.'[43] Here, that which is given to experience is given as 'pure givenness, precisely because it no longer discerns any objectifiable given therein'.[44] Marion uses the example of music:

> It falls to music, or rather to listening to music, to provide privileged occurrences of this sense of the phenomenon . . . A memory of previous performances no doubt allows me to identify the melody more quickly and to assess the orchestral ensemble, but it does not allow me to abolish the arising, therefore the event. The music offers the very movement of its coming forward, its effect on me who receives it without producing it, in short, its arising without real content. Consequently, it comes upon me in such a way that it affects me directly as pure givenness mediated by almost no objectifiable given, and therefore imposes upon me an actuality immediately its own . . . Let me name this phenomenological extremity where the coming forward exceeds what comes forward a *paradox*.[45]

Likewise, Richard's reaction to the music seems to rise from his inability to contain it conceptually: though he recalls that music is known to cure madness, in his case he fears the opposite. Despite his negative reaction, Richard accepts its gift as a sign of love. And contemplating this gift, Richard comes face to face with a paradox: love in 'this all hating world'. Though he still seeks to translate the experience into material terms, calling it a 'strange brooch', Richard's momentary contemplation of the gift of music brings him the closest he will come to a revelation of the immaterial, through the excess of intuition that Marion identifies with the saturated phenomenon. In wishing a blessing on the 'heart that gives it me' Richard momentarily opens himself to the possibility of the other person outside the prison of language. It occurs, phenomenologically speaking, in Richard's experience with the temporality of the music, at the only moment in the play when he is alone, when the music impinges upon his experience, distracting him from his linguistic conceit. To this point Richard has consistently tried to impose his consciousness on the world, to render meaningful the objects of his intentional consciousness. But that may not be the subject Shakespeare gives us in Richard's experience with the music. As Marion argues,

> if the 'subject' is defined as constituting objects, then it can only objectify the Other (Descartes, perhaps Sartre) or appresent him in ordinary inter-objectivity and therefore miss him as such (Husserl). If by contrast, he accomplishes this purely by his own self-resolution, he comes only across the Other according to his own-for-the-Other, without joining with him (Heidegger). It's entirely different with the gifted: defined as he who receives and receives himself from the given, he can receive, according to the ordinary procedures of givenness (no predetermined horizon, no a priori principle, no constitution), among other givens . . .[46]

Only alone and presented with the ephemeral temporality of music can Richard experience the phenomenal world in its plenitude, unpopulated by the objects of his imaginative mind – the world given to his experience in the name of love ('a blessing on the heart that gives it me!'). In this solitary space, and only for a moment, Richard is '[no] longer concern[ed with] intersubjectivity or interobjectivity, but intergivenness'.[47] Marion calls 'intergivenness' one of the most 'advanced developments' of phenomenology, and that which opens philosophy to the concept of love by allowing for the revelation of the Other 'in his unsubstitutible particularity'.[48]

Of all Shakespeare's tragic heroes, Richard is quite possibly the one we would least expect to recognise givenness in Marion's sense. And yet the king's surprising reception of the gift of music in the final moments of his life is crucial to the play's aesthetic power. The moment is fleeting. In the lines that follow, and even as he finally takes action against his murderers and gives up his life, Richard falls back on the controlling poetic conceits he rehearsed throughout the play – first condemning his horse for treason and then urging his soul to ascend to heaven while his 'gross flesh sinks downward, here to die' (5.5.112). Nevertheless, his ability, albeit momentarily, to receive the gift of love and accept its paradox may help explain the feeling that in his depiction of Richard's fall Shakespeare offered us something more than an exploration of history or tragedy as the deserved end of a weak monarch or the consequences of a blindness to self-knowledge. Finally abandoning the visible for the invisible, Richard becomes worthy of the substantial grief he described without conviction in the deposition scene. Grief, if it is ever actualised in the play, is made manifest in the prison scene where it is finally given through the experience of love. Where grief was an empty signifier for Richard throughout the play, a word to hurl at his adversaries in displays of self-pity, without an audience, and facing his own very real decline, it finally becomes something real, if not material. A similar delay in actualisation occurs for Hal in *1 Henry IV*, which is the subject of the next chapter.

Notes

1. The scene has attracted a mountain of critical attention. For some of the studies that share my interests here, see, in particular, Scott McMillin, 'Shakespeare's *Richard II*: Eyes of Sorrow, Eyes of Desire'; Ernst H. Kantorowicz, *The King's Two Bodies*, pp. 24–41; Christopher Pye, *The Regal Phantasm*; Philip Lorenz, 'Christall Mirrors: Analogy and Onto-Theology in Shakespeare and Francisco Suarez'; and Gary Kuchar, *The Poetry of Religious Sorrow in Early Modern England*, pp. 31–77.

2. On analogy in the play, see Lorenz, 'Cristall Mirrors', pp. 108–19.

3. Richard's conclusion, 'There lies the substance' (4.1.292), further complicates an already difficult negotiation between the material and immaterial, as the line could be read to suggest that the soul is substance and that the grief is thus embodied in the substance of the soul; or, Richard could mean that the substance of his speech lies in recognising the distinction between his immaterial grief and the visible laments that can never truly represent it.

4. The revival of *Richard II* in support of the Earl of Essex's ill-fated rebellion is only the most overt reminder during Shakespeare's career of the importance of representation in maintaining monarchical legitimacy. Even Leeds Barroll, in an essay questioning the connection between the Essex revolt and the play, admits: 'That Richard II was a suggestive subject in these years is, I think, beyond debate' ('A New History for Shakespeare and His Time', p. 105).

5. When the play first appeared in quarto in 1597, it bore the title *The Tragedy of King Richard the Second*. A quarter century later, the Folio identified the play with the more neutral title *The Life and Death of King Richard II*, grouping it with the histories.

6. Johnson, qtd in Bloom (ed.), *William Shakespeare's Richard II: Modern Critical Interpretations*, p. 4. Some thirty-five years later Charles Dibdin would repeat the claim, suggesting that

'we cannot trace in it his usual force, either as to the characters or the language' (qtd in Forker [ed.], *Richard II: Shakespeare The Critical Tradition*, p. 90).

7. Halverson, 'The Lamentable Comedy of *Richard II*', in Farrell (ed.), p. 262.

8. Kott quoted in Halverson, 'Lamentable', p. 263. Of course, most critics are not willing to go this far. Though Ruth Nevo also compares Richard to Lear, hers is a qualified comparison: at the end of the play, she argues, Richard is 'reduced to something as near as the impure tragedy of the histories will get to unaccommodated man', but his resistance to the murderers 'is the simplest kind of catharsis' ('The Genre of *Richard II*', p. 35).

9. Nietzsche, *Birth of Tragedy*, trans. Kaufmann, p. 33.

10. Ibid., p. 42, emphasis original. The story is related by Plutarch and Kaufmann notes the repetition in Sophocles, *Oedipus at Colonus*.

11. Ibid., p. 43.

12. Ibid.

13. See Kantorowizc, *The King's Two Bodies*.

14. In his early edition of the play Nahum Tate gave this speech to Carlisle, rendering it, in Forker's terms, a 'choric expression of royalist orthodoxy' (p. 3), rather than a reflection on Richard's belief in divine right. In a similar vein, I don't see this as an expression of belief, but rather an appeal to institutional power.

15. See, for example, Dorothea Kehler, 'King of Tears: Mortality in *Richard II*'.

16. This was Walter Pater's sense of the play, and of Shakespeare's historical kings generally: 'Shakespeare's kings are not, nor are meant to be, great men: rather, little or quite ordinary humanity, thrust upon greatness, with those pathetic results, the natural self-pity of the weak heightened in them into irresistible appeal as the net result of their royal prerogative' (Pater, in Forker, p. 298).

17. Pater calls the mirror scene an 'inverted rite': the king 'perform[s] a mock undoing of precisely what cannot be

un-done: the anointing that made him a sacred king' (qtd in Kantorowicz, *The King's Two Bodies*, p. 36).

18. His handling of the murder of Gloucester and its consequences indicates that he is aware of the political reality that Northumberland must explain to the Queen in response to her plea for Bolingbroke to spare Richard's life: 'That were some love, but little policy' (5.1.84).

19. Kuchar, *Religious Sorrow*, p. 61.

20. Kuchar argues that Richard 'begins the play presuming a continuity between word and thing, intention and substance, [but] he ends it by recognizing an irremediable gap between them' (*Religious Sorrow*, p. 59). I agree with Kuchar's initial premise, but come to a different conclusion about the resolution of the play.

21. Nietzsche, *Birth of Tragedy*, trans. Kaufmann, p. 60.

22. When York exclaims that he 'is too far gone with grief', Richard's response is incredulous: 'Why, Uncle, what's the matter?' (2.1.184, 186). Also see Kuchar, *Religious Sorrow*. In performance, Richard's line 'My eyes are full of tears; I cannot see' (4.1.236) is often delivered by a dry-eyed actor.

23. McMillin, 'Eyes of Desire', p. 40.

24. Ibid., p. 42.

25. Heller-Roazen, *The Inner Touch*, pp. 136–7. He notes that earlier examples of 'internal senses' have been recorded. Fazlur Rhaman traces the use of the term 'internal' with the common sense to the Stoics and then Alexander of Aphrodisias. See Ibn Sīnā, *Avicenna's Psychology*, pp. 77–8. Katharine Maus, *Inwardness and Theater in the English Renaissance*, notes, among other examples of inwardness, the phrase 'inward heart' (p. 17). I share her sense that the period's interest in inwardness is not necessarily related to 'subjectivity' in the sense usually deployed by cultural theorists from the twentieth century forward (see p. 30).

26. Avicenna's medical works continued to be used as textbooks in Europe through the end of the sixteenth century. On Avicenna's theory of the inward sense, see Heller-Roazen, *The Inner Touch*: 'Avicenna cast the inner power not only as the

foundation of all the senses but also as their center, the point from which they all "emanated," engendered in the shared procession from a primary power' (p. 154). For Avicenna's influence on scholastic thought, see Jon McGinnis, *Avicenna*, pp. 244–54.

27. Banchetti-Robino, 'Ibn Sīnā and Husserl on Intention and Intentionality', p. 74. She concludes that the unique theory has its roots in Avicenna's medical training: 'Therefore, since it can be shown that, for Ibn Sīnā, there is a physiological element to the reception and retention of the sensible forms of external objects, one would have to conclude that intentionality has, ultimately, physiological origins' (p. 74). I discuss this further in the last part of this book.

28. Avicenna, *Psychology*, p. 30. See Banchetti-Robino, 'Ibn Sīnā and Husserl', p. 72, for a discussion of this passage.

29. Avicenna, *Psychology*, p. 35. McGinnis, *Avicenna*, explains that for Avicenna, 'a human comes to know or understand something when the intellect receives the intelligible object or concept of the thing . . . Some individuals just do not "get things," while others do, some get things faster, some slower. When this capacity or disposition to get things is strong, Avicenna terms it "insight" or "intuition" . . . The person with insight is, with relative ease, able to make initial contact or conjunction with the Active Intellect, which again brings about intellectual perception' (p. 147).

30. The scene establishes the Queen and her inward sense as a kind of chorus for the play, a fact that is of special importance when considering its development in light of Nietzsche's identification of the origins of tragedy with the musicality of the dithyrambic chorus.

31. The term 'unkinged' appears again, crucially, in Richard's prison soliloquy.

32. For the relation of this performance to one of James's before parliament, see Lorenz, 'Christall Mirrors', pp. 102–3.

33. Harold Bloom identifies this line as 'the earliest Shakespearean litany of nihilism, predating *Much Ado About Nothing* and prophesying Hamlet, Iago, and Leontes' (*Shakespeare*

and the Invention of the Human, p. 269). See Kirby Farrell, 'Introduction: Play, Death, and History', pp. 1–22.

34. Here Nietzsche might identify the moment when art, that 'saving sorceress', appears in the form of the 'satyr chorus of the dithyramb' (p. 60). In Francis Golffing's translation, the role of the dithyramb is to 'turn his fits of nausea into imaginations with which it is possible to live' (p. 52). On the importance of the music, see Richard Altick, 'Symphonic Imagery in *Richard II*', and Pieter D. Williams, 'Music, Time and Tears in *Richard II*'.

35. For an account of the contradictory way that music was seen as both immaterial (cosmic harmony) and material (sensuously enthralling), see Scott Trudell, *Unwritten Poetry: Song, Performance and Media in Early Modern England*, pp. 1–13 and *passim*.

36. Marion develops his theory of saturated phenomena in *Being Given: Toward a Phenomenology of Givenness* and *In Excess: Studies of Saturated Phenomena*.

37. Marion, *Being Given*, p. 5.

38. In this sense, Marion hopes to include in his phenomenological project both the miraculous form of Revelation found in an example like Christ's Transfiguration as well as the mundane form of revelation suggested by the word's root, to 'reveal'. See Westphal, 'Transfiguration as Saturated Phenomenon', pp. 26–8.

39. Heidegger turned attention from the experience of phenomenal objects in general to the experience of being in the world (*Dasein*), whereas Levinas questioned the turn to being and urged attention to the experience of the other ('ethics as first philosophy'). See Marion, *Being Given*, pp. 259–69.

40. Hintikka, 'The Notion of Intuition in Husserl', pp. 173–4.

41. The Norton decision to include the stage direction 'music stops' at line 61 seems unwarranted. Even in the Folio, with its additions to the stage directions, there is no direction for the music to stop, and Richard's continued focus on the music here suggests that he has no control over it.

42. Nietzsche, *Birth of Tragedy*, trans. Kaufmann, p. 55.

43. Marion, *Being Given*, p. 215.
44. Ibid., p. 216.
45. Ibid.
46. Ibid., p. 323.
47. Ibid.
48. Ibid., pp. 323–4.

CHAPTER 4

"TIS INSENSIBLE, THEN?': CONCEPT AND ACTION IN *1 HENRY IV*

> Honour! tut, a breath:
> There's no such thing, in nature: a mere term
> Invented to awe fools.
>
> Ben Jonson, *Volpone*

In the previous chapter, we examined a character almost allergic to action. For the first half of the play Richard deferred authority to a God of his imagination, one who would bring armies of angels to fight in his name. Rousing invocations of his divine authority are the closest he comes to mounting a defence against rebellion. Even Richard's closest allies must remind him to raise an actual army to resist the encroaching Bolingbroke. Once defeated by the loss of supporters against the strength of Bolingbroke's insurgence, Richard's sense of action continues to be restrained to the level of utterance, as he insists on recasting the calamity of his fall in terms of his own victimisation. His only staged action – with perhaps the exception of his shattering of the mirror in the deposition – comes too late, as he rises up against his murderers just before his own death. Lack of action leads to Richard's downfall, but action itself leads to death, a reality foreshadowed by Richard's own conclusion on the death of kings, that they are 'all murdered'. While Richard is unable to bring his image of divine kingship into being through his words, he is able to strip bare the political events of the play, exposing the mechanisms of power for what they are.

In the play that follows in the historical narrative, Shakespeare can be seen to explore precisely the opposite dynamic. If action was secondary to articulation in *Richard II*, *1 Henry IV* explores a case in which action determines conception, and the concept at question is once more the very identity and existence of the title character. The question of genre is again central, for if *Richard II* is at least in part a tragedy, *1 Henry IV* is partly comedy. In an influential description of *1 Henry IV* Cleanth Brooks and Robert Heilman describe the play as 'one of the wisest and fullest commentaries on human action possible [in] the comic mode'. They go on, nevertheless, to conclude that 'Shakespeare has no easy moral to draw, no simple generalisation to make', suggesting that in choosing the comic mode, Shakespeare opted to emphasise the ethical ambiguity of human actions over any guiding principle of moral propriety.[1] Alternately, in his introduction to his Arden 2 edition, A. R. Humphreys argues that the play does not fully embrace the moral ambiguity that Brooks and Heilman claim: 'There is history here as well as comedy – history which requires responsible action.'[2] Humphrey's comment is prompted by his belief, shared by a range of critics, that Shakespeare had to side with Hal, with history, over both Hotspur's misplaced valour and the endearing, but untenable misrule of the comic Falstaff. In Humphrey's view, it is Hal's action around which the play revolves: will the wayward prince act with the honour of an heir apparent? From this position, all other action in the play is included to offer a contrast to Hal's heroism, thus making coherent sense of the historical events that are Shakespeare's subject.[3]

Hal's victorious action in battle signifies his honour and, by implication, the divine justification of his cause. Read in this way, Hal's victory actualises his potential, underwriting his heroism as an expression of his true substance.

Although such a reading is in keeping with the authorised historical account, critics have stressed that this narrative of heroic redemption is troubled by the play's subplots, characterised, in Phyllis Rackin's account, not by linear narrative time, but by 'analogy, parody, contrast, and juxtaposition'.[4] The contrast with Hotspur is perhaps most notable. If Hal's development is to successfully recuperate the monarchy, he must earn honour at Hotspur's expense. Because Hotspur's defence of Mortimer's right to the throne has some merit – it is a claim that is arguably equal to King Henry's – Hal must purchase his honour at the cost of Hotspur's life on the battlefield at Shrewsbury.[5] But, as Rackin points out, Hotspur's uncompromising devotion to chivalric honour represents an outmoded form of political action, and his failed rebellion exposes 'the impossibility of the old feudal ideas in the pragmatic new world of *Henry IV*'.[6] Though both seek to justify their authority in relation to the concept of honour, Hal's pragmatic method of acquiring it displays an awareness of its constructedness that Hotspur lacks in his unbridled desire for the ideal.

Falstaff, on the other hand, offers an alternative philosophy of action that is much more threatening to the political order, generally speaking. David Kastan makes this point persuasively in arguing that 'the comic plot serves to counter the totalising fantasies of power, to expose and disrupt the hierarchies on which they depend'.[7] For Kastan, the tension between the comic subplot and the main historical plot arises from the fact that 'the history of state politics inevitably and purposefully erases other histories . . . histories whose very existence contests the story that the hegemonic state would tell of itself'.[8] Kastan's argument that the play resists the subversion of alternatives to the official political history is convincing, as is Rackin's characterisation of Hotspur as a representative of a fading political order. Both accounts, characteristic of other New Historicist readings of power in the drama of the period, seek to point out the discontinuities in Shakespeare's representation of the authorised historical narrative. Highlighting such discontinuities illuminates our understanding of the ways in which literary texts, and other forms of cultural representation, influence and are influenced by both the established historical narrative and its alternatives.

The present chapter builds on the contributions of such New Historicist readings by turning attention to the play's engagement with the experience of temporality. Time and the conditions of temporal versus eternal existence have long been recognised as a thematic focus of the play.[9] And, as we have seen, temporality, manifested by material change, generation and corruption, was a feature of existence that had to be accounted for across the material/immaterial divide. How something could persist through changes is a key to Aristotle's definition of substance, as is the question of when something is the thing that it is in actuality rather than potentiality. Historical representation is a particularly interesting platform through which to explore questions relating to the reality of existence over time, for the events are known, though only through the mediation of subsequent accounts.

Rackin addresses the temporal dimension of early modern historiography specifically, arguing that the Henry IV plays represent a shift from a medieval conception of time in *Richard II* organised by 'historical connection under the aspect of eternity' to an early modern one marked by the 'empty time of modern narrative and modern consciousness which relates disparate events only by calendrical coincidence'. The import of this shift, in her view, is that 'The spatial boundaries that define modern nations replace the chronological links that define feudal dynasties.'[10] This is a helpful explanation of the shifting ground of historical representation in early modern England, especially for those interested in understanding England's emergence as a conceptually coherent nation, a prerequisite for its development into a colonial power in the centuries to come. Foregrounding spatial as opposed to temporal understanding as a feature of the history offered up in the Henry plays nevertheless turns attention away from one of historical representation's key features: that history is dependent on linguistic narrativity for its intelligibility. To examine the experience of time in *1 Henry IV* is not to deny Rackin's claim that the different forms of historiography on display in Shakespeare's *Richard II* and *1 Henry IV* reflect a formal shift from chronicle to chorography in the early modern era that substituted 'land for king as the embodiment of national identity and space for time as its medium'.[11] Rather, by turning attention from the play's representation of political authority and national identity to its phenomenology of temporal experience, it is possible to consider Shakespeare's reflection on the interrelatedness of material experience and immaterial ideality. In *1 Henry IV*, Shakespeare explores this relation through a thematic focus on the contrast between embodied action and incorporeal identity.

Action, History, Temporality

The interrelation of action, history and temporality has long attracted the attention of philosophers of history, and the rise of phenomenology in the late nineteenth century animated twentieth-century debates that increasingly focused on temporality and language. While the complex relationship between temporality and history is a recurring theme in twentieth-century phenomenology, nowhere is it more central than in the work of Paul Ricoeur. Throughout a long and extremely prolific career, Ricoeur returned with regularity to the dynamic relationship between historical representation, which he came to associate with narrative, and temporality, which he imagined to be at the heart of the human experience of life. As Hayden White summarises, 'the overarching thesis' of Ricoeur's magnum opus, the three-volume *Time and Narrative*, 'is that temporality is "the structure of existence that reaches language in narrativity" and that narrativity is "the language structure that has temporality as its ultimate referent"'.[12] This thesis reflects Ricoeur's interest in merging hermeneutics and phenomenology by focusing on the phenomenal experience of interpretation in time. Though Ricoeur is ultimately concerned with the experience of narrativity, and with plot as narrative's configuring element, human action is naturally central to his analysis. As he notes in a discussion of the 'reciprocal constitution of action and of the self':

> A character is the one who performs the action in the narrative. The category of character is therefore a narrative category as well, and its role in the narrative involves the same narrative understanding as the plot itself . . . [T]he identity of the character is comprehensible through the transfer to the character of the operation of emplotment, first applied to the action recounted; characters, we will say, are themselves plots.[13]

For Ricoeur, the relationship between character and action points to further connections between action and plot, plot and narrative, and narrative and temporality. This way of conceiving of the temporality of history as bound up with the relations among characters, actions and plots has important implications for a reading of Shakespeare's histories, and particularly *1 Henry IV*, a play explicitly concerned with 'consequential action', those actions that ultimately constitute historical events in Ricoeur's terms:

> To be historical, an event must be more than a singular occurrence, a unique happening. It receives its definition from its contribution to the development of a plot. Reciprocally, a plot is a way of connecting event and story. A story is *made out of* events, to the extent that plot makes events *into* a story.[14]

Ricoeur's theory of action as emplotment and thus as constitutive of narrativity points to another way of reading the play's treatment of honour, action and history, for honour is conceptually inextricable from narrative temporality. Honour has no meaning without reference to actions and events, and, as Ricoeur's philosophy of history demonstrates, actions and events cannot be disentangled from the narratives through which they are made intelligible. Rather than view the play's commentary on honour as representative of changing attitudes towards chivalric responsibility, focusing on narrative temporality reveals the play's deeper interest in the human experience of time beyond or beneath the authorised historical account.

In Shakespeare's play we are presented with competing narratives about gaining, losing and retaining honour. These narratives are clearly focused on the temporal modalities of those states: as reflections of past actions, present convictions and future aspirations. This thematic focus has implications for the question of being and substance that is the subject of this part of the present study. Specifically, is honour 'a breath', as Corvino asserts in Ben Jonson's *Volpone*? It would be hard to argue with his conviction that 'there is no such thing in nature', though by this Jonson's character presumably means to invoke the distinction between objects of sense and intellect. Honour is clearly an object of the latter and not the former, which would seem to place it firmly in the realm of the immaterial. And yet the temporal designations that mark the possession of honour – 'I have lost my honour, Othello's occupation's gone!' – depend on material manifestation for their intelligibility. This framing of events in relation to past, present and future is at the heart of history, or what Ricoeur calls 'historicality'. As White explains,

> To experience time as future, past, and present rather than as a series of instants in which every one has the same weight or significance as every other is to experience 'historicality.' This experience of historicality, finally, can be represented symbolically in narrative discourse, because such discourse is a product of the same kind of hypotactical figuration of events (as beginnings, middles, and ends) as that met with in the actions of historical agents who hypotactically figurate their lives as meaningful stories.[15]

In *1 Henry IV*, we witness historical agents both acting in ways that will 'figurate their lives', and also overtly narrating the process of that figuration. Following Hannah Arendt, Ricoeur notes that:

> Action deserves its name when, beyond the concern for submitting nature to man or for leaving behind some monuments witnessing to our activity, it aims only at being recollected in stories whose function it is to provide an identity to the doer, an identity that is merely a narrative identity. In this sense, history repeats action in the figure of the memorable. Such is the way in which history itself – and not only fiction – provides an approximation of what a phenomenology of time experience may call repetition.[16]

Repetition is crucial to Ricoeur's phenomenology of time experience. In order to establish the centrality of narrative to the human experience of time, Ricoeur proposes three levels of time experience, drawing on and ultimately parting from Heidegger's analysis in *Being and Time*. The first level is being 'within-time', by which he means simply the experience of living in time, having an awareness of time passing, for example, but without any overt attempt to reflect on that experience.[17] This is the simplest, and most self-evident, form of temporal experience. Ricoeur cites Augustine's claim that he knows time unless he is asked to define it: 'If nobody asks me, I know; but if I were desirous to explain it to one that should ask me, plainly I know not.'[18] This 'within-time-ness' is the first step of Ricoeur's account of the human experience of time, in which the experience of time is evident (as one event occurs after or before another) but not assessed. The paradigmatic discursive form of this kind of time is the chronicle, in which events are organised chronologically but without being configured by any narrative logic.[19]

This first-order experience of time is followed by the level of 'historicality' mentioned above, in which the events are emplotted to figure coherent narratives:

> narrative does more than just establish humanity, along with human actions and passions, 'in' time; it also brings us back from within-time-ness to historicality, from 'reckoning with' time to 'recollecting' it. As such, the narrative function provides a transition from within-time-ness to historicality.[20]

Repetition of the historically memorable action in language is the key to the next and most profound level, what Ricoeur calls 'deep temporality'. In the process of repetition, narrative reveals action as an experience of history, of temporality, but which is only available in the experience of narrative itself:

> The question . . . is whether we may go so far as to say that the function of narratives – or at least of some narratives – is to establish human action at the level of genuine historicality,

that is, of repetition. If such were the case, the temporal structure of narrative would display the same hierarchy as the one established by the phenomenology of time experience.[21]

In White's terms, Ricoeur's analysis leads to the conclusion that 'every great historical narrative is an allegory of temporality':

> in narrative fiction, the experiences of both 'within-time-ness' and 'historicality' can be dissolved in the apprehension of the relation of 'eternity' to 'death,' which is the content of the form of temporality itself . . . Thus conceived, narrative fiction provides glimpses of the deep structure of historical consciousness and, by implication, of both historical reflection and historical discourse.[22]

Drawing on Heidegger's account of historicity, Ricoeur attributes this function of narrative to repetition:

> Through repetition, the character of time as stretching-along is rooted in the deep unity of time as future, past, and present, the backward move toward the past is retrieved in the anticipation of a project, and the endless-ness of historical time is grafted on the finite structure of being-toward-death.[23]

It is here that Ricoeur parts ways with Heidegger, seeking to explore what he calls 'the aporetics of time' as an antidote to the circularity of Heidegger's existential hermeneutics. By acknowledging the 'ultimate unrepresentability of time, which makes phenomenology continually turn to metaphors and to the language of myth', Ricoeur preserves some of the mysteriousness of time that clearly interested Shakespeare.[24] That the human experience of temporality is always haunted by death, against which all material figuration is positioned as a bulwark, suggests that the relationship between the material and the immaterial is among the central concerns of any attempt at historical representation. Honour, as the concept that mediates between these two realms in *1 Henry IV* – connecting human actions to conceptual identity and historical legacy – makes a perfect case study for reflection on Shakespeare's depiction of the phenomenal experience of time.

Material Action and Immaterial Honour

The theme of honour emerges in the play's first scene just after we learn of the troubles in the North, as King Henry considers Hotspur's conduct on the battlefield. For the present purpose, I am interested in the distinction the King establishes when he compares Hotspur and Hal – the former is 'A son who is the theme of honour's tongue', while 'riot and dishonour stain the brow / of my young Harry' (1.1.80, 84–5). The King's distinction is between the immaterial concept of honour ('the theme of honour's tongue' as the conceptual and linguistic rendering of honour), and the material 'stain' on Harry's 'brow'. The play's meditation on honour culminates in the fifth act with a return to this distinction, first in Falstaff's 'catechism' on honour and then in the final exchange between Hotspur and Hal. Significantly, the image that prompts the King to describe Hotspur as 'the theme of honour's tongue' is a field of bloodstained Scottish corpses, 'Ten thousand bold Scots, two-and-twenty knights / Balked in their own blood' (1.1.68–9).

This scene – the visible testimony of Hotspur's valorous action against the rebellious Douglas written in blood on the bodies of the vanquished – serves to balance the morbid news Westmorland has just delivered of the defeat of Mortimer by Owen Glendower:

> A thousand of his people butchered,
> Upon whose dead corpse there was such misuse,
> Such beastly shameless transformation,
> By those Welshwomen done as may not be
> Without much shame retold or spoken of. (1.1.42–6)

The implication, of course, is that the Welsh butchery of the English is shameful while the English butchery of the Welsh is honourable. Notably, this remains implicit, as the story on which it depends cannot 'without much shame [be] retold or spoken of', presumably because the act of narration would somehow repeat the original shameful actions.[25] Both honour and dishonour are thus written onto the bodies of the dead here, the story of virtuous or corrupt action narrated in the language of voiceless flesh. Tellingly, it is Sir Walter Blunt who witnesses the aftermath of Hotspur's valour and brings news of the 'honourable spoil' of the prisoners to the king, for it is Blunt's corpse that will serve as Falstaff's example of honour embodied in act 5.

The distinction set up between immaterial, conceptual motives for action – virtue, honour, divine justice and their opposites irregularity, rudeness, shamelessness – and the material bodies in action 'stained' with signifying 'blood', 'riot' or 'dishonour' establishes the play's epistemological meditation on the philosophy of action as a matter of interpretation. The most concentrated example of this comes in Falstaff's 'catechism' on honour in 5.1, culminating in his memorable claim that 'Honour is a mere scutcheon', an insubstantial symbol displayed after death (5.1.138).[26] In the introduction to Arden 3, Kastan notes that Falstaff 'is unquestionably unreliable and self-indulgent, but also . . . his behavior marks a commitment to life (at least his own) over a set of thin abstractions that often deny it'.[27] Falstaff's argument against honour represents the largest obstacle that the errant and sensually oriented Hal must face in his transformation from degenerate prince to heroic King, for it is ultimately immaterial, abstract honour that must materially 'prick' Hal on to act as he knows a king must act, to act according to the established abstractions that his old friend repeatedly demystifies.

But if one's moral character, one's honour, is a consequence of one's actions, we must ask what Hal could possibly mean when he promises his father, 'I shall hereafter … be more myself' (3.2.92–3).[28] At this mid-point in the play, Hal's 'self' is precisely as his father describes it: he has lost his honour, 'with vile participation' (3.2.86–7), that is, as a result of his actions. As the king points out, Hotspur 'hath more worthy interest to the state / Than thou, the shadow of succession' (3.2.98–9). As in the opening scene, the comparison of honour and dishonour relies on a distinction between the material and immaterial, but here the relationship is even more complicated. A 'shadow of succession', Hal is an heir in name only, a word, a breath without material substance.[29] Hotspur's 'worthy interest to the state' is based on a material discourse of accumulation: 'this Hotspur, Mars in swaddling clothes', has gained his name by defeating Douglas three times; Douglas had previously earned the 'military title capital / Through all the kingdoms that acknowledge Christ' by 'high deeds', on the battlefield (3.2.110, 107). Hotspur literally 'got' – as in took possession of – his 'never-dying honour' through action. But even as the King links Hotspur's honour to his actions, we witness the process of its narrativisation: Hotspur's honour is 'never-dying', emplotted in a narrative of heroic action that is the envy of a King ashamed of his own story.[30] It is no wonder, then, that Hal's assurance of future behaviour means little to the King, when Hal insists: 'I shall hereafter, my thrice-gracious lord, / Be more myself' (92–3). Hal's reference to 'himself' – unproven in action – can appear to King Henry as nothing more than an empty promise.[31] When his rhetoric turns to external deeds, however, it is a different story.

Hal's ability to speak the language of honour, to 'wear a garment all of blood, / And stain my favours in a bloody mask', offers the particularity that Henry ostensibly hopes for. It is in this speech that Hal most clearly articulates his understanding of the need to materialise immaterial honour through a narrative of accumulation. His language

here is focused on the body, and his logic explicitly relies
on the metaphor of property exchange:

> For every honour sitting on his helm,
> Would they were multitudes, and on my head
> My shames redoubled; for the time will come
> That I shall make this northern youth exchange
> His glorious deeds for my indignities.
> Percy is but my factor, good my lord,
> To engross up glorious deeds on my behalf;
> And I will call him to so strict account
> That he shall render every glory up,
> Yea, even the slightest worship of his time,
> Or I will tear the reckoning from his heart. (3.2.142–52)

This material language of exchange both grounds Hal's
defence of himself to his father and pushes the play's discourse of honour further into the realm of abstraction. Hal
guarantees his account with an impossible promise: 'I will
die a hundred thousand deaths / Ere I break the smallest par-
cel of this vow' (3.2.158–9). Hal's honour is guaranteed by
the sheer number he will kill in defence of the King's right –
more than either Douglas or Hotspur had killed, according
to the reports in the opening scene. The quantitative logic
wins the day, as the King concludes that 'A hundred thousand rebels die in this' (3.2.160). At precisely this moment
in the exchange, Sir Walter Blunt enters, signalling, perhaps
the material presence of the body intruding on the idealised
discourse of heroic death – either killing or dying for one's
honour. Blunt is the both the bearer of the news of Hotspur's
bloody triumph in the first scene and the ironic material symbol of 'honour' for Falstaff who sees in the corpse of Blunt
'no vanity' (5.3.32–3).

Hal's concept of honour depends on a violent and visceral
language for its power – he will tear the 'reckoning' from

Hotspur's heart. However, just as Hal's promise to 'die a hundred thousand deaths' is rhetorically powerful but materially impossible, his promise to 'tear the reckoning' from Hotspur's material body relies on a refusal of materiality in favour of an immaterial ideality, a conceptual ledger of military valour. Moreover, this immaterial honour that underwrites Hal's narrative is generated by a discourse concerned almost obsessively with time: 'the time will come', that Hal 'shall make', 'will call', and Percy 'shall render' and 'will die', 'Ere' he breaks his word. All of this temporal ordering, configures the plot to come, that which we are in fact in the process of recollecting, as narrative. In Ricoeur's terms, we witness Hal 'reckoning' with time: 'the heroes of the narrative "reckon with" time. They "have" or "don't have" time "to" (do this or that). Their time may be "won" or "lost"'.[32] In the process of such a reckoning with time in narrative, 'Story-telling . . . reveal[s] the existential traits of within-timeness over and against the abstraction of linear time.'[33] Hal's promise in this speech comes in the form of storytelling; he tells a story that 'will redeem' his character from that described by his father moments before: 'I will redeem all this on Percy's head / And in the closing of some glorious day / Be bold to tell you I am your son' (3.2.132–4). While the emphasis on materiality appears to ground Hal's subsequent narrative in the language of human action, it is in fact his acknowledgement of temporality that guarantees the outcome. It is important that Hal hasn't actually done anything honourable at this point. His only honourable action comes in his willingness to articulate an acceptance of his essentially temporal existence – his relationship to death.

In doing so he explicitly invokes a narrative of repetition. The word 'redeem' is crucial here. As Paul Jorgensen points out, the term is deployed in a complicated way in the play. The instance most critics focus on occurs in Hal's soliloquy at the end of the second scene, when he promises a future change in his behaviour, 'redeeming time when men think least I will' (1.3.195). Hal's promise is usually glossed as some form of 'making amends for misspent time', but according to Jorgensen, 'To the Elizabethan audience, to redeem (or "rescue") time would be clearly understood as meaning to take full advantage of the time a man is given here on earth for salvation.'[34] Jorgensen's point is that early modern audiences would not have thought it possible to 'make up for lost time', as time wasted was lost irretrievably. But the Latin etymology suggests repetition: *redimere* 'to buy back' or to 'gain again'. The *OED* cites *1 Henry IV* in support of five different senses of the word current at the end of the sixteenth century, including the sense Hal uses in his soliloquy: 'To make the best of use of (time); to prevent (time) from being lost or wasted'.[35] The definition supports Jorgensen's point that rather than 'get time back', Hal's sense is future oriented: to 'redeem time' is to *redeem from time* one's potential salvation. This is also in line with Hotspur's effort to incite Northumberland and Worcester to rebel, arguing that there is still time to act: 'Yet time serves wherein you may redeem / Your banished honours and restore yourselves / Into the good thoughts of the world again' (1.3.179–81). Importantly, the complexity of the term is a product of its juxtaposition of the seemingly discordant elements of gain (or acquisition) and repetition, that which allows the term to mean both 'ransom' (or payment) *and* recovery. It also seems important that the word 'redeem' appears in two of Shakespeare's sources – Holinshed's *Chronicles* and Ephesians – in two very different senses. According to Holinshed, when King Henry refused to ransom Mortimer, 'Henrie Hotspur said openly: Behold, the heir of the realm is robbed of his right, and yet the robber with his own will not redeem him.'[36] Shakespeare's King Henry refuses to ransom Mortimer, with the line 'Shall our coffers, then, / Be emptied to redeem a traitor home?' (1.3.84–5). Here the material sense

of the term is emphasised, though later in the play the use of
the word will shift to the immaterial. That shift is suggested
in the scriptural reference from Ephesians that lies beneath
Hal's use of the term in 1.2: Paul begins with a reminder
of Christ's role as redeemer, 'In whom we have redemption
through his blood, the forgiveness of sins, according to the
riches of his grace' (Eph. 1: 7). While King Henry remains
focused on material riches – the contents of the royal coffers – the passage from Ephesians transforms material blood
into grace, just as Christ's material presence is transformed
into immaterial salvation in the narrative of the Passion.
A subsequent scriptural use of the term confirms this movement from material experience to narrative:

> . . . after that ye heard the word of truth, the gospel of
> your salvation: in whom also after that ye believed, ye were
> sealed with that holy Spirit of promise,
>   Which is the earnest of our inheritance until the
> redemption of the purchased possession, unto the praise of
> his glory. (Eph. 1: 13–14)

The movement of time is captured here through the figure
of exchange, commerce that relies on a temporal logic for
its coherence: the 'earnest' is an immaterial 'holy Spirit of
promise' that serves as guarantee until the 'purchased possession' is redeemed. It is this logic that underlies the verse that
apparently piqued Shakespeare's interest: 'See then that ye
walk circumspectly, not as fools, but as wise, redeeming the
time because the days are evil' (Eph. 5: 15–16).

The concept of redemption configures Hal's development
as the result of a self-reflexive narrative. Though we learn at
the beginning that Hal will 'redeem time', redeem from time
his own 'self', it only becomes clear that he can do this in the
context of a narrative that is bounded by his own death. That
some form of the term 'redeem' appears at the beginning,

middle and end of Hal's progress in the play is important for
the current discussion of the narrativity of time experience.
I have discussed the first instance of the term in Hal's story,
his claim that he will redeem time, and I have mentioned
the second, when he promises his father that he will 'redeem
all this on Percy's head'. This second instance appears in
the *OED* as the only example of an obscure and rare sense
meaning 'To avenge, repay (a wrong)'.[37] Yet this fails to capture the sense of the word as Hal uses it here, clearly echoing
his earlier soliloquy. If by redemption he is righting a wrong,
it is not a wrong done him by Hotspur. In fact, his respect for
Hotspur remains strong throughout the play. What he hopes
to avenge is the blot on his own reputation that had led his
father to imagine the worst about him – that he is capable
of the double crime of patricide/regicide. If he must avenge
anyone for this 'wrong', however, it is himself, as he is the
source of his own poor reputation ('I will so offend to make
offence a skill'). The fact that his own goal of redemption
here is self-reflexive points to the structure of the narrative
in which we witness his self-transformation, which is, by his
own account, not a matter of change but of a consistency of
identity revealed through repetition:

> Yet herein will I imitate the sun,
> Who doth permit the base contagious clouds
> To smother up his beauty from the world,
> That, when he please *again to be himself*,
> Being wanted he may be more wondered at
> By breaking through the foul and ugly mists
> Of vapors that did seem to strangle him. (1.2.172–8,
>   my emphasis)

The Prince's self is constant through the changes that the play
depicts. When he first 'uphold[s]' the material actions of his
companions, their 'unyoked humor', he impugns his image,

his outward reputation, creating the opportunity to be himself *again* when he will redeem time by being 'more himself', making good on his promise to redeem 'all this' in violent action against the admittedly valiant Hotspur. It is not surprising, then, that when the time comes in the form of an opportunity for action – to save King Henry's life – the concept appears again, now in the words of another: 'Thou hast redeemed thy lost opinion, / And showed thou mak'st some tender of my life, / In this fair rescue thou hast brought to me' (5.4.47–9). Unlike the King's first use of the term which emphasised its material sense (the coffers), here King Henry's reference is to the immaterial 'opinion' that had been lost to time.[38]

It is just after this exchange that Hal meets Hotspur on the battlefield, the moment that he will truly 'reckon with time', as he must face the real possibility of his death. When he meets this challenge, when the narrative reaches its climax, Hal literally wears the 'garment all of blood' that he imagined in his speech promising future action in 3.2. Just before the exchange with Douglas in which he rescues the King, Hal is urged by King Henry to rest: 'I prithee, Harry, withdraw thyself, thou bleed'st too much' (5.4.1). The 'garment all of blood' that serves as a kind of material guarantee of Hal's honour here is of course precisely what Falstaff refuses to wear throughout the play. Falstaff, the play's emblem of materiality, mortal man, considers the material benefits of attaining honour to be slight: 'a trim reckoning'. His view replaces Hal's heroic, active and powerful image of tearing the reckoning of honour from Hotspur's heart with the very real corpse of Sir Walter Blunt: 'There's honour for you. Here's no vanity' (5.3.32–3). For Falstaff, Sir Walter's 'grinning honour' is much more powerful than any heroic, but immaterial, ideal of Hal's could ever be. While both Hal and Falstaff define honour as a product of action, the motivation to act with honour derives from a refusal of the material world – of vanity – that Falstaff is unwilling to let go unexamined. Sir Walter is 'no vanity' because his is no longer of this world; Falstaff embraces the ironic implication that those who seek immaterial honour by devaluing material existence as pure 'vanity' imperil themselves to a future oblivion. Faced with the choice between knowable, material cowardice and immaterial honour only accessible in death, Falstaff chooses the former.

Text, Interpretation and the Phenomenology of Temporal Experience

The three attitudes towards honour on display in the play rely on the interrelated nature of materiality and immateriality in time. For Hotspur, the immaterial concept must be made material through action; even at his most poetic, his language echoes his material understanding of the term: he will 'pluck bright honour from the pale-faced moon', as if it were a tangible thing (1.3.201). Falstaff, on the other hand, focuses on the movement from material to immaterial, concluding that action leads to bodily injury and death, simply confirming the significance of mortal existence against an unknowable immaterial ideal. Without any material referent forthcoming as a result of honourable action, Falstaff can only conclude that honour is immaterial, hardly worth risking one's life in search of, despite the fact that death is inevitable for all. Falstaff's attitude is thus in the end an evasion of temporality. Hal's honour is more dynamic, more overtly temporal than Falstaff admits, as he enacts the honour he has promised in language and follows through on the actions that underwrite the immaterial honour he promises. In each case, action is the subject of interpretation. Here, Ricoeur's theory of action as text (meaningful, but also singular and in need of interpretation) is useful, for bridging the gap between linguistic abstraction and meaningful action lies at the heart of the Henriad's effort to recuperate a conception of monarchy – and aristocratic honour – shaken by the Wars of the Roses. Ricoeur describes the connection between text and action as follows:

> human action is in many ways a quasi-text. It is exterior-
> ized in a manner comparable to the fixation characteristic
> of writing. In becoming detached from its agent, the action
> requires autonomy similar to the semantic autonomy of a
> text; it leaves a trace, a mark. It is inscribed in the course
> of things and becomes an archive and document. Even
> more like a text, of which the meaning had been freed
> from the initial conditions of its production, human action
> has a stature that is not limited to its importance for the
> situation in which it initially occurs, but allows it to be
> reinscribed in new social contexts. Finally, action, like a
> text, is an open work, addressed to an indefinite series of
> possible 'readers'. The judges are not contemporaries, but
> subsequent history.[39]

Ricoeur goes on to note that just as action is a kind of text, 'certain texts – if not all texts – have as a referent action itself'.[40]

Certainly, Falstaff's catechism on honour is a kind of text, and I would argue it is a text that has as its referent human action. In response to Hal's quip that Falstaff 'owest God a death', Falstaff muses in soliloquy:

> 'Tis not due yet. I would be loath to pay him before his day.
> What need I be so forward with him that calls not on me?
> Well, 'tis no matter; honour pricks me on. Yea, but how if
> honour prick me off when I come on? How then? Can hon-
> our set-to a leg? No. Or an arm? No. Or take away the grief
> of a wound? No. Honour hath no skill in surgery, then? No.
> What is honour? A word. What is in that word 'honour'?
> What is that 'honour'? Air. A trim reckoning! Who hath it?

He that died o' Wednesday. Doth he feel it? No. Doth he
hear it? No. 'Tis insensible, then? Yea, to the dead. But will
it not live with the living? No. Why? Detraction will not
suffer it. Therefore I'll none of it. Honour is a mere scutcheon. And so ends my catechism. (5.1.126–39)

Falstaff's meditation on honour parodies the accumulative
logic of Hal's and Hotspur's accounts and emphasises the
finality of death above any earthly gain – even such immaterial gain as that of reputation. But rather than allow Falstaff's
demystification of honour to render Hal's attempt to redeem
his honour naive and morally empty, I am suggesting that the
play pits such materialist epistemologies that are haunted by
their immaterial, unknowable other against one that takes
immateriality seriously, despite acknowledging that the only
access to the immaterial is through the material. Thus the
answer to Falstaff's question ''Tis insensible, then?' is yes,
but not only to the dead (as Falstaff believes). And it is precisely this quality of immaterial honour – its insensibility –
that allows Hal's version to win the day, in part because all
meaning is insensible, including Falstaff's negative conception of honour.

On one level, of course, Falstaff's emphasis on sensuous
materiality is a marker of his moral failure as a Christian –
his 'vanity', or investment in the material world, prevents
him from embracing immaterial virtues that could guide him
away from sin.[41] However, the fraught relationship between
materiality and immateriality that I have been highlighting
complicates the simple opposition he hopes to maintain. Falstaff is at his most materialist when he considers the essence
of honour, when he asks directly: 'What is honour?' His conclusion, that it is 'A word', leads him to seek for something
like the matter that would make up the word: 'What is *in*
that word, honour?' It is tempting to take Falstaff's answer
'Air' to mean 'nothing': for example, 'What is the substance

of honour? Nothing'. But as Carla Mazzio has recently reminded us, 'air' was a fairly important *something* in the period. Air was, in fact, the 'mythic and Galenic medium of thought, intellect, communication'.[42] Mazzio draws our attention to Gertrude's willingness to equate the substance of words – breath – with life in *Hamlet*: 'if words be made of breath / And breath of life, I have no life to breathe / What thou has said to me' (3.4.199–201).

If air is life, it is also potentially dangerous to life. Critics since Kittridge have noticed that contaminated air, most often contaminated in a way that made it visible to the eye, was considered a breeding ground for pestilence.[43] Early in *1 Henry IV*, we recall that in comparing himself to the sun, Hal identifies his companions with 'the base contagious clouds / [that] smother up his beauty from the world' (1.2.193–4). By identifying honour with air in hopes of demystifying honour as nothing, Falstaff in fact associates it with something, albeit something ostensibly insensible, mysterious and prone to corruption. It is not difficult to extend the corruption of breath/air/life to the corruption of language as we get Falstaff's meditation on the subject in the form of a catechism, a text to be repeated and 're-sounded'. According to Jonathan Sparke, in an essay introducing John Seddon's English translation of the Heidelberg catechism (1588),

> to catechize is nothing els, but first in apt woords to teach one to conceive and to resound or repeate, the first and necessary principles of Christian religion, soundly; and then secondly, by explaining of them, to cause him to understand them, wisely; and lastly, by some fit place or places of scripture, to enable him, to confirm them pithily: al which, this catechisme, with the help of those Commentaries, if thou wilt voutsafe, to take any paines therein, wil enable thee very wel to performe.[44]

In a fundamental way, Falstaff's catechism is about the philosophical problem of reference: how do we know that what we say refers to what is? This is one of the key concerns driving Ricoeur's philosophy of history, for in pointing out that fictional narratives and historical narratives are both 'true', he argues that it is the experience with narrative that deepens our understanding of 'what is' or what it means to experience 'what is' more than any theory of correspondence can ever do. Sparkes's emphasis on 're-sounding', on making sensible the immaterial tenets of the Christian faith, offers an interesting backdrop against which we might consider Falstaff's catechism. By invoking the form of catechism, Shakespeare – through Falstaff – associates his meditation on the problem of reference with theological exegesis, a mode of early modern discourse in which the relationship between materiality and immateriality was particularly unsettled. In the aftermath of the Reformation, attempts to make the immaterial material, even for the purposes of religious edification, faced theological as well as philosophical opposition.

The Protestant rejection of the materiality of the Roman church famously prompted the Counter-Reformation question, 'Where was your church before Luther?' The Jesuit Lawrence Anderton considered this question philosophically in his 1633 treatise *The Non-Entity of Protestancy*. Among Anderton's claims for the illegitimacy of the Protestant church is its reliance on negation:

> Protestancy ... hath no true reality, or subsistency in it selfe, but is a mere vaporous, intentional, and Imaginary Conceite, and consequently in itself false. For if things be only true, as they have a real being, and therein affirmative; and false, if they want such a being and therein negative ... how then can Protestancy, which consists only in denials and negations, which have no being, be real, or true?[45]

Anderton takes his lead from Aquinas here: 'That is false, which is not to be apprehended as it is a thing but as it is not.'[46] Falstaff teaches us that honour is nothing through negation: it is not skilful in surgery, it is not sensible, etc. And the body of Sir Walter Blunt is material proof of what is not vanity. Sir Walter's very material body, his dead corpse, invites comparison with Falstaff's understanding of his conscripted soldiers. When questioned by Hal about the suitability of his soldiers, Falstaff quips morbidly: 'Tut, tut, good enough to toss; food for powder, food for powder. They'll fill a pit as well as better. Tush man, mortal men, mortal men' (4.2.64–6). His callous disregard for the lives of his soldiers doesn't seem to coincide with his deeper feelings about mortality, however. Only a few lines earlier he has admitted in soliloquy that he feels guilty about his blatant disregard for the process of conscription, which he has corrupted by taking bribes to let abler men out of the battle. His attitude towards bodies, corpses that will 'fill a pit', is considerably more apprehensive: 'I like not such grinning honour as Sir Walter hath' and 'I am afraid of this gunpowder Percy, though he be dead' (5.3.57–8, 5.4.118–19).

Falstaff's fear is of the immaterial, that which lies beyond the material realm in which he feels most comfortable. It is a fear that is future directed, but without the willingness to face the uncertainty of that future. This is in contrast to Hotspur's attitude towards the immaterial, which is one of almost complete dismissal. Hotspur is unmoved by Glendower's claims of access to the occult. When Glendower brags: 'I can call spirits from the vasty deep', Hotspur responds, 'Why, so can I, or so can any man, / But will they come when you do call for them' (3.1.52–4). Hotspur's mocking response reveals not only his unwavering respect for action above all else, but also his lack of respect for the spoken word and any ideas that cannot be immediately confirmed by virtue of their relevance to action. Hotspur's unrelenting desire for action reaches its peak in act 5, when, declining to read letters apparently because he's in a rush to get to battle, he happily leaves reflection on the possibility of his impending death. He welcomes the interruption of a second messenger: 'I thank him that he cuts me from my tale, / For I profess not talking; only this: / Let each man do his best' (5.2.90–2).

All of this leads to the exchange between Hal and Hotspur promised in act 3, the action that completes Hal's narrative of self-actualisation. Upon receiving the mortal wound from Hal, Hotspur exclaims consistently, if ironically, his preference for immaterial honour over his material body: 'I better brook the loss of brittle life / Than those proud titles thou hast won of me; / They wound my thoughts worse than thy sword my flesh' (5.4.76–8). Hotspur associates his 'proud titles' with his 'thoughts' in what appears at first to be a defence of immaterial honour over the material body. Yet his next lines qualify the opposition, apparently realising that his entire conception of honour had been grounded in material action: 'But thought's the slave of life, and life time's fool; / And time, that takes survey of all the world, / Must have a stop' (5.4.79–81). Hotspur's initial identification with his titles and thoughts gives way to the material logic of his conception of honour – here he is susceptible to Falstaff's critique, for upon his death he will lose both access to and control of his titles, his honour. By his own logic, he becomes, in the phrase completed by Hal, 'food for worms' (5.4.85), entirely material. But, as Hal appears to recognise, Hotspur's titles were won in a past that cannot be 'lost' just as 'wasted' time cannot be redeemed. Hotspur's dying speech confirms Hal's earlier logic of accumulation and exchange at the same time that it points to a paradox. That Hotspur has become entirely material cannot or must not undo the meaningfulness of his actions. The inability to reduce time to its material effects is one of the profound aporias of temporality identified by Ricoeur in his exploration of narrative and time.[47]

Hal's decision to hide Hotspur's face with his favours can be read as an effort to hide the material body on which honour is always inscribed in blood in order to ensure that we read the text of Hotspur's actions – the narrative Hal supplies: 'take thy praise with thee to heaven. / Thy ignominy sleep with thee in the grave' (5.4.98–9). The alternative would be to focus on the meaningless materiality of his corpse. Kastan argues that Falstaff's return from feigning death at this moment destroys 'the emblem [of Hal's honour] with his own irrepressible refusal to be subordinated to any principle of order. In rising and stabbing Hotspur's body, he undoes the reassuring dialectic – and history's judgment – that would insist upon Hal's triumph'.[48] Without disagreeing, I would suggest that Falstaff's presence here ominously confirms the play's suspension of judgement on the mysteries of time. If a valiant Hotspur can live on even as his body returns to the earth, so too can the life-loving Falstaff live on despite his inevitable rejection and death in the concluding instalments of the Henriad. Ricoeur's sense of the 'ultimate unrepresentatibility of time' breathes life into the narratives through which we attempt to capture temporal experience. If Shakespeare does not side with Hal over Falstaff, he certainly seems to disagree with Hotspur's claim that 'time . . . must have a stop'.

In this way, the play points to the theological mysteries that I will take up in the next part of this book. Hotspur's binary thinking (action/talk, honour/dishonour, and ultimately life/death) has a stability to it that one does not find in either Falstaff or Hal. Critics have noted that despite his seemingly earth-bound nature, Falstaff quotes or alludes to scripture more than any other Shakespearean character. His fear of death suggests that he worries about what he cannot experience with the senses. Similarly, while one might accuse Hal of superstition as he thanks himself 'for doing fair rites of tenderness' by respecting the corpse of his vanquished enemy, the gesture invokes a future judgement that Hal is reluctant to challenge. The self-absorbed, even Machiavellian manipulator, often seen as ushering in a secular humanist form of political strategy, acknowledges something here that is beyond himself. The reverence for such 'rites' has a religious feeling to it, and it is to religion that I now turn.

Notes

1. Cleanth Brooks and Robert B. Heilman, *Understanding Drama* (1946), p. 386, qtd in A. R. Humphreys, 'Introduction', Shakespeare, *Henry IV, Part I*, ed. Humphreys, p. lvi.

2. Humphreys, 'Introduction', p. lvii.

3. Scott McMillin has shown that productions of the play emphasising Hal as the central character emerged in the second half of the twentieth century; see his *Henry IV, Part One* Shakespeare in Performance series. Nevertheless, more recent critics have argued for the centrality of Falstaff and Hotspur. Bloom, *Invention of the Human*, argues, for example, that 'The two parts of *Henry IV* do not belong to Hal, but to Falstaff, and even Hotspur, in the first part, is dimmed by Falstaff's splendor' (p. 272). For an argument in favour of the centrality of Hotspur, see Roberta Barker, 'Tragical-Comical-Historical Hotspur'.

4. Rackin, *Stages of History*, p. 136.

5. Northumberland confirms that King Richard had named Mortimer his heir at 1.3.155.

6. Rackin, *Stages*, p. 136.

7. David Scott Kastan, '"The King Hath Many Marching in His Coats," Or What Did You Do in the War Daddy?', p. 245. Kastan is responding in part to Stephen Greenblatt's argument in *Shakespearean Negotiations* that the play subverts authority only to contain that subversion in the resolution (p. 65).

8. Kastan, 'Marching', p. 245.

9. The importance of time in the play attracted considerable attention from critics in the 1960s and 1970s, which eventually gave way to New Historicist accounts focused more

directly on the relationship between history and power or political authority. See, especially, Paul Jorgensen, *Redeeming Shakespeare's Words*; Frederick Turner, *Shakespeare and the Nature of Time*; Wylie Sypher, *The Ethic of Time: Structures of Experience in Shakespeare*; Gary F. Waller, *The Strong Necessity of Time: The Philosophy of Time in Shakespeare*; and Maurice Hunt, 'Time and Timelessness in 1 *Henry IV'*.

10. Rackin, *Stages*, p. 137. Her argument here is influenced by work on early modern chorography as essentially spatial history (in Richard Helgerson's account) and Benedict Anderson's work on the early modern nation. On the connection between 'plot' and 'plat' emphasising the spatial character of early modern thinking about temporality, see Lorna Hutson, 'Fortunate Travellers', p. 86.

11. Rackin, *Stages*, p. 138.

12. White, *The Content of the Form*, p. 171. White is quoting Ricoeur, 'Narrative Time', p. 169. This essay, also published in a slightly different form as 'The Human Experience of Time and Narrative', forms the kernel of the first volume of Ricoeur's three-volume *Time and Narrative*. His argument begins with Augustine's theory of time in the *Confessions* and then merges that reading with Aristotle's account of plot and action in the *Poetics* before moving on to an engagement with twentieth-century phenomenology and a critique of Heidegger.

13. Ricoeur, *Oneself as Another*, pp. 140, 143.

14. Ricoeur, 'Human Experience of Time', p. 106, emphasis original. Much recent attention has been given to Alain Badiou's theory of the event in *Being and Event*. For a critique of Badiou that presents Ricoeur's hermeneutics as an alternative, see Sebastian L. Purcell, 'After Hermeneutics?'

15. White, *Content of the Form*, p. 179. For an elaboration on this idea, see White's *Figural Realism: Studies in the Mimesis Effect*.

16. Ricoeur, 'Narrative Time', p. 187.

17. This coincides with the perceptual stance that Husserl calls the 'natural attitude'. See the discussion of Husserl in the Introduction above and also Chapter 6 below.

18. Augustine, *Confessions* XI, XIV, qtd in Ricoeur, 'Human Experience of Time', p. 103.

19. See White, *Content of the Form*, p. 176. There is some debate about whether or not early modern English chronicles such as Shakespeare's source have a narrative logic. See, for example, Annabel Patterson, *Reading Holinshed's Chronicles*. Nevertheless, Holinshed's text is ordered according to chronological time, following the reigns of the monarchs.

20. Ricoeur, 'Narrative Time', p. 178. Also see *Time and Narrative*, vol. 1, p. 62.

21. Ricoeur, 'Narrative Time', p. 180.

22. White, *Content of the Form*, p. 180.

23. Ricoeur, 'Narrative Time', p. 182.

24. Ricoeur, *Time and Narrative*, vol. 3, p. 243.

25. Kastan points out that the matter *is* actually spoken of in gory detail by Abraham Fleming, writing in Shakespeare's source, Holinshed's *Chronicles*: 'the Welsh women cut off their privties, and put one part thereof into the mouthes of everie dead man, in such sort that the cullions hoong downe to their chins; and not so contented they did cut off their noses and thrust them into their tailes as the laie on the ground mangled and defaced' (Holinshed quoted in *King Henry IV, part 1*, ed. Kastan, p. 144).

26. The *OED* defines 'scutcheon' as 'escutcheon' or an armorial coat of arms. Most editors add that such armorial shields were regularly displayed at funerals and monuments.

27. Kastan, 'Introduction', Arden 3, p. 51.

28. Greenblatt reads this promise as a false promise of self-revelation that in turn becomes merely another moment (later in the play) for Hal to put on a mask. See *Shakespearean Negotiations*, p. 46.

29. This was also Richard's problem, as the deposed king had put too much stock in the concept of divine right, thinking that

he did not need to act. King Henry is acutely aware of this danger and warns Hal in this scene.

30. Consider that Holinshed's chronicle account of Hotspur's victory continues on to mention that 'the lord Persie, hauing bestowed the prisoners in suer keeping, entered Tiuidale, wasting and destroieng the whole countrie ...' (Holinshed, *Chronicles of England, Scotland, and Ireland*, vol. 3, p. 21). This less flattering account is simply chronological, lacking the figuration proper to narrative.

31. I'm concerned here with what Matthew Smith, in a discussion of *Hamlet*, calls the 'inaccessibilities' of the play, those things to which we have no tangible access, usually the 'internal' state of a character's self. In such cases, as Smith argues, we in the audience are left to base our judgement of character on the actor's external actions. Philosophically this amounts to deducing cause from effects, a necessity for those interested in proving the existence of spirits. See my discussion of spirit in the third part of this book. Smith, 'Describing the Sense of Confession in *Hamlet*', p. 9.

32. Ricoeur, 'Human Experience of Time', p. 108.

33. Ibid., p. 109.

34. Jorgensen, *Shakespeare's Words*, p. 59.

35. *OED*, v. 10, 'Redeem'.

36. Holinshed, *Chronicles*, vol. 3, p. 22.

37. *OED*, 2.c

38. *OED*, 7.b. 'To regain, recover (an immaterial thing)'.

39. Ricoeur, 'Explanation and Understanding', pp. 160–1.

40. Ibid., p. 161.

41. For an analysis of pre-Reformation theological influences in the play, see Ellen M. Caldwell, '"Banish all the wor(l)d": Falstaff's Iconoclastic Threat to Kingship in *1 Henry IV*'.

42. Mazzio, 'The History of Air', p. 179.

43. Humphreys, *1 Henry IV*, notes Kittredge's comment that 'Pestilence was thought to be generated in fog, mist, and clouds' (p. 20). I discuss air, *pneuma* and spirit (life), in more detail in Chapter 8.

44. Ursinus, *A Catechism, or short kind of instruction* (Heidelberg Catechism), B1r.
45. Anderton, *Non-Entity of Protestancy*, C5r–C5v.
46. Ibid., C3r.
47. See *Time and Narrative*, vol. 3, pp. 261–74.
48. Kastan, 'Introduction', Arden 3, p. 73.

PART II

BELIEVING

CHAPTER 5

THE VISIBLE AND THE INVISIBLE: SEEING THE EARTHLY – BELIEVING THE SPIRITUAL

I can comprehend *naturam naturatam*, created nature, but that *natura naturans*, God himself, the understanding of man cannot comprehend. I can see the sun in a looking-glass, but the nature, and the whole working of the sun I cannot see in that glass. I can see God in the creature, but the nature, the essence, the secret purposes of God, I cannot see there.

John Donne, *LXXX Sermons*, no. VII[1]

Thus far, my discussion of the material and immaterial has focused on the way this opposition functioned in early modern ontology. This subject was the supposed purview of the philosophers known in the period as metaphysicians, a distinction derived from the title of Aristotle's *Metaphysics*, despite the fact that the subject matter was drawn from a range of philosophical authorities who rarely respected a bright line between physics and metaphysics.[2] As we saw in Chapter 3, Shakespeare portrayed Richard's obsession with his identity in explicitly ontological terms: either he is king or he is 'nothing'. Hal's challenge, more subtle perhaps than Richard's, was to bring honour into existence, to substantiate it, through action. Focusing on whether Richard's self or Henry's honour exists brings one aspect of the early modern fascination with the immaterial into focus. But of course, in the Renaissance as in the late medieval period before it, the theological implications of ontological propositions could not be avoided. Shakespeare portrays Richard's identity problem as a product of faulty theology as much as vexed ontology. And, in order for the recuperation of Hal's reputation to have any force, his material victory over Hotspur had to make manifest an honour and destiny that lacked material support up to that point in the play. It is difficult to avoid the implication that the roustabout Hal overcomes the much more militaristic Hotspur because he is divinely ordained to do so. Was Hal a naturally superior warrior in some essential way? Perhaps. But, due to the nature of history and time governing the logic of the play, he had already won before the play began, despite the fact that it is difficult, if not impossible to assign this victory to the material conditions of his early life.

Speculation about the nature of material existence inevitably raised questions about the status of the non-material realm. Today it is possible to take a strong materialist position, the claim that everything that exists exists materially, or more commonly, a form of 'naturalism' that rules out much of the immaterial realm that preoccupied the early modern period as 'supernatural', and thus the product of superstition.[3] But for early modern theologians and their medieval predecessors, the proposition that materiality is a condition for existence was clearly untenable, as was the idea that the natural world delimited existing reality. Much of what concerns theology is explicitly immaterial, and many of the natural philosophers who focused intently on the changing nature of the material world were also theologians who not only accepted but prioritised the reality of immaterial things, most importantly God, but also all 'things in heaven', as well as liminal things like angels. The need to balance natural philosophy's goal of creating knowledge through an analysis of the natural, material world with the theological principle that earthly existence is corrupt and earthly knowledge incomplete forced early modern natural philosophers to place special pressure on the distinction between things material (earthly) and immaterial (spiritual). A typical example is the French Calvinist Lambert Daneau, whose *Physica Christiana* (1576) was translated into English by Thomas Twyne in 1578 as *The Wonderful Workmanship of the World*. Daneau's work is in dialogue form, written, according to the dedicatory epistle, to 'advance the commodity of studious young men'. The first section, entitled 'An Excellent Discourse of *Christian Natural* Philosophy', begins by answering the question 'What is natural philosophy?' as follows:

> It is the true knowledge or discourse concerning the Creation and distinction of all this whole world with the partes thereof, of the causes by whiche it was wrought, and likewise of the effectes whiche follow thereon, apperteinyng to the praise of God the Creatour.[4]

After pointing out that the Church Fathers referred to this undertaking as 'natural philosophy' (a point made in response to the charge that natural philosophy was the purview of 'Heathen Philosophers'), Daneau goes on to make an important distinction:

> *nature*, in the common use of the Greek tongue, is, for the moste parte, applied to such thynges as doe consist, not of essence onely, of whiche sort God is, but are compounded with certein accidents adjoined, such as are all the things that wee beholde with our eyes, and whereof this visible worlde consisteth: that knowledge seemeth more properly to bee termed natural philosophy, which is busied in the handling of the mixt, conpounded, and material thinges,

that it may bee distinguished from Divinitie. Wherefore,
Natural Philosophy, saie thei, is the knowledge of Materiall
and Instrumentall beginnynges.[5]

Exploring the nature of material things is not only safe for the
faithful, it is encouraged as long as it is clearly distinguished
from 'Divinitie'. Natural philosophy thus deals with those
things which fall outside the purview of theologians, except
insofar as the created world is evidence of the divine creator.
As we will see, this is a crucial exception. Further, Daneau
invokes a disciplinary distinction that rests on the categorical
division of things into two distinct classes: the material and
immaterial, visible and invisible. Associated with the divine,
the invisible (immaterial) is the ultimate goal of Christian
contemplation, even if attention to the natural world may
provide an experience of 'the effectes whiche follow thereon,
apperteinyng to the praise of God'.

It is only in the theological context that immateriality is
defined positively – as spiritual – rather than through negation. The purity of the spiritual makes it non-earthly, rather
than the other way around. In this positive account of immateriality, the spiritual is distinguished from the natural as
'supernatural'. Belief in the supernatural constitutes belief
in something fundamentally different from the things that
make up the natural world. In C. S. Lewis's terms, one's conception of nature is contingent on one's beliefs:

> The Naturalist believes that a great process, or 'becoming',
> exists 'on its own' in space and time, and that nothing else
> exists – what we call particular things and events being only
> the parts into which we analyse the great process or the
> shapes which that process takes at given moments and given
> points in space. This single, total reality he calls Nature. The
> Supernaturalist believes that one Thing exists on its own and
> has produced the framework of space and time and the pro-
> cession of systematically connected events which fill them.
> This framework, and this filling, he calls Nature.[6]

The key distinction for early modern Christian natural philosophers was that between single and multiple, pure and 'mixt'. As we saw in Chapter 2, God *is*, His essence is existence, while the creatures of the created world are composites of form and matter (soul and body). Unity and multiplicity grounds a series of analogies, structuring, for example, the distinction between postlapsarian humanity (the corrupt, multiple condition of earthly, mortal existence) and prelapsarian innocence (a unified state to be regained through eternal salvation). This provided a moral element even to those areas of enquiry that would seem to be the most neutral of proto-scientific subjects: botany, chemistry, geology and so on. The merging of theology and science is clear in the area of alchemy, a seemingly natural science focused on chemical and physical distillation, with the aim of reducing compounds to their elements, but with the ultimate goal of reaching the truth of all truths (the philosopher's stone). According to the medieval alchemical tradition, the art required a practitioner who was pure of heart. George Ripley begins his *Compound of Alchemy* (1471) by imploring his students to 'Live clene in soule, to God doe none offense / Exhalt thee not but rather keep thee low, / Ells wyll thy God in thee noe Wysdome sowe'.[7] Even more dramatically, John Norton warns in his *Ordinal of Alchemy* (1477) that 'Excesse for one halfe quarter an howre / may destroy all'.[8] This was, of course, a way to dodge complaints about charlatan alchemists out to defraud hopeful believers in the occult. According to the alchemists, it should come as no surprise that such impure, spiritually corrupt men are unable to unlock the secrets of nature. God created nature, and thus it is God who must reveal its secrets to man.

The language of the alchemists is strikingly close to the language of the divines, highlighting how important the interrelation between the material and immaterial realms was considered to be. In a religious tract on maintaining faith entitled 'A brief discourse touching the extinguishing of Spirit', John Dod writes: 'If there be nothing in a man but that which by nature and industrie may bee attained unto, then surely he hath not in him the spirit of God; for that is above nature, and worketh supernatural effects.'[9] Like the impure alchemist who will never find truth (the philosopher's stone) by plumbing the depths of the material world, the impure Christian will never find truth (salvation) without the immaterial spirit of God. But even the alchemists who were pure of heart missed the theological point about their project: their focus on the material world would forever deny them access to the greater truth they seek. Material purity is a useful analogy to the actual purity to be found in the spiritual realm, but it is ultimately material, and by virtue of this materiality, it is corrupt.

The critique of alchemy rests on a return to analogical thinking, for the point is to mark the limits of human capacity, and thus exalt that which exceeds human reason. The argument is clear in the French Calvinist Phillipe de Mornay's defence of faith as the path to truth:

> It remaineth then in the end, that wee must atteine to that by Fayth, which wee cannot atteyne vnto by Reason; that wee must mount vp by liuely beleef aboue our vnderstading, vnto the things whereunto the eye of our mynd is not able to reach . . . And what is this fayth in God, but a beleeuing that our welfare lyeth in him? What is the beleeuing, but the hoping for it? What is hope, but the desiring of it? What is the desire of it, but the not hauing of it? And to bee short, what is the continuall beleef of it heere, but a bewraying that heere we can neither haue it nor see it? If we haue not faith; what haue we but ignorance? And if we haue faith; what haue wee but onely a desire and longing; considering that the greater our fayth is, the more wee despise these bace things; and the greater our desire is, the more we hate our selues, and the more earnestly doe we loue God . . .[10]

The distinction between reason and faith serves to demarcate a realm of knowledge available to reason via the natural world from the realm of higher truth, which is available to the understanding imperfectly through belief:

> Whereas wee seeke for an ende or resting point, the world is made for man, man for the Soule, the Soule for the mynd, the mynd for a much higher thing than it self, and what els can that be but God? As for that which we vnderstand here as concerning God by our naturall wisdome; it is but ignorance; and that which we conceiue by our supernaturall power, but beleefe; and beleefe maketh not things perfect, but only moueth the vnderstanding.[10]

Importantly, belief is still derived from the contemplation of the natural world. What that world withholds is an experience of the fullness of God's perfection. At the dawn of modernity, when it appeared that the physical and spiritual worlds were increasingly considered to be separate and distinct, concern over their interaction actually intensified.

The primary early modern explanation of how material and immaterial things could both exist and interact was that they must have different modes of being. As we have seen, the immaterial mode of being is most often called 'spiritual', or 'supernatural', demarcating it from the realm of tangible, material things. In George Jenney's description, the spirit is the necessary third term that makes sense of the natural/ supernatural distinction:

> by our spirit is not meant any thing which naturally is our own, either of soule or body, concerning the substance of that which we had by creation, or the created faculties of either of them: but by our spirit is meant a supernatural qualitie of holinesse [. . .] indeede it is our conscience which is sanctified by the bloud & spirit of Christ.[11]

To properly grasp this way of thinking about the immaterial it is important to distinguish it from the closely related concept of nothingness discussed in Chapter 2. Literally speaking, 'nothing' is not any thing, it is non-existent, and thus it is not an entity or substance of any kind. By contrast, spiritual entities that are immaterial lack matter but not existence and substance. The common view is summed up in a piece of seventeenth-century religious verse by the minister and amateur poet Nicholas Billingsley:

> Man's Soul a substance is spiritual
> And immaterial and immortall too
> In Adam and in all men [since the fall]
> By god him selfe [whose power can all things do]
> Created of meer nothing and it still
> Remaineth one and indivisible[12]

In a treatise on Galatians 5: 17, William Perkins comments on the way the material and immaterial elements of the human person are intertwined:

> And we must know, that they are not severed asunder, as though the flesh were placed in one part of the soule, and the spirit in another: but they are joined and mingled togither in all the faculties of the soule. The minde, or understaning part, is not one part flesh, and an other spirit, but the whole minde is flesh and the whole minde is spirit; partly one and partly the other. The whole will is partly flesh and partly spirit: the flesh and the spirit, that is, grace and corruption, not severed in place but onely in reason to be distinguished. As the ayre in the dawning of the day is not wholly light or wholly darke as at midnight & at nooneday: neither is it in one part light, in another part darke: but the whole ayre is partly light, and partly darke throughout.[13]

Despite their interconnectedness, to identify the spiritual as immaterial is to grant a realm of actuality (of being) modally distinct from the material, sensuous world. And to accept that the spiritual and earthly are different modes of being, calling for different methods of enquiry, is to shift the question from an ontological one to an epistemological one. In his 'Preface to the Reader', de Mornay makes the case for our knowledge of this realm of being through analogy:

> But we say that mans reason is able to lead vs to that point; namely, that we ought to beleue euen beyond reason, I meane the things whereunto all the capacitie of man cannot attaine. And like wise, that when things are reuealed unto vs, which reason could neuer haue entered into nor once imagined, no not euen when it was at the soundest; the same reason (which neuer could haue found them out) maketh vs to allow of them: the reason I say (whereunto those mysteries were insuisible afore) maketh them credible vnto vs: surely euen after the same maner that our eye maketh vs to see that in the visible things, which we ought to beleue of the invisible, without the which the visible could haue no beeing: that is to wit, the inuisible God, by the visible Sonne, & also to see many things when the Sun is vp, which were hidden afore in darknesse: not that the eie-sight was of lesse force, or the thing it selfe lesse visible afore: but because the Sonne is now vp, which lighteneth the aire with his brightnes, which is the meane both wherby the eie seeth, & wherby the thing is seen.[14]

De Mornay's point is that we don't doubt the existence of things that escape our perception – objects do not cease to exist in darkness – and thus we should grant existence to immaterial things that cannot be proven to lack being simply because they lack sensuous materiality.

Today, belief in an immaterial realm is either exported to the field of theology or characterised as superstition. Steven Pinker characterises non-empirical beliefs as unreasonable, because they are rarely 'calibrated by their fit to the world', something that can only be done through modern science: 'Traditional causes of belief – faith, revelation, dogma, authority, charisma, conventional wisdom, hermeneutic parsing of texts, the glow of subjective certainty – are generators of error, and should be dismissed as sources of knowledge.'[15] At the turn of the seventeenth century, however, the disciplinary segregation of natural science and faith was tenuous. While the charge of superstition was common in religious polemic, belief in immaterial things was among the least likely ways to garner such a charge. On the contrary, one was much more likely to be accused of superstition for attending too fervently to things material: the Protestant accusation that the Roman Church valued material ornament over true faith, for example, or the charge that alchemists heretically claimed access to the supernatural through physical and chemical experimentation. Edmund Spenser opens the second book of *The Faerie Queene* with a jab at those who only believe what they can see with their own eyes, 'that nothing is, but that which [they] hath seen', despite the likelihood that in 'later times things more unknown shall show'.[16] The regularity of new discoveries underscored the period's growing knowledge about the material world, prompting natural philosophers, astronomers and geographers to promise more revelations about the invisible mysteries of the natural world. Yet this project of discovery, perhaps most famously announced in England by Bacon, often exempted the whole spiritual realm as both real and inaccessible to human knowledge, except indirectly.[17] The unknown and unseen were thus perfect analogies for the immaterial, but they were not identical to it. Something unseen could become visible in the light or under the microscope, and things unknown could be discovered, but the immaterial, spiritual realm could only be imputed by its effects in the material world or its relationship to that world as a kind of inaccessible, but essential counterpart. Thus, while very few doubted the existence of immaterial things, intense debates erupted over how such things related to the material world they experienced through the senses.

Clearly, the various ways in which the immaterial was invoked in the period were in tension. The immateriality of non-existence, nothingness and non-being was obviously not the same as the immateriality of God, the immortal soul and heaven (eternal being). Nor were immaterial things like thoughts the same as immaterial eternal truths like God. But access to that most important immaterial reality was to be found only indirectly, through the materiality of earthly experience. That is, the immateriality of the spiritual realm, so essential to Christian thought, came into focus most clearly when contrasted with the corrupt materiality of earthly experience. Analogy is the obvious vehicle for understanding the relation, and it is not surprising that analogical thinking dominated the Christian Middle Ages.

Recognising the corruption of earthly existence compared to God's perfection has always been a component of Christian devotion, and one could argue that the history of Christianity is largely a story about the forms this recognition can take in human expression, ranging from the ascetic's rejection of the material world to the mystic's embrace of sensuous nature saturated with an inscrutable God. In an important way, the Reformation combined both extremes, rejecting the ascetic's withdrawal from the world while at the same time condemning human depravity as hopelessly ignorant without the supernatural intervention of God's grace. One can find this synthesis in de Mornay's Calvinist defence of the role of reason in discerning invisible truths from the observation of the natural world, a position shared with medieval mysticism. St Bonaventure, for example, encouraged attention to the natural world as the path to understanding God, arguing that 'the invisible things of God are clearly seen, from the creation of the world, being understood by the things that are made'.[18]

There is no doubt, however, that emphasis on the value of material things 'seen' and 'made' for human analogical understanding of invisible, immaterial, spiritual things undergoes a transformation in the Reformation. In his first catechism, Calvin would include the following, bleak account of human perception: 'whatever way we turn our eyes, we can see nothing but what is impure, profane, and abominable to God'.[19] Calvin's position is no doubt on the extreme end here even for him. But by increasingly emphasising the corruption and fallibility of human sense and reason, even while acknowledging reason's place as the most ennobled of God's gifts to humanity, Protestants necessarily shifted attention to the immaterial as the locus of potential enlightenment. This happened even as the study of the natural world (and thus natural philosophy) was becoming increasingly empirical, challenging the orthodoxies of traditional authorities. These developments would endanger the fragile marriage of natural philosophy and theology brokered by medieval scholastic efforts to articulate a physics that would not contradict the tenets of the church. As natural philosophy slowly abandoned its reliance on authorities and arguments from logic in favour of empirical observation, immaterial things became harder to justify as a part of the natural world. One solution, as seen in the references to Daneau and de Mornay cited above, was to cordon off discussions of the spiritual as beyond the reach of human reason, even while stressing the value of exploring the laws of the sublunary world.[20]

The greatest challenge in equating the spiritual exclusively with the immaterial is that to do so threatens to push the spiritual out of human reach. The Jesuit Lawrence Anderton, discussed above, addresses the problem explicitly by attacking Protestantism as an innovation and resting his argument on what he views to be the Reformation's insistence on negation: 'Protestancy consisteth only in the denyalls and Privations of

Affirmative points of our Christian, and Romane Fayth.'[21] Anderton's target is the Protestant critique of the Roman Church as defined by its material trappings – its buildings, vestments and ornaments. In his response to Sir Thomas More, William Tyndale argued that the church of scripture referred to 'the whole multitude of all scripture, them that receive the name of Christ to believe in him'.[22] Such a position sought to shift the locus of spiritual experience from the material church to the immaterial belief of the faithful. The shift from the material church to the *corpus mysticum* looked back as much as it shifted the thinking forward.[23] For despite Protestant emphasis on the misguided materiality of Roman Catholic worship, the immaterial nature of God and the presence of the invisible in the visible had long been the focus of medieval mysticism, and its accompanying emphasis on an inscrutable God.[24] And as Jennifer Waldron has argued, the return to an emphasis on the invisible church did not mean that Protestants rejected the idea that the material world could offer access to spiritual knowledge. Rather it redirected the attention of believers from the misleading materiality of human artifice to the wondrous creation of God, on display most clearly in human bodies. Formed in the image of God, the miraculous human body was the best material analogy to the spiritual perfection missing from the earthly realm.[25]

The challenge of conveying spiritual truths through the rhetoric of the material world was nevertheless significant. Christ's embodiment provided the most powerful response to the challenge, while also identifying the place where theology and metaphysics unavoidably meet. Without the literal materialisation of the word made flesh (John 1: 14), articulations of the immaterial, spiritual truth would rely entirely on figuration – on analogy, metaphor and comparison. The relationship between metaphysics and theology is made manifest in the event of the incarnation. In Paul Tillich's concise account, 'Metaphysics is the rational inquiry into the structure of being, its polarities and categories as they appear in man's encounter with reality', while theology

> deals with the concrete revelatory experience in which human beings have been grasped by an ultimate concern . . . This is the reason why the early Christian theologians called Jesus as the Christ the *Logos*. *Logos* is the principle of the divine self manifestation in nature and history. There is no *theo*-logy where there is no concrete, revelatory experience. And there is no theo-*logy* where there is not the universal claim for truth. This unity of the concrete-existential and the universal-essential gives theology its special position, its greatness and its dangers.[26]

While these can seem to be distinct areas of enquiry, Tillich points out that:

> Neither the theologian nor the philosopher has unconditional certainty about the contents of his faith or the results of his reasoning. In both of them doubt and the courage of affirmation are within each other. Therefore, the history of philosophical and theological thought is overwhelmingly a history of interdependence of theology and metaphysics and not of their lying side by side.[27]

The Pauline comparison of earthly vision to looking 'through a glass darkly' suggests the mediating role of concrete experience in conveying spiritual truth. In the favoured state of perfection 'when that which is perfect is come', such mediation will fall away and we will see 'face to face' (1 Cor. 13: 12). Paul's analogy between earthly and spiritual vision maintains the distinction between a familiar earthly experience and an inaccessible eternal state. The early reformer Roger Hutchinson stressed the distinction in defending the two natures of Christ: 'Otherwise God's face signifieth the unuisible nature of Christes Diuinitie, as Exod. doth declare, *you shall see my hinder partes, but my face you can not see*, that is thou shalt see Christes humanitie, but his Diuinitie can not be seene.'[28] The analogy operates by stressing rather than reducing the distance between the two modes of existence. The fact of Christ's rising and return to heaven is required for the analogy to have force. It is the event that demonstrates the possibility of miraculous contact between the material and immaterial.[29] But the further we are from the event, the greater the need for other means by which to validate the actuality of the immaterial in a material world. After the age of miracles, direct, discernible contact between the material and spiritual realms was no longer thought to occur with regularity, if at all. Repeatedly returning to Christ's material embodiment and divinity grounds the discourse in terms that accommodate, albeit mysteriously, both the material and immaterial modes of existence simultaneously.

From the earliest days of Christianity, theologians faced considerable pressure to reconcile metaphysical claims with the most basic of Christian doctrines: the Trinity and the resurrection. This takes us to another important way in which the nature of 'substance' was debated throughout the Middle Ages and Renaissance. Treatises on the nature and essence of God consistently establish the Trinity in the language of substance, as originally defined at the First Council of Nicaea. The nature of God's substance was among the central reasons for convening the council, as a means of settling the disputes over the nature of God and Christ associated with the Arian heresy. Meredith Hanmer's 1577 translation of Eusebius reveals the fine line that early Christian theologians walked to maintain the doctrine of the Trinity as a doctrine of one God. The appearance of the translation in Reformation England suggests the ongoing interest reformers had in these early debates, viewing them as evidence of a pure early church, free from later corruption. Eusebius' Creed initially read:

> We beleue in one God the father almighty, maker of all things visible & inuisible, & in one Lord Iesus Christ the word of God, God of God, light of light, life of life, the only begotten sonne, the first begotten of all creatures, begotten of God the father before all worlds, by whome all things were made, who for our saluation was incarnate & conuersant among men, who suffred & rose the third day, who ascended vnto the father and shall come againe to iudge both the quicke & the dead. We beleue also in one holy Ghost, beleuing more-ouer euery one of these to be in essence & substance. the father to be a father in deede, the sone to be a sone in deede. the holy ghost to be a holy ghost in deed.[30]

The emperor Constantine, who had convened the council in the hopes of stemming schismatic conflict, demanded an amendment, asking the bishops to add the phrase 'of one substance' to the Creed:

> The vvhich he him selfe explicated in these vvordes: to be Of one substance, may not be taken accordinge vnto corpo-rall affections, neytherto consist of the Father by diuision, neyther by incision or parting asunder. It may not be that an immateriall, an intellectuall, and an incorporeall nature should admitt or be subiect to any corporall passion, for it behoueth vs to conceaue such mysteries vvith sacred and secrett termes. Our most sage and vertuous Emperour rea-soned of these thinges after this sort.[31]

The revised Creed, the one that would go forward and have a powerful influence on Trinitarian doctrine, read as follows:

> We beleue in one God the father almighty maker of all things visible & inuisible, and in one Lord Iesus Christ the sonne of God, the onely begotten sonne of the father, *that*

is of the substance of the father, God of God, light of light, very God of very God, *begotten not made, being of one substance with the father*, by whome all things were made, both the things in heauen & the things in earth. who for vs men & for our saluation came downe, & was incarnate, he was made man, he suffred & rose the third day, he ascended into the heauens, he shall come to iudge both the quicke & the dead. And we beleue in the holy Ghost.[32]

The need for such carefully qualified language was a result of the central event in Christian history. There was no trouble conceiving of an immaterial God prior to Christ's incarnation. Classical theories of substance were able to rest on the analysis and observation of the natural world and remain based in logic and theory. But the need to reconcile such theories with the tripartite Christian God led to schism. Eusebius details the problem raised by the revision of the Creed:

Therefore they which say that there was a time when he was not, before he was begotten, or that he had his beginninge of nothinge, or that he is of an other substance or essence, or that affirme the sonne of God to be made, or to be conuertible or mutable: these the Catholicke & Apostolicke church of God doth pronounce for accursed when they had prescribed this forme of faith, we ceased not diligently to demaund of them how they vnderstoode that sentence, To be of the substance of the father. & that: to be of one substance with the father. Wherevpon there rose obiections & resolutions, so that the right sense of the foresayd sentences was curiously sought out. They sayd that, to be Of one substance, signified nothing else then to be of the father, yet not to be as a part of the father. This seemed vnto vs very well to agree with the exposition of that blessed doctrine which teacheth the sonne to be of the father, yet not to be part of his substance.[33]

It is the perfection (unity and indivisibility) of God as immaterial and substantial – inaccessible but really existing – that constitutes the distinction between the divine and the human. Early modern works on the divine essence consistently foreground this point. Thomas Morton's description is typical:

> God is immateriall and incorporeall, not existing as we do in earthly and corruptible bodies, or as the Angels doo in some more pure, solide and firme subiects, which may in some sense bee called bodies, or in the most subtile and pure matter that can be imagined, but as a pure actuall and substantiall forme, subsisting of it selfe.[34]

God's immateriality is indisputable and absolute, as is His identity as 'a substantiall form, subsisting of it selfe'. If God were to consist of anything material, even the most 'pure matter', He would cease to be the perfect God. Christ's materiality and substantial identity are thus a great mystery.

Though this is a theological debate it is soundly metaphysical, as the concern is with the nature of discrete substances. In order for God to be a substance, He cannot be subdivided. As we have seen, indivisibility is a key feature of the Aristotelian definition of substance. But both the Holy Spirit and Christ are 'of one substance' with God, creating a mystery. The trick, of course, is that all are one, precisely the kind of conclusion a metaphysics of substance sought to avoid. This would be among the most important topics for scholastic theologians. Peter Lombard, whose *Sentences* were the primary text in medieval universities for centuries, devoted his first book to the topic.[35] The long tradition of commentary on the subject consistently revolved around the concept of substance in increasingly contorted efforts to provide a reasonable account of a topic fundamentally unsuited to such treatment. This is apparent in the tension between belief – 'we believe' – and reason – 'this seemed unto us to agree very well with the exposition . . .' – in the Nicene Creed's defence of the divine substance.

Just as the immateriality of God is essential to His substance, Christ's materiality is essential to His identity as saviour. While those of different confessions would vary in their emphasis on Christ's divinity or mortality, accepting the two modes of identity in one God is an essential matter of faith, just as the Holy Spirit is of God but not the same as the Holy Father.[36] The liminal nature of the Holy Spirit is in many ways the most important for the present study, as it was the interaction between the material and immaterial that posed the greatest problem in the early modern period, in which there were few, if any, true atheists, who doubted either the existence of the immaterial God or that Christ was the word made flesh, an embodied human who suffered and died a material death. The material or immaterial character of the Holy Spirit was less clear, especially as it was the key to the interaction of the material and immaterial – it is that by which God is in all things without taking on their corrupt materiality. The basis for human exceptionalism, the distinction between ensouled animals and humans, likewise rests on the liminal category of human intellect (the least material element of early modern psychology), a feature lacking in animals possessing sensitive, but not rational souls.

Speculation and anxiety about the interaction of material and immaterial things rose not from the belief that an immaterial realm was an outdated superstition, but that it was the more valuable, if inaccessible object of pious Christian desire. It is not surprising, then, that the term *spirit* came to represent the substance most vexed in terms of its material or immaterial character. Spirits exist on the border between the material and the immaterial. Spirits will be a special concern of the final part of this book, but before getting to that topic, it will be useful to turn once again to the subject of time, here emphasising its theological valence over its philosophical one. The poets considered in this part of the book, John Donne and George Herbert, are deeply concerned with temporality, especially as it relates to the experience of material and immaterial things that is my focus in this study. The next chapter concentrates on Donne's highly original and deeply searching exploration of the subject in the *First Anniversary*, first published as *An Anatomy of the World* in 1611.

Notes

1. Donne, qtd in Ryan, *The Reputation of St. Thomas Aquinas among English Protestant Thinkers of the Seventeenth Century*, p. 18. His source is John Donne, *The Works of John Donne, D.D., with a Memoir of His Life*, ed. Henry Alford, vol. 1, p. 129.

2. As we have seen, for Aristotle the distinction between physics and metaphysics is notoriously slippery, and there is considerable overlap in the two books in his corpus that bear those titles.

3. In defending the compatibility of science and faith, the physicist Steven M. Barr writes, 'The basic tenet of so-called "scientific materialism" is that nothing exists except matter, and that everything in the world must therefore be the result of the strict mathematical laws of physics and blind chance' (*Modern Physics and Ancient Faith*, p. 1). Though such categorical materialists are hard to find, the view is held more or less by some important mainstream thinkers. See, for example, Steven Pinker, *Enlightenment Now: The Case for Reason, Science, Humanism, and Progress*, p. 392.

4. Daneau, *Wonderfull vvoorkmanship of the world*, b1r.

5. Ibid., b1v–b2r.

6. C. S. Lewis, *Miracles: A Preliminary Study*, pp. 19–20.

7. Ripley in Elias Ashmole, *Theatrum Chemicum Britanicum*, R3r.

8. Norton in Ashmole, *Theatrum Chemicum Britanicum*, H3v.

9. Dod, *Seven Godly Sermons*, Bb3r.

10. De Mornay (du Plessis-Marly), *trewnesse of the Christian religion*, X8v. This is a translation of *De la verité de la religion chrestienne*.

10. Ibid.

11. Jenney, *A Catholic Conference between a Protestant and a Papist*, F3r.

12. Billingsley, 'Ανθρωποποιια: *Theological reflections on God's Admirable master-peece; or profitable instructions from the creation of man, relating to his visible/invisible nature, his body/soul*, BL Sloane 1161, f. 46v. Billingsley flirted with nonconformity, and this manuscript was passed down by the ejected minister Richard Baxter, who wrote on the flyleaf, 'The poetry of this book I leave to the judgment and relish of the reader; the philosophical and theological matter, as far as I had leisure to peruse it, is such as is agreeable to the authors that are most commonly esteemed.'

13. Perkins, *Two Treatises*, C8v.

14. De Mornay, 'Preface to the Reader', **6v.

15. Pinker, *Enlightenment*, p. 393.

16. Spenser, *Faerie Queene*, Book II, Proem, s. 3, ll. 5, 3.

17. See Bacon, 'The Proficience and Advancement of Learning, Divine and Human', in *The Philosophical Works*, p. 175.

18. St Bonaventure, *The Mind's Road to God*, sec. II, par. 13.

19. I. John Hesselink, *Calvin's First Catechism*, p. 9.

20. As Kellie Robertson notes, this approach was associated with Augustinian and Neoplatonic commentators in the Middle Ages, as opposed to Aristotelian-influenced thinkers like Aquinas. See *Nature Speaks*, chs 1 and 2.

21. Anderton, *Non-Entity of Protestancy*, *4r.

22. Tyndale, *Answer to Sir Thomas More's Dialogue*, p. 12.

23. See Jennifer Rust, *The Body in Mystery: The Political Theology of the Corpus Mysticum in the Literature of the English Reformation*.

24. See Sarah Beckwith, *Christ's Body: Identity, Culture, and Society in Late Medieval Writings*, ch. 1, 'The Transcendent and the Historical: Inventing the Discourse of Mysticism'.

25. See Waldron, *Reformations of the Body*, esp. ch. 1. The emphasis on Christ's body in the Middle Ages continued to inform the view that the body offered a glimpse of the divine throughout the early modern period.

26. Paul Tillich, 'Relation of Metaphysics and Theology', p. 58. The true object of metaphysics was hotly debated from antiquity through the medieval period, with the two prime candidates being God and existence as such. See McGinnis, *Avicenna*, p. 253.
27. Tillich, 'Relation', pp. 62–3.
28. Hutchinson, *The Image of God*, A8v.
29. This accounts for the intense focus of medieval Christian mystics on the body of Christ as the path to spiritual knowledge. See Beckwith, *Christ's Body*, p. 15.
30. Eusebius, *The auncient ecclesiasticall histories*, S6r.
31. Ibid.
32. Ibid. Emphasis added.
33. Ibid.
34. Morton (of Berwick), *Treatise of the Nature of God*, G2v.
35. See Lombard, *The Sentences: Book 1, The Mystery of the Trinity.*
36. Paul Cefalu has recently argued that there was a significant interest in the Johannine corpus in the seventeenth century, resulting in a theological emphasis on the divine over the human Christ, a position referred to as 'high Christology'. See *The Johannine Renaissance*, ch. 1. I discuss this in more detail below in Chapter 7.

CHAPTER 6

'WHEN THOU KNOWEST THIS, THOU KNOWEST': INTENTION, INTUITION AND TEMPORALITY IN DONNE'S *ANATOMY OF THE WORLD*

If man were anything, he's nothing now.
John Donne, *An Anatomy of the World*[1]

Almost from the moment of their publication, Donne's *Anniversaries* have been criticised for what appears to be a disproportionate relationship between vehicle and tenor: the death of Elizabeth Drury, a young girl Donne had never met or seen, as representative of the spiritual corruption of the world and the future hope of the salvation of the soul.[2] In the *First Anniversary*, first published in 1611 as *An Anatomy of the World*, the inadequacy of Drury's death as the model for Donne's representation of 'the frailty and decay of this whole world' is especially acute (*FA*, t.p.). The poem's excesses have led many to question Donne's intentions for the poems, despite his own claim (reported by Ben Jonson) that he was 'describing the Idea of a Woman and not as she was', a position he also stressed in a letter to Sir Henry Goodyer: that he had striven for 'the best [he] could conceive'.[3] Both defences rest on an understanding of ideation that privileges reflection over correspondence. Donne's subject in the *Anniversaries*, if we are to take him at his word, is not Elizabeth Drury, but his own conceit of earthly corruption and its potential redemption conceived upon reflection – in Frank Manley's phrase, 'an image of his own imagination to be filled with whatever it possessed'.[4]

The subject of this chapter is the relationship established in the poem between the best that Donne 'could conceive' – presumably derived from his reflection on experience – and belief in a place 'where the stuffe is not such as the rest' (*Second Anniversary [SA]*, 500). In the process, Donne explores the limits of materiality, the 'most immaterial parts' (247) of the temporal world, only to find that they fail to offer access to the true object of his contemplation: the utterly immaterial realm beyond mortal existence. Donne's conceit is the product of his experience of an earthly world marked by 'frailty and decay', a world 'Corrupt and mortall in thy purest part' (*FA* t.p., 62). This entirely material and corruptible world has a counterpart, however, another world of perfection and purity, which ought to be the object of any good Christian's attention. Unfortunately, this world's other is entirely inaccessible to experience and even comprehensible conceptualisation: 'Only who have enioyd / The sight of God, in fulnesse, can think it' (*SA* 440–1). Though it is possible to see in Donne's representation of the relationship between the two worlds a sympathy for Platonic idealism, the poems themselves complicate a reading of the spiritual as simply transcending the earthly, existing above or outside of the corrupt world and thus immune to its modifications. Rather, Donne conceives of the commerce between the worlds in temporal as much as spatial terms. The poems offer access to the inaccessible, however circumscribed and indirect, through a difficult temporal logic that paradoxically reveals the irregardable, immaterial, eternal world in its visible, temporal, material other. While Donne asks his reader at times to 'look vpward' (*SA* 65), more often the call is to look *back* to a long lost and now inaccessible state of perfection as a promise of what is to come in an unknowable future. In Donne's *Anniversary* poems, the temporal dimension of embodied experience structures the search for knowledge of eternal, theological truths; metaphysics serves theology and theology constitutes metaphysics.

The difficulty in accounting for Donne's approach to metaphysical theology stems in part from what critics have seen as Donne's critical engagement with the 'new philosophy' in the *Anniversaries*: his inclusion of an astonishing range of allusions to developments in medical, alchemical, astrological and geographical thought at the turn of the seventeenth century. The ostensible conclusion of his survey of such developments in the *First Anniversary* is that the 'new philosophy', which 'calls all in doubt', is a disaster, leaving the world 'all in pieces, all coherence gone' (205, 213). The conceit of the poem appears to be that progress is in fact decay, the advancement of learning a retreat of knowledge. For this reason, the *Second Anniversary* is often taken to represent the other side of a dualistic world-view, the salvific 'Progress of the Soule' an alternative to the corruption and incoherence of the material world.[5] Without denying the virtue of this account, I will argue that the experience of corruption and ultimately incoherence in the *First Anniversary* is actually the key to the wisdom offered in both poems.[6] In epistemological terms, despite the constant reference to knowledge of the natural world in the *First Anniversary*, the knowledge sought by Donne's speaker is of the spiritual rather than natural world. Because the former cannot be revealed to the mortal, temporal subject except through the latter, we are faced with a paradox in which the diminution of the world as thoroughly corrupt results in its ironic elevation as the path to salvation and perfection.

It is for this reason that my focus in this chapter is on the *First Anniversary*, Donne's diagnosis of the world's spiritual sickness through a figurative 'anatomy', rather than the cure promised in the *Second Anniversary*, or *The Progress of the Soul*. My argument is that Donne's anatomy can be understood as a phenomenological analysis of how the sensuous, material experience of the world provides access to eternal and immaterial truths explicitly withheld from the senses but available to human experience more broadly defined. The poem's difficulty arises in large part from Donne's attempt to bridge the gap between the two realms by focusing almost exclusively on language related to the material realm. As we have seen in earlier chapters, commerce between the material and immaterial is a mystery explored intensely by scholastics who framed the issue in terms of the manner in which the rational soul enabled one to contemplate different kinds of objects. The key term for the schoolmen was *intentio* (commonly translated as 'intention'), and the tradition was one with which Donne was well acquainted.[7] As discussed above, the term is also central to modern phenomenology, and the concept of 'intention' is the most important of Brentano's borrowings from the scholastic tradition to be taken up and re-envisioned by Husserl and later phenomenologists.[8] Donne, an admirer of medieval thought, writing at a moment of significant change in attitudes towards the natural and spiritual worlds, is a particularly interesting case study. The publication of the *Anniversaries* in 1611–12 places them on the hinge between Donne's early love poetry, focused on the vicissitudes of sensual and material experience, and his devotional writing dedicated to the spiritual realm. While Judith Anderson cautions against characterising the *Anniversaries* as evidence of this 'pivot' as 'a little too neat', I suggest that they are one piece of evidence concerning a shift in the object of Donne's contemplation – in phenomenological terms, the object of his intention.[9]

Objects of Intention

Intention (*intentio*) is a technical term in both scholasticism and phenomenology. Herbert Spiegelberg calls its philosophical sense 'extra-practical', to distinguish it from the ordinary language sense indicating a 'desire to act' or a purpose.[10] In scholastic thought, 'extra-practical' intention (*intentio*) appears when there is a need to indicate the mediation that occurs between objects of sense (things) and objects of cognition (ideas) in the process of understanding. For this reason, scholastic *intentio* has been described as 'the mark of cognition'.[11] In Aquinas's cognitive theory, where *intentio* plays a central, if not always consistent, role, the production of knowledge is a directional process that moves from the material to the immaterial by degrees. The Aristotelian inheritance is clear. The process begins with the objects of material sense experience (*esse naturale* or natural being), made present to the understanding through their likeness or *species* (as *esse intelligible* or intelligible being), which are then the occasion for the actualisation of expressions as *intentio* or intentional expressions possessing intentional being (*esse intenionale*); only when the object is grasped by cognition, when its *esse intentionale* is activated (as an *intentio*) in thought, does it become a potential object of knowledge. Importantly, while the form remains identical at each stage, what changes is the mode of being (its relation to materiality). Thus, the intentional object is identical to the object of sense, only in a different mode of being. This is how Aquinas could maintain that the form of the object is in the knower, that 'each thing is known in so far as its likeness is in the one who knows'.[12] The theological implications of this account of knowledge should be immediately apparent, for Aquinas's adoption of an Aristotelian metaphysics puts considerable pressure on the relationship between form and matter, as well as on the nature of likenesses, essences and existents.

Among the challenges complicating the use of the term *intentio* in scholastic thought was identifying at which point precisely the object of sense became an immaterial object as it passed through the phases of perception, cognition and understanding. As Avicenna had argued before him, Aquinas maintained that objects of sense are increasingly stripped of their materiality as they become intelligible objects of the understanding. What is *in* the one who knows is not the material of the sensuous object. Aquinas's account in the *Summa Contra Gentiles* is worth quoting at length:

An external object, coming to be an object of our understanding, does not thereby exist in our understanding in its own proper nature: but the impression (*species*) of it must be in our understanding, and by that impression our understanding is actualised, or comes actually to understand. The understanding, actualised and 'informed' by such an impression, understands the 'thing in itself'. The act of understanding is immanent in the mind, and at the same time in relation with the thing understood, inasmuch as the aforesaid 'impression', which is the starting-point of the intellectual activity, is a likeness of the thing understood. Thus informed by the impression (*species*) of the thing, the understanding in act goes on to form in itself what we may call an 'intellectual expression' (*intentio*) of the thing. This expression is the idea (*ratio, logos*) of the thing, and so is denoted by the definition. So it must be, for the understanding understands alike the thing absent and the thing present; in which respect imagination and understanding agree. But the understanding has this advantage over the imagination, that it understands the thing apart from the individualising conditions without which the thing exists not in *rerum natura*. This could not be except for the understanding forming to itself the aforesaid 'expression'. This 'expression' (*intentio*) in the understanding, being, we may say, the term of the intellectual activity, is different from the 'intellectual impression' (*species intelligibilis*), which actualises the understanding and which must be considered the starting-point of intellectual activity; and yet both the one and the other, both the 'impression' (*species*) and the 'expression' (*intentio*), are likenesses of the 'thing in itself', which is the object of the understanding.[13]

The relationship of the object to its material instantiation is gradually removed at each of the stopping points of the process, until the 'thing in itself' (essence) is revealed in its immaterial fullness. Much has been written about the 'impression' (*species*) in this theory, but in what follows I will focus on the 'expression', which Aquinas refers to with *intentio*.[14]

In modern phenomenology the scholastic term *intentio* was revived by followers of Brentano, eventually taking on a more stable meaning, specifically: 'the conscious relationship we have to an object', as Robert Sokolowski puts it.[15] Confusion over the use of the term by later scholastic thinkers (some of whom rejected it altogether), points to the difficulty of the phenomenological problem it was initially deployed to address. Despite its inexact use in scholastic philosophy, Spiegelberg notes that the term was always 'closely associated with knowledge'.[16] And while modern phenomenologists are always trying to bridge the gap between incomplete perception and true knowledge, for the schoolmen, true knowledge was always considered in the context of the knowledge of God. The scholastic concept of intention is thus an elaborate solution to an especially acute problem of correspondence. On the immediate level, the question is how the world received through the senses corresponds to the world as represented in conscious thought, even if the putative material stimulus for the ostensibly immaterial thought is inaccessible to sense (as in the case of a multitude that cannot be taken in by the senses as a whole).[17] Ultimately, however, the theory accounts for correspondence more generally, specifically to the way the material world corresponds to eternal Christian truth, the manner in which one can have knowledge of God. The third part of this book focuses more directly on how shifting early modern theories of cognition and correspondence affected the period's epistemological discourse. But here, my focus is on the theological implications of the inherited scholastic account, one to which Donne returned throughout his career. In particular, I will explore how Donne's use of analogy as a means of correlating perceptual experience and conceptual understanding pushes questions about the relationship between materiality and immateriality to the foreground. The result is a poetic exercise in the contemplation of the inaccessible – the immaterial other of the frail and corrupt world available to phenomenal experience through the complex interaction of intention and intuition in time.

Microcosm/Macrocosm

The centrality of analogy to the *First Anniversary* is well established, though, intriguingly, it has been identified as both a strength and a weakness of the poem. The claim – lodged memorably by Ben Jonson – that Donne's *Anniversary* poems suffer from elegiac extravagance, rising to 'blasphemy', is based on the belief that Donne's analogy comparing the death of Elizabeth Drury to the whole world's corruption is unbalanced. Jonson's quip that had Donne's 'Anniversarie . . . been written of ye Virgin Marie it had been something' suggests that the failure of the poem is a failure of analogical thinking.[18] Yet the question remains as to whether Donne was in fact trying to achieve the balance many expect of analogy.[19] The assumption is that the poem is an attempt to compare the incomplete particularity of the material world available to the embodied individual through experience to the inaccessible and eternal truths of the immaterial world that exceed human perception, truths that will only become available in an unknown future. St Paul's analogy of mortal and eternal vision is paradigmatic: 'now we see through a glass, darkly; but then face to face'.[20] Paul assures us that the imperfection of sensuous perception is to incomplete mortal understanding as the unmediated perception of God is to eternal understanding. Analogical thinking presses us to find the similarities in disparate things: rain is to a crop as love is to a marriage, for example. But analogy can draw attention to dissimilarity as well: rain is nothing like love. The manner in which Donne deploys analogy in the *Anniversaries* suggests that it is this odd feature of analogy itself that serves as the occasion for his elaborate philosophical exploration of correspondence. This is apparent at the moment we expect Donne to deploy the commonplace analogy of microcosm to macrocosm in the *Anatomy*: the death of Elizabeth Drury to the general decay of the world – the microcosm or 'little world' of her body and soul compared to the macrocosmic order of the world as a whole. And in fact, the only use of the term 'microcosm' in his poetry appears in the *First Anniversary*.[21] Yet Donne complicates the analogy, famously reversing the expected movement from the 'little world' of the personal body to the whole world in which that person is situated. Rather than move from small (micro) to large (macro), Donne instead describes his subject, Elizabeth Drury as 'She to whom this world must it self refer / As Suburbs, or the Microcosme of her' (235–6).[22]

In medieval Christian thought, the microcosm/macrocosm analogy gave expression to the accessibility of the universal in the particular – or of the divine in the natural – allowing for the world to be read as a legible script of God's word, a stabilising truth against the modifications of material existence. The unity suggested by the microcosm/macrocosm understood in this way was always secondary and inaccessible, as the distinction between macro and micro was the occasion for the deeper and inaccessible truth to appear to the understanding. Perhaps as a result, the analogy also lent itself to mysticism and the occult, as the basis for the mystic's search for hidden meaning in the world and the alchemist's goal of divining the perfection of the world from its material impurities. The analogy was attractive in such a wide range of registers in part because of its promise to balance the subjective experience produced by the limited mortal perspective with a universal truth that, while inaccessible, is nonetheless in evidence in the perfection of the correspondence between all parts of the created world. The evidence, like the 'shee' of Donne's poem, is what is not available in the actual micro/macro analogy, as Donne himself suggests in the tenth meditation of the *Devotions*:

> This is *Nature's nest of boxes*; The Heavens containe the Earth; the Earth, Cities, Cities, Men. And all these are Concentrique; the common center of them all is *decay, ruine*; only that is *Eccentrique*, which was never made; only that place, or garment rather, which we can *imagine* but not *demonstrate*, That light, which is the very emanation of the light of God, in which the *Saints* shall dwell, with which the *Saints* shall be appareld, only that bends not to this *Center*, to *Ruine*; that which was not made of *Nothing* is not threatened with this annihilation. All other things are; even *Angels*, even our *soules*; they move upon the same poles, they bend to the same center . . . annihilation.[23]

Excluded from this system of containers is that which falls outside the created world. An analogy that celebrates what it excludes serves Donne's project in the *Anniversaries* well, as it highlights the gap between postlapsarian, temporal existence available to the embodied individual and the eternal (and thus atemporal) existence that both precedes mortality and is yet to come. The nature of temporality itself is implicated, as the temporal advance of corruption in the created world is caught up in the temporal process of its creation: 'For, before God had made up all the rest, / Corruption entered . . . / So did the world from the first hour decay' (193–4, 201). In what follows I will focus on the importance of temporality, but first it is worth noting how spatial, material and extended relationality guide the analogy in its conventional form.

Consider Helkiah Crooke's description of the brain in his *Microcosmographia* (1615):

> And therefore *Plato* did worthily call it, because hee could give it no higher a title, *The devine Member*. For what the Heaven is in the worlde, the same in man is the Braine. The Heaven is the habitation of the supreme *Inteligence*, that is of God; and the Braine the seate of the *Soule*, that is the *demi-God* of this *Little-world*.[24]

Crooke's emphasis on spatial relations is not particularly surprising considering his work is a medical encyclopaedia, concerned with mapping the human body. But he was also following convention.[25] The description of the spatial relation is telling: brain is to man as heaven is to the world, but more importantly heaven contains ('is the habitation of') the 'supreme Intelligence' (God), while the brain contains, is 'the seate of the Soule' or 'demi-God'. The 'Little-world', or microcosm, is understood in relation to the larger world, or macrocosm, at the same time that it is contained within it. This double relation recalls Donne's characterisation of the world as the microcosm or 'Suburbs' of the macrocosmic Elizabeth Drury – the world both contained within and adjacent to her absent presence.[26] Donne's use of 'suburb' suggests a less common contemporary use identified in *OED*: 'The marginal or subordinate part of an immaterial thing; the point of transition between states, eras, etc'.[27] This use, in other words, shifts the meaning of suburb from the more common spatial relation to a more obscure conceptual and temporal one.

Donne's manipulation of the analogy in the *First Anniversary* is striking. The human microcosm, containing all elements of the world in little, the vehicle through which an imperfect knowledge of the world is made possible, collapses at the death of Elizabeth Drury. Without the unifying presence of the 'shee' who is gone, the elements are scattered rather than combining to form a coherent whole, even one that implicitly excludes the crucial 'extropique' uncreated paradise to come:

> Nor ought more this worlds decay appeares,
> Then that her influence the heau'n forbeares,
> Or that the Elements do not feele this,
> The father or the mother barren is. (*FA* 377–80)

Donne's evocation of the physical and spatial correlation that structures the microcosm/macrocosm analogy through his decision to present the poem as an anatomy deceptively promises to position the speaker as a kind of detached scientific observer. In fact, however, the speaker's point of view is deeply subjective, anchored to the moment of contemplation (spurred by the poem's occasion) and limited to the speaker's perspective. The emotional power of the poem is a product of this situated speaker's limited access to the knowledge promised, rather than any emotional reaction to the death of a girl Donne never met.

Temporality, Memory and Causality

The poem's emphasis on temporality is important to an understanding of Donne's analogical method. There is a great deal of commentary on Donne's treatment of time in the *Anniversaries*, and in the *Anatomy* in particular.[28] The two primary strands of this line of criticism examine the poem's emphasis on either memory or causality. A focus on memory is invited by the strange way in which Donne's subject (Drury) is bodily absent and yet a lingering presence:

> Though shee which did inanimate and fill
> The world, be gone, yet in this last long night,
> Her Ghost doth walke; that is a glimmering light,
> A faint weak loue of vertue and of good
> Reflects from her, on them which vnderstood
> Her worth; And though she have shut in all day,
> The twilight of her memory doth stay; (68–74)

The function of memory is suggestive here, especially if taken as part of the poem's larger analogical structure: the memory of Drury's presence is to her absence as the memory of Christ's presence is to God's absent presence in the temporal world.[29] Achsah Guibbory notes that Donne privileged the faculty of memory over the understanding and the will, the other two faculties of the soul. While the three faculties were aligned by tradition with the tripartite God, Donne 'finds memory the most reliable for leading man to God'.[30] Guibbory attributes Donne's preference to its supposed stability compared to understanding and will, noting that he links memory to the experience of memorials and ceremonies, identifying their emphasis on repetition as a strength. Memory's repeatability is a feature of its structure; it is linked to experience but radically severed from it. One can conclude that Donne's predilection for memory rises from his sense of this doubleness. Unlike the understanding, subject to the imperfection of human reason and capable of yielding conflicting judgements when faced with the same experience, or the will which threatens to seek its object blindly, memory is related to its object at a temporal remove.[31]

Donne's emphasis on memory reflects the influence of the theological tradition, stretching back to Augustine's meditation on the complex experience of time in the *Confessions*. The importance of memory as a key to temporal complexity in the Christian tradition appears early on in the *First Anniversary*, when Donne introduces the power of Drury's 'memory',

> Which, from the carcasse of the old world, free,
> Creates a new world; and new creatures be
> Produc'd: The matter and the stuffe of this,
> Her vertue, and the forme our practise is.
> And though to be thus Elemented, arme
> These Creatures, from hom-borne intrinsique harme,
> (For all assum'd vnto this Dignitee,
> So many weedless Paradises bee,
> Which of themselves produce no venomous sinne,
> Except some forraine Serpent bring it in)
> Yet, because outward stormes the strongest break,
> And strength itself by confidence grows weake,
> This new world may be safer, being told
> The dangers and diseases of the old: (FA 75–88)

The 'new world' created by Drury's memory is both a return to a lost paradise and the creation of a new one. The reference to the Fall evokes a vulnerability that is presumably irrelevant in the world to come, when 'all assum'd vnto this Dignitee, / So many weedless Paradises bee'. Nevertheless, the speaker is willing to hedge bets on the perfection of the state to come, especially its imperviousness to 'outward stormes', thus justifying a focus on the memory of the Fall, and its consequences of sin and death, the 'danger and diseases of the old' world. Emphasis on the temporal ensures the logic of the poem's analogy: the present is to the past as the present is to what will be.

Critics have also pointed to Donne's emphasis on the relationship between time and causality in the *Anniversaries*. The relationship is complex, as the poems explore both the cause of Drury's death (generally speaking, as a result of mortality) and the consequences of her death. Lines such as, 'For though the soule of man / Be got when man is made, 'tis borne but then / When man doth die' (451–3), suggest an answer to the poem's earlier question: 'Whether the world did lose or gain in this [her death]' (15).[32] The question's potentially jarring dismissal of the loss of one so young is supposedly avoided through the conventional reference to eternal salvation, foregrounding the temporal repetition involved in the cycle of birth and death, repeated and overcome in resurrection, the rebirth symbolic of the death of death ('death thou shalt die').[33] But there is also a perspectival puzzle: the soul of man is 'begotten', and man is 'made', presumably by God, only later ('but then') to be born in a purer state at death. All of the points in the temporal chain appear to involve the transformation of states of matter, at the same time that they are explicitly associated with the power of God, a power free from mutability. Generation and decay are the conditions of mortal existence, but they are products of creation, the power reserved exclusively for God.[34]

What lies beyond mortal experience is a state of existence utterly devoid of mutability and temporality. For Donne, the temporal and eternal are absolutely distinct; Gary Waller notes Donne's account of eternity in the *Devotions*: 'if we consider eternity, into that time never entered; eternity is not an everlasting flux of time, but time is a short parentheses in a long period; and eternity would have been the same as it is would time had never been'.[35] Donne's sense of time here is deeply indebted to Plotinus's distinction between time and eternity in *The Enneads*: 'Eternity and Time; two entirely separate things, we explain, "the one having its being in the everlasting Kind, the other in the realm of Process, in our own universe". . . .'[36] While maintaining this distinction in the *Anniversaries*, Donne appears to draw directly on Augustine's meditation on time in Book 11 of the *Confessions*, in which he reduces the tripartite structure of time as past, present and future, to forms of the present:

> But that which is cleere now, and plain, is, *that neyther tymes past, nor tymes future,* have any being. Nor is it properly sayd, that there *are,* three *Tymes.* But thus per-adventure, it might properly be sayd, that there are *three Times;* The *present, concerning things past;* the *present, concerning things present;* and the *present, concerning things future.* For there are three such kinds of things, as these, in the mind; but I see them not any where els. The *Present* of things *Passed,* by *Memory;* the *Present* of things *Present,* by *Inspection;* the *Present* of things *Future,* by *Expectation.*[37]

In constructing a phenomenology of temporal experience, Augustine overcomes time by considering it in ontological terms, as a thing made, like the other things in the world God created. Plotinus's synthesis of Platonic and Aristotelian metaphysics offered Augustine a way to preserve the unity of eternal time while offering an analogy to the eternal in temporal experience. Just as eternity is without duration, temporal existence is always present, even when it treats of the past and future. The Aristotelian contribution is to view what Plotinus calls 'process' as a series of distinct actualities. Something only has being when it is in its actual state, though that does not preclude contemplation of its potentiality. It is a paradox that fascinated Donne. The eternal (undifferentiated) state is the desired end, of course, but it is impossible to conceive of without reference to its temporal other. A focus on mutability is the necessary starting point, and memory, the actualisation of the past in the present, is the most reliable defence against the uncertainty of the temporal flux that structures mortal, material experience.[38]

Perception as Paradox

The scholastic and phenomenological accounts of the intertwining of intention and intuition provide two ways of
assessing Donne's approach to the material and immaterial
divide in the *Anniversaries*. As a start, it is clear that the
poet draws on a scholastic, Aristotelian account of sense
experience in the *First Anniversary*. Consider the following
important passage:

> Shee by whose line proportion should bee
> Examine'd measure of all Symmetree,
> Whom had that Ancient seen, who thought soules made
> Of Harmony, he would at next have said
> That Harmony was shee, and thence infer,
> That soules were but Resultances from her,
> And did from her into our bodies go,
> As to our eyes, the forms from objects flow; (309–16)

Understanding derived from perceptual experience is a
result of the translation of objects into forms, which flow to
our eyes. But Donne deploys this explanation to construct
a more complicated comparison. The passage develops a
complex analogy to account for the relationship between
the speaker's ostensible subject (Drury as she was in the
world and is no longer) and his intended object: what we
are to understand as her memory. Just as the poem identifies the ideality of its subject – the 'shee by whose line proportion should bee' – we are asked to reverse the analogy
chiastically: she is what makes proportion intelligible, at
the same time that her intelligible proportionality defines
her as the ideal (and makes her what she is). Her material
proportion, 'beauties best' (306), is discernible obliquely
through a range of sensuous qualities – symmetry, colour,
line (310, 340, 256, 309) – but as those qualities become

legible to the observer their disproportion obscures the ideal from which beauty is supposed to flow:

> Sight is the noblest sense of any one,
> Yet sight hath only colour to feed on,
> And colour is decayd: summers robe growes
> Duskie, and like an oft dyed garment showes. (353–6)

In emphasising the surface appearances available to vision, Donne seems to privilege a transcendent and inaccessible ideal over a world of faint and inferior shadows. Yet the poem's emphasis on temporality complicates the transcendent reading, suggesting the influence of the scholastic, Aristotelian explanation of change in the context of a metaphysics of immanence.

Particularly striking is Donne's insertion of a temporally distinct witness into the analogy at a key point: the 'Ancient . . . who thought souls made of Harmony'. Variously identified by critics as Pythagoras or Simmias, but more likely standing in as a generalised figure for ancient thought, this observer provides the reader of the *First Anniversary* with a witness to the lost event that establishes the poem's paradoxical causality.[39] Though proportion is 'dead' *now*, that is, for readers of the poem, were it possible to witness it *then*, in its pure state, one would understand how it could be a cause. The temporal markers in the passage are difficult: proportion's lines '*should be*' examined in comparison to her ('shee'); '*had* that Ancient seen'; 'he *would at next have* said'; 'Harmony *was* shee'; 'and *thence* infer'; 'souls *were* but *Resultances* from her'.[40] The passage's analogy relies on Donne's construction of a hypothetical past experience imagined for the ancient witness as the proof of a theory of the soul in fact 'inferred' in retrospect: if he had seen her, he would have recognised her as the essence of Harmony, and thus, by his own theory of the soul, the source of all souls.

The temporal revelation of perfect proportion relies on its absence; its incompleteness offers the key to the conceptual ideal, rather than obscuring it from view, as when we are told that 'Shee, after whom, what forme soe're we see, / Is discord, and rude incongruitee' (323–4). The idea that 'soules' are 'but resultances' of her is available only to the past observer, for 'shee' is gone, her harmonious perfection no longer available to sensuous experience. The analogy produces a temporal paradox in which her absent presence is the key to understanding that the world is the resulting microcosm, and 'shee' the macrocosmic cause. Donne replaces the conventional spatial analogy of the macrocosm/microcosm, in which the organisation of the body corresponds part by part to the organisation of the cosmos, with a temporal analogy in which the focus turns to cause and effect, dependent on temporality, but not necessarily in the manner one might expect. The language is specifically that of generation:

> Nor in ought more this worlds decay appeares,
> Then that her influence the heau'n forbeares,
> Or that the Elements doe not feele this,
> The father or the mother barren is. (377–80)[41]

Rather than imagine a spatially external cause (God) inferred as prior to the existing material reality, the poem's temporal causality depends on an Aristotelian understanding of the formal cause as immanent in things at a given point in time. Donne had mused on this as early as the *Paradoxes*:

> Discord is never so barren that it affords no fruit, for the fall of one State is at the worst the increase of another; because it is as impossible to find a discommodity without any advantage as corruption without generation. But it is the nature and office of Concord to preserve only; which property when it leaves, it differs from it selfe, which is the greatest Discord of all.[42]

As with other observations in the *Paradoxes*, this leads Donne to argue that positive knowledge is actually available only through contemplation of its privation. In the *First Anniversary*, it is the absence of Elizabeth Drury in the world that serves as the occasion for an exploration of what the world actually is.[43]

Part of the temporal/causal problem is the question of how the 'shee' of the poem could be both the fount of souls and have one herself. The question is a chicken and egg problem, famously answered in Aristotelian terms by the argumentative Surly in Ben Jonson's *Alchemist*: 'the egg's ordained by nature, to that end: / And is a chicken in *potentia*'.[44] Following Aristotelian natural philosophy Surly understands the problem according to the explanation of mutability in the *Metaphysics*. For a practical thinker like Surly, the explanation applies to the natural world and thus reveals the Alchemist's aim as a sham, against the laws of nature. The natural end of a lesser metal cannot be, according to this logic, the purest metal, gold: you can't 'hatch gold in a furnace' (2.3.127). In response, Subtle turns Surly's Aristotelian explanation of substance and change against him, arguing that it is the same as that used by Alchemists to justify a belief in their art; just as an egg is a chicken in *potentia*, impure 'mixed' substances have the potential to be gold if properly purified. Jonson's satire rests on the insight that language is manipulable, that the Aristotelian account of nature can be true at the same time that it can be abused.

But the subject of Donne's poem is spiritual rather than natural, raising the stakes considerably. In theological terms, the imperfection of the mortal world is utterly complete. The teleology Aristotle identifies for all natural things can be extended to theological concerns, but only in the broadest of terms, specifically as a general theory of causality. The unique exemplar of a cause which is not itself caused is the prime mover of *Metaphysics* Book Lambda. The existence of such an entity is a theoretical necessity, without which Aristotle's entire natural philosophy and metaphysics would falter. But it is one that is inferred through intuition rather than observation. One does not see the prime mover. Christian commentators on Aristotle would naturally align this theoretically necessary entity with the Christian God, but theologians had an additional advantage. Unlike Aristotle who had to posit a prime mover on the evidence of his analysis of movement on a smaller scale, Christians could refer to a time that God was materially manifest. In Christ, God's perfection is paradoxically combined with mortal imperfection. To witness this mystery is to learn something that can only be learned indirectly, as the very experience exceeds human understanding. The indirect experience of the incomprehensible as the utterly true is Donne's subject in the *First Anniversary*, but to evoke this indirect experience is to shift the focus of one's attention to a different intentional object.[45]

Donne comments on the gap between perfect ideality and imperfect worldly perception at the heart of the paradox he associates with his subject's essential form:

> She from whose influence all Impressions came,
> But by Receivers impotencies, lame, (415–16)

The loss of harmony in the world, the world's imperfect, decayed state, is figured here as a result of an insufficiency in the human faculties of perception and understanding. Recognising 'shee' as 'harmony' is to focus on Elizabeth Drury's material absence, while privileging the immaterial, eternal and also static objects of thought (Harmony, Proportion and finally Soules) she represents.

Just as Donne figures Elizabeth Drury earlier in the poem as the macrocosm containing (or perhaps adjacent to) the world, the form of which in turn represents her in little, here she is simultaneously the knowledge resulting from the object of thought and the object that gives rise to that knowledge. In Aquinas's description of cognition quoted above, there is an emphasis on temporal progression: first the impression, 'the starting point of the intellectual activity', must be in the understanding (this is the *species*), then 'thus informed' the understanding 'goes on' to form the 'intellectual expression' (*intentio* or intention), which can subsequently become the object of intellectual action or cognition leading to knowledge. In drawing on the scholastic and Aristotelian account here, Donne foregrounds experience of the material as the path to the immaterial. One would imagine that the point would be to shore up the correspondence between experience of the world and knowledge of the world, even if the goal is to emphasise that the relationship is asymmetrical. Surprisingly, however, Donne exploits the complexity of the account's temporal structure as reliant on a gradual movement from material to immaterial in order to alter the notion of correspondence more generally.

One finds a comparable strategy in what modern phenomenologists call the 'eidetic reduction'. Experience of the world begins in what Husserl called the 'natural attitude' in which one experiences the world as it is given:

> I find continually present and standing over and against me the one spatio-temporal fact-world to which I myself belong, as do all other men found in it and related in the same way to it. This 'fact-world', as the world already tells us, I find to *be out there*, and also *take it just as it gives itself to me as something that exists out there*. All doubting and rejecting of the data of the natural world leaves standing the *general thesis of the natural standpoint*. 'The' world is as fact-world always there; at the most its odd points 'other', than I supposed, this or that under such names as

'illusion', 'hallucination', and the like, must be struck *out of it*, so to speak; but the 'it' remains ever, in the sense of the general thesis, a world that has its being out there. To know it more comprehensively, more trustworthily, more perfectly than the naïve lore of experience is able to do, and to solve all the problems of scientific knowledge which offer themselves upon its ground, that is the goal of the *sciences of the natural standpoint*.[46]

To deny the existence of the 'fact-world' would be to deny the practical attitude towards the world in which we act according to the way we expect the world to behave from past experience. While such an attitude is essential for everyday life, rather than offering actual knowledge of the world, this natural (or naive) position is an obstacle to true knowledge; in such a state it is possible to go on about one's life, but it is impossible to receive the pure knowledge available only to philosophical intuition. Pure knowledge is only to be found upon reflection, a philosophical mode in which one 'brackets' the natural attitude to analyse the objects of thought (the intentional objects) in their completeness, not as they are 'out there' but as they appear in consciousness. The availability of the intentional object to philosophical intuition in its entirety underscores the fact that ordinary experience in the natural attitude is always incomplete.[47]

Donne systematically dismisses the idea that human knowledge of the world has progressed. Citing the advancement of medicine, he points to the less than comforting conclusion of physicians that 'There is no health; physicians say that we / At best, enjoy but a neutrality' (FA 91–2). This 'fact' is for Donne evidence of the incompleteness of knowledge gained through the new science rather than assurance of its claim to truth.[48] The key insight in Donne's survey of the knowledge of the natural world is that increasing knowledge produced by the 'new philosophy' – granular detail about the body from anatomy, the heavens from astronomy, chemical compounds from alchemy and chemistry, and so on – is proportionally indexed to a less coherent picture of the world. The more one focuses on these new facts about the world, the less one knows the truth about the world in which such facts are inconsequential. The insight prompts Donne to shift attention to a different object of contemplation in his quest for true knowledge of that world:

> And that except thou feed (not banquet) on
> The supernatural food, religion,
> Thy better growth grows withered, and scant;
> Be more than man, or thou'art less than an ant. (*FA* 186–90)

To underscore the value of the supernatural, Donne must begin by demonstrating that the knowledge of the natural world is by definition incomplete knowledge.

Corruption is essential to the created world almost from its inception, as Donne describes in his retelling of the Fall:

> Then, as mankinde, so is the worlds whole frame
> Quite out of joynt, almost created lame:
> For before God had made vp all the rest,
> Corruption entred, and deprau'd the best:
> It seis'd the Angels: and then first of all
> The world did in her cradle take a fall,
> And turn'd her brains, and tooke a generall maime
> Wronging each joynt of th'vniversall frame. (191–8)

The account emphasises the complex temporality explored throughout the poem: original sin, the source of corruption in the world, 'entred' *even before* the act of creation was complete, *decaying* the world progressively to the extent that the perfection prior to this corrupt condition is 'almost' omitted from the story altogether. Donne's speaker figures corruption's movement spatially from part to part, likening it to the spread of a disease through a body. Importantly, this progressive spatial movement is also temporal, bringing the account into the present:

> The noblest part, man, felt it *first; and than*
> Both beasts and plants, curst in the curse of man.
> So did the world *from the first houre* decay,
> That euening *was beginning* of the day,
> *And now* the Springs and Sommers which we see,
> Like sonnes of women after fifty bee. (199–204, my emphasis)

The account makes clear that things in the created world have been imperfect from the beginning, though the speaker's oft-quoted conclusion that the 'new Philosophy calls all in doubt' (205) suggests something is different now. I suggest that the difference is where we are in the narrative, one that is bound to repeat, just as innocence gave way to sin and then was redeemed by Christ. The world is at a low point, *now*, ''Tis all in pieces, all coherence gone' (213).

According to the speaker of the *Anatomy*, contemporary claims of progress in the human acquisition of knowledge are misguided, based on illusions that paper over the repetition of error and corruption endemic to earthly imperfection. Janel Mueller identifies the same diagnosis in Donne's earlier unfinished satire, *Metempsychosis or The Progress of the Soul*:

> Donne purports to give an account of the way the world really is – the predatory and destructive motives that govern all behavior once the agent comes to enough awareness and consent to take an active part in experience . . . The force and vitality of Donne's presentation result from an absorption in the earthly (and earthy) that is maintained even as life in the body and the world emerges as something more and more to be despaired of . . . [49]

This immersion in the world, despite its thoroughgoing corruption, is a source of vitality in part because in it one can
find the truth that exceeds its materiality, always present, yet
unnoticed:

> In the *Metempsychosis* Donne's utterance becomes for the
> first time explicitly redemptionist, seeking and finding
> the hero that epic (and his heart) demanded. The Savior,
> the figure so prominently missing from the Third Satire,
> is invoked here as 'That All, which alwayes was all, every
> where; / Which could not sinne, and yet all sinnes did beare;
> / Which could not die, yet could not chuse but die' (74–6)[50]

Donne's inclusion of this redemptive figure in the midst of his
exploration of inescapable and recurrent earthly corruption
in the *Metempsychosis* prefigures his more developed treatment of the subject in the *Anatomy*. As in the earlier poem,
the truth goes unnamed in part because of its paradoxical
nature, its status as the now absent Saviour, the 'shee' that
is dead is impossible knowledge, perfection in an imperfect
world.[51]

Phenomenology of the Invisible

Donne's exposition reveals that it is the attempt to seek
knowledge of the material world as a thing in itself that is
misguided. Somehow one must overcome the obstacle of the
created world to seek true knowledge, as Donne would suggest overtly in the *Second Anniversary*:

> Forget this rotten world; And vnto thee,
> Let thine owne times as an old story be.
> Be not concern'd: study not why, nor whan;
> Do not so much, as not beleeue a man.
> For though to erre, be worst, to try truths forth,
> Is far more busines, then this world is worth. (*SA* 49–54)

Donne's method mirrors both scholastic theories of spiritual knowledge and modern phenomenology's attempt to establish pure knowledge (knowledge of essences) from phenomenal experience. Both philosophical approaches attempt to include within their ken aspects of human experience that exceed material observation at moments when a close attention to the structure and make-up of the natural world complicated epistemological and ontological claims about immaterial, invisible entities. Donne's caution against the urge to 'try truths forth', to test them in the material world, is akin to the phenomenological call to bracket the natural attitude in order to bring consciousness of the world itself into focus. Both also privilege intentionality in order to overcome the weight of the material world, and both include a theory of intuition that complements intentionality in a way that allows the truth of the world to subsist free from the preconceptions of systematic thought. Intuition refers to that which is given to consciousness, while intentionality defines one's relationship to that given.

Writing at a moment when intense interest in the natural world threatened to eclipse conventional knowledge about the supernatural, Donne's poems reflect a similar anxiety about the possibility that attention to the material features of the world might occlude valuable reflection on the immaterial. Though they emerged out of fundamentally different historical conditions and theological contexts, medieval scholasticism and modern phenomenology can be seen to bookend the early modern period's encroaching interest in the explanatory power of the material world. While the scholastics sought to adapt natural philosophy and ancient metaphysics to theological ends (ensuring a place for the spiritual and the immaterial in scientific observation), the phenomenologists were reacting in part to the elision of the immaterial from increasingly naturalistic philosophical and psychological positions in the nineteenth century. The scholastics' philosophical account of knowledge acquisition in the natural world was designed explicitly to complement the centrality of spiritual revelation in everyday life. This appears to contrast with phenomenology, which emerged as a response to late nineteenth-century psychology (Brentano) and logic (Frege), in a post-Enlightenment context dominated by empiricism and positivism. In its earliest form, phenomenology involved the adaptation of scholastic terminology and concepts to secular, scientific ends. At the same time, however, in Husserl's hands the science of phenomenology was a science in the pre-modern sense as much as the modern empirical one. In fact, empiricism was an explicit target of Husserl's phenomenology. He argued that empiricism and naturalism limited the knowable world to its material, physical manifestation. In his account of Husserl's theory of intuition, Levinas argues that 'Husserl goes beyond the naturalistic ontology which hypostatises the physical objects and conceives of the whole of reality on this model.'[52] The 'transcendental phenomenology' Husserl offered in the place of naturalism was initially misconstrued as a form of Platonism or psychologism, but it actually shares more with Aristotle's account of sensation and understanding, positioned as it is between materialism and idealism through its emphasis on the category of experience. While experience in the naturalistic or empiricist sense consists of the experience of the senses and the cognitive processing of such, phenomenological experience stresses the role of consciousness: 'experience . . . has shown itself as absolute being always carrying the guarantee of its own existence, as the locus where all being is constituted and as essentially intentional'.[53] Concern with knowledge as knowledge of being turns phenomenology towards the theological, a fact that has been a source of criticism since its earliest articulation in Husserl's hands.

We have already seen how medieval theologians adapted Aristotle's metaphysics to Islamic and Christian ends, despite the obvious fact that his system pre-dated both religions.

Phenomenology's relationship to theology is equally complex. Brentano's interest in Aristotle and the scholastics may have contributed to his decision to become a Catholic priest. And, theological questions are central to the thought of many of phenomenology's key figures. Despite Heidegger's turn to an apparently atheistic ontology and his discredited moral standing, his existential phenomenology, a response to Husserl's transcendental idealism, had a broad influence on twentieth-century theology.[54] Emmanuel Levinas's philosophical work was routinely called into question as theology masquerading as philosophy. And Jean-Luc Marion makes no effort to hide the Catholic agenda that underwrites his phenomenology.[55] Part of the reason for this is that the idea of pure knowledge always carries theological freight. The first modern phenomenologists were willing to risk the charge of mysticism – which they strenuously denied – in order to challenge the orthodoxies of logical positivism and naturalism. For medieval scholastics like Aquinas the theological nature of truth was self-evident. Donne's affection for St Thomas is clear, at least on this point, and his approach in the *Anniversaries* reflects his intellectual debt to the schoolmen.

Thus, while the focus on knowledge in the *First Anniversary* would suggest that Donne's concern is primarily epistemological, both scholastic theology and modern phenomenology reveal that the relationship between intention and intuition effectively collapses the distinction between ontology and epistemology. Ontological questions are the purview of a theologically oriented epistemology. As we saw in Chapter 3, despite the language of divine right, Shakespeare's meditation on Richard's identity crisis sidesteps the more perplexing theological questions even as it foregrounds Richard's ontological anxiety.[56] Richard's problem is that he is almost incapable of reflection without a prop. In the *Anniversaries*, on the other hand, Donne focuses his reflection on absence as the path to understanding. The bulk of the *First Anniversary* is concerned with how the perception of the world can, on reflection, reveal truths unavailable to the senses that appear to exceed what is given to experience. Where phenomenology helps make sense of Donne's strategy is in its inclusion of objects of consciousness – intentional objects – along with natural, material objects. Phenomenology accounts for the various levels of engagement with 'all the levels of conscious life', from what Husserl calls 'hyletic data' (the material qualities of sense objects) to intentional objects, which include the objects of conscious reflection derived from sense experience as well as those embedded in consciousness itself. As we saw in Part I, for Husserl intuition is, in Jaakko Hintikka's phrase, 'immediate knowledge of any sort', the key being 'immediate'.[57] The objects given to experience through intuition can be both material and immaterial. As Levinas puts it,

> I may remember a memory of a perception. An intuitive look may travel through the various levels of articulation of a *noema* (this is an inherent possibility) and may stop at any one of them. It is also necessary that the intuitive looks be limited to the complexity of what is given and respect its intrinsic meaning without introducing anything indirectly – as through reasoning, for example.[58]

Noema here is a technical term deployed by Husserl to stand for the object that appears to consciousness in experience. As Levinas's description suggests, experience is complex, as the object is articulated at various levels. The intuition of a sense perception (heat, for example) is the immediate knowledge of that characteristic (when one nears a flame). But one can also remember the feeling of the heat when nearing a flame and thus have immediate knowledge of a different phenomenological facet of that same object.

Levinas sums up the phenomenological account of intuition in the following terms: 'phenomenological reflection is an intuitive look directed at life in all the fullness of life's concrete forms. It is an attempt to understand life and, on that basis, to understand the world, life's intentional object.'[59] For the phenomenologist, to understand life is to understand the world rather than the other way around. And life here is a specific object of analysis. As Michel Henry puts it,

> Life is . . . not a something, like the object of biology, but the principle of every thing. It is a phenomenological life in the radical sense where life defines the essence of pure phenomenality and accordingly of being insofar as being is coextensive with the phenomenon and founded on it . . . So Life always founds what we call 'being' rather than the contrary.[60]

Similarly, Donne sets out to understand the world by understanding life in this sense. His anatomy of the world is focused not on what an analysis of the world can reveal but on what life can reveal about the world. Thus, while it would seem that, for Donne, 'the world' is indeed the intentional object he seeks to understand in the *First Anniversary*, it is by emphasising reflection he is able to surpass worldly knowledge (that which is available to the new philosophy, for example) and contemplate the world's essential truth. In this way, Donne is able to bring together two senses of immaterial mystery: the immaterial aspects of the created world and the utterly immaterial world of eternal perfection. If analogy widens the gap between terms even as it effects their comparison, Donne's poetic approach in destabilising analogy intertwines the two as if through a kind of ephemeral touch.

Here it is helpful to note a recent qualification of the view that *intentio* in Aquinas is the 'mark of cognition'. Robbie Moser argues that, for St Thomas, intentional being (*esse intentionale*) is subordinate to immaterial being (*esse immateriale*). In the case of intentional being, 'it is proper for *esse*

intentionale to exist as representational within a knower . . .
there is a fullness of being proper to any thing, and to attain
this fullness of being is to attain a perfection'.[61] This is important when considering how knowledge functions in relation
to the sensible/intelligible distinction in Thomas's thought,
and it helps explain Donne's complicated efforts to drain the
material world of any purchase on essential, as opposed to
temporal, knowledge. He thus writes of the completeness of
the world's 'general sickness':

> . . . this worlds general sickness doth not lie
> In any humour, or certaine part;
> But, as thou sawest in a rotten hart,
> Thou seest a Hectique fever hath got hold
> Of the whole substance, not to be contrould.
> And that thou hast but one way, not t'admit
> The worlds infection, to be none of it.
> For the worlds most immaterial parts
> Feel this consuming wound, and ages darts. (240–8)

Like Shakespeare's Richard, Donne imagines the only
escape from mortal corruption, the material world, is to be
outside of it completely. Yet, Donne complicates Richard's
desire to escape the world, to not be, by adding a temporal dimension that foregrounds the theological. Richard's
ontological musings focus entirely on the future (no man
'shall be pleased till he be eased / with being nothing'),
while Donne's reflect on the cause of the 'general sickness',
which though complete now, was introduced in the past
when 'corruption entered, and depraued the best'. To 'be
none of it' is not only to be outside earthly corruption, but
it is to be prior to the same; just as corruption entered the
world at a point in time, the way 'not t'admit / the worlds
infection' is to exist 'eccentrique' to this world, before or
after this temporality, the temporal being 'a short paren-
thesis in a long period'.[62]

Donne's inclusion of the 'worlds most immaterial parts' among the entities that 'feel this consuming wound' both emphasises the completeness of the corruption of the world and hints at the nature of its truly immaterial other. The use of the superlative is telling. How can something be 'more' immaterial than another thing, much less the 'most immaterial'? The answer would seem to lie in the concept of gradation that we have already seen in discussions of the distinction between material and immaterial things. As we approach the immaterial, substances become more refined, subtle, to the point where they are described, as in the case of some bodily spirits and sometimes angels, as the 'most subtle' of things. In suggesting that even the most subtle, immaterial entities of the world are corrupt, the speaker leaves nothing of the created world worthy of the attention of one who seeks uncorrupted truth. Yet, the superlative also indicates that there is a limit point to the immateriality of the temporal world, and that those things that are 'most immaterial' are at this limit. Nevertheless, beyond this limit there is another 'eccentrique' world, the one Donne valorises in the *Devotions*, the world we can 'imagine but not demonstrate'.[63] But if even the most 'subtle immaterial parts' of this world are corrupt, that would include imagination, as the imagination is a faculty of the soul still identified with earthly rather than eternal immateriality. The limits of the human imagination are explicitly included in the speaker's indictment of earthly corruption: 'What Artist now dares boast that he can bring / Heauen hither, or constellate any thing . . . The art is lost, and correspondence too' (391–2, 396).

Near the end of the *First Anniversary*, having discredited nearly every attempt to erect even provisional knowledge of the world, Donne turns directly to the opposite of knowledge: 'incomprehensibleness'. It is here that Donne proposes that it is in the experience of the incomprehensible that one may come closest to having knowledge of the world.[64] It is the proper object of his intention, rather than one to be avoided in favour of some coherent truth: 'Nor could incomprehensibleness deterre / Me, from thus trying to emprison her' (469–70). Ending the poem in a middle place, Donne chooses temporal movement over static truth: 'heaven keepes soules, / the grave keeps bodies, verse the fame enroules' (473–4). Donne's choice of parataxis in these last lines is striking. Heaven and earth are static 'facts of the world' here, but verse moves temporally, and the three exist alongside one another. In Donne's hands the eternising conceit points less to the poet than to the activity of versification, drawing on the etymological root of verse as 'to turn'.[65] In fact, the poem's repetition of the formula, 'when thou knowest this, / Thou knowest', enacts a kind of turning, a refrain invoking the temporal oscillation between the stopping points of knowledge and experience. Knowing here is believing: what we are told we 'learn' is that 'man is a trifling thing', the world is a 'cripple', a 'monster', a 'ghost' and 'a cinder' (184, 238, 326, 370, 428). Donne's speaker suggests that only when you know 'shee' is dead – reflect on and obtain knowledge of her absence – can you know what he knows to be exemplified in the incompleteness of his objects of comparison: man is not advancing knowledge (he is trifling), the world is not coherent, complete, it is a cripple (lacking), a monster (disproportioned), a ghost (a trace) and a cinder (remains). In each case, we are asked to set aside the positive knowledge offered by astronomy, science, alchemy and so on in favour of something that cannot be explained, something invisible but that has an inexplicable commerce with the visible. The invisible is fundamentally intertwined with the visible in a manner that exceeds understanding, an insight central to scholastic thought as well as Reformation devotional practice, and a feature of experience that continues to animate the development of modern phenomenology.

Despite the intense meditation on the materiality of the world and the human capacity to comprehend it, Donne's interest in the *First Anniversary* is in the immaterial as much as the material, and, most importantly, their points of contact, their intertwining. In the *Anatomy* Donne suspends the two modes of being through an emphasis on recurrence, a version of eternal return as the necessary object of Christian devotion. The final gesture in the poem is a return to memory, signalled by the speaker's reference to the Mosaic song of Deuteronomy (31–3), ordered by God to remind the people of His law:

> God did make
> A last, and lastingst peece, a song. He spake
> To Moses, to deliuer vnto all,
> That song: because he knew they would let fall,
> The Law, the Prophets, and the History,
> But keepe the song still in their memory. (461–6)

The forgetting that is the root of the collapse of knowledge chronicled in the *Anatomy* is inevitable (God 'knew they would let fall / The Law . . .') but so is the retention of the song kept 'still in their memory'. I would suggest that these are the two sides of the material/immaterial dyad that so preoccupied Donne. What will be forgotten, again and again, is the 'matter fit for chronicles' ('The Law, the Prophets, and the History'). What will always abide is that which exceeds that history, the matter fit for Donne's verse song.

If verse 'enroules', it does so not by preserving a past or moving forward to an inevitable *telos*: ends are clearly available in heaven and the grave. To write on a roll, as the term suggests, is also to imply return, a folding back over what has come before. Unlike a codex with its fixed recto and verso, mapping the text neatly in a linear narrative, when a scroll is rolled and unrolled, earlier and later points in the text touch one another, unseen, at unexpected intervals, suggesting return and disrupting any sense of progression.

Donne's reference to the scroll and use of the present tense ('verse enroules') places emphasis on the enacted verse, to the phenomenal experience of writing a line, but more specifically of singing and hearing a song. As Scott Trudell reminds us: 'In a culture that commonly described music in terms of a cosmological ideality that humans could not reproduce or even hear, song was often understood to be radically immaterial.'[66] Trudell goes on to note that, somewhat contradictorily, music was also thought to be among the most vivid of sense experiences. The comparison of the *Anatomy* to the Mosaic song is introduced by the speaker in response to the anticipated objection that his subject is 'matter fit for Chronicle, not verse' (460). The comparison recalls Sir Philip Sidney's elevation of poetry over history, the latter dealing only with the 'bare, was', while the former is closely associated with the moving power of music.[67]

In the concluding lines of the *First Anniversary*, verse stands in for continuous reanimation, the promise of reactivating its subject through a repetition that provides stasis only through motion, as the movement forward is always also a return.[68] Like the song of Moses intended to keep God's word living with the people, the 'middle nature' of verse, the 'fame' Donne's verse 'enroules', combines the immaterial and sensuous as perfectly as can be achieved in this world, and as such it constitutes wisdom, that imperfect, perhaps even irrational but theologically essential knowledge of the world, the best Donne 'could conceive'.

Notes

1. John Donne, *The Variorum Edition of the Poetry of John Donne, Vol. 6: The Anniversaries and the Epicedes and Obsequies*, ed. Gary A. Stringer et al., l. 171. References to the *Anniversaries* will be to this edition by line number and given in the text.

2. See, for example, Frank Manley's account in *John Donne: The Anniversaries*: 'The main problem with the *Anniversaries* is that they are unable to support the weight of their own hyperbole. They collapse under their own burden of praise' (p. 10).

3. Jonson, 'Ben Jonson's Conversations with William Drummond of Hawthornden', in *Ben Jonson*, ed. C. H. Herford and Percy Simpson, vol. 1, pp. 128–78, qtd in *Variorum*, vol. 6, p. 240; Donne to Goodyer (1612), *The Letters to Several Persons of Honour (1651): A Facsimile Reproduction with an Introduction by M. Thomas Hester*, p. 75 qtd in *Variorum*, vol. 6, p. 240.

4. Manley, *Anniversaries*, p. 2.

5. For a strong defence of Donne's dual project in the two poems see Judith H. Anderson, *Light and Death: Figuration in Spenser, Kepler, Donne, and Milton*, ch. 6. Elizabeth D. Harvey and Timothy M. Harrison, in 'Embodied Resonances: Early Modern Science and Tropologies of Connection in Donne's *Anniversaries*', see Donne's project as less clearly successful.

6. The appearance of the *First Anniversary* as the *Anatomy* complicates the argument that the two poems must be read together. Part of my argument is that the *First Anniversary* contains everything one needs to know, the second being simply an elaboration on and clarification of the implicit message of the first.

7. Herbert Grierson notes that 'Donne was steeped in Scholastic Philosophy and Theology', *The Poems of John Donne*, vol. II, p. 4, qtd in Ryan, *Reputation of St. Thomas Aquinas*, p. 12. Ryan details many of Donne's allusions to Aquinas. See also Manley's annotations to the *Anniversaries* in which he identifies many references to Aquinas.

8. See above, Introduction, pp. 22–4.

9. Anderson, *Light and Death*, p. 155.

10. Spiegelberg, *The Context of the Phenomenological Movement*, pp. 3–4.

11. See Robbie Moser, 'Thomas Aquinas, Esse Intentionale, and the Cognitive as Such', p. 763.

12. Aquinas, *Summa Theologica*, first part, question 12, article 9.
13. Aquinas, *On the Truth of the Catholic Faith (Summa Contra Gentiles)*, ch. 53, paras 3–4.
14. For an excellent discussion of species, see Clark, *Vanities of the Eye*, pp. 9–38.
15. Sokolowski, *Introduction to Phenomenology*, p. 8.
16. Spiegelberg, *Context*, p. 8.
17. Husserl stresses that all perception is incomplete: 'A certain inadequacy belongs, further to the perception of things, and that too is an essential necessity. In principle a thing can be given only "in one of its aspects," and that means incompletely, in some sense or other imperfectly . . .' (*Ideas I*, p. 124).
18. Jonson quoted in Donne, *Variorum*, vol. 6, p. 240.
19. Anderson, *Light and Death*, focuses explicitly on analogy in the two poems, arguing that the unstable use of analogy in the *First Anniversary* sets up its 'salient, significant, and constructive' use in the *Second Anniversary*, pp. 150–1.
20. 1 Corinthians 13: 12. The analogy between limited vision and immature attention ('when I was a child . . .') radically juxtaposes a well-known experience (the maturing of thought) with an impossible one: the direct experience of God.
21. He would go on to invoke the concept without using the term in the Holy Sonnet 'I am a little world made cunningly', returning to the idea that all is corrupt: 'blacke sin hath betrayd to endless night / My Worlds both parts, and Oh both parts must dy' (Donne, *Variorum*, vol. 7, pt. 1. Westmorland text).
22. Among the senses of 'microcosm' *OED* includes the following: 'More generally: a place, situation, etc., regarded as encapsulating in miniature the characteristic qualities or features of something much larger' (2 c). Interestingly, Donne's *First Anniversary* is the earliest source for this sense of the word.
23. Donne, *Devotions on Emergent Occasions*, p. 51, emphasis original. I am grateful to Timothy Harrison for drawing my attention to this passage.
24. Crooke, *Microcosmographia*, Qq5r.
25. See, for example, John Davies of Hereford, *Microcosmos: The Discovery of the Little World, with the government thereof* (1603).

26. In his sermon preached at the Spital Cross on Easter Monday, 1622, Donne writes, 'The properties, the qualities of every creature are in man, the Essence, the Existence of every Creature is for man, so man is every Creature. And therefore the Philosopher draws man into too narrow a table, when he says he is Microcosmos, an Abridgment of the world in little: Nazianzen gives him but his due, when he calls him Mundum Magnum, a world in which all the rest of the world is but subordinate' (*Sermons*, ed. Potter and Simpson, vol. IV, pp. 3, 104, qtd in Herbert, *The Complete English Poems*, ed. Tobin).

27. *OED*, suburb, 2.b.

28. Gary Waller, for example, notes Donne's 'fascination with time' in the poems ('John Donne's Changing Attitudes to Time', p. 85). For a recent discussion, see Judith H. Anderson, 'Matter and Spirit, Body and Soul, Time and Eternity in Donne's Anniversaries'.

29. See Patrick J. Mahony, 'The Anniversaries: Donne's Rhetorical Approach to Evil'.

30. Guibbory, 'John Donne and Memory as "the Art of Salvation"', p. 261.

31. Guibbory quotes Donne's worry that the will is the 'blindest and boldest' of the faculties (Donne, *Sermons*, ed. Potter and Simpson, vol. II, p. 235, qtd in Guibbory, 'John Donne and Memory', p. 262).

32. See, for example, Earl Minor, *The Metaphysical Mode from Donne to Cowley*, pp. 63–5.

33. Donne, *Variorum*, vol. 7, pt. 1, 'Death be not proud', l. 14.

34. The spiritual corollary to generation is regeneration, also a power reserved exclusively for God.

35. Donne, *Devotions*, Meditation 14, qtd in Waller, 'Changing Attitudes', p. 85.

36. Plotinus, *Enneads*, p. 213.

37. Augustine, trans. Toby Matthew, *The confessions of the incomparable doctour S. Augustine*, Qq4v–Qq5r. In his 1631 translation, partly an effort to challenge Matthew's translation on doctrinal grounds, William Watts (*Augustines confessions translated*, pp. 772–3) places the three kinds of time in the soul rather than the mind, and for Matthew's 'Inspection', he offers 'Sight'.

38. Marshall Grossman identifies a somewhat more elusive feature of the poem's temporality in what he describes as its chiastic movement from metaphor to metonymy (from Species to Genus and Genus to Species). See Grossman, *The Story of All Things*, pp. 154–96.

39. On the identity of 'that Ancient', see Donne, *Variorum*, vol. 6, p. 430.

40. Emphasis added.

41. Ramie Targoff discusses the generation of the soul in the poem at length in *John Donne: Body and Soul*, noting Donne's engagement with Traducianism (the theory that the soul is generated in the body) versus a theory of infusion, in which the soul is created by God and infused into the body (the theory favoured by Augustine) – see pp. 82–3.

42. Donne, *Selected Prose*, ed. Neil Rhodes, p. 46. Donne makes a similar argument in the 4th and 7th Paradoxes 'That Nature is our worst guide' and 'That the gifts of the body are better than those of the mind or of fortune'.

43. Colie, *Paradoxia Epidemica*, argues that the *Anniversaries* 'hold in balance many oppositions and contradictions: they are, in short, paradoxical poems, poems about paradoxes, and poems within the paradoxical rhetoric' (p. 414).

44. Jonson, *The Alchemist*, 2.3.133–4.

45. I share Judith Anderson's view that the poem's final turn to 'incomprehensibleness' is crucial, signalling as it does that '*She* . . . is well beyond . . . physical grasp . . . beyond definition, or limit' (*Light and Death*, p. 167). Anderson takes this as a defining element of the *First Anniversary*, 'which is stuck, excepting only squibs of light, in a twilit physical world' (p. 170). She contrasts this to the *Second Anniversary*'s use of figurative language 'in a way, to an extent, and with a complexity not found in the *First*' (p. 170). My argument is that the work of figuration in the *First Anniversary* is every bit as complex, and even more so for its reliance on the material as its conduit to the immaterial.

46. Husserl, *Ideas I*, p. 96, emphasis original.

47. On the phenomenological reduction, see Crowell, 'Transcendental Phenomenology'.

48. Note the similar way in which human progress is figured as decline in his subsequent claims about the shortness of human life (111–34) and the smallness of stature (135–54) compared to the biblical accounts of long life (Methuselah living 969 years) and the age of Giants, in which humans towered over all other creatures.

49. Mueller, 'Donne's Epic Venture in the "Metempsychosis"', pp. 135–6.

50. Ibid., p. 136.

51. Anderson, *Light and Death*, notes the 'credible consensus' that 'Shee' represents 'with varying twists and emphases, the image of God' (p. 164). See the section in the *Variorum* on the topic, pp. 293–317.

52. Levinas, *Theory of Intuition*, p. 153.

53. Ibid. The phenomenological position contrasts sharply with Descartes' position, which denies the world until reviving it through the recognition of cognition. The world is never in question for the phenomenologist.

54. See, for example, Judith Wolfe, *Heidegger and Theology*.

55. The same could be said for Michel Henry, Kevin Hart and John Caputo. Though Merleau-Ponty would appear to be one of the less theological of the major phenomenologists, the received view of this may be changing. See Christopher Ben Simpson, *Merleau-Ponty and Theology*.

56. With the possible exception of his embrace of the 'strange brooch' of love in the prison scene, Richard appeals to divinity without interrogating it as properly theological. His early claims of his divinely anointed power are more about power than the divine, as is his final command to his soul: 'Mount, mount, my soul! Thy seat is up on high' (5.5.111).

57. Hintikka, 'The Notion of Intuition in Husserl', p. 173.

58. Levinas, *Theory of Intuition*, p. 139. The limitation to intrinsic meaning is precisely the limit Marion seeks to exceed in his articulation of saturated phenomena, discussed in Chapter 3 above.

59. Ibid.

60. Henry, *Material Phenomenology*, p. 3.

61. Moser, 'Cognitive as Such', p. 776.
62. Donne, *Devotions*, Meditations 10 and 14. See above pp. 190 and 195.
63. Ibid., Meditation 10, p. 51.
64. Anderson, *Light and Death*, also sees this as a crucial turn in the poem. See above, note 45 to this chapter.
65. OED, *Verse* n., etym: from the Latin *vertĕre,* to change or turn.
66. Trudell, *Unwritten Poetry*, p. 11.
67. Sidney, *Defence of Poesy*, D3v. Sidney identifies the height of ancient poetry with scripture, including the psalms, the Song of Songs and 'Moses and Debora in their Hymnes' (C1v). Sidney later calls on Aristotle's argument that 'poetry . . . is more philosophical and more studiously serious than history' to support his case, noting that 'His reason is, because *poesy* dealeth with καθόλου, that is to say, with the universal consideration, and the Historie with καθ εκάστον, the particular' (D3r).
68. My conclusion differs from both Harvey and Harrison's, who see Donne's attempt to be 'doomed to failure' (p. 1002), and Anderson's who sees the kind of success I identify with the *Anatomy* only in the *Second Anniversary*. I argue it is here that Donne most closely approaches the authentic truth he begins to explore in *Metempsychosis*, and that the *Second Anniversary* is not an improvement but a step back.

CHAPTER 7

'A BRITTLE CRAZY GLASS': GEORGE HERBERT AND THE EXPERIENCE OF THE DIVINE

Crazy: 1. Full of cracks or flaws; damaged, impaired, unsound; liable to break or fall to pieces; frail, 'shaky'. (Now usually of ships, buildings, etc.)

OED, 'Crazy', 1

Like Donne, George Herbert engaged with the distance between his earthly experience and the divine object of his desire through poetry animated by the distinction between the material and immaterial. In Joseph Summers's account, 'It was by means of form that the material could be used in the service of the spiritual, that the senses could be properly employed for the glorification of God.'[1] Ostensibly written in the same year that Donne composed his earliest Holy Sonnets and a year before the publication of his *First Anniversary*, Herbert's 'New Year's Sonnets' argue that poets ought to turn from human to divine love. Writing in the aftermath of the Elizabethan sonnet craze, the young poet asks, 'Cannot thy love / Heighten a spirit to sound out thy praise / As well as any she?' (6–8).[2] While the suggestion that poets turn their attention away from the exhausted subject of Petrarchan courtly love is unsurprising at this moment in English literary history, Herbert's early devotion to religious poetry, and the specific terms in which he announces his intentions, foreshadow a poetic career in which the productive tension between material experience and the desire for the immaterial will be central.

Herbert's sequence of Latin poems on the Passion, *Passio Discerpta*, offers another example of the devotional poet's early meditation on physicality and embodiment.[3] Through a series of short poems that focus on the material particularities of the Passion – the crown of thorns, the cross, the nails, the bloody sweat, the whip and so forth – Herbert gives voice to the materiality of the world felt in Christ's suffering. Edmund Miller notes that the poems' 'Baroque tendency to dwell in the sensuous' is unlike what we find elsewhere in Herbert's poetry.[4] Yet the emphasis on the sensuous elements of Christ's suffering plays an important role in the overall message of the sequence. Near the end of the series, in a poem on 'The Rent Veil', Herbert's speaker inveighs against misguided Jewish worship in celebration of God's intervention in the Temple and thus the material world – Christ's resurrection felt as a rupture of the old and new forms of worship:

> Frustrà, Verpe, tumes, propola cultûs,
> Et Templi parasite; namque velum
> Diffissum reserat Deum latentem,
> Et pomoeria terminósque sanctos
> Non vrbem facit vnicam, sed Orbem.

> In vain, O Circumcised Prick, you swell, o huckster of
>   ceremonies,
> And Temple parasite; for the Veil
> Rent reveals the hidden God,
> And makes the holy borders and sacred boundaries
> Circumscribe not just one city, but the World. (1–5)[5]

Herbert's message is ecumenical, but his disdain for the material trappings of worship is nonetheless pronounced. In

Greg Miller's translation, the 'Circumcised Prick' of the first line emphasises Herbert's play on the proud 'swell' of the preacher with an explicitly material, sexually loaded, visual performance. Herbert's speaker goes on to force the distinction between the material and immaterial in making the case for God's omnipresence after the Resurrection:

Et pro pectoribus recenset aras,
Dum cor omne suum sibi requirat
Structorem, & Solomon vbique regnet.

And he counts altars as bosoms,
As every heart for itself seeks its own
Builder, and Solomon everywhere reigns. (6–8)

The reference to Solomon suggests that Herbert had in mind the admiration of the ancient King he shared with his friend Francis Bacon, to whom he dedicated several Latin poems.[6] Where Bacon peeled back layers of authority to look at the world anew and explore its mysteries through experiment, Herbert would do the same to worship. Commenting on what the poem views as the wrongheadedness of the Jewish worship depicted in the ancient Temple, Herbert's speaker opts for simplicity:

Nunc Arcana patent, nec inuolutam
Phylacteria complicant latrîam.
Excessit tener Orbis ex Ephebis,
Maturúsque suos coquens amores
Praeflorat sibi nuptias futuras.
Vbique est Deus, Agnus, Ara, Flamen.

Now Mysteries lie open, nor do
Phylactories complicate unintelligible worship.
The World's tender age has passed greenness,
And the mature age its own loves ripening
Brings to an early flowering its future marriage.
And everywhere is God, Lamb, Altar, Priest. (9–14)

This portion of the poem stresses the temporal complexity of the event. An unavailable 'future marriage' is made available 'now', revealing the truth of what is to come in a manner impossible to see when blinded by the material accumulations that had accrued to religious practice: the 'phylacteries' like hedge mazes covering true worship. The striking similarity of the 'unintelligible worship' of the Temple – complicated by material trappings, its inner rooms reserved for the Priest alone – and the medieval church's dependence on the Latin mass and the rood screen to obscure the ritual could not have been lost on Herbert and his readers. Material things literally get in the way of worship here. The reliance of Jewish worship on 'phylacteries', materially encased texts of the sacred law, is a symptom of the decline away from the truth now available in the world – 'now' literally being the moment of Christ's sacrifice. The temporal emphasis is crucial: the moment that the veil is rent represents a turning point in the materiality of worship. One might ask if Herbert's speaker would have considered the Priest's traditional practice blameworthy before this event, though to continue as such after the fact is clearly wrong. A failure to recognise the meaning of the miraculous rending of the veil is equivalent to the failure to recognise the true Christ, both identified with an impossible materiality that should be immediately clear.

But the poem does not evade the difficulty of the temporal logic on which it draws. The revelation of the 'hidden God' ('Deum latentem') prefigures the later change that is both now and to come as the 'young world' ('tener Orbis') is depicted in the process of maturation, its loves 'ripening' ('coquens amores') and thus prefiguring a future union ('nuptias futuras').[7] Though Miller and Freis suggest that this poem 'feels different in kind than other poems in the sequence and perhaps any other poem by Herbert', I would suggest quite the opposite.[8] The baroque character of the poems in the *Passio Discerpta* sequence is appropriate to its subject – Christ's human suffering and sacrifice, the events which in turn underwrite all of the poems in *The Temple*. Yet the baroque is necessarily absent from the later work, due to its focus on the temporal present. As the central event in the story of God's interaction with the human experience of the material world, the Passion is the paradigmatic point of contact between the material and immaterial, withheld in the interval of time that remains between the sacrifice of the human Christ and the joining of all with God after the Judgement. Though ostensibly extreme in their baroque sensibility – as Miller and Freis indicate, 'bordering on mannerist' – I would argue that the poems in the *Passio Discerpta* are ultimately concerned with an attitude towards these events that has been described as 'high Christologi-cal'.[9] The conclusion to 'The Rent Veil' is that the divine God is everywhere. And, in the final poem of the sequence, 'On Christ's Sympathy with the World', Herbert writes:

> Non moreris solus: Mundus simul interit in te,
> Agnoscítque tuam Machina tota Crucem.
> Hunc ponas animam mundi, Plato: vel tua mundum
> Ne nimium vexet quaestio, pone meam.

> You do not die alone: the World at the same time in you
> dies too
> And the whole Scheme acknowledges your Cross.
> You may assert he is the world's soul, Plato; or lest your
> Questioning shake the world excessively, assert he is
> my soul. (1–4)

The final gesture returns to the subject of individual devotion, precisely the subject on which Herbert will focus explicitly in *The Temple*. At the same time, however, the poet empha-sises that the temporal remainder is the burden of the world. Herbert's speaker obliquely admits that the revelation of God at the moment that the veil was rent is no longer accessible, and the condition bequeathed to the Christian subject is to accept a world in which God remains hidden ('latentem'), albeit hidden everywhere and in everything. This does not mean, however, that God is absent from this world, in Herbert's account. The temporal 'scheme' initiated by Christ's sacrifice is not equivalent to the disenchantment of the world that is often associated with the Reformation.[10] For Herbert, the experience of the world is a phenomenological affair that continuously doubles back on itself in moments of clarity and obscurity. The primary object of Herbert's devotional practice is found in this productive confusion: Herbert has not left behind an older interest the mystery of the world, though his focus is more often on the 'mystery of the word', as Gary Kuchar argues.[11] The rest of this chapter will be devoted to an exploration of the strangeness of this 'object', outlining how Herbert's attention to it can be understood as an attempt to straddle the divide between material and immaterial, and ultimately opting to abandon the distinction.

Entering 'The Church'

If Donne's elaborate conceit in *The Anatomy of the World* can be understood as part of his attempt to reconcile the experience of the material world with belief in a pure state of being that is categorically incompatible with that experience, *The Temple* introduces the same problem structurally. The temporal epistemology of the *Anniversaries*, '*when* thou knowest this, thou [*will*] knowest', is enacted repeatedly in *The Temple*. Herbert's 'little book' invites an attention to the Christian experience of the flawed material world that will refocus the attention of the reader on that world's immaterial other. *The Temple* can be read as a phenomenological tutorial, an elaborate answer to the Reformation question, 'Where was your church before Luther?' The 'Church' that the reader is invited to enter is the self, the soul, but also the *corpus mysticum*, the invisible body of the collective church of Christian faithful, figured after the material churches in which Herbert developed his vocation.[12] Reading *The Temple* encourages one's involvement in the community comprising the invisible church by stimulating reflection on the phenomenological experience through which one comes to know the material church, its community of members and its physical textures.

In a sermon preached at Whitehall between 1622 and 1624 on Ezekiel 34: 19, Donne describes the relationship between the material and immaterial church that Herbert explores in *The Temple*:

> But these sheep in our text, were his flock, that is, his Church. Though they durst not communicate their sense of their miseries, and their desires to one another, yet they were a flock. When *Elias* complained, *I, even I onely am left*, and God told him, that he had *seven thousand* besides him, perchance *Elias* knew none of this *seven thousand*, perchance none of this *seven thousand and* knew one another, and yet, they were his flock, though they never met. That timber that is in the forest, that stone that is in the quarry, that Iron, that Lead that is in the mine, though distant miles, Counties, Nations, from one another, meet in the building of a materiall Church; So doth God bring together, living stones, men that had no relation, no correspondence, no intelligence together, to the making of his Mysticall body, his visible Church . . . So were our Fathers in *Rome*, though they durst not meet, and communicate their sorrows, nor fold themselves so in the fold of Christ Jesus, that is in open, and free *Confessions*. They therefore that aske now, *Where was your Church before Luther*, would then have asked of the *Iews* in *Babylon*, Where was your Church before *Esdras*; that was in *Babylon*, ours was in *Rome*.[13]

Herbert's approach in *The Temple* draws on the same juxtaposition of the 'material Church' to the *corpus mysticum* that Donne deploys in this sermon. The movement is thoroughly phenomenological in its emphasis on both temporal experience (structured by 'then' and 'now') and an emergent understanding of the relation between the visible and invisible, material and immaterial.

Entering Herbert's collection through 'The Church Porch', the reader is asked to prepare the self for the experience to come upon entering the church proper, the success of which is by no means a foregone conclusion. Admonitions against worldliness in 'The Church Porch', such as 'Kneeling ne're spoil'd silk stocking; quit thy state' (407), make clear that 'All worldly thoughts are but theeves met together / To couzin thee' (424). But this, like many seemingly simple statements in Herbert's poetry, cannot be taken to suggest that one ought to abandon worldly thoughts or an engagement with material experience. In fact, the case is quite the opposite, as the lyrics in 'The Church' will demonstrate, an engagement with worldly thoughts is the only path to that which cannot be found in the material world. This paradox is explored repeatedly as the reader is invited to find solid theological ground on the quicksand of Herbert's verse.

The Christian reader 'taught' by the 'precepts' of 'The Church Porch' 'how to behave / thy self in church', and now invited to 'taste / the churches mystical repast' ('Superliminare', 2–4), is greeted by the physicality of the first lyric in 'The Church'. The reference to sensuous materiality in 'The Altar', signalled by the title and foregrounded through its form as a shaped poem, is immediately undercut as the altar's material stone is transfigured into an immaterial heart.[14] Unlike the image of a perfect altar offered in the poem's visual pattern, the altar described in the opening lines is already broken, and it is not an altar at all, instead being 'Made of a heart, and cemented with tears' (2). The shift introduces the poem's and *The Temple*'s true subject by figuring the immaterial Christian heart as special kind of temporal substance: like stone, the human heart is subject to corruption and decay, but unlike material stone it is durable when (and only when) sanctified by God. In Richard Strier's reading, the subsequent turn, suggesting that the altar in question is the carefully crafted poem rather than a physical feature of the church, is similarly undercut by the final reference to 'this altar' (16) clearly referring back to the heart of the petitioning speaker. He argues that the poem's 'final line puts human art in its place by decisively turning away from it just as it attains its perfection'.[15] This is clearly true. My argument is not that Herbert is focused on anything but the human Christian heart here, but only that he cannot begin to approach that subject without confronting the problematic interrelatedness of material and immaterial things. The figure of the 'hardened heart' is conventional to the point of being a dead metaphor, but it is a metaphor nonetheless. Despite the fact that only God 'did frame' the speaker's altar-heart, the materials are familiar from material experience: stone, cement, tears. The distinction between the material and immaterial is an animating force behind Herbert's devotional practice from the outset.

The collection's uncharacteristically long second poem, 'The Sacrifice', places special stress on a central point to which Herbert will return throughout *The Temple*: that even at the moment that God is closest to man, at the instant of His material death on the cross, the chasm that exists between human and divine is unimaginably vast. The refrain of 'The Sacrifice' is consistently posed as a question inviting comparison: 'was ever grief like mine?' And the answer is presented unequivocally at the moment of Christ's death, 'Never was grief like mine' (216, 252).[16] That the material suffering of the passion is consistently associated more broadly with Christ's 'grief' rather than with his particularised pain differentiates the poem's focus from the visceral, baroque physicality of the *Passio Discerpta*.[17] This is not to say that Christ's material suffering is absent from 'The Sacrifice'. All of the elements are there, of course, but they are immediately subsumed by the immaterial lesson to be gleaned from this misery: 'Ah! how they scourge me! Yet my tendernesse / Doubles each lash' (125–6); 'Then with a scarlet robe they me aray; / Which shews my bloud to be the onely way' (157–8).

The centrality of Christ's sacrifice to the overarching message of *The Temple* is to be expected, but for the present purpose I draw attention to the way Herbert positions the sacrifice in the dynamic of material and immaterial interaction. The opening lines place the poem's meditation on Christ's grief in explicitly these terms:

> *Oh all ye*, who passe by, whose eyes and minds
> To worldly things are sharp, but to me blinde;
> To me, who took eyes that I might you finde:
> Was ever grief like mine? (1–4)

The question that becomes the poem's refrain is rhetorical, addressed as it is to the sharp 'eyes and minds' of worldly observers. Those who witnessed Christ's sacrifice would clearly see that none could experience grief like his. But the imperfect knowledge of the passers-by blinded them to his true identity. Rosemond Tuve argues that Herbert draws here on liturgical conventions, specifically the Good Friday Reproaches that share the formal feature of a repeated refrain from Christ on the Cross.[18] In the logic of *The Temple*, the blindness of the passers-by is extended to the readers of the sequence. The repetition is essential.

While the initial blindness led to Christ's sacrifice, an event required for salvation, the blindness of the present age is a result of the fact that the experience has been lost to time. No longer witnesses to the material suffering of

Christ, Herbert's readers live in a world that is cut off materially from the event that defines it. The promise of Christ's sacrifice, described in 'The Rent Veil' as the event that 'discloses the hidden God', has been overwhelmed by the materiality that had previously obscured it. Consider Richard Sibbes's admonition in *A Miracle of Miracles* (1638):

> So saith Saint *Paul*, 2 Cor. 1. *God that raised Christ*, restored me againe, that had *received the sentence of death*: when we receive sentence of death in our persons, looke to him that raised Christ from the dead, and to the grand promises *to come*. They before Christ comforted themselves in times of all distresse by the grand promise of Christ to come. But, now the Messias *is come*. And (which may much more strengthen our faith,) he *hath* suffered and *given* his body to death for us, and therefore why doubt we of Gods good will in any petty matters whatsoever?[19]

The temporal dichotomy outlined in 'The Rent Veil' and found again here in 'The Sacrifice' underwrites the distinction between the material world of experience and the immaterial object of devotion throughout *The Temple*.[20] Opening with 'The Altar', Herbert locates the collection in the present of Christian worship. God's creation, figured as a broken altar, 'Made of a heart', 'a stone, / As nothing but / Thy pow'r doth cut' (2, 6–8), requires grace to be dematerialised, to realise the promise of a salvation, visible now only to the immaterial God. The lyrics of *The Temple* all address this condition in one manner or another, gesturing towards a future as yet unrealised in which the fallen condition of Herbert's speakers will, like the misguided material worship in the Jewish temple, be replaced with a pure communion with God unencumbered by the material corruptions of earthly experience.

The Time Between

In 'Sion', a poem located near the centre of the sequence, the temporal movement from Old to New is figured similarly, along material and immaterial lines.[21] 'When most things were of purest gold', Solomon's great temple was a marvel of material devotion, 'The wood was all embellished / With flowers and carvings, mysticall and rare' (3, 5). But, 'All Solomons sea of brasse and world of stone / Is not so deare to thee as one good grone' (17–18). In place of the material temple, made of stones 'not temples fit for thee', Herbert erects a living temple of 'grones' that are 'quick' (21). As he details, in 'Sighs and Grones' and 'Gratefulnesse' the groans of the living are representative of an inadequate, but properly directed yearning for God. The erection of material temples to God may have begun in good faith, but they inevitably pull one downward towards the earth ('brasse and stones are heavie things' ['Sion', 19]), while the groan of the living Christian is 'full of wings, / And all their motions upward be' (21–2).

'Justice [II]' brings this temporal memory to the individual level. Giving Christ voice as the speaker of 'The Sacrifice' established the temporal distance separating Herbert's contemporaries from the event of Christ's sacrifice, through an analogy with the onlookers at the moment of the Passion, blind to the meaning of the event. 'Sion' offers a similar account of the inadequacy of ancient understanding to properly honour the Glory of God. In 'Justice [II]' the phenomenological experience of the speaker is foregrounded even as it is mapped onto the same epochal history of Christian devotion. Justice was a 'fright and terror . . . of old, / When sinne and errour / Did show and shape thy looks to me' (1–4). The temporal shift in the poem is both expected and jarring: 'But now that Christ's pure vail presents the sight, / I see no fears' (13–14). The speaker is at once the converted

Christian, 'now' at the moment Christ's death rent the veil and revealed the hidden God, *and* the devoted, penitent Christian living 'now' in the age after this event, in which Christ has replaced the material veil with his living flesh. The speaker's conclusion is also figured temporally: 'before', justice called on me, 'Now I still touch / And harp on thee' (19–21). Many commentators have noted that the poem's temporal schema recalls that described by St Paul in 1 Corinthians 13: 12: 'For now we see as through a glass darkly: but then shall we see face to face.' As I have noted elsewhere, the phenomenology of time is complex in Paul's analogy.[22] We are to draw on experience – 'When I was a child I spake as a child, I understood as a child, I thought as a child; But when I became a man, I put away childish things' (13: 11) – but the satisfaction of the first half of the analogy (we have all experienced the movement from childhood to adulthood) is explicitly deferred in the second: not only do we not 'now' see 'face to face', but it is impossible to do so until an inaccessible future is come. The temporal problem addressed by the poem is profound in its emphasis on experience. At the moment when the speaker overcomes the earlier fear of Old Testament justice, he has 'no fears' (14). Yet this 'now' of the poem is situated in the temporal rather than eternal context. The difficulty will be in sustaining the experience over time. Jesus' articulation of the temporality of Old and New in the Sermon on the Mount similarly holds in suspension the moment of His coming and the ultimate Judgement: 'Think not that I am come to destroy the Law or the Prophets. I am not come to destroy but to fulfil them. For truly I say to you, Till heaven and earth perish, one jot or one tittle of the law shall not escape, till all things be fulfilled' (Matt. 5: 17–18). At the moment one finds comfort in the assurance that God is 'for me', 'now', as Herbert's speaker confidently states, one must also accept the conditions of earthly life, in which salvation is deferred 'till all things be fulfilled'.

This deferral is precisely the topic of 'Time', in which Herbert's somewhat impatient speaker, now assured that the judgement he will receive at death will be positive, hopes for death to hurry up and get to business. The poem's final turn is a rebuke, as death quips that the speaker is deluded: 'He doth not crave lesse time, but more' (31). While this line can be read as a reference to the speaker's misguided understanding of eternity as 'more' time, I would argue that Time's frustration at the speaker ('What do I do here before his door?') realigns the personified Time with Death, indicated by the 'sithe' of the second line. The final line is thus Time's warning to a speaker who has yet to learn the lessons of earthly, mortal experience, is not ready for death, and must return to the task of living well. One doesn't get to 'jump the life to come', as Macbeth would have it. Acceptance of the deferral of eternity is an essential component of the devotional life.

The speaker of 'Time' is presumptuous, as the positioning of the next two poems suggests. In 'Gratefulnesse' Herbert returns to the present, and the speaker's ongoing struggle to 'a thankful heart obtain' (27), something not yet accomplished, and in fact not entirely possible while burdened with the material body. Such a heart can only be obtained 'Of thee', and thus accepting this is the closest one can come, a realisation that concludes the survey of possibilities in the following poem, 'Peace'.

The temporal problem is closely related to the problem of assurance that pervaded the theological landscape in the early seventeenth century. As Gary Kuchar has noted, Herbert developed his devotional poetics at a moment when the rigidities of the first wave of English Puritanism had begun to soften. Where 'Elizabethan puritans made assurance of salvation the center of devotional life', some Jacobean divines began to stress the incomprehensibility of God so dear to Augustine, one of Herbert's key influences.[23] The result was that doubt of one's salvation could be viewed not as evidence of one's non-elect status, but rather as an effect of God's inscrutable ways, and poetic form was particularly germane to the expression of the human experience with inscrutability. In 'Assurance', Herbert entertains doubt of salvation by personifying the thought only to accept it as part of God's plan. Herbert's speaker is powerless on his own, having 'not half a word' of comfort against his 'foes' (here 'fears', specifically of abandonment). Herbert's speaker appears to have abandoned the central lesson of covenant theology.[24] But the covenant was never one between equal partners. Since the covenant forged at Christ's crucifixion bound the believer to his God in submission, the Christian's experience is ever guided by God's hand:

> Thou art not onely to perform thy part
> But also mine; as when the league was made
>   Thou didst at once indite,
>   And hold my hand while I did write (27–30)

There is a place for doubt here, as it plays a useful role in avoiding the sin of presumption, for God is both the only path and unknowable in this world. As Kuchar notes, Herbert 'deftly balances the virtue of assurance with the vice of presumption'.[25]

In focusing on doubt and fear Herbert emphasises the value of human experiences that seem to call into question communion with an ineffable God as hedges against the presumption of self-assurance (through works for example). As Lisa Gordis points out, this emphasis on the difficulty of assurance is in keeping with the mainstream strain of covenant theology. She cites Michael McGiffort, who describes George Gifford as a covenant theologian and also an orthodox Calvinist: 'Gifford contended that because the covenant was "founded upon free grace, it is detestable impiety to hang it upon the works of men'.[26] McGiffort identifies the origins of covenant theology in Reformers' desire to preserve rather than dilute the Calvinist conception of absolute grace. And Gordis points to John von Rohr's account of covenant theology as evidence of its role in mainstream English Calvinism:

> Rohr sees the system of covenant theology as reflecting a basic tension in Puritan thought: 'On the one hand, as heir of the implicit, if not always explicit voluntarism inherent in Protestantism's call for faith and obedience as the believer's response to God's proclaimed Word, it affirmed boldly the role of human responsibility and the element of contingency in the divine–human relationship. And on the other hand, as heir of early Protestantism's somewhat more fully explicit emphasis upon God's sovereignty in relation to human affairs, it saw ultimate human destiny as divinely and unconditionally determined by God's decree.'[27]

Herbert's worldly orientation suggests a nuanced understanding of this tension. Dwelling on the inadequacy of material experience is essential to Herbertian devotion precisely because it is the only option in a fallen world, but that does not make it emblematic of the kind of worry over the distance between God and Man that one finds at times in the work of a poet like Donne. The experience of inadequacy is the experience of the time between, an interval Herbert often foregrounded formally in the lyrics of *The Temple*.

Experiencing Inadequacy

The hopeful conclusion of 'Assurance' relies on the speaker's acceptance of human inadequacy to overcome doubt without God's support. Only together can poisonous doubt be overcome, and only through the event of Christ's sacrifice is that communion assured. The poem's conclusion emphasises the temporal dynamic explored in the previous section and reiterates the challenge to the devoted Christian, who is both saved and not yet able to fully experience salvation. The final stanza of 'Assurance' begins 'Now foolish thought go on' and ends 'Now love and truth will end in man' (37, 42, my emphasis). The repetition of 'now' returns us to the moment of the sacrifice, the moment that the veil is rent, and consequently the moment of contact between the material world and its immaterial other. This moment anchors the speaker's confidence on Christ as an everlasting 'rock', even as the poem emphasises the corruptible nature of all material things: 'Yea, when both rocks and all things shall disband, / Then shalt thou be my rock and tower' (34–5). The oscillation between the 'then' of these lines and the 'now' of the poem serves to dignify the otherwise weak quality of material things, even the most sturdy of which will eventually 'disband'. Many of the lyrics in *The Temple* take the present as their starting point, despite an implicit acceptance of this future 'then' that will ultimately displace the unsettling 'now'. A central question for the devotional poet is how to properly inhabit the present, defined by human inadequacy and the inaccessibility of the immaterial divine. The inadequacy of Herbert's speakers figures prominently in *The Temple*, and especially in 'The Temper [I]', 'Grace', 'The Windows', 'Submission', 'Misery', 'Dullness', 'Love-Joy', 'The Holdfast', 'The Priesthood' and 'The Elixir'.

'Misery' is perhaps the most extreme statement of this kind of inadequacy in *The Temple*. Richard Strier points out that the poem highlights 'sensuality as the source and most characteristic manifestation of sin'. The emphasis on sensuality signalled in the poem's 'overly materialistic' vocabulary is, in Strier's view, uncharacteristic of Herbert's approach to sin elsewhere in *The Temple*.[28] But the materialistic emphasis on human imperfection is repeated again and again in poems that foreground the difference between God and man. In 'Misery', even the devotee is unable to praise God properly: 'My God, Man cannot praise thy name: / Thou art all brightness, perfect puritie / . . . How shall infection / Presume on thy perfection?' (31–2, 35–6). In fact, the very attempt is sinful. The speaker's presumption to regard perfection leads to its corruption: 'As dirty hands foul all they touch / And those things most, which are most pure and fine' (37–8). The echoes of the impious alchemist are clear here. The path to an experience of 'perfect puritie' must go through the 'mixed' material world of things. The least accessible thing is that which passes over from the material to the immaterial, the philosopher's stone is not a stone at all, but a future state; God is not accessible flesh, except in one remarkable instance, and when that is the case He is immediately corrupted by mortality and ultimately death.[29]

While the darkness of 'Misery' is certainly hard to miss, the point of the poem is not to dwell on the speaker's miserable state but to acknowledge its role in an experiential dialectic. The final two stanzas recall the development of 'Affliction [I]', often described as the most biographical of the lyrics in *The Temple*. The speaker there begins by recalling the joyous feeling of Christian submission: 'What pleasures could I want, whose King I served?' (13). Time disabuses the speaker of this euphoria, 'But with my yeares sorrow did twist and grow', until 'Sorrow was all my soul' (23, 29). The lowest point in the poem comes in the penultimate line, as the speaker appears to believe he is forsaken by God ('Though I am clean forgot'). Syntactically, however, the final lines reanimate the temporal element of the devotional mode addressed above: 'Ah my deare God! though I am clean forgot, / Let me not love thee, if I love thee not' (65–6). The plea recalls the speaker of Donne's Holy Sonnets, 'Batter my Heart' for example, in which the inadequacy of the speaker to guarantee even his own devotional authenticity signals recognition of his utter dependence on God's grace. The temporal element is essential, as only by mediating the temporality of mortal experience and that of eternal salvation can the speaker be both forgotten and capable of redemption.

Herbert condenses the development of 'Affliction [I]' in the final two stanzas of 'Misery':

> Indeed at first Man was a treasure,
> A box of jewels, shop of rarities,
>   A ring, whose posie was, *My Pleasure*:
> He was a garden in a Paradise:
>   Glorie and grace
>   Did crown his heart and face.
>
>   But sinne hath fool'd him. Now he is
> A lump of flesh, without a foot or wing
>   To raise him to the glimpse of blisse:
> A sick toss'd vessel, dashing on each thing;
>   Nay, his own shelf:
>   My God, I mean my self. (67–78)

What appears to be a general history of the Fall is transformed by the final line into a personal reflection on the speaker's state in sin. Like the speaker of 'Affliction [I]', who worries God has 'clean forgot', the speaker here is nothing more than 'A lump of flesh', an entirely material, and thus worthless 'thing'. The missing features required of one who would properly love God, the 'foot or wing' that might 'raise him to the glimpse of blisse', are God's, not his – they are immaterial, not material. Reduced to indeterminate, material 'flesh', the speaker lacks definition, a foot, which could be read as a 'foot-hold' or 'footing', recalling the image of Christ as an everlasting rock on which Christians might stand. Without proper footing, he sinks, and without 'wing' – explicitly linked to God elsewhere in *The Temple* – he cannot rise.[30] The speaker's inadequacy is palpable, but the remedy is clear. Rumination over the inscrutable ways of God serves to bring that inscrutability into focus. To learn the lesson is in part to ask the question.[31]

Rather than simply state the inadequacy of man to praise God, the speaker of 'The Temper [I]' poses the question to God ('How shall I praise thee') before going on to measure the distance between himself and his Lord, noting the gulf that divides them. The precision of the poem lies in the way it performs the inadequacy of the comparisons that seemingly demonstrate the speaker's difference from God. Noting that 'the world's too little for thy tent, / A grave too big for me', the speaker puts himself on the same plane with God to illustrate how unalike they are:

> Wilt thou meet arms with man, that thou dost stretch
>> A crumme of dust from heav'n to hell?
>> Will great God measure with a wretch?
>>> Shall he thy stature spell? (13–16)

The poem's emphasis on measurement illuminates its method. As we saw in John Dee's account of the different kinds of things available to contemplation – material, immaterial and mathematical – measurement operates in a middle place of the third kind. As Dee puts it, mathematical things are 'thinges immateriall: and neverthelesse, by materiall things hable somewhat to be signified'.[32] The pun of the poem's title is especially important here. 'Temper' can refer to the process of physically altering something material (metal, for example) to perfect it for a purpose, but it can also refer to temperament, as the poem's original title in the Williams manuscript suggested ('The Christian Temper'). The poem's shift from the tempering of steel in the first stanza to the tempering of the heart in the penultimate stanza invokes this middle place in the figure of music (numbers), as the speaker compares the process of God's tempering of his heart to the tempering of an instrument: 'Stretch or contract me thy poor debter: / This is but tuning of my breast / To make the music better' (22–4). As the poem progresses, the speaker abandons the material comparisons, breaking down the distinction between the immaterial God and material petitioner altogether, and replacing multiplicity with unity, a place, 'there' where 'Thy power and love, my love and trust / Make one place ev'ry where' (26–8).

The speaker's conclusion in 'The Temper [I]' is echoed in 'Submission' where the speaker's initial doubts of God's methods are abandoned in favour of a radical acceptance of inadequacy without communion with God. The gift of creation is the only hedge against the speaker's dissatisfaction with his material conditions:

> But that thou art my wisdome, Lord,
>   And both mine eyes are thine,
> My minde would be extreamly stirr'd
>   For missing my designe. (1–4)

Despite the comfort of God's 'wisdome' and acknowledgement of his 'gift' of life, the speaker is nevertheless willing to air his doubts about God's plan, wondering 'were it not better' to reward him in this world than frustrate his ambitions. But ultimately the speaker is unwilling to 'Disseize thee of thy right' to know what's the best way to tutor the speaker to properly praise God. Only in the recognition of his grief over lack of preferment does the speaker truly 'see' that his vision is imperfect: 'How know I, if thou shouldst me raise, / That I should then raise thee?' (13–14). Again, we find one of Herbert's speakers struggling with the problem of presumption. Only chastened by his unrealised ambition is the speaker able to consider the flaw in his thinking: 'Perhaps great places and thy praise / Do not so well agree' (15–16). In recognition of his inadequacy, the speaker submits to God. Stating 'I will no more advise', the speaker instead requests divine assistance, 'a hand' to raise him up, in recognition that God 'hast both mine eyes' (18–20).[33]

The pattern is repeated with a difference in 'The Hold-
fast', in which the initial joy of the speaker's self-conscious
submission to God is cast in a sinister light: 'I threatened
to observe the strict decree / Of my deare God with all my
power & might' (1–2). By this point in *The Temple*, it would
be clear to readers that any human speaker's 'power & might'
alone is insignificant in matters of devotion. The speaker
needs to be reminded of this by an interlocutor who offers
God's power as an alternative and as the proper object of the
speaker's attention. Yet the speaker's willingness to 'trust . . .
in him alone' is also revealed to be a devotional error: 'Nay,
ev'n to trust in him, was also his: / We must confess that
nothing is our own' (5–7). The subsequent turn from 'trust'
to 'confession' results in amazement:

> Then I confesse that he my succour is:
> But to have nought is ours, not to confesse
>   That we have nought. I stood amaz'd at this (8–10)

As in 'Misery', where without God mankind is reduced to a
'lump of flesh', the speaker here is faced with what appears
to be the abject materiality of earthly existence ('to have
nought' is to be mortal, all is vanity). This moment is the
opportunity for the turn – both in the poem and in the speaker's devotional comportment – as a friend intervenes with
comfort, to 'expresse, / That all things were more ours by
being his' (12). Critics of the poem have noted the difference
between the interlocutor of line 3, whose tone is chastising,
and the 'friend' of line 11, who aims to comfort (and is thus
often identified as Christ), but it is possible to read both as
figures of the Holy Spirit, the Paraclete or comforter left by
Christ on his departure.[34] Strier's suggestion that the two
speakers '*are* the God whose "all things" are' supports this
reading, as the voices of both correction and comfort must
be of God.[35] Strier concludes that the poem is about grace,

and though this seems right, for the present purpose it is also an example of Herbert's interest in maintaining faith in the face of a difficult mystery: that the things that are are nought ('that nothing is our own'), and that this revelation is the path to the things that are ('all things . . . being his'). Though technically this could be seen as an argument for faith alone, Herbert seems to view it more practically as an invitation to engage fully with the world of things – both those in earth and in heaven.

The difficulty resolved in the final stanza of 'The Hold-fast' is presented as an extreme version of self-abnegation, as even total devotion – trust, confession, etc. – are shown to be of the speaker and thus too earthly to truly honour God. The problem is prefigured earlier in 'Dullness', where Herbert questions his own path as a poet. 'Dullness' recalls Herbert's youthful call for poetry to turn from earthly to spiritual love, and yet his speaker here finds the latter task more difficult than expected. Weighed down by mortality, the speaker muses on his inability to equal the 'wanton lover' who can 'praise his fairest fair', while he feels 'As if [he] were all earth' (5–6, 2). Aware that he is 'lost in flesh' (21) the speaker asks for God's grace in a measured way:

> Lord, clear thy gift, that with a constant wit
> > I may but look toward thee:
> *Look* onely; for to *love* thee, who can be,
> > > What angel fit? (25–8, emphasis original)

The move here is remarkable, as the sense of the stanza relies on a careful balance of physical and spiritual vision. The stanza recalls the opening of 'Submission', in which the gift of 'wisedome' is associated with a God-given vision mapped on to the physical body: 'both my eyes are thine' (1–2). Here the desire that God 'clear' the speaker's vision is figured as a matter of clearing the 'sugred lies' of material, fleshly experience from one's vision in order to find a 'constant wit' capable of focusing on the object of devotion, God.[36] The next two lines turn to that act of perception, again figured as physiological vision – *looking* rather than seeing – the hedge against presumption that the speaker can in fact see God (to 'love thee' being something beyond the power of even the liminal angels). To linger at the level of the look, to 'look onely', is to stay mortal while focusing on God.

Transfiguring the Material

All of this emphasis on the inadequacy of man to praise God is informed by the biographical story that lay behind *The Temple*, and Herbert's own journey to the priesthood is the explicit subject of two poems that take up the problem of inadequacy in relation to the role of Herbert's own calling and ordination. In 'The Priesthood', generally acknowledged as a poem composed while contemplating the priesthood, but before ordination, Herbert foregrounds his inadequacy: 'I am both foul and brittle; much unfit / To deal in holy Writ' (11–12).[37] The almost certainly biographical musings of the speaker in the opening stanzas of this poem are subsequently subsumed by more general observations about the proper attitude one should take towards ordination, again hinging on the evacuation of personal worth in favour of an utter submission to God's will and grace. Though the speaker does not 'wonder' that 'earth in earth delight', he accepts his 'brittle' state, and vows to wait 'untill my Maker seek / For some mean stuffe whereon to show his skill' (37–8). Herbert's use of 'brittle' here is interesting.[38] Against the assumption earlier in the poem that the 'holy men of God' are 'pure things', 'such vessels' capable of serving God 'who all the world commands', the speaker goes on to accept the necessity of his imperfection, the 'brittle', 'mean stuffe' of which he is made: 'The distance of the meek / doth flatter power' (39–40).

The 'brittle' substance through which God will convey His message is also the subject of 'The Windows', in which Herbert has posed the same question about the priest's worthiness to convey God's word: 'Lord, how can man preach thy eternall word? / He is a brittle, crazie glasse' (1–2).[39] Unlike the poems discussed in the previous section, Herbert does not withhold the answer here, providing it in the next lines of the first stanza: 'Yet in thy temple thou dost him afford / This glorious and transcendent place, / To be a window, through thy grace' (3–5). The answer is that God's grace allows the preacher to become a window to His word: 'making thy life shine within / The holy Preachers' (7–8). In place of the corrupt mortal body, the poem offers the divine body, as is evident in the poem's reference to 2 Corinthians: 'for ye are the temple of the living God; as God hath said, I will dwell in them, and walk in them' (2 Cor. 6: 16). Here, worry over the fragility of the human condition, its seeming separation from eternal truth and lack of assurance of salvation, is overcome by Christ's presence, the word become flesh. Yet the simplicity of the poem's message is complicated by its central conceit, here the figure of the preacher as the stained-glass church windows. The speaker's consideration of the eternal word – 'thy story' 'anneal[ed] in glass' – evokes centuries of theological controversy. The contrast between eternal word and mortal man is further developed through the comparison of the true God and the false idol, the distinction that occasions Paul's account of the human temple in the passage from Corinthians just quoted, for Paul asks: 'And what agreement hath the temple of God with idols?' before responding, 'for ye are the Temple of the living God . . .' (2 Cor. 6: 16).[40]

'The Windows' is often grouped with other poems in *The Temple* dealing with the material features of the physical church, especially 'The Altar', 'Church-Monuments', 'Church-Lock and Key', 'Church Music' and 'The Church

Floor'. As we have seen in the case of 'The Altar', Herbert establishes at the outset that his church is not a physical one, but instead that identified by Apostolic and Reformed theologians as the communal body comprised of Christian believers.[41] Nevertheless the move does not blunt the role that the physical church plays in *The Temple*, a fact underscored by Herbert's decision to begin the sequence of lyrics with a pattern poem that draws attention to its sensuous form.[42] Deploying a series of conceits that focuses attention on the materiality of devotional experience, seemingly distinct from the human temple, allows Herbert to offer a double reflection on both the place of worship and one's place in that material space. Just as 'The Altar' both is and is not about a church altar, 'The Windows' both is and is not about church windows.[43]

On a purely poetic level, stained glass windows are a metaphor for effective preaching: the windows are the vehicle and the holy preacher the tenor. In his reading of the poem, Richard Strier stresses the tenor to the exclusion of the vehicle: 'the poem really is about preachers and preaching, and really is not about anything else'.[44] This hyperbolic conclusion is based on a virtuosic reading that culminates in an emphasis on the final lines in which Herbert 'entirely drop[s] any reference to stained glass'.[45] But as with any metaphor, each component is implicated in the process by which meaning is generated.[46] The poem may end up leaving the material stained glass windows behind, but it couldn't have reached that conclusion without them. The poem's emphasis on the phenomenological experience with material windows is no accident, not only because Herbert valued the material trappings of the English church, as some have recently argued, but also because sensuous response, in this case to the illuminated windows, is at the heart of Herbert's poetic enterprise.[47]

It is worth recalling that Herbert was deeply invested in the physical church itself, taking personal financial responsibility for the reconstruction of his parish church at Bemberton, and a frequent visitor to Salisbury Cathedral, with its wonderful stained glass windows.[48] His well-documented love of church music is further evidence of the importance of the sensuous in his devotional life. Herbert's invocation of the physical process of making stained glass – annealing the stories told in the windows into their 'brittle, crazy' substance – nevertheless raises the question of how such images ought to be used. The veneration of images was clearly prohibited by all authorities on the subject of idolatry. The most potent defence of images in churches descended from brief remarks by Pope Gregory the Great in a seventh-century letter to Serenus, the Bishop of Marseilles. In response to Serenus's iconoclastic breaking of saints' images, prompted by his fear that they had become objects of adoration, Gregory wrote:

> For to adore a picture is one thing, but to learn through the story of a picture what is to be adored is another. For what writing presents to readers, this a picture presents to the unlearned who behold, since in it even the ignorant see what they ought to follow; in it the illiterate read. Hence, and chiefly to the nations, a picture is instead of reading.[49]

Comparing the preaching of 'thy eternal word' to windows, suggested in the poem's title and descriptive language of the poem, Herbert clearly evokes this centuries-old debate. The English reformers of the previous century who took sides on the role of images in religion would have been well known to Herbert. In the 1583 edition of Foxe's *Actes and Monuments*, an appendix includes 'A treatise of M. Nich[olas] Ridley against the worshipping of images' (since attributed to Archbishop Grindal with a debt to Heinrich Bullinger), in which we find the following:

> Experience of the tymes since hath declared whether of these two sentences were better. For since Gregories time the Images standyng in the Westchurch, hath bene ouer-flowed with Idolatry, notwithstanding his or other mens doctrine. Whereas if serenus iudgement had vniuersally taken place, no such thyng had happened. For if no Images had bene suffred, none could haue bene worshipped, and consequently no idolatry committed by them.[50]

Such suggestions that a blanket ban on images in religion was the answer to idolatry featured prominently during the century leading up to the publication of *The Temple*. As many accounts of iconoclasm attest, church windows were often the explicit target.

According to the *Homily against peril of Idolatry*, two-dimensional art was less of a threat than 'one dumbe idol or image standing by it selfe', for 'men are not so ready to worshyppe a picture on a wall, or in a window, as an embossed and gylt image, set with pearl and stone'. Yet historically, the *Homily* continues, the path to idolatry is clear: 'But from learning by paynted stories, it came by lytle and lytle to idolatrie. Whiche when godly men (aswel emperors and learned bishoppes, as others,) perceived, they commaunded that such pyctures, images, or idols, should be used no more.'[51] The sentiment of the *Homily* reflects the careful balance of the Elizabethan settlement, hoping to move past the violent iconoclasm of the Edwardian Reformation while still keeping potentially idolatrous images from the churches. But the question of images in churches would not go away. Archbishop Laud's attempt to defend himself from charges of idolatry by referring to reformers' enthusiasm for Foxe's heavily illustrated *Book of Martyrs* fell on deaf ears.

And only ten years after *The Temple* was published, Laud's efforts to beautify the Anglican church were utterly reversed by an Ordinance of Parliament for the 'Removal of Pictures, Images, & etc', calling for the 'utter destruction' of:

> all Crucifixes, Crosses, and all Images and Pictures of any One or more Persons of the Trinity, or of the Virgin *Mary*, and all other Images and Pictures of Saints, or superstitious Inscriptions, in or upon all and every the said Churches or Chapels, or other Places of Public Prayer, Church-yards, or other Places to any the said Churches and Chapels or other Place of Public Prayer belonging.[52]

Though the relative calm of the 1620s and early 1630s when Herbert was writing and revising *The Temple* may have mitigated the pressure to denounce images in the church, 'The Windows' does not avoid the controversy as much as overcome it. The problem with images, according to nearly all reformers who objected to them, was their ability to distance one from the word of God. According to the 1582 *Short Catechism for Householders*, the second commandment forbids three kinds of image worship: the belief that God 'be like either man or woman, or any other thing'; to worship an image in order to 'be the better put in mind of God by the image'; and third, to 'worship not God in any other outward worship, according to our own fantasies, but as God commandeth us in his word'.[53] All three modes of erroneous worship hinge on the distinction between the immaterial and material (God vs 'man or woman'; God vs 'image'; 'word' vs 'outward worship'), the one presumed to be utterly unlike the other.

This hard-line view of idolatry softened as the Reformation wore on, and in the early decades of the seventeenth century such a position became increasingly associated with Puritan divines and nonconformists hoping to 'complete the work of Reformation', and working against an Anglican church which quietly restored some of the 'outward worship' decried by the iconoclasts of the Elizabethan and Edwardian eras.[54] This is the context in which Herbert wrote, and to characterise him as an iconoclast would be inaccurate.[55]

Yet, as I have suggested, 'The Windows' both is and is not about material images, just as it both is and is not about windows. What we are in fact invited to look at in the poem is the preacher, rather than any picture in a window. Why then does Herbert need the windows at all? One answer can be found in the wisdom of the idiosyncratic Enlightenment thinker Giambattista Vico, whose account of the nature of the human mind can offer a way in to Herbert's poem that allows the material windows and the history of the image controversies to stand alongside its central message about effective preaching, a message that is irreducible to either the poem's tenor or vehicle. Metaphor is at the heart of Vico's 'new science', aimed at a genetic understanding of human thought and perception. He anticipates modern phenomenology in tracing the origins of human culture to a mind, in Marcel Danesi's description, 'that did its work on the basis of bodily experience, not analysis and deduction'.[56] Unlike God, who, Vico writes, 'in his purest intelligence, knows things, and, by knowing them, creates them', poets create 'by virtue of a wholly corporeal imagination. And because it is quite corporeal, they did it with a marvelous sublimity' which led to their being named '"poets" which is Greek for "creators"'.[57] This 'wholly corporeal imagination', what Vico calls 'poetic wisdom', is the origin of all great poetry, which has the following 'three-fold labor': '(1) to invent sublime fables suited to the popular understanding, (2) to perturb excess, with a view to the end proposed, (3) to teach the vulgar to act virtuously, as the poets have taught themselves.'[58]

Poetic wisdom, for Vico, refers to the mind's 'capacity to "make sense" of perceptions', which are then transformed by metaphor into concepts.[59] Margaret Freeman has explicitly linked Vico's account of metaphor to modern phenomenology and recent cognitive theory:

> Sensory *topoi* developed when the first humans discovered sameness in repetition. Thus, Vico says, when humans experienced fear repetitively in responding to thunderstorms, a sensory *topos* created a memory that enabled meaning to emerge by imaginatively creating an identification first between the emotion of fear and the sensation of thunder and then between the image of thunder and the name given to thunder, Jove . . . This imaginative identification is internal to the mind, unlike the logical functions of induction and deduction, which are predicated on objectifying perceptions of the external world. It reflects the more basic, primordial, precategorial level of emotion and sensory memory of Maurice Merleau-Ponty's . . . phenomenology and the more recent understanding of the cognitive unconscious [of Antonio] Damasio.[60]

The distinction that is valuable to the present discussion of Herbert is that between comparison and attribution. In Freeman's characterisation:

> According to Vico, then, conceptual thought first arose from metaphor – not the conceptual metaphor of analogy but the sensory metaphor of attribution or identity. Contemporary theories of metaphor . . . do not make this distinction, seeing metaphor in general as analogically and conceptually based . . . By contrast, Vico says that when human beings first developed the metaphor "jove is thunder" they were not finding similarity or comparing Jove with thunder but were attributing existential, sensory identity between thunder and Jove. This distinction between analogical and attributive reasoning lies, I believe, at the heart of the difference between science and aesthetics.[61]

In the *New Science*, Vico tells us that 'Because of the indefinite nature of the human mind, wherever it is lost in ignorance man makes himself the measure of all things.'[62] There is, of course, nothing one could be more ignorant of than the nature of God's 'eternal word'. Herbert no doubt shared the view of his friend Lancelot Andrewes who mocked those Calvinists who dared to presume knowledge of 'GOD's secret *Decrees*'.[63] Vico goes on to say that 'It is another property of the human mind that whenever men can form no idea of distant and unknown things, they judge them by what is familiar and at hand.'[64] Similarly, Herbert notes in *The Country Parson*, perhaps taking his cue from Sir Philip Sidney, 'particulars ever touch and awake more than generals'.[65] Following his own advice, the poet has the ability to touch and awaken his reader through a particular figure, here a stained glass window, what Sidney would call a 'speaking picture', into which God's story has been annealed.[66] The poet's ability to affect his reader is likened to the preacher's ability to affect his parishioners, which Herbert describes in the remarkable lines of advice to the country parson: 'by dipping and seasoning all our words and sentences in our hearts before they come into our mouths, truly affecting and cordially expressing all that we say, so that the auditors may plainly perceive that every word is heart-deep'.[67] In 'The Windows', the preacher's undipped words ring 'watrish, bleak, & thin' (10), whereas when the 'light and glory' of 'thy life' 'shine within' the preacher's living temple, his speech 'More rev'rend grows, and more doth win' (8, 7, 9).

In the same chapter of *The Country Parson*, Herbert urges the preacher to choose 'texts of devotion, not of controversy, moving and ravishing texts whereof the Scriptures are full'.[68] For as Herbert writes, the preacher is responsible for 'some choice observations drawn out of the whole text as it lies entire and unbroken in the Scripture itself', unlike 'the other way of crumbling a text into small parts, as, the person speaking or spoken to, the subject and object, and the like, has neither in it the sweetness, nor gravity, nor variety, since the words apart are not Scripture but a dictionary'.[69] From Herbert's early seventeenth-century Calvinist perspective, understanding of God's word was only available to the parishioner through the gift of grace. The preacher's role was less to persuade the parishioner of the meaning of the scripture under consideration and more to provide an opportunity for the parishioner to receive that gift. The role of the preacher was on a level with the listeners and subordinate to that of the Holy Spirit in the service. For as Mary Morrissey argues, if the listeners failed to respond to the sermon appropriately, 'The alternative, that the success or failure of a preacher was measured by the effect of his sermons on his hearers, was untenable because it would leave the operation of God's "Ordinance" wholly in the hands of fallible men.'[70]

Rather than elaborate on the distinction between the living temple of the preacher as window and the physical windows that are the occasion for the metaphor, the final stanza of 'The Windows' further develops the figure of the window as the path to understanding – the 'crazy', flawed, cracked glass is the only conduit to the 'eternal word'. Juxtaposed paratactically, 'doctrine and life, colours and light' – the preacher as living temple and the windows as illuminated form – 'bring / A strong regard and awe', precisely the danger images pose, but also the proper way for one to respond to a sermon when enlightened by the Holy Spirit. Even in Gregory's original defence of images, 'to adore a picture is one thing', namely idolatry, 'but to learn through the story of a picture what is to be adored is another', namely devotion. Herbert's concern that 'speech alone / Doth vanish like a flaring thing', ringing only 'in the ear', finally establishes the proper object of the preacher's attention, the 'conscience' of the final line.

The vehicle of the windows is crucial for Herbert to make his point in this poem. The three participants in the sermon – preacher, listener and Holy Spirit – are each represented in the window metaphor. The listener is the one looking at the window onto which is annealed 'thy story' (the subject of the sermon), the composite subsequently figured as the preacher's word, which is only comprehensible if the Holy Spirit shines through to make it visible.[71] Far from not being about stained glass windows, only Herbert's own somatic familiarity with stained glass windows could provide him with the experience required to identify the precise vehicle required for the subject of this poem.[72]

In 'Love-Joy' Herbert returns to the process of annealing so important in his characterisation of the preacher in 'The Windows'. Cefalu highlights the poem's vine reference – the subject of the image depicted on the windows that are the occasion for the poem – arguing that it invokes the Gospel of John, and thus gestures away from the material, which is signalled in the stained glass window, with its image of grapes made visible through the annealing process. The Fourth Gospel emphasises high Christology and Christ's abiding love. Cefalu argues that 'Love-Joy' provides 'a veritable paraphrase of John's vine allegory', through which the Apostle articulates his conception of divine love. At the heart of the allegory is the verse 'I am the true vine, and my Father is the husbandman' (John 15: 1). The allegory involves an incremental orientation towards the knowledge of God, as Cefalu explains: 'One loves God when one recognises that Christ is the embodiment of that love, after which one experiences the fullness of joy that signals a sharing of love among God, Christ, and the brethren.'[73]

The speaker of 'Love-Joy' recounts an experience of revelation that is facilitated by a chiastic intertwining of material embodiment and spiritual enlightenment, as the mortal speaker and the spiritual interlocutor exchange positions in the process of observing the window.[74] 'Love-Joy' becomes 'Joy-Charity [Love]', and ultimately Jesus Christ, combining both. As the speaker comes to see Christ as the embodiment of love (the initial recognition signalled in the interpretation that 'J' and 'C' are 'joy' and 'charity'), he is not corrected but confirmed in his view. 'You have not miss'd', his interlocutor tells him, 'It figures *JESUS CHRIST*' (7–8). As important for the poem's subject is the nature of the object of the interpretation, repeatedly referred to as 'it' (the one standing by asks 'what it meant'; 'It seemed' to the viewer; 'It figures'). 'It' apparently refers to the window in which the speaker sees 'a vine drop grapes with J and C / Anneal'd on every bunch' (2–3). The speaker's revelation that 'It seem'd to me / To be the bodie and the letters both / of *Joy* and *Charitie*' (5–7), confirmed by the 'man' in the final line, effectively suspends the distinction between the material and immaterial, a role reserved for Christ as both God and man. To be the body and the letters is to be the flesh and the word, as Kimberly Johnson and Robert Whalen have noted in their discussions of this poem.[75] For the present purpose I am interested in the way that the poem's ostensible subject – an immaterial and inaccessible divinity – drives a meditation on materiality: the materiality of the vine and grapes, the letters through which the message is conveyed, and the window before which the embodied speakers contemplate the meaning of the image. Rather than transcending the moment of sensory perception in the revelatory final conclusion, the poem invites one to linger in the experience from which this revelation arises.

In the context of the iconoclastic controversies, those willing to accept images generally argued that the material image was a conduit or catalyst to the immaterial truth that lay beyond it. One could 'learn' from the image what lay beyond it, as Gregory argued, or as Herbert puts it in 'The Elixir':

> A man that looks on glasse,
>   On it may stay his eye;
> Or if he pleaseth, through it passe,
>   And then the heav'n espie. (9–12)

The reference is here again to Corinthians and Paul's analogy of looking 'through a glass darkly', the last two lines of the stanza suggesting that heaven lay on the other side. But, as Paul's analogy makes clear through its temporal cues, the movement is not spatial (from here to there) but temporal (from now to then). Perhaps most important is that 'now' is all we have in this world; 'then' is always to come. The promise of passing through the glass to 'espie' heaven is always deferred for Paul, and thus also the devout Christian, Herbert's intended reader. 'The Elixir' of the poem's title is thus both material and immaterial. The elixir is identified as a 'tincture' at line 15, associating it with 'a supposed spiritual principle or immaterial substance whose character or quality may be infused into material things'.[76] The immaterial substance is likely to be God's grace, though its connection to the poem's other alchemical references ('elixir', 'stone', 'told') identify it as an intermediary. The poem's original title in the Williams MS, 'Perfection', also combines the alchemical and devotional meanings of 'purification' discussed above in Chapter 5. In addition to the alchemical Philosopher's stone or elixir, critics have linked the tincture to the water of baptism, Christ's blood and the Eucharist.[77] The other sense of 'tincture' as 'staining' or 'dyeing' supports these readings.[78] The term's root, 'tinct', also has implications for both spiritual and material alteration, as I will discuss in more detail in Chapter 9.

The human desire to discover an elixir capable of perfecting, purifying or distilling the material corruption of the world to reach a unity (gold, truth and so on) is as foolish as it is ubiquitous in the period. Herbert's poem draws attention to this vanity to eschew it in preparation for the acceptance of God's grace. There is always, nevertheless, a temporal element to Herbert's devotional practice. In both its substantive forms, the poem begins with the speaker's request of God 'teach me', suggesting something to be learned. Once learned, a 'servant with this clause' is not yet perfected, but only assured, as the result of the lesson is to make 'drudgerie divine' (17–18). Read in this light, the third stanza's reference to a man who can pass through the glass and see heaven at his 'pleasure' is a chimera. Ironically, as we saw in 'The Windows' and 'Love-Joy', the point is not to seek access to that which lies beyond, but to understand that the gift, which needs no transmutation, is right before one's eyes.

Earth and Spirit Both

Considering the abiding effort to break down the opposition between the material and immaterial throughout *The Temple*, it is worth taking a moment to explore how Herbert deploys the distinction. Several of the lyrics are explicitly structured according to the opposition's implicit hierarchy. 'Antiphon [II]', for example, is organised around the opposition between men 'below' and angels 'above', representing the two 'folds' of existence (material and spiritual, earth and heaven).[79] On the figural level, the 'folds' in question are the enclosures containing the communities of men and angels respectively, a reference to the scriptural characterisation of God as shepherd. The figure of spatial separation supports the temporal logic of the poem, in which the ontological modes of the two communities identify them as separate, but with the potential promise of future integration. The poem's first three stanzas are divided among the voices of the Chorus, Men and Angels in alternating lines of what

Helen Vendler calls the 'most peculiar example of *terza rima* in English'.[80] Though Vendler finds this a torturous structure, the intertwining of realms explicitly defined by their hierarchical opposition reveals the brilliance of Herbert's use of the distinction he seeks to undercut. When, in the poem's final lines, the voices of the men and angels disappear, it is clear that they have been absorbed into a new synthesis, signalled by Herbert's departure from the earlier structure. The men and angels do not answer the Chorus's final lines as one would expect from the form of the first three stanzas. The formal omission enacts the poem's account of divine wisdom: 'Praised be the God alone, / Who hath made of two folds one' (22–3). As the lines directly reference John 10: 16 – 'There shall be one fold, and one shepherd' – they also serve to highlight the temporal element of the poem: only God has the power to 'make' two into one, and from the human point of view this is something that 'shall be' but is yet to come.

What is the case *now* is temporal, earthly existence, as Herbert explores most explicitly in 'Vanitie [I]', the first three stanzas of which constitute Herbert's most direct engagement with the natural philosophy of his day in *The Temple*. The poem is often discussed in relation to his friendship with Francis Bacon, a man about whom Herbert wrote Latin poetry and whose *Advancement of Learning* he helped translate into Latin.[81] The poem catalogues human efforts to gain knowledge of the world through material observation: the astronomer 'views' the 'stations [of the spheres]', the diver 'cuts through the working waves', and the chemist 'strips the creature naked' (2–3, 9, 16). All this attention to the discovery of knowledge in the materiality of the world is an obstacle to spiritual edification. Despite the fact that God 'Embosomes in us' 'his glorious law' (24, 23), we seek certainty in the dead earth: 'Poor man, thou searchest round / To finde out *death*, but missest *life* at hand' (27–8).[82]

Herbert's reliance on the distinction between the material and immaterial here can be understood in relation to his effort to distinguish between competing interpretive orientations towards the world in order to offer guidance for devotion at a moment when the explanatory power of empirical observation was increasingly given pride of place. Following Gerald Bruns, Kuchar describes Herbert's approach as a 'hermeneutics of teaching versus a hermeneutics of meaning'.[83] Kuchar sees an affinity between the Herbertian orientation (a hermeneutics of teaching) and the later tradition of phenomenological hermeneutics.[84] The third stanza of 'Vanitie [I]' is of particular interest for the present argument about the role of the immaterial in early modern experience, as it showcases how Herbert elevates what Vico calls poetic wisdom over scientific discovery. In the first two stanzas, Herbert addresses those who look up to the heavens and then those who look down into the stuff of the earth (specifically, the deep of the sea, 'the working waves', in search of the 'dearely-earned pearl'). The vanity of both efforts is relatively clear and also relatively easy to differentiate from the search for spiritual knowledge. But in the third stanza, the 'subtil Chymick' seeks a knowledge of first principles that comes closer to the kind of knowledge sought by the devoted Christian. As we have seen, a purity of heart and pious comportment was a requirement of the alchemist to succeed in unlocking the mysteries of the world through the discovery of the philosopher's stone. Theoretically, this unifying 'elixir' is not unlike God's law that is 'embosomed' in the hearts of men. But that is where the comparison ends. The chemist and alchemist alike search the material world for what can only be found in the immaterial realm. As Herbert writes in 'The Foil',

> If we could see below
> The sphere of vertue, and each shining grace
> As plainly as that above doth show;
> This were the better skie, the brighter place. (1–4)

But it's not. The 'Chymick' gets the harshest treatment in 'Vanitie [I]' because he believes that through his method of distillation ('stripping the creature naked', i.e. to its elements) he will discover its 'callow principles' or basic laws. The description of the principles as 'callow' establishes a comparison of purified elements to fledgling birds, creatures defined by their ability to fly, but not possessing that capacity. Flight is, of course, one of Herbert's favourite tropes for spiritual ascent, here invoked as an absent quality. Both the chemist and the properly devoted Christian seek after laws, but the laws derive from different sources. Seeking the laws of nature through material observation will lead only to an understanding of death, unless one's efforts are directed towards life, the eternal and spiritual thing that resides elsewhere and is accessible only obliquely through such an engagement with materiality.

How, then, does one traverse the material–immaterial divide? Where is the capacity for flight located? For many readers of *The Temple*, the answer is that Herbert's poetics are, in Robert Whalen's terms, a 'poetics of immanence'.[85] Building on rather than departing from this view, I want to stress the way that Herbert continually returns to the point of contact between the earthly and spiritual, material and immaterial. References to flight and wings serve as a salve against *The Temple*'s references to the earth-bound inadequacy of fallen humanity, the need, as in 'Easter Wings', to 'imp my wing on thine' in order to commune with God. Flight suggests both an upward and a transformative movement from earthly to heavenly, a movement towards a purity and unity unavailable materially and marked by its association with air. As Donne explored in 'Air and Angels', the intermediate sphere is all important:

> For, nor in nothing, nor in things
> Extreme, and scatt'ring bright, can love inhere;
> Then as an angel, face and wings

Of air, not pure as it, yet pure doth wear,
So thy love may be my love's sphere. ('Air and Angels', 21–5)

Intermediaries and points of contact play an important role in *The Temple*, and Herbert's reliance on them offers further insight into his attitude towards the material/immaterial distinction.

The best-known example of Herbert's use of wings and flight in service of a salvific vision is 'Easter Wings', the poem that visually performs the oscillation between the material and immaterial prefigured by Christ's incarnation and sacrifice. The poem's balance of movement towards and away from God with the movement from material dearth – the shortest lines representing the furthest distance from God, when the speaker is 'most thin with thee' – to immaterial fullness turns on the figure of the bird in flight. The speaker yearns to 'rise' like the larks, like Christ, 'harmoniously', become song on the air, as the pun on air as medium and music serves to 'further the flight' (10) in the speaker. The move is repeated in 'Church Music', in which the speaker, wounded by 'displeasure', is comforted by music, 'Sweetest of sweets': 'Now I in you without a bodie move, / Rising and falling with your wings' (1, 5–6). Movement without a body is a philosophical impossibility, or a theological mystery. It is not surprising that Herbert associates this mystery so closely with air and breath, which are consistently poised on the borderline between the material and immaterial.

In its repetition of 'breath', 'Mortification' identifies breath as the life-giving force (*anima*), until the final stanza in which the loss of breath teaches one of eternal life. Breath is the threshold that separates life and death, mortal life representing death and death at the end of the process of mortification figured as the path to life.[86] Breath also figures prominently in 'The Odour, 2. *Cor*. 2'. The poem's opening line reaffirms the association of sound and 'sweetness', but by the end of the stanza the sweetness is fragrant.[87] Critics have noted the intense sensuality of this poem, and most recently, Kuchar has stressed how Herbert dramatises the experiential nature of prayer as a physical act: 'it creates the effect that the speaker's process of spiritual rebirth is happening as he prays'.[88] The intertwining of the sensuous and the divine is repeatedly identified with a point of contact: 'My Master' 'shall call and meet' 'My Servant' as breath, spirit, 'That call is but the breathing of the sweet' (21, 24, 25). And again, in the final stanza, 'This breathing would with gains by sweetning me / (As sweet things traffick when they meet) / Return to thee' (26–8). As the immaterial is impossible to reach materially, the meeting place between the two becomes the essential focus of devotion. Too much in either direction risks error, either presumption (claiming experience of that which cannot be experienced) or vanity (claiming that experience of the material world is all there is or is anything at all without God).

Herbert's desire to overcome the distinction between the material and immaterial is always tempered by his acknowledgement that the distinction governs temporal, mortal experience. The temporal problem, with which I began, is also where I will end. In 'Clasping of Hands', Herbert celebrates the idea that the distinction between the speaker and God will be dissolved in the event of salvation. The poem's first stanza ends with the speaker's worrisome conclusion about the nature of making a distinction between self and God, 'If I without thee would be mine / I neither should be mine nor thine', suggesting that the desire for autonomous selfhood is a rejection of God (9–10). This fear is resolved at the end of the poem, but in the form of a radical desire for union with God: 'O be mine still! Or make me thine! / Or rather make no Thine and Mine' (19–20). This desire for ecstatic union is conventional, but it is nevertheless radical precisely because it relies on a rejection of the nature of distinction itself. Like the repeated justification of affliction and mortal suffering as requirements for salvation, the distinctions on which Herbert structures the many lyrics I have discussed in this chapter are prerequisites for the concept of perfection, unity and proper communion with God.

As one nears the end of *The Temple*, Herbert's verse increasingly emphasises a careful balance of the material and immaterial, often by returning to the central mystery surrounding the relationship between Christ's body and God's divinity. As I have already discussed in Chapter 5, the mystery animated much of the theological controversy of the Elizabethan Reformation. Religious controversy in the period repeatedly returned to the problem of defining a devotional practice that maintained the doctrinal necessity of God's immateriality and Christ's material body. The general relationship of the soul and body is central to the debates, but nowhere was there more subtlety of argument than in the struggles over the nature of the Eucharist. Herbert scholars have paid a great deal of attention to the representation of the Eucharist in *The Temple*.[89] As Jeanne Clayton Hunter puts it, 'At the heart of George Herbert's poetry lies the eucharistic Christ.'[90]

Not surprisingly, commentary on Herbert's treatment of the Eucharist has focused on the two poems titled 'The H. Communion' (in the Williams MS and *The Temple*), often in dialogue with the 'The Elixir', 'The Invitation', 'The Banquet' and 'Love [III]'. A typical observation is that despite the period's intense debates over the nature of the Eucharist, Herbert seems consistently uninterested in the substance question. This view is supported by the Williams MS version of 'The H. Communion', the more doctrinally combative of the two poems, which includes the memorable lines, 'ffirst I am sure, whether bread stay / Or whether Bread doe fly away / Concerneth bread not mee' (7–9).

As Paul Cefalu puts it in reference to the wine in 'The Banquet', 'Herbert makes no fuss at all over what exactly is

contained in the cup.'[91] While this is true, the Eucharist does
provide Herbert with an important opportunity to contemplate
the point of contact between the material world of the flesh
and the immaterial world of spiritual salvation. In the penultimate stanza of 'The H. Communion' (Williams), the speaker
offers an explicit expression of the gulf between the material
and spiritual realms:

> Into my soule this cannot pass
> fflesh (though exalted) keeps his grass
>   And cannot turn to soule.
> Bodyes & Minds are different Spheres
> Nor can they change their bounds & meres,
>   But keep a constant Pole. (37–42)

The chasm separating these two realms is unbridgeable
here, as it will remain in the version included in *The Temple*.
In revising the poem, Herbert appears to shift the emphasis
from any concern with the material to a meditation on the
Eucharist as spiritual food: 'But by the way of nourishment
and strength / Thou creep'st into my breast' ('The H. Communion', 7–8).[92] The gulf so prominent in the earlier poem
remains, though with a difference. A revised version of the
penultimate stanza of the Williams MS poem appears as
the third stanza of 'The H. Communion' (*Temple*), now
celebrating the positive presence of God in the flesh, rather
than its inherent corruption. The earlier poem's insistence
that 'fflesh (though exalted) keeps his grass' is softened,
as the still material, 'fleshly hearts', are now armed with
the Eucharistic 'elements' that serve as bulwarks against
corruption:

> Yet can these not get over to my soul,
>   Leaping the wall that parts
>   Our souls and fleshly hearts;
> But as th' outworks, they may controll

My rebel-flesh, and carrying thy name,
                    Affright both sinne and shame.
                        ('The H. Communion' (*Temple*), 13–18)

This allows Herbert's speaker to turn explicitly to the subject of Grace:

Onely thy grace, which with these elements comes,
                    Knoweth the ready way,
                    And hath the privie key,
            Op'ning the souls most subtle rooms;
While those to spirits refin'd, at doore attend
                    Dispatches from their friend. (19–24)

The brilliance of this stanza is in its articulation of the cross-ing point between material and spiritual in utterly material terms: to 'leap' the 'wall' only grace can show the way, pro-vide the 'key', open the 'doors', attended by bodily 'spirits refin'd'. The speaker's faith in God's gift of grace gives him the comfort that he might move with 'ease', like Adam before the Fall, from a material to a spiritual state, as from room to room, 'Which I can go to, when I please, / And leave th' earth to their food' (37, 39–40).

Strategic indifference to the substance question is thus itself a theological position. Herbert's evasion on the doc-trinal and dogmatic questions of the day has previously supported the conventional view that he chose to accept unquestioned an Anglican middle way. The second half of the twentieth century saw this view challenged, and begin-ning in the 1980s Herbert scholars began to reveal just how deeply Herbert was engaged in the theological debates of his day.[93] As Brian Cummings puts it, in what is now a con-sensus view, attention to the religious context reveals that '*The Temple* is difficult to interpret according to rigid cat-egories because he has absorbed so much theology.'[94] In par-ticular, his debts to Calvin and Luther and the influence of

English Protestant divines ranging from Lancelot Andrewes to Richard Sibbes have illuminated our understanding of his complex approach in *The Temple*. More recently, Herbert's theology has been reassessed in relation to another of his primary influences, St Augustine, not in an attempt to identify his theology with what Tuve had called the Christian 'tradition', but to acknowledge the role of Augustine's thought in the devotional habits and rhetorical style of both mainstream and radical Calvinists in the early decades of the seventeenth century.[95]

In keeping with this project of reassessment, Paul Cefalu has recently drawn attention to the centrality of the Johannine corpus as a key feature of the English Reformation. In Cefalu's view the focus on the Johannine texts suggests Herbert's attraction to a high Christology that is consonant with the Augustinian notion of divine inscrutability as well as with Calvinist theology. Concerning the Eucharist, the result is that Herbert's 'emphasis is on the force of the sacrament to enable the speaker to rise to the ascended Christ; the emphasis is not on Christ's descent in bodily form to the elements of the Eucharist'.[96] This helps explain Herbert's seeming indifference to questions concerning the nature of the material Host, while confirming that such indifference was not the result of a lack of theological conviction, but rather a thoroughgoing commitment to the expression of the impossible gift of grace. The result, as Cummings notes, is a defining feature of *The Temple*, Herbert's attempt 'to capture what could hardly be captured'.[97]

As we have seen in both 'The Foil' and 'Vanitie [I]', the earthly search, though necessarily focused on one's experience of the material, natural world, is not aimed at discovering the laws of that world. The lesson is repeated again and again in *The Temple*, until the reader is invited to witness the proper communion with God. In a reversal of the warning to the utterly worldly against entering the church in 'The Church Porch', 'The Invitation' calls to those whose eyes have been tutored to look at the world *with* rather than *for* God:

> Come ye hither all, whose love,
>   Is your dove
> And exalts you to the skie:
> Here is love, which having breath
>   Ev'n in death
> After death can never die. (25–30)

Breath here traverses life and death, no longer, apparently, the breath of life so reluctantly relinquished in 'Mortification' – that which binds one to the mortal world and the value of which is vanity. Life after mortal death renews the breath of life as the paradoxical conduit linking material existence to eternal salvation.

'The Banquet', a companion poem to the 'Invitation', further develops Herbert's dissolution of the distinction between sensuous materiality and ecstatic union with God. The subject is the Holy Communion, figured as the banquet to which the addressee was invited in 'The Invitation'. Again, we find the figure of the wing as a metonymic means to ascension, and the association of sweetness with the odour of divinity. Recalling the synesthetic intertwining of 'The Odour. 2. Cor. 2', the wine of the sacrament is celebrated for its ability to traverse modes of existence:

> O what sweetness from the bowl
>   Fills my soul,
> Such as is, and makes divine!
> Is some starre (fled from the sphere)
>   Melted there,
> As we sugar melt in wine? (7–12)

The poem is an exercise in the suspension of debate over substance, as the sensuous sweetness of material sensation is immediately transformed into the sweetness of God's love which fills the devoted speaker's soul. The simile that makes up the last three lines of the stanza appears to question the substance of the wine, asking what precisely is 'melted there' in the bowl that could have such efficacy. Yet, the simile's own answer emphasises the miraculous and mysterious rather than the particular: 'some starre' suggests something like a 'piece of the heavens', has left its place to give the wine its efficacious power. But the comparison's turn to the mundane sugaring of wine highlights a material mystery: how does the hard substance of the sugar appear to 'melt' in the wine without heat? It turns out that both poles of the comparison are of the created and thus material world – the heavens and the earth each having their share of mystery. But Herbert has already shown the reader of *The Temple* that these are not the mysteries of God; knowledge of the natural world is not the object of devotion: 'Doubtlesse, neither starre nor flower / Hath the power / Such a sweetnesse to impart' (19–21). The communion with God occurs at the moment the wine touches the tongue of the speaker: 'Sweetly he doth meet my taste' (39). But this moment of contact immediately reconstitutes the distance between the speaker and his God. 'Wine becomes a wing at last', giving the speaker the means to ascend 'to the skie' and 'see / What I seek, for what I sue; / Him I view, / Who hath done so much for me' (44–8). Only with God can the speaker see God; Christ's real substance in the wine has become the wing on which the speaker can experience his ecstatic vision: 'Him I view'. Yet how can this be? We are consistently told that the sight of God is to be deferred to the future, only 'then' will we see 'face-to-face'. The 'wonder' that the last stanza celebrates reveals what the speaker has actually 'seen' in the experience of communion. As his vision is cleared once he is lifted up 'To the skie, / Where I wipe mine eyes, and see', the truth of Christ's sacrifice is revealed to the speaker, 'Him . . . Who hath done so much for me'. The shift from physiological to spiritual vision constitutes the speaker's transformation, and it is a shift that relies on the distinction between the material and immaterial even as it results in the expected dissolution of the distinction.

My argument throughout this chapter has been that a key element in Herbert's poetic project is in accepting the impossibility of experiencing immateriality while remaining confident in its priority over material experience. The confidence of the speaker of 'The Banquet' to 'Strive in this, and love the strife' signals precisely this acceptance. Herbert's speaker here would apparently share Bacon's view that 'there are two things which are known to God the author of the Scriptures, but unknown to man; namely, the secrets of the heart, and the successions of time'.[98] Considering Bacon's hope of striving towards complete knowledge of the natural world, his position on matters theological was equally expansive: not only are the things known to God unknown to man, they are categorically unknowable.

In 'Love [III]', the last poem in 'The Church', Herbert condenses the experience of Christian unworthiness and hope that his speakers have fluctuated between throughout the sequence. But here Love is present, and for every doubt there is a response: 'my soul drew back' 'But quick-ey'd Love . . . Drew nearer to me'; 'I cannot look on thee' ' Who made the eyes but I?' (1, 5, 10, 11). The speaker's acquiescence in the final line, 'So I did sit and eat', signals the abandonment of the desire for knowledge on the model of human reason and experience. Like Cordelia's response to King Lear, the love here is free, there is 'no cause'.[99] Strier's argument that the poem is about *agape* is helpful, as the distinction between earthly love and *agape* parallels that between a particularised material experience and a universal power that suffuses the world but also transcends it.[100] Many critics have identified the both/and logic of the final poem as representative of Herbert's approach

throughout *The Temple*; my point here is that the poetic power
Herbert generates from his use of the both/and approach is
derived from the central role that the material/immaterial distinction played in early modern thought.

Though 'Love [III]' ends the section of *The Temple* identified as 'The Church', it is worth considering Herbert's decision
to include two codas to his sequence of lyrics, one quite long,
'The Church Militant', and one extremely slight, 'L'envoy'.
Though a full account of these poems is beyond the scope of
the present study, I would suggest that the two poems represent the tension between the material and immaterial that
I have been discussing throughout this book. The weight of
the material struggle is represented in a recounting of church
history and division in 'The Church Militant'. The challenges
facing the church are significant, and, it would seem, representative of the 'strife' accepted by the speaker of 'Love [III]'.
The counter in the small final lyric, 'L'Envoy', calling on God
('*King of Glory, King of Peace*') to overcome a personified
'Sinne', seems insubstantial by comparison. That is, of course,
the point. All of Sinne's efforts to sow doubt in the faithful are
materially directed: 'Bragging that thy bloud is cold, / That
thy death is also dead', 'That thy flesh hath lost his food, /
And thy Crosse is common wood' (6–7, 9–10). The appeal
to God is explicitly future-directed. Though asked to 'choke
him', implying a loss of breath and thus voice (presumably the
vehicle of Sinne's efforts to 'devour [God's] fold'), the plea is
qualified as God is asked to hold Sinne's breath in reserve:

> But reserve his breath in store,
> Till thy conquests and his fall
> Make his sighs to use it all,
> And then bargain with the winde
> To discharge what is behinde. (12–16)

It seems unlikely that Herbert would end with the image of
his God bargaining with a material entity, even if that entity

is the wind. It is thus Sinne who, with his last breath, is apparently doing the bargaining. And what are the fruits of his efforts? The wind will 'discharge what is behinde', that is, what is 'to come'. To 'discharge' is to relieve of a burden, but it is also to bring to an end. The burden of the material world, that which is now, will be discharged in a future that is to come, one that will also mark the end of time.[101]

Notes

1. Summers, *George Herbert: His Religion and Art*, p. 73.
2. *The English Poems of George Herbert*, ed. Helen Wilcox. All references to Herbert's poetry will be to this edition unless noted otherwise. In the letter to his mother, in which these poems appear, Herbert announces his dedication to religious poetry exclusively. See Isaac Walton's *Life of George Herbert*, in *The English Poems of George Herbert*, ed. John Tobin, p. 274. On the shift to the divine sonnet, see William L. Stull, '"Why Are Not 'Sonnets' Made of Thee?" A New Context for the "Holy Sonnets" of Donne, Herbert, and Milton', pp. 129–35.
3. In the following I will draw on two modern translations of the *Passio Discerpta*. The first is in *The Latin Poetry of George Herbert: A Bilingual Edition*, trans. Mark McCloskey and Paul R. Murphy. The second is Greg Miller's translation in *The George Herbert Journal* 39 (2015/16), pp. 99–117. Miller cites Amy Charles in dating the composition of the sequence to 1622; see Greg Miller with Catherine Freis, 'Introduction', *George Herbert Journal* 39 (2015/16), p. xvi. In-text citations are to the Miller/Freis translation except where noted.
4. Edmund Miller, 'Herbert's Baroque: The *Passio Discerpta*', p. 202.
5. McCloskey and Murphy's earlier translation provides a helpful comparison:

> You Jew,
> Huckster of worship, sponger

Of the Temple, you strut in vain,
For the ripped veil
Discloses the hidden God,
And makes the outer walls, and the sacred
Inner Temple grounds themselves,
Not one city only, but a world.

McCloskey and Murphy, p. 77.

6. See Miller and Freis, 'Introduction'.

7. The image of ripening love could evoke the vine imagery so important in the Gospel of John. On the importance of the vine imagery elsewhere in Herbert, see Cefalu, *Johannine Renaissance*.

8. Miller and Freis, p. xix.

9. The distinction is one of emphasis. In the high Christological view, based on the account of Christ in the Gospel of John, Christ's divine nature is emphasised over His humble humanity, as in the Synoptic Gospels. See Cefalu, *Johannine Renaissance*, pp. 2–5 and *passim*.

10. See, for example, Regina Schwartz, *Sacramental Poetics at the Dawn of Secularism: When God Left the World*.

11. See Gary Kuchar, *George Herbert and the Mystery of the Word: Poetry and Scripture in Seventeenth-Century England*.

12. On the *corpus mysticum*, see Rust, *Body in Mystery*, Beckwith, *Christ's Body*, and Kuchar, *Mystery*, ch. 2. Herbert's involvement with the upkeep of physical churches is well documented, but has been emphasised by Ceri Sullivan in new work on Herbert's administrative role in church maintenance. See her essay, 'Cement, Summers, Pulleys, Plummets, Pipes, Timber, and Screws: George Herbert's Building Works'.

13. John Donne, *Fifty sermons*, p. 214, emphasis original.

14. See Paul Dyck, 'Altar, Heart, Title Page: The Image of Holy Reading'. Dyck notes that critics have puzzled over the apparently perfect typographical altar as the form through which Herbert describes the 'broken' altar of the heart (p. 541). Also see Martin Elsky, 'George Herbert's Pattern Poems and the Materiality of Language'.

15. Strier, *Love Known*, p. 195.
16. See Strier, *Love Known*, p. 48 on Herbert's emphasis on the mysteriousness of this event; also, Kuchar, *Mystery*, pp. 207–14.
17. William Empson, *Seven Types of Ambiguity*, describes the poem as dealing with 'the most complicated and deeply-rooted notions of the human mind' (p. 233). For a discussion of Empson's reading and quarrel with Rosemond Tuve, see Strier, *Resistant Structures*, p. 18.
18. See Tuve, *A Reading of George Herbert*, esp. pp. 24–5. Tuve's argument is for a conservative and 'tradition'-driven Herbert, a view challenged by Strier in *Resistant Structures*, pp. 13–26. Strier's point is that tradition can be invoked and challenged rather than simply reinscribed. The reference to the Reproaches seems to be on solid ground either way.
19. Sibbes, *A Miracle of Miracles, or Christ in our nature*, B3v–B4r, emphasis original.
20. P. G. Stanwood has explored some of the same issues of Herbert's treatment of time that I am concerned with here. See his 'Time and Liturgy in Herbert's Poetry'. For other treatments of time in *The Temple*, see Mark Taylor, *The Soul in Paraphrase*, pp. 76–84; Hannah Eagleson, 'Inhabiting Time: Donne, Herbert, and the Individual Body'; William Bonnell, 'Anamnesis: The Power of Memory in Herbert's Sacramental Vision'; Stanley Stewart, 'Time and *The Temple*'.
21. On the location of the poem in *The Temple*, see Herbert, *English Poems*, ed. Wilcox, p. 381.
22. See my *Image Ethics*, pp. 124–5.
23. Kuchar, *Mystery*, p. 14. Kuchar is drawing on a significant body of scholarship, beginning in the 1990s, that has reshaped our understanding of the theological character of some of Herbert's most important contemporaries, including Richard Sibbes and Lancelot Andrewes. Consistently indebted to Calvin, the understanding of late Elizabethan and early Stuart theology that has emerged is one that gradually became more open to an emphasis on the inscrutability of God.

24. Throughout *Love Known*, Strier argues that Herbert rejected covenant theology as compromised Calvinism in favour of an unmediated form of Calvinism that is closer to Luther. In 'Assurance' Strier sees Herbert's emphasis to be on 'God's promises and not . . . a "covenant"' (p. 112). Strier's argument is based largely on Perry Miller's influential account of covenant theology in 'The Marrow of Puritan Divinity'. The idea that covenant theology was a departure from Calvinism is rejected by Lisa Gordis, 'The Experience of Covenant Theology in George Herbert's 'The Temple'. Gordis's argument is that Herbert struggled with rather than resisted or rejected covenant theology.

25. Kuchar, *Mystery*, p. 120.

26. Gordis, 'Experience', p. 391, quoting Michael McGiffort, 'Grace and Works: The Rise and Division of Covenant Divinity in Elizabethan Puritanism', p. 478. George Gifford, *A Short Treatise against the Donatists of England Whom We Call Brownists* (1590), A2r.

27. Gordis, 'Experience', p. 391, quoting John von Rohr, *The Covenant of Grace in Puritan Thought*, p. 1.

28. Strier, *Love Known*, pp. 4–5. Strier does acknowledge that Herbert's poetry is 'not entirely free from this strain' (i.e. the connection between sensuality and sin).

29. Wilcox notes that the poem was preceded by 'Mortification' in the Williams MS, in which it was titled 'The Publican'.

30. Wilcox notes the connection to 'Easter Wings', in which the speaker hopes to rise with God's wing: 'If I imp my wing on thine' (19). I take this up below.

31. See Stanley Fish, *The Living Temple: George Herbert and Catechizing*.

32. Dee, *Preface to Euclid*, *4v.

33. Wilcox notes that Michael Schoenfeldt still sees an attempt to bargain on the part of the speaker here (*Prayer and Power: George Herbert and Renaissance Courtship*, p. 90). I agree that the speaker remains apart from the spiritual purity sought, dependent on grace to truly free him from the doubts that trouble the early stanzas of the poem. Compare the

desired assistance yearned for here (in an almost Donnean mode) to 'Grace', which compares the falling of the dew on grass, a commonplace that cannot be effected by the grass, to the falling of God's grace on man, asking God not to be out-done by the dew, and thus emphasising again the inadequacy of the comparison chosen. 'Grace' draws again on the inad-equacy of the earthly agent to effect his salvation, but its tone is less equivocal.

34. See Paul Cefalu's discussion of the Holy Paraclete in Johan-nine theology, *Johannine Renaissance*, ch. 3. Cefalu highlights the role of the Paraclete as protection against 'backsliding and tribulations' (p. 131).

35. Strier, *Love Known*, p. 72. Strier's reading of the poem as a positive celebration of grace is pitched against Stanley Fish's argument that it explores the problems of faith (Fish, *Living Temple*). Strier notes that the final two lines of the poem can't be assigned, as they could either be a continuation of the friend's interjection or the speaker's reflection.

36. Clearing one's vision is a recurrent theme in *The Temple*, often figured, following scripture, as dust in one's eyes. See, especially, 'Frailty', and 'Ungratefulness'.

37. See Amy Charles, *A Life of George Herbert*, p. 141.

38. Herbert draws on the sense of the term as indicative of mate-rial instability. See *OED* 'frail, transitory', adj. 4.

39. Strier connects the two poems. See *Love Known*, p. 129.

40. See Waldron, *Reformations of the Body*, on the Reformation emphasis on the living body as representative of God's crea-tive power (p. 24 and *passim*). John Foxe records the follow-ing in a dialogue between Nicholas Ridley and Hugh Latimer on the subject of images in churches in the 1583 edition of *Actes and Monuments*: 'What concord hath christ with Beliall? Either what part hath the beleuer with the Infidel? or how agreeth the temple of God with images? For ye are the temple of the liuing God as God himselfe hath sayde: I will dwell among them, and will be theyr God, and they shalbe my people' (2 Cor. 6: 14; Foxe, *Actes and Monuments*, bk. 11, p. 1746).

41. A typical account is found in Thomas Rogers, *The English Creede* (1585): Article 19 Of the Church: Proposition 1: 'There is a Church of Christ, not only inuisible, but also visible' (pt. 1, p. 55).
42. Dyck, 'Altar, Heart, Title Page', makes this point persuasively.
43. Richard Strier argues the poem 'is not about windows', a position I take issue with below. See Strier, 'Ironic Ekphrasis', p. 101.
44. Ibid., p. 103.
45. Ibid.
46. Following I. A. Richards (*The Philosophy of Rhetoric*), Marcel Danesi describes the interaction: the referents of both the tenor and vehicle 'retain a separate part of their meanings but create a new meaning domain which generates an array of shared semantic attributes' (*Vico, Metaphor, and the Origin of Language*, pp. 124–5).
47. On Herbert and sensuous response, see Michael Schoenfeldt, 'Herbert and Pleasure'. Schoenfeldt notes that despite the attention to suffering, '*The Temple* nevertheless includes a remarkable investment in sensuous and sensual pleasures' (pp. 145–6). Also see Kimberly Johnson, *Made Flesh: Sacrament and Poetics in Post-Reformation England*, ch. 1; Taylor, *Soul in Paraphrase*, esp. ch. 3; and Robert Whalen, *Poetry of Immanence: Sacrament in Donne and Herbert*.
48. Ceri Sullivan has documented Herbert's close involvement with the upkeep of church properties in 'George Herbert's Building Works'.
49. *A Select Library of Nicene and Post-Nicene Fathers of the Church*, vol. 8, pt. 2, p. 53.
50. Foxe, *Actes and Monuments* (1583 edn), DDDDD4v.
51. John Jewel, *The Second Tome of Homilies* (1570), D6r–D6v.
52. 'Ordinance for removing superstitious Pictures, Images, & etc'. *Journal of the House of Lords*, vol. 6, p. 200.
53. *A Short Catechism for Householders* (1582), quoted in Aston, *England's Iconoclasts*, p. 458.
54. See Summers, *George Herbert*, pp. 50–1.
55. See, for example, the critical disagreement between Strier (*Love Known*, p. 150) who argues that the poem could

have been 'written by an iconoclast', and Clifford Davidson, who stresses Herbert's defence of the physical church,
and windows in particular ('George Herbert and Stained
Glass Windows').

56. Danesi, *Vico*, p. 52.

57. Giambattista Vico, *The New Science of Giambattista Vico:
Unabridged Translation of the Third Edition (1744)*, p. 117,
§376. Sidney's discussion of *Vates* in the *Defence* is along the
same lines.

58. Vico, *New Science*. On the connection to Bacon and Herbert
on the idea of the truth value of fables, see Arnold Stein,
George Herbert's Lyrics, pp. xxx–xxxvii. Stein notes that
there is an assumption in Bacon that 'the expressions of the
"pre-logical" mind criticize what the mind has made of itself
and that the original is somehow real in a way that the conscious intellect is not' (p. xxiii).

59. Danesi, *Vico*, p. 52. Danesi's argument about Vico's theory
of metaphor is that it stresses 'the iconic and verbal parts of
the brain' (p. 132), rather than associating metaphor with
language primarily. Metaphor transforms percepts into concepts, but 'Percepts are formed at the deep level of consciousness as iconically transformed sense impressions and affective
responses' (p. 132).

60. Freeman, 'The Aesthetics of Human Experience', p. 722.

61. Freeman, 'Aesthetics', p. 723.

62. Vico, *New Science*, p. 60, §120.

63. Andrewes, Easter Sermon, No. 15, qtd in Brian Cummings,
The Literary Culture of the Reformation, p. 317.

64. Vico, *New Science*, p. 60, §122.

65. Herbert, *Complete English Poems*, ed. Tobin, p. 209.

66. Even as he admits that Herbert uses 'an ostentatiously technical term' that refers to a very specific material process, Strier
argues that 'all this annealing, etc. is not "within" glass, but
"within / The Holy Preachers"' ('Ironic Ekphrasis', p. 102).
Strier misses a step here as only through his own very careful
analytical transfer of the material process to the metaphorical
target can Strier make sense of what is obviously a line about
the annealing of a story (a narrative image) into a stained

glass window. Even if we accept that the comparison is to the combinatory effect of God's grace and virtuous life in the Holy Preacher, the transfer from window to preacher in the metaphoric process must come after one has an understanding of the process of annealing a story into glass.

67. Herbert, *Complete English Poems*, p. 209.
68. Ibid.
69. Ibid., pp. 210–11.
70. Morrissey, 'Scripture, Style, and Persuasion in Seventeenth-Century English Theories of Preaching', p. 691.
71. See Sullivan, 'Herbert's Building Works', on the importance of 'annealing' as a marker of Herbert's direct reference to the material processes for making stained glass in the early modern period by painting and annealing (pp. 184–5).
72. Vico writes, 'The most luminous and therefore the most necessary and frequent [trope] is metaphor. It is most praised when it gives sense and passion to insensate things . . . by which the first poets attributed to bodies the being of animate substances, with capacities measured by their own, namely sense and passion, and in this way made fables of them. Thus every metaphor so formed is a fable in brief' (*New Science*, p. 129, §404, also quoted in Freeman, 'Aesthetics', p. 722). Vico's title is a reference to Bacon's *Novum Organon*, and he developed his first four axioms after Bacon's four idols (see *Giambattista Vico: Keys to the New Science*, ed. Thora Ilin Bayer and Donald Phillip Verene, p. 8).
73. Cefalu, *Johannine Renaissance*, p. 195.
74. On this point, see Kuchar, *Mystery*, p. 148. Kuchar connects the poem to 'The Bunch of Grapes' and notes its emphasis on participatory reading.
75. See Johnson, *Made Flesh*, pp. 47–9 and Whalen, *Poetry of Immanence*, pp. 130–1; Elsky, 'Materiality of Language', p. 253.
76. OED 6a. The full definition continues: 'which are then said to be tinctured; the quintessence, spirit, or soul of a thing. *universal tincture*, the Elixir' (emphasis original). Wilcox notes this sense, but excludes 'supposed' from the beginning of the definition.

77. Eggert, *Disknowledge*, considers 'The Elixir' Herbert's poem 'most explicitly on the subject of the Eucharist' (p. 97), and notes that the poem turns attention back to the material substance of the Holy Supper. The claim is a bit surprising, as the two poems entitled 'The H. Communion' (B and W) are the most directly concerned with the Eucharist. I discuss Herbert's attitude to the Eucharist in more detail in the next section.

78. See Wilcox for the range of associations, pp. 642–3.

79. 'The Foil' is another example in which Herbert invokes 'above' and 'below' only to complicate the hierarchy.

80. Vendler, quoted in *English Poems of George Herbert*, ed. Wilcox, p. 337.

81. The Latin translation on which Herbert worked was published in 1623 as *De augmentis scientiae*.

82. Kuchar, *Mystery*, identifies this poem as Herbert's 'greatest warning against turning mysteries into problems' (p. 227). Elsewhere, Kuchar notes that Herbert was well aware of Augustine's warning that it 'is a miserable bondage of the soul to take the signs in the stead of things that be signified; and not to have the power to lift up the eye of the mind above the bodily creature' (Kuchar, 'Poetry and the Eucharist in the English Renaissance', p. 131; Kuchar quotes St. Augustine, *On Christian Doctrine*, cited in John Jewel, 'Of Real Presence', in *The Works of John Jewel* [Cambridge: Cambridge University Press, 1845], p. 448).

83. Kuchar, *Mystery*, p. 229.

84. Kuchar groups Kierkegaard, Heidegger and Gadamer on the side of phenomenological hermeneutics against deconstructionists such as Derrida and de Man (*Mystery*, p. 229).

85. See, in particular, Whalen's description of Herbert's efforts to fuse material and spiritual aspects of experience (*Poetry of Immanence*, pp. 145, 148).

86. For a discussion of temporality and form in this poem, see Barbara Herrnstein Smith, *Poetic Closure: A Study of How Poems End*, pp. 112–17.

87. On the poem's use of synaesthesia, see Kuchar, *Mystery*, pp. 239–44.

88. Ibid., p. 249.
89. In addition to Eggert, *Disknowledge*, Johnson, *Made Flesh*, Whalen, *Poetry of Immanence* and Cefalu, *Johannine Renaissance*, important discussions of Herbert's attitude towards the Eucharist include Sophie Read, *Eucharist and the Poetic Imagination in Early Modern England*; Ryan Netzley, *Reading, Desire, and the Eucharist in Early Modern Religious Poetry*; Donald R. Dickson, 'Between Transubstantiation and Memorialism: Herbert's Eucharistic Celebration'; and R. V. Young, 'Herbert and the Real Presence'.
90. Hunter, '"With Winges of Faith": Herbert's Communion Poems', p. 57. Hunter cites C. A. Patrides' comment that 'The Eucharist is the marrow of Herbert's sensibility' (Patrides, ed., *The English Poems of George Herbert* [Towson, NJ: Rowan & Littlefield, 1975], p. 17).
91. Cefalu, *Johannine Renaissance*, p. 69. As Whalen, *Poetry of Immanence*, puts it: 'Herbert was among those English divines whose reluctance to articulate explicitly the *modus* of divine presence did not prevent them from revering the material aspects of sacramental ritual' (p. 114). Katherine Eggert notes Herbert's treatment of the Host elsewhere in *The Temple*: 'Just as "The Agony" ends with an airy and inconclusive wave toward the physical connection between Christ's blood and the Holy Communion's wine, "The Elixir" stops at the moment it declares the Eucharist the philosopher's stone, with no elaboration of what properties in the stone effect transmutation.' In Eggert's view, especially considering his friendship with Bacon, 'Herbert's profound interest in nature ought not to stop when it comes to the makeup of natural matter' (*Disknowledge*, p. 98).
92. See Cefalu, *Johannine Renaissance*, p. 74.
93. Hunter, 'Communion Poems', makes the argument for Herbert's debt to Calvinism. Strier's argument for Herbert's thoroughgoing Lutheranism appeared almost simultaneously, though Strier is clear that Herbert's Lutheranism is consonant with aspects of Calvinism (see *Love Known*, p. xv). On the complications arising from the Calvinist elaboration of Luther's thought, see Cummings, *Grammar and Grace*, pp. 232–80, and on Herbert in particular, pp. 308–27.

94. Cummings, *Grammar and Grace*, p. 322.

95. Tuve makes the case for Herbert's reliance on conventional aspects of the medieval Christian tradition in *A Reading of George Herbert*. See Strier, *Resistant Structures*, ch. 1, for a trenchant critique of Tuve's argument.

96. Ceflau, *Johannine Renaissance*, p. 69.

97. Cummings, *Grammar and Grace*, p. 327.

98. Bacon, *De Augmentis Scientiarum*, in *The Philosophical Works of Francis Bacon*, ed. Robertson, p. 634. This is the work that Herbert had a role in translating. See 'Spedding's Preface', in Robertson, p. 416, and Charles, *A Life*, p. 78.

99. Strier, *Love Known*, p. 82.

100. See Strier, who notes that *agape* is a creating power (*Love Known*, p. 79), and Cefalu, *Johannine Renaissance*, ch. 4.

101. See *OED*, Discharge, 1.a. 'To remove a load', 2.a. 'To relieve of something burdensome', and 2.c. 'To put an end to'.

PART III

THINKING

CHAPTER 8

COGNITION AND ITS OBJECTS, OR IDEAS AND THE SUBSTANCE OF SPIRIT(S)

Idea is a bodilesse substance, which of it selfe hath no subsistence, but giveth figure and forme unto shapelesse matters, and becommeth the very cause that bringeth them into shew and evidence.

Socrates and Plato suppose, that these *Idea* bee substances separate and distinct from Matter, howbeit, subsisting in the thoughts and imaginations of God – that is to say, of Minde and Understanding.

Aristotle admitteth verily these formes and *Idea*, howbeit, not separate from matter, as being the patterns of all that which God hath made.

The Stoicks, such as were the scholars of *Zeno*, have delivered, that our thoughts and conceits were the *Idea*.

Plutarch, *Morals*, trans. Philemon Holland[1]

And now we might add something concerning a certain most subtle Spirit which pervades and lies hid in all gross bodies; by the force and action of which Spirit the particles of bodies mutually attract one another at near distances, and cohere, if contiguous; and electric bodies operate to greater distances, as well repelling as attracting the neighbouring corpuscles; and light is emitted, reflected, refracted, inflected, and heats bodies; and all sensation is excited, and the members of animal bodies move at the command of the will, namely, by the vibrations of this Spirit, mutually propagated along the solid filaments of the nerves, from the outward organs of sense to the brain, and from the brain into the muscles. But these are things that cannot be explained in few words, nor are we furnished with that sufficiency of experiments which is required to an accurate determination and demonstration of the laws by which this electric and elastic Spirit operates.

Sir Isaac Newton, conclusion to
Principia Mathematica[2]

The Naturalists have been engaged in thinking about Nature. They have not attended to the fact that they were thinking. The moment one attends to this it is obvious that therefore something other than nature exists.

C. S. Lewis, *Miracles*[3]

In sonnet 44, Shakespeare uses what might be called a thought experiment to explore the relationship between mental activity and embodied experience in elemental terms:

If the dull substance of my flesh were thought,
Injurious distance should not stop my way,
For then despite of space I would be brought,
From limits far remote, where thou dost stay.
No matter then, although my foot did stand
Upon the farthest earth removed from thee,
For nimble thought can jump both sea and land
As soon as think the place where he would be.
But ah, thought kills me that I am not thought,
To leap large lengths of miles when thou art gone,
But that, so much of earth and water wrought,
I must attend time's leisure with my moan,
   Receiving naught by elements so slow
   But heavy tears, badges of either's woe.

Shakespeare defines 'thought' by its lack of materiality here, its ability to operate outside of the temporal and spatial limitations that define experience in the material world. Ironically, only through reflection on embodiment is the speaker reminded that the dream of thought's freedom is unattainable to one bound by the 'dull substance' of 'flesh'. The movement of the poem is Herbertian. Just as the liberatory realisation of immaterial thought can be conceived of and admired, it fades from view, serving as a reminder of the absolute distance separating mortal, temporal existence from something truly free, immaterial, divine.[4]

In the following sonnet, Shakespeare approaches the distinction from the other direction:

> The other two, slight air and purging fire,
> Are both with thee, wherever I abide,
> The first my thought, the other my desire:
> These present-absent with swift motion slide.
> For when these quicker elements are gone
> In tender embassy of love to thee,
> My life, being made of four, with two alone
> Sinks down to death, oppressed with melancholy,
> Until life's composition be recured
> By those swift messengers returned from thee,
> Who even but now come back again assured
> Of thy fair health, recounting it to me.
>   This told, I joy; but then, no longer glad,
>   I send them back again and straight grow sad.

If the earthly, mortal speaker is anchored to place and time primarily by the heavy elements of earth and water, it is the 'other two', air and fire, that promise something beyond the prison of the body. Indeed, as we saw repeatedly in the previous section, despite the early modern Christian's condition, condemned for a time to live in an afflicted state of imperfection and sin, the alternative was very much available to contemplation if not experience. The swiftness of air and purgative nature of fire both characterise the immaterial as closely as is possible in the language of mortal, material experience. In sonnet 45, the lighter elements offer what might be called a glimpse or brush with immateriality, briefly resulting in freedom from melancholy and imperfection; assured of the 'addressee's health', the speaker's life is 'recured', suggesting a reconstitution, a putting back together of that which had been separated, presumably by the very distinction between 'dull flesh' and the 'swift messengers' that fly between the speaker and the addressee.

The Separate Worlds of Sense and Thought

The separability of thoughts from bodies was a crucial question in the period. Faculty psychology explained that thinking involved the embodied activity of cognition, through which the mental processing of sense experience produced knowledge. It was a complex discourse developed over centuries. Even so, the explanation that such modally different 'things' as the objects of sense could become ideas through a kind of transformative process raised questions about the nature of those things. How can a thought produced by embodied cognition (sensuous interaction with the material world) subsist when the material stimulus is no longer present? If thought is dependent on sensation, how can we think about things we have never seen or experienced through the senses? Even more troubling, how can we think about things that don't, and possibly can't, exist? Such questions all stem from the central unanswered question: How do sensible things (material things) *interact* with the thoughts we have about them (mental things)? These questions preoccupied philosophers and physicians throughout the Middle Ages and continued to play a central role in theories of cognition in the early modern period. They provide the tension that drives some of the most memorable scenes in Shakespeare's plays: Macbeth's struggle with a 'dagger of the mind' (2.1.38), for example, or Brutus's contemplation of the assassination of Caesar, in which he describes his thought as a 'phantasma' existing in the 'interim', 'Between the acting of a dreadful thing / and the first motion' (2.1.63–5).[5]

For medieval thinkers, the ancient concept of the *phantasm*, Brutus's 'phantasma', played a critical role in providing answers to the questions raised above. The phantasm remained a key component of early modern theories of cognition, the legacy of a productive synthesis of Aristotelian metaphysics, Galenic humoralism, Arabic natural philosophy and medicine, and scolastic theology. The term corresponds roughly to what we would now call a 'mental image', though in medieval and early modern natural philosophy and medicine it is a highly technical term that undergoes a variety of modifications over the course of its development. Giorgio Agamben traces the term to Plato's *Philebus* in which the philosopher describes as *phantasms* the images of things drawn in the soul by the artist phantasy.[6] The subject of the dialogue at this moment is the problem of accurate perception in time. The example Socrates offers is when one tries to determine what an object is at a distance while walking towards it. The observer may first ask herself what the object may be, and then silently try out different possibilities – it is a 'carving', for example. At this moment, Socrates claims, the mind is 'like a book':

> I think memory interacting with perception together with the things undergone in connection with them write as it were statements in our minds (*psyche*). When what is undergone writes the truth (*alethes*) we acquire true (*alethes*) judgements or statements; when this as it were internal scribe of ours writes falsehoods, the result is the opposite of the truth (*alethes*).[7]

Plato adds another layer in the mind, 'another worker', 'A painter, who follows the scribe and paints pictures in the mind (*psyche*) of what the scribe writes.'[8] These painted images, in familiar Platonic fashion, are thus twice removed from reality. Clarifying for his interlocutor, Protarchus, Socrates explains: 'I am thinking of when a person isolates what he previously judged or said from sight or any other form of perception and as it were sees in his mind's eye the images of what was judged and stated.'[9] Plato's interest here is ultimately in the true or false pleasure one derives from this experience, but for the present purpose it is important to consider the idea that one can 'isolate' images in the 'mind's eye' and that these images are the objects of contemplation concerning judgements. If these images or phantasms are isolated from perceptual experience, are they immaterial or merely internalised in the material body in a manner that cordons them off from that experience?

This question is central to the development of the cognitive theory that would ultimately make its way to early modern England. The first step was Aristotle's elaboration on the role of the phantasm in his theory of cognition, explicitly addressing, though not resolving, the question of its materiality. As Agamben notes, what appear to be metaphors in Plato's hands Aristotle has 'in a certain sense taken literally, and inserted into an organic psychological theory, in which the phantasm has a very important function'.[10] Agamben refers here to the development of the concept in *De anima*, in which he gives us the dictum that all ideas derive from sense:

> The objects of thought are in the forms that are perceived ... This is also the reason why if one perceived nothing one would learn and understand nothing, and also why it is necessary that, whenever one is contemplating, it is some image that one is contemplating; for the images are like sense-data but without matter.[11]

As Agamben notes, 'The function of the phantasm in the cognitive process is so fundamental that it can in a certain sense be considered the necessary condition of intellection.'[12]

But as Aristotle's final characterisation of the mental images attests, their status is peculiar: they are immaterial ('without matter') but 'like sense-data'. The precise location of the phantasm on the material/immaterial spectrum was a particularly thorny problem for Aristotle's Arabic and scholastic commentators, those who would shape the theories of cognition that remained influential throughout the early modern period. Aristotle leaves open the question of a complete separability of immaterial objects.[13] In an important step for the development of medieval cognitive theory, Avicenna took the Neoplatonic version of the Aristotelian phantasm and developed a hard distinction between the internal and external senses (internal faculties of the soul and the external senses of the body).[14] Avicenna went to great lengths to detail a theory of cognition in which the internal faculties are described as 'disrobing' the phantasm of its material accidents.[15] The movement from external sense experience to internal mental activity is thus a movement from the material to the immaterial. This is necessary in part because Avicenna went well beyond Aristotle in his definition of the rational soul, which the former defined as follows:

This rational soul is a substance subsisting in itself, and is imprinted neither in a human body nor in any other corporeal entity. On the contrary, it is separable and abstracted from material and corporeal entities. It has a certain association with the human body as long as the person is alive, but this association is not like the relation of a thing to its receptacle; it is rather, like the relation of a wielder of an instrument to the instrument. [This substance] comes into existence together with the body but it does not perish when the body perishes and dies.[16]

This definition of the soul works on the same principle as Avicenna's theory of cognition. As Jon McGinnis explains,

> the essence of a material thing is intelligible, contends Avicenna, only to the extent that it has been completely abstracted from those particularizing characteristics that are the concomitants of matter, for example, having a particular shape, size, sensible colour, and so on. Once the essence has been stripped of all the particularizing characteristics, there is a universal, and it is precisely because of the intelligible object's universality that it must be immaterial.[17]

Following Aristotle, self-actualisation and the perfection of the soul requires one to habituate one's self to 'good habits' and the purgation of 'wicked qualities of character', to which Avicenna adds the theological element that this must be done by 'purification through knowledge of God'.[18] The result is that the soul 'becomes like a polished mirror upon which are reflected the forms of things as they are in themselves without any distortion'.[19] Subsequently, Averroës (Ibn Rushd) further complicated the function of the phantasm with the metaphor of a multifaceted mirror. As Agamben explains,

> Averroës showed with the image of the two facets of the mirror that cannot be looked at simultaneously, [that] it is possible to contemplate the phantasm in the imagination (*cogitare*) or the form of the object in the sense, but not both at the same time.[20]

In other words, Averroës effectively used a spatial metaphor to make a point about temporal experience. In the mortal, temporal condition, one can only have access to a succession of perceptual experiences, either sensual or mental (contemplating the form of the sense object or the mental phantasm), but the separation of these two modalities points to their fundamentally different nature: the one, material, available to the senses, the other immaterial, available to the intellect. In the process of describing the aspects of his cognitive theory, Averroës described the mirror as 'the mediating air'.[21] Though in all accounts phantasms facilitated the relationship between the sensible and intelligible – material sense experience in the world and intellection in the rational soul – depending on which authority one followed, they could be either material or immaterial entities.

As Averroës's complex mirror analogy and reference to 'mediating air' suggest, despite intense interest in and debate over the nature of phantasms and their relationship to material sensation and incorporeal ideation, natural philosophers, physicians and theologians could not adequately explain the point of contact between the seemingly immaterial mind and the 'dull substance' of the body except through reference to an intermediary. This intermediary substance was most often indicated by the term 'spirit'. The role of the intermediary spirit is ancient, and it saturates the discourse on cognition into the Enlightenment. In the early modern era, 'spirit' denoted a wide range of things both material and immaterial. The most material of these things were 'natural spirits' responsible for movement in the body, a substance common to humans and 'beasts' alike. At the other extreme was the Holy Spirit, one of the three persons of God, immaterial by definition. In between these poles, 'spirit' designated a complex collection of objects, most of which straddle the divide between material and immaterial, often serving explicitly as an intermediary between the two. Angels and demons were called spirits, as was the animating force in living things, liquor, breath, the soul (sometimes), and as Newton's description attests, that force which is 'hidden' in all material things that enables motion and change.[22] Considering its fluidity of meaning, it is not surprising that 'spirit' has as many figurative uses as it does literal ones: the 'spirit' rather than the 'letter' of the law; the 'spirit' of the age; personality – one's 'spirit' that can't be denied, and so on. My argument in this part of the book is that such multiform senses of spirit reveal an anxiety over the manner in which immaterial forces interact with the world of material things, and that this anxiety served as an engine for poetic innovation concerning the nature of thinking (cognition and ideation) in the period.

Spirit, Spirits and the Holy Spirit

Though the many senses of 'spirit' are diverse enough to make any attempt at discerning commonality challenging, I focus in what follows on some important ways in which the term's most popular uses are related. All senses touch on spirit's 'subtle' nature. This quality accounts for its close affinity with air, and in turn can be seen in its association with breath, and subsequently life. The early modern term 'spirit' elides the ancient distinction signalled by the Greek terms *pneuma* (spirit, wind, breath, soul) and *psyche* (spirit, mind, soul, breath of life, ghost).[23] Though the distinction marked by the two terms in classical texts was often crucial – distinguishing between a world animating force and that associated with an individual animal – it was also muddled by closely associated etymologies and a history of popular usage. The early modern English term 'spirit' (from the Latin *spiritus*, a translation of the Greek *pneuma*) is often used to mark the distinction between material and immaterial things.[24] The *OED* identifies at least three early modern senses of the term that explicitly foreground the distinction between the material and immaterial:

1. Incorporeal or immaterial being, as opposed to body or matter; being or intelligence conceived as distinct from, or independent of, anything physical or material. (I.1.d)
2. The disembodied soul of a (deceased) person, regarded as a separate entity. (I.2.b)

3. The immaterial intelligent or sentient element or part
of a person, frequently in implied or expressed contrast
to the body. (III.11.a)

These three senses align roughly with three seemingly immaterial objects that were the subject of intense scrutiny in the early modern period: supernatural spirits, the soul and the mind. Daemonologists, including John Deacon and John Walker, Sebastian Michaelis, and Pierre Le Loyer, wrote extensively on the existence of supernatural spirits, while theologians of all confessions grappled with the nature of the soul and the tripartite Christian God, and physicians and natural philosophers attended to the problem of embodied cognition and its mental objects.[25] As Elizabeth Harvey notes, 'early modern spirits move transgressively between worlds'.[26]

Theologians understood spirit in its most immaterial sense – as that which underwrites or guides belief in the immaterial and unseen for those bound by mortal materiality. In the description of the puritan divine John Dod:

The spirit 'shall convince the world of sin' (after John the Evangelist), and then make one humble, letting us 'see the corruption of our judgment', how in things belonging to God wee be as bruit beasts, not able to discern things that differ, nor to put a sound difference between good and evil, then doth it let us see that our reason is unreasonable, nay that it is hurtfull unto us, a great enemie to faith, and a great patron of infidelity and unbeleefe.[27]

Theologians also extended this definition of immaterial spirit to the soul, as the Jesuit Robert Persons explains in a philosophical defence of the immortality of the soul. 'Mans soule', he writes,

is a spirit and immateriall substance, whose nature dependeth not of the state of our mortall bodie, for so by experience wee see dailie, that in olde men and wythered sickly

bodies, the minde and soule is more quicke, cleere; preg-
nant, and liuely then it was in youth, when the bodie was
most lustie.[28]

Persons adds that the objects of the soul's 'desire' are also
immaterial:

> The same is also proued by the vnquenchable desire which
> our minde hath of learning, knowledge, wysedome, and
> other such spirituall and immateriall things, wherin her
> thyrst by nature is so great, as it cannot be satisfied in thys
> life, neyther can the obiects of sence and bodily pleasures,
> or any other comoditie or delight of this materiall world,
> content or satiate the restlesse desire of thys immateriall
> creature.[29]

On the other hand, for those most concerned with material
bodies – especially natural philosophers and physicians – the
need to account for phenomena that could not be explained
through observation allowed the ancient theory of material
spirits to persist into the eighteenth century. Seeking to limit
the weight of empirically unconfirmable speculation in causal
accounts, physicians fell back on explanations of invisible
forces that relied on the language of gradation. The point
of contact between mind and body was an extremely subtle stuff, the thinnest of material substances. Such accounts
descended from Galen, though the ancient physician's system
had been filtered through Islamic Aristotelian and medieval
Christian authorities blending theology with Galen's natural
philosophy.

Thus, while the sixteenth-century French physician Jean
Fernal could proclaim in Aristotelian fashion that 'Whatever we perceive in our mind drew its whole origin from
the senses',[30] he would also go on to discuss the connection
between mind and body aided by the most rarefied spirit:

Academics were first to realise that it was impossible for utterly different natures to enter a combining association, except by the intervention of some suitable intermediary. They considered that before our soul ... (the work of the supreme craftsman of things) appeared and entered into this compact solid body, it was clad in some shining body, pure and starlike, as a simple garment, and this, being immortal and eternal, could never be parted from the mind, which could not become an inhabitant of the world without it.

Then they went on to place another body around the mind, a thin and simple one, but rather impure, less shining and bright than the previous one. This one is not the work of the supreme craftsman, but composed from a mixture of elements, particularly the more rarefied ones, from which it acquires the name airy and ethereal. Pent now in these two bodies, the mind is banished into this third body, a mortal and transient one, or rather it is exiled into a foul gloomy prison, and becomes a visitor to the earth, until it bursts out to return nimbly to the freedom of its fatherland, and becomes a citizen of heaven.[31]

The link between the body and the immaterial soul/mind is the most refined form of 'spirit' – an explanation retained from Galenic theory – 'a very suitable link between [body and mind], intervening to reconcile and hold opposed natures together'. This particularly rarefied spirit is able to serve as the link because

it is exceedingly intimate with both, and not being completely devoid of body, can be placed in a course body. But being more rarified and bright, it can be linked to the mind. Sharing thus in both after a fashion, it bonds a nature without body to corporeal nature, the immortal to the mortal, the pure to the impure, the divine to the earthly.[32]

Fernal's evidence for the existence of the most rarified spirit – the intermediary between mind and body – is an absence:

> Anyone who has not yet fully grasped its substance and standing after considering the structure of our body, should visit the arteries, and gaze into the cardiac cavity and the cerebral ventricles; he will see them empty and virtually devoid of humor, but not created so large by nature without a reason; when he turns his mind to them, I think he will soon grasp mentally that a very rarefied air filled them during the animal's life, but while it breathed its last, was so very light that it escaped unperceived.[33]

The theory of the 'breath of life' is familiar here, explaining both the manner in which the soul departs the body and the reason we need to breathe, for according to Fernal, 'If we had no rarefied and spirituous substance in us, there would undoubtedly be hardly any need for us to inhale.'[34]

In his philosophical poem *Nosce Teipsum*, Sir John Davies sums up the need for the intermediary spirit in the process of cognition:

> Then what vast body must we make the *mind*?
> Wherein are men, beasts, trees, towns, seas, & lands,
> And yet each thing a proper place doth find,
> And each thing in the true proportion stands?
> Doubtlesse this could not be, but that she turnes
> Bodies to spirits by *sublimation* strange;
> As fire conuerts to fire the things it burnes,
> As we our meates into our nature change.
> From their grosse *matter* she abstracts the *formes*,
> And drawes a kind of *Quintessence* from things,
> Which to her proper nature she transformes,
> To beare them light on her celestiall wings;
> This doth she, when from things particular,
> She doth abstract the *vniuersall* kinds,

Which bodilesse, and immateriall are,
And can be lodg'd but onely in our minds;
And thus from diuerse accidents and acts,
Which do within her obseruation fall,
She goddesses, and powres diuine abstracts,
As *Nature, fortune,* and the *vertues* all.[35]

In order for the logic of spatial bodies to persist despite the
ability of the mind to hold multitudes, Davies notes the need
for a mysterious transformation to occur, a process 'by sub-
limation strange' that turns bodies to spirits. Thoughts here
are explicitly defined as abstractions, '*formes*' 'Bodiless and
immateriall', begotten in the mind of 'her proper nature',
while the 'diverse accidents and acts' in the material realm
serve as their raw material. Facilitating their interrelation are
the spirits, an order closer to the abstract forms, but still in
touch with the gross matter from which they are sublimated.

Such spirits make an appearance at a crucial moment in the
closet scene in *Hamlet* at precisely the moment when Hamlet
is confronted by another kind of spirit, the ghost of his father.
This is, of course, the second time in the play that Hamlet
sees the Ghost, but it is the first in which he is alone in seeing
the apparition. When Hamlet demands of Gertrude, 'Do you
see nothing there?' her response is unequivocal: 'Nothing at
all, yet all there is I see' (3.4.136). Gertrude affirms a sensuous material ontology – everything that exists is perceptible.
This is partly what has underwritten the Ghost's believability
up to this point, as the multiple witnesses in the earlier scenes
seemed to confirm that the spirit is not a figment of Hamlet's imagination. What Hamlet apparently sees in the closet
scene is the same spirit, his father's ghost, visible to him 'in
his habit as he lived'. But now Hamlet's vision has taken
on a dubious material reality, for the vision appears to him
alone.[36] Seeing nothing, Gertrude invokes the other kind of
spirit. Watching Hamlet 'bend his eye on vacancy', she sees

him changed: 'Forth at your eyes your spirits wildly peep'.[37]
The appearance of one kind of spirit, the Ghost, leads to visible evidence of another, specifically Hamlet's bodily spirits,
a collection of highly refined material substances invisible to
the eye but internally present, and here apparently signalled
by Hamlet's facial expression, which is changed by their
presence and power.[38]

If bodily spirits were clearly material, even if only 'subtly'
so, ghosts, demons and angels were consistently considered
to be immaterial spirits, incorporeal entities that may or may
not have the ability to take on material form. Indeed, Hamlet calls on such sprits to protect him from the spirit of the
Ghost on his first encounter ('Angels and ministers of grace
defend us!'). The question of whether demonic sprits could
have bodies was deeply contentious and closely related to
the question of the embodiment of Angels. Theologians had
to accept that angels were once able to take on bodily form,
due to scriptural references, but by the Renaissance most rel-
egated this ability to the time of miracles, long past.[39] In the
case of non-angelic sprits, the concern was with the material
presence of demons and the threat of demonic possession,
which some similarly dismissed as no longer possible. For
those holding a belief in demons, the question of possession –
using the body of a person temporarily – was a way to finesse
the question. In his *Pneumalogia*, appended to an account
of a possession trial in France, Sebastian Michaelis explains
that spirits are to be discerned primarily from their effects in
the material world:

> This question bereth with it more difficulties then any other,
> either in philosophy or divinity next after the question of
> Divine nature: first because spirits do approach nearer unto
> the nature of God then any other creature; as also because
> it is impossible to see or comprehend them but onely by
> their effects.[40]

Michaelis makes clear that it is the lack of bodies that makes them so difficult to comprehend:

> Since then spirits have no bodies, they cannot be seene by the eye nor received into any external sense: and thereupon it ariseth, that a man cannot forme them in his imagination, unless it bee because we see them simply by their effects.[41]

The fact that spirits were viewed as problematic *substances* is particularly important for the present discussion because spirits of this supernatural sort seemed to be able to move between the realms of the immaterial and material in ways that complicated the very distinction between the two. The kind of spirits to which Gertrude refers convey a similar ambiguity. If demons and angels descend from the immaterial to the material realm, the 'bodily spirits' to which Gertrude attributes Hamlet's frenzied mind approach the material/immaterial divide from the other direction. In medical discourse, natural, vital and animal spirits served as the animating forces of all living things. The lower forms of these spirits – natural and vital – were responsible for animation and involuntary actions like breathing and digestion, and they were literally considered more material than those attending on thought and will, those animal spirits located in the brain. The French surgeon Ambroise Paré, writing at the end of the sixteenth century, explains the material gradations of the medical spirits as follows: the most refined is the animal spirit, so called 'not because it is the Life [margin: anima], but the chief and prime instrument thereof . . . it hath a most subtile and Aery substance' which is 'made and laboured in the windings and foldings of the veins and Artereyes of the braine'.[42] When the animal spirit is obstructed, the person can appear lifeless, 'sometimes wanting both sence and motion'.[43] 'Next to the animal spirit in dignity' is the 'vital' spirit, which originates in the heart and provides essential heat to the body through the blood. At the bottom of the spectrum we find the natural spirit, which 'hath its station in the Liver and Veins. It is more grosse and dull than the other, and inferior to them in the dignitie of the Action and the excellencie of the use'. Whereas the role of the vital spirit is to 'nourish the heate which resides fixed in the substance of each part [of the body]', the natural spirit serves 'to helpe the concoction both of the whole body, as also of each severall part, and to carry blood and heate to them'.[44] Only at the most refined level were the animal spirits able to bridge the gap between the material body and the immaterial soul.

By the end of the sixteenth century, the scholastic solutions to the problems of material/immaterial interaction were becoming strained. Nevertheless, objections to the seemingly contradictory uses of the term 'spirit' throughout the period, explicitly denoting both material and immaterial substances – often when referring to the same objects – were momentarily held in suspension by virtue of a theory of gradation inherited from the medieval tradition: the soul was spirit in its purest form, while the more nutritive functions of spirit resulted from mixture with corruptible material. Consider the description of spirits in Anglicus Bartholomaeus' thirteenth-century *De proprietatibus rerum*, translated into English by John Trevisa and published in the sixteenth century as *Batman upon Bartholome*:

> Then one and the same spirit corporeal, subtill, and airily, through diverse lims, is named by diverse names. For by working in the liver it is called Spiritus Naturalis, in the heart Vitalis, and in the head Spiritus animalis. We may not believe that this spirit is mans reasonable soule: but more truly the chaire or upholder thereof, and proper instrument. For by meane of such a spirit, the soule is joined to the body: and without the service of such a spirit, no act, the soule may perfectly exercise in the bodie.[45]

As we have seen in the examples from Jean Fernal and Ambroise Paré, this account remained current throughout the sixteenth century. In the first decades of the seventeenth century, we find the medical encyclopaedist Helkiah Crooke describing the bodily spirits as 'the thinnest of substances', following the medieval authorities on the function of the spirit in the relationship between the body and the soul. Yet Crooke acknowledges that the understanding of spirits is by no means settled science: 'Because in the Schooles of Physicians the Controversie concerning the naturall spirit is sufficiently bandyed, I will not spend much time in a thing so notorious: onely for their satisfaction to whom these subtleties are most strange and lesse obvious, I will give a taste or short assay concerning the nature of spirits':

> the distance is not so great between the highest Heaven and the lowest Earth, as is the difference betwixt the Soule and the Bodye. It was therefore verie necessarie that a spirite should bee created, by whose intermediate Nature, as it were by a strong though not indissoluble bonde the Divine soule might be tyed to the bodie of earth . . . Our definition of a spirit shall be this, *A subtle and thinne body always mooveable, engendered of blood and vapor, and the vehicle or carriage of the Faculties of the soule.*[46]

Crooke's solution for bridging the 'great distance' is to follow Galen in defining the corporeal spirit as the 'thinnest of all' substances, but a material substance nonetheless.[47] The semantic overlap between these subtle bodies and those of spirits and demons is unavoidable.

A familiar passage from *Macbeth* is helpful in making my point. Consider Lady Macbeth's invocation of spirits in act 1:

> Come, you spirits
> That tend on mortal thoughts, unsex me here,
> And fill me from the crown to the toe top-full

Of direst cruelty! Make thick my blood;
Stop up the access and passage to remorse,
That no compunctious visitings of nature
Shake my fell purpose, nor keep peace between
The effect and it! Come to my woman's breasts,
And take my milk for gall, you murdering ministers,
Wherever in your sightless *substances*
You wait on nature's mischief! (1.5.38–52)

A conventional reading of the passage is that Lady Macbeth
calls on demonic spirits to give her the will to murder. Such a
reading interprets her invocation as externally directed, and is
usually supported with the description of the spirits as 'sightless substances' that 'tend on mortal thoughts'. But of course,
such spirits can also refer to the material spirits that served
as the guardians of the soul's faculties in the body, the spirits
that Aristotle described as consisting 'of the tiniest particles,
so small that each individual bubble cannot be detected by the
eye'. They are sightless, unseen, invisible, but not immaterial.
Rather than a purely occult conception of immaterial spirits –
associated explicitly with witchcraft – or an overtly materialist
psychology in which the physical spirits in the body are responsible for all things emotional and cognitive, the passage draws
on a productive confusion that suggests both were equally
powerful explanations of otherwise mysterious phenomena.

Thinking Spirit in Cymbeline

Before turning to Shakespeare's staging of the tension between
embodied cognition, spiritual intermediaries and immaterial
ideas in the following chapters, I want to sum up the previous discussion by reviewing the complex role of spirit in
Shakespeare's *Cymbeline*, a play in which spirit is invoked
in almost all of its contemporary senses. Awakening to the
headless body of the recently slain Cloten in act 4, Imogen
struggles to orient herself to the visible world before her:

> I hope I dream,
> For so I thought I was a cave-keeper
> And cook to honest creatures. But 'tis not so.
> 'Twas but a bolt of nothing, shot at nothing,
> Which the brain makes of fumes. (4.2.296–300)

Imogen's first impulse in the face of this horrific scene is to deny her perceptual experience, hoping it lacks material substance, that it is a 'dream'. Almost immediately abandoning this first impulse, she decides that it is her memory of life with the exiled Belarius, Arveragus and Guiderius that is dream-like, 'a bolt of nothing', 'which the brain makes of fumes'. Intriguingly, after trying to wish the scene away by appealing to the pity of the Gods, she laments 'The dream's here still: even when I wake it is / Without me as within me; not imagined, felt' (4.2.305–6). This 'dream' is not the immaterial 'nothing' of her memory (incidentally, her 'real' experience according to the action of the play); it is the material corpse of the headless man lying beside her in the grass and flowers. In her attempt to reconcile perception and cognition in this scene, Imogen turns frenetically from the material to the immaterial, ultimately settling on terms that combine elements of both. The 'bolt of nothing' which is 'shot at nothing', is made by the brain of something: 'fumes'. Importantly, 'fumes', another term for 'vapours', were a form of 'spirit', a subtle combination of air and moisture, existing on the borderline between the material and the immaterial.[48]

The scene is prefigured by the Queen's doctor, Cornelius, when he describes the potion that has produced the effect Imogen has just experienced. He reveals his true intention to deceive the Queen in a comforting aside:

> I do not like her. She doth think she has
> Strange lingering poisons. I do know her spirit,
> And will not trust one of her malice with
> A drug of such damned nature. Those she has

Will stupefy and dull the sense awhile,
Which first, perchance, she'll prove on cats and dogs,
Then afterward up higher; but there is
No danger in what show of death it makes
More than the locking-up the spirits a time,
To be more fresh, reviving. She is fool'd
With a most false effect; and I the truer,
So to be false with her. (1.5.33–44)

Ironically and unwittingly, after dropping the poison box for
Pisanio to find, the Queen describes the potion accurately.
Though thinking it contains 'most poisonous compounds /
Which are the movers of a languishing death', as Cornelius
has just told her, she tells Pisanio that it is a 'cordial' that has
'Five times redeemed [the King] from death' (1.5.8–9, 64, 63).
The Queen's attempt at deception, describing a poison as a
restorative, echoes Cornelius's deception of the Queen. Why
Pisano trusts her account of the box's contents is one of the
play's more confusing elements, especially considering his disdain for her. Despite his claim that he'll 'choke' himself before
he 'prove untrue' to Posthumus, he goes on to give the box to
Imogen, ostensibly accepting the Queen's account of its contents at face value: 'Here is a box – I had it from the Queen – /
What's in't is precious. If you are sick at sea, / Or stomach-
qualmed at land, a dram of this / Will drive away distemper'
(3.5.187–91). It is this exchange that makes possible the tab-
leaux in which Shakespeare unites life and death, juxtapos-
ing the headless corpse of Cloten with the awakened Imogen,
newly restored to life. The 'show of death' brought on by
the potion, as Cornelius predicted, depended on its power of
'locking up the spirits a time', the same spirits responsible for
restoring the awakened Imogen to 'life'. A doctor, Cornelius
is clearly referring to the bodily spirits.

   The 'locking up' of Imogen's animating spirits, the
bodily humours and 'very rarified air' that give her life,

finds a figurative corollary in the play's subplot involving the kidnapped sons of Cymbeline: Arviragus and Guiderius. Though Belarius raised them in Wales without knowledge of their royal parentage, he bemoans, 'How hard it is to hide the sparks of nature!' – the evidence of their royalty:

> This Polydore,
> The heir of Cymbeline and Britain, who
> The king his father called Guiderius – Jove,
> When on my three-foot stool I sit and tell
> The warlike feats I have done, his spirits fly out
> Into my story: say 'Thus mine enemy fell,
> And thus I set my foot on 's neck,' even then
> The princely blood flows in his cheek, he sweats,
> Strains his young nerves, and puts himself in posture
> That acts my words. The younger brother, Cadwal,
> Once Arviragus, in as like a figure
> Strikes life into my speech, and shows much more
> His own conceiving. (3.3.79, 86–98)

The 'spirits' that 'fly out' into Belarius's story combine several of the senses of the term I have discussed thus far. In a play in which characters are utterly unable to dissemble – a fact that makes it all the more dramatic that Posthumus fails to see that Imogen could never have betrayed him – Guiderius's 'spirits' are something like a projection of his essential self or soul onto his material body.[49] While that essence may remain hidden by the common Welsh weeds he wears, it is discernible in his outward actions, the effects of the spirits on his figure. Here, like his transformed brother, he 'strikes life into [Belarius's] speech', peopling the story of heroism with the body of a prince. This enlivened body is animated by spirits, as is apparent from the physiological effects made visible on his body and interpreted by Belarius as the 'sparks of nature' Guiderius is unable to hide: his 'princely blood flows in his cheek, he sweats, / Strains his young nerves'. The moment highlights the connection between invisible essence (the princeliness that has been hidden in exile) and visible embodiment – the boys' 'figures' animated by the physiological spirits that move their passions.

After Guiderius beheads Cloten to Arviragus's praise, Belarius again notes the hidden workings of nature: 'O thou goddess, / Thou divine Nature, how thyself thou blazon'st / In these two princely boys!' (4.2.168–70). Again focusing on their 'blood', which he sees to be moved ('enchafed'), he considers the connection between the seen and unseen:

> 'Tis wonder
> That an invisible instinct should frame them
> To royalty unlearned, honour untaught,
> Civility not seen from other, valour
> That wildly grows in them, but yields a crop
> As if it had been sowed. (4.2.175–80)

All of this animated, princely blood is soon contrasted to the presumably dis-spirited bodies of both Cloten and Imogen. Marking their return to inanimate materiality, the brothers speak a song in eulogy that is primarily concerned with the disburdening of worldly care upon death.[50] Towards the end of the song, however, their attention turns to spirits of another kind:

> GUIDERIUS No exorciser harm thee,
> ARVIRAGUS Nor no witchcraft charm thee.
> GUIDERIUS Ghost unlaid forbear thee.
> ARVIRAGUS Nothing ill come near thee. (4.2.275–8)

Though the animating spirits have left the bodies of the two (of course, in Imogen's case, only apparently), the uncertain modality in which the spirits of the dead persist raises the spectre of different cares than those experienced in the world they have just left. Where the first part of the song confidently reassures the living of the carefree state to which the departed have passed, the last section highlights an anxiety about the unknowability or inaccessibility of the immaterial spirit world.

This other kind of spirit makes an explicit appearance later in the prison scene when Posthumus is visited by the ghosts of his family and the divine is made manifest in the form of Jupiter descending on an eagle. As many have noted, the scene parallels the one with which I began in which a beleaguered Imogen awakens to what she imagines must be a dream: Posthumus's (actually Cloton's) material body bereft of its animating spirit. In Posthumus's case, the disembodied spirits of his family are presented to him in a dream, which is itself of dubious materiality.[51] The appearance of Jupiter at the behest of the family of ghosts constitutes a breaching of the material world by its immaterial other. The spirits specifically ask that Jupiter 'peep through thy marble mansion', to intervene in Posthumus's earthly suffering.[52] Jupiter's rebuff of the 'petty spirits of region low', coming as it does from a divine source, inflects the play's thematic focus on spirits with the term's religious dimension: 'How dare you ghosts / Accuse the thunderer, whose bolt, you know, / Sky planted, batters all rebelling coasts?' (5.4.63–6). Though the line is given to a pagan god, considering the play's historical setting at the time of the birth of Christ, Jupiter's divinity evokes that of the Christian God. Jupiter's modus operandi, to 'cross' those 'whom best I love', recalls the early modern language of Christian devotion, an allusion that is underscored by Jupiter's claim that under His dominion Posthumus will be 'happier much by his affliction made' (5.4.71, 78).

Upon awakening from his dream, Posthumus ponders the visions he has seen which now lack substance, for awake he 'find[s] nothing' (5.4.99). When he notices the tablet left by Jupiter and placed on his breast by the ghosts of his family, his impulse is to suspect spirits: 'What faeries haunt this ground?'

(5.4.103). The conceptual work that is done by the layering
of different kinds of spirits in the play reflects the way language, and particularly poetic representation, was driven by
the mystery of material–immaterial interaction. In the earlier
scene, made possible by the manipulation of humoral spirits,
Imogen brings her imagination to bear on a material scene
that lacks coherence. In the prison, Posthumus is confronted
with the material trace of an experience with the immaterial.
Each of these encounters is mediated by spirits of differing
kinds. On the one hand, the playwright emphasises the role
of the bodily spirits that raise the blood and sweat of the
princely brothers, and which weaken in Imogen, prompting
her to take the potion designed to 'lock her spirits up'. On
the other, we are invited into a world in which immaterial
spirits guide the events of the world, including an all-encom-
passing divine judge that has already set right the injustices
of the world only now unfolding materially before the eyes
of the mortal characters. That this latter, immaterial spirit is
only accessible indirectly – through dreams or imagination –
helps to explain the profoundly complex interrelatedness of
the various forms of spirit current in the period. The most
refined form of bodily spirits are so 'subtle' that they can
contact the soul, and yet they remain 'bodies'. The 'nothing' left behind to Posthumus after his dream visions turns
out to be something quite important, the material vehicle for
the prophecy later interpreted by the soothsayer, a seer into
other worlds. Similarly, the 'bolt of nothing' that frustrates
Imogen upon her awakening is the product of 'fumes', airy
substances, like spirits. And, of course, Imogen will herself
be described as 'a piece of tender air' in the prophecy left for
Posthumus by Jupiter.

Spirits of many different kinds haunt the language and
action of *Cymbeline*, suggesting that the play's offer of resolution or redemption through revelation may be a consolation
for an audience anxious about the nature of the unseen that

was felt to be so important to daily life. I agree with Elizabeth Harvey when she concludes that in *Cymbeline* and *The Tempest* 'Shakespeare anatomizes liminal states . . . in order to reveal the workings of spirits as a central feature of early modern embodiment.'[53] I would add that in addition to providing insight into the experience of embodiment, Shakespeare's anatomy of liminal states has implications for the period's fascination with what might exceed embodiment – an area of unknowable possibility, utterly inaccessible to sense. It is clear that Shakespeare's approach seeks to 'display the otherwise invisible subtle bodies or spirits that continually shape human experience',[54] though my sense is that this is not always intended to 'reveal' and 'display', that is, to make available in material form. It can also serve to value the mystery of what cannot be revealed. As the significant epistemological shifts of the early modern period had destabilised previous accounts of material and immaterial interaction, the space between widened, opening itself to poetic exploration and innovation. This exploration is the subject of the next two chapters.

Notes

1. Plutarch, *Morals*, trans. Philemon Holland, Yyy5r. This instance is cited by *OED*. See *OED* 'Idea', I.1.

2. Newton, *Newton's Principia*, trans. Andrew Motte, p. 507. First published in Latin as *Philosophiae naturalis principia mathematica* (London, 1687).

3. C. S. Lewis, *Miracles*, p. 51.

4. The connection between the secular and theological understanding of the relationship of sense and thought is unavoidable in the period. Shakespeare's most quoted lines on poetic imagination yoke the two together casually, as the poet glances 'from heaven to earth and earth to heaven' before making something of nothing through imaginative thought, giving 'to airy nothing / A local habitation and a name' (*Midsummer Night's Dream*, 5.1.13, 16–17).

5. Despite the importance of the concept of the phantasm in faculty psychology, this is the only appearance of the term in Shakespeare. See Roychoudhury, *Phantasmatic Shakespeare*, pp. 1–26, and Jonathan Bate, *How the Classics Made Shakespeare*, ch. 10, 'The Defense of Phantasms', pp. 160–84.

6. Agamben, *Stanzas: Word and Phantasm in Western Culture*, p. 74.

7. Plato, *Philebus*, pp. 34–5 (38b–39a).

8. Ibid., p. 35 (39a).

9. Ibid., pp. 35–6 (39a–39b).

10. Agamben, *Stanzas*, p. 75.

11. *De Anima*, trans. Lawson-Tancred, p. 210 (432a).

12. Agamben, *Stanzas*, p. 76.

13. In *De anima* Aristotle writes: 'Abstract objects, as they are called, the mind thinks as if it were thinking the snub-nosed; *qua* snub-nosed, it would not be thought apart from the flesh . . . So when the mind thinks the objects of mathematics, it thinks them as separable though actually they are not. In general, the mind when actively thinking is identical with its objects. Whether it is possible for the mind to think of unextended objects when it is not itself unextended, must be considered later' (*On the Soul*, trans. Hett, p. 179 [431b]). Of Aristotle's closing question, Lawson-Tancred writes, 'It is a question he neither answers himself nor provides us with the materials for answering' (p. 249n125).

14. The key intermediary text here is 'The Theology of Aristotle', an Arabic translation of Plotinus's *Enneads* that attempted to reconcile Plotinus with Aristotle and Christianity and Islam. Its influence explains the interpenetration of Neoplatonic and Aristotelian thought in the Arabic context. See Peter Adamson, *The Arabic Plotinus: A Philosophical Study of 'The Theology of Aristotle'*.

15. See Agamben, *Stanzas*, p. 79.

16. Avicenna (Ibn Sīnā), 'On the Rational Soul', p. 74

17. McGinnis, *Avicenna*, pp. 120–1.

18. Avicenna, 'Rational Soul', p. 74.

19. Ibid., pp. 74–5.

20. Agamben, p. 83. Averroës's position was not without its difficulties, as it led to the controversial argument for a universal intelligence, separated from but accessible by the individual. This would be at the heart of Aquinas's anti-Averroest position.

21. Averroës quoted in Agamben, *Stanzas*, p. 81.

22. There is a wealth of recent scholarship on the medical spirits. For the present purpose, the following are especially important: Clark, *Vanities of the Eye*; Paster, *Humoring the Body*; Katherine Rowe, 'Humoral Knowledge and Liberal Cognition in Davenant's Macbeth'. On the interrelation of different kinds of spirits (though without an emphasis on the theological), see Elizabeth Harvey, 'Passionate Spirits: Animism and Embodiment in *Cymbeline* and *The Tempest*'. Most of these accounts have focused on the material effects of spirits or on the way the unseen was imputed as the force behind embodied experience. My focus here is on maintaining the immaterial as a crucial category motivating the early modern representation of these effects and experiences.

23. Theories of *pneuma* are found in a broad range of ancient works from the Presocratics (elemental air), medical works of Hippocrates and Galen (associated with breath), and the Stoics ('breath of life'). In his *Dictionary* of 1598 John Florio defined *pneuma* as 'a spirit, a winde, a blowing, an inspiration' (Aa3v). On the theories of *pneuma* as deployed in early modern drama, see Christopher Crosbie, *Revenge Tragedy and Classical Philosophy on the Early Modern Stage*.

24. Aristotle connects the 'vital heat' to 'connate *pneuma*' (*On the Generation of Animals*, p. 163 [736a]), which he describes as a compound substance, a mixture of air and moisture, associated especially with semen – 'a compound of *pneuma* and water (*pneuma* being hot air)'. In describing this substance, Aristotle goes on to say that 'the cause of the whiteness of semen is that it is foam, and foam is white, the whitest being that which consists of the tiniest particles, so small that each individual bubble cannot be detected by the eye'. As W. S. Hett

notes, in the Aristotelian system, *connate pneuma* 'formed a link between the immaterial and the material' (*On the Soul*, p. 392).

25. The subject of supernatural spirits was controversial, as it involved taking a position on the extent to which the interpretation of scripture should be undertaken literally. Among the early modern writers to address the issue were John Deacon and John Walker, *Dialogical Discourses of Devils and Spirits* (1601); John Darrell, *A Suruey of Certaine Dialogical Discourses* (1602); King James I (England), *Daemonologie* (1597); and Pierre Le Loyer, *A Treatise of Specters* (1605). Reginald Scot's *Discoverie of Witchcraft* (1584) is among the earliest sceptical treatises on the subject, though many more would follow, the best known to Shakespeare scholars being Samuel Harsnett's *A declaration of egregious popish impostures* (1603). On the controversies, see Kathleen Sands, *Demon Possession in Elizabethan England* and F. W. Brownlow, *Shakespeare, Harsnett, and the Devils of Dehnham*.

26. Harvey, 'Passionate Spirits', p. 372. Harvey's focus is on the relationships among external ghosts and spirits (like the faeries imagined in *A Midsummer Night's Dream*) and internal medical spirits. She argues that 'bodily spirits, ambient air, and external spirits were related not analogically, but through the attenuated touch of the ethereal substance they shared' (p. 370). I extend her argument in the following discussion to include more overtly 'spiritual' spirits, including the Holy Spirit. My aim is, in part, to consider the implications of early modern theological pneumatology for our understanding of *pneuma* in the history of science and medicine. Theological pneumatology can be overtly analogical. On the continued role of spirit theory in debates that continued into the eighteenth century, see Justin E. H. Smith, 'Spirit as Intermediary'.

27. Dod, *Seven Godly Sermons*, Bb3v–Bb4r.

28. Parsons (Persons), *The seconde parte of the booke of Christian exercise* (1590), D2r.

29. Ibid.

30. Fernal, *The Physiologia of Jean Fernal (1567)*, p. 229. Fernal cites Lucretius in defence of this position.

31. Ibid., p. 263.

32. Ibid.

33. Ibid., p. 265.

34. Ibid.

35. Sir John Davies, *Nosce Teipsum* (1599), pp. 24–5.

36. This detail has attracted a great deal of attention, especially because it contrasts with the appearance of the Ghost to Hamlet, Horatio, Bernado and Marcellus on the battlements earlier in the play. The text raises important questions for staging here, as well – for example, is the Ghost visible to the audience?

37. The term 'peep' is telling here, as it carries two primary meanings: to 'emerge or protrude' as well as to perceive with the eyes, 'to steal a glance'. It appears again in *Macbeth*, when Lady Macbeth, after asking for the assistance of 'spirits that tend on mortal thoughts', calls on the night to fall lest 'heaven peep through the blanket of the dark / To cry, "Hold, hold!"' (1.5.51–2). I discuss this passage in more detail below.

38. I explore the relationship between bodily spirits and facial expression in more detail in the next chapter.

39. The age of miracles is loosely identified with the age of the Apostles. In the Reformation, and following Luther, there was scepticism about miracles purportedly performed after the first century. This does not mean that interest in the inexplicable waned. See, for example, Philip M. Soergel, *Miracles and the Protestant Imagination*.

40. Michaelis, *Pneumalogia*, Hh5v. The *Pneumalogia* was originally printed in 1594 in France. In the address 'To the Reader' the English translator 'W. B'. indicates that the only reason for printing the book is to ensure 'that wee may both discerne and deride these fopperies, it has been thought fit, that this Treatise should be turned into the English tongue, that our people may see with what fraffe their neighbors are fedde' (ibid., ¶4r). Despite the apparent rejection of the book's contents, its translation and publication suggests the continued

interest in the nature of spirits, even by educated English readers. The publisher in this case, William Aspley, also published Shakespeare's *Much Ado about Nothing* and would go on to join the partnership responsible for printing the First and Second Folios of Shakespeare.

41. Michaelis, *Pneumalogia*, Hh6r. He goes on to cite Aristotle: 'Aristotle doth affirme and proove, that those few Spirits whom he had knowledge of, were certainly free from any Masse or pressure of bodies, and were substances separated and abstracted from all composition of elements: for well he knew that a corporeall forme ought to be proportioned unto the body wherein it doth act and produce motion' (Hh6v). There is a whole body of scholarship on demons, magic and angels that is relevant to my concerns here, but beyond the scope of the present study. See, for example, Sands, *Demon Possession*; John S. Mebane, *Renaissance Magic and the Return of the Golden Age*; Floyd-Wilson, *Occult Knowledge*; Stuart Clark, *Thinking with Demons*; and Stephen Greenblatt, 'Shakespeare among the Exorcists'.

42. Paré, *The workes of that famous chirurgion Ambrose Parey*, D1v. Paré first published his *Works* in Paris in 1575.

43. Ibid.

44. Ibid.

45. Bartholomaeus, *Batman vppon Bartholome his booke De proprietatibus rerum*, E4r.

46. Crooke, Q3r–Q3v.

47. Ibid., Q3v. For Galen, as James J. Bono explains, *pneuma* ('breath' commonly translated as 'spirit') 'derives chiefly from the air taken into the body (through inspiration) and from the blood . . . It is, consequently, of a corporeal, that is material nature, though the matter in question is of an exceptionally fine and rarified sort, rather like hot vapor.' See his 'Medical Spirits and the Medieval Language of Life', p. 92.

48. The game of vapours in Jonson's *Bartholomew Fair* provides a contemporary example.

49. Everyone is immediately recognised for what they are in this play. When Imogen is disguised as Fidele, for example, the

brothers value her over their father, correctly intuiting their blood relation to her (lacking in their relation to Belarius). Everyone recognises that Cloten is an idiot, the Queen is evil, Imogen is true, and so on.

50. Some have speculated that the actors playing the boys were not good singers, thus prompting the conceit that they would speak the song. Considering the occasion, however, and the relationship of songs to time, and thus mortal life, and 'air' (songs as *ayres*), speaking the song at death is thematically appropriate. On the important ways that mediation obtains in differences between music, speech and written word, see Trudell, *Unwritten Poetry*. Harvey ('Passionate Spirits', p. 378) notes Cloten's emphasis on the 'penetrating' nature of song ('airs') in describing his plan to seduce Imogen.

51. The persistence of the prophetic tablet beyond the dream sequence emphasises the ambiguity of the dream's immateriality.

52. Compare to Gertrude's exclamation that Hamlet's spirits 'wildly peep', discussed above.

53. Harvey, 'Passionate Spirits', p. 383.

54. Ibid.

CHAPTER 9

'THINKING MAKES IT SO': MIND, BODY AND SPIRIT IN *THE RAPE OF LUCRECE*, *HAMLET* AND *MUCH ADO ABOUT NOTHING*

The soule indeede is so diuine, that raising and mounting itself sometimes aboue all natural formes, it comprehendeth by an admirable, absolutely free, and incompulsiue power, all incorporeall things seuered and divided from all matter and substance.

Helkiah Crooke, *Microcosmographia*[1]

The justification for Claudio's infamous rejection of Hero at the altar in *Much Ado About Nothing* raises an epistemological problem that Shakespeare returned to often: the gap between perception and knowledge, particularly the knowledge of another person. Claudio declares, 'Oh, what authority and show of truth / Can cunning sin cover itself withal!' before going on to charge that despite her 'exterior shows', Hero 'knows the heat of a luxurious bed; / Her blush is guiltiness not modesty' (4.1.34–5, 39–41).[2] Claudio then draws attention to the signifying power of Hero's 'seemingly' guiltless face, only to emphasise that her appearance does not reflect her inner character:

Out on thee seeming! I will write against it:
You seem to me as Dian in her orb,
As chaste as is the bud ere it be blown;
But you are more intemperate in your blood
Than Venus, or those pamp'red animals
That rage in savage sensuality. (4.1.55–9)

A principal irony in the scene is the fact that Claudio's
certainty – that he *knows* the truth about Hero's character –
is a product of his own eyes, the very evidence he rejects
in the process of Hero's public shaming.[3] Even more telling, perhaps, is that he is willing to draw attention to Hero's
ambiguous appearance in support of his claim: 'Behold how
like a maid she blushes here! / Oh, what authority and show
of truth/ Can cunning sin cover itself withal' (4.1.33–5).
Unlike Hamlet who *is* as he *seems* despite his suggestion
that the two are not necessarily connected, Claudio is certain
that Hero *is not* what she *seems*: 'Would you not swear, /
All you that see her, that she were a maid / By these exterior shows? But she is none . . . her blush is guiltiness, not
modesty' (4.1.37–9, 41). Later in the scene, Friar Francis will
also point to Hero's appearance, but he will do so to make
his case for her innocence. The scene begs the question: how
can Claudio know what he has seen in the dark from a distance with more certainty than what his eyes tell him in the
light of day before the altar? And, assuming he is looking at
the same person, why can the Friar be so sure that Claudio
is wrong?

The scene highlights the relationship between perception,
cognition and ideation, a dynamic that drives the central conflicts in the play. Specifically, in what manner does the sensuous perceptual body inform thought or cognition, the mental
activity associated variously in the period with the physical
brain, the intermediary mind and the immaterial rational
soul? In *Much Ado About Nothing*, Shakespeare invites his

audience to contemplate the relationship between outward, material appearance and inward, immaterial character in both the Hero–Claudio and Beatrice–Benedict plots, a relationship that preoccupied early modern natural philosophy, medicine and theology, and which resulted in the complicated, and often contradictory, accounts discussed in the last chapter. Of particular interest here is the status of the immaterial in these explanatory systems, and specifically, the question of how Shakespeare exploited contradictions in contemporary accounts of immateriality to open up theatrical possibilities in a play aptly titled *Much Ado About Nothing*. The well-known pun of the play's title – nothing/noting – points to the mental activity of processing the input of the senses through cognition at the same time that it references the seeming immateriality of the thoughts produced by such activity. While the title phrase has come to mean something like a lot of energy wasted on a non-issue, the issues it raises are far from inconsequential. Before turning to *Much Ado*, it is useful to consider how some of the same body–mind interactions play out in works that end less happily: *Hamlet* and *The Rape of Lucrece*. Having done so, I will then turn to the specific question of how these theories of physical and mental activity inform an early modern understanding of perceptual recognition and misrecognition before examining *Much Ado*'s exploration of these themes.

Locating the Subject: Material Change and Immaterial Subsistence

At the altar, Claudio makes a distinction between Hero as she appears 'by these external shows' (like 'Dian in her Orb') and Hero as she is (an 'animal' who 'rages in savage sensuality'). The difference is the result of a material touch identified explicitly by Don Pedro with the 'vile encounters' she has had 'a thousand times in secret' with the 'ruffian' whose meeting with Hero at her chamber window the three witnessed for themselves at Don John's urging. The particular details of these secret encounters are, as Don John would have it, 'not to be named . . . not to be spoke of' (4.1.94), without some injury to the very concept of chastity. We also know, of course, that they never happened, that the Prince and Count are being set up by the play's villain. Importantly, the ruse is based on the assumption that if such encounters had occurred, Hero would indeed be ruined and the wedding justifiably called off.[4] At one moment in the play Hero is 'a jewel', the 'sweetest lady that ever [Claudio] looked on', and at the next she is 'an approved wanton', 'a common stale' (1.1.53–4, 4.1.43, 64). The 'proof' offered in the scene at the altar is enough to make Leonato wish for his only daughter's death, the change in her is so palpable that 'The story . . . is printed in her blood' (4.1.120). Leonato foregrounds the material touch in his account of her fallen reputation. Bemoaning the loss of his idyllic beloved daughter, he laments that

> She is fallen
> Into a pit of ink, that the wide sea
> Hath drops too few to wash her clean again
> And salt too little which may season give
> To her foul tainted flesh. (4.1.137–41)

The relevant sense here is touch, as Hero's purported crime is physical contact with another man. The play is filled with references to contaminating touch and contagion, beginning with Beatrice's comparison of Benedict to a 'disease', 'sooner caught than the pestilence' (1.1.68–9), and continued in the characterisation of love as a sickness and the identification of Hero as a gift corrupted (a rotten orange). Feigning relief when Don Pedro and Claudio agree to spy at Hero's window, Don John exclaims, 'Oh plague right well prevented!' (3.2.114).

Leonato's identification of Hero's 'tainted flesh' with the 'ink' that stains it further evokes period discussions of contagion as corrupting touch, associated with the concept of the stain or taint. 'Taint', from 'attaint/attain' and the related 'tinct', highlights the alteration of visible form upon infection, an idea easily extended to the figurative – the convention of the 'tainted' mind or soul used to describe a state of corruption, for example. Here, *The Rape of Lucrece* is exemplary. Though Lucrece's 'stained' soul is unseen, like Hero's, its cause can be traced to Tarquin's material touch: 'The wolf hath seized his prey, the poor lamb cries; / Till with her own white fleece her voice controlled / Entombs her outcry in her lip's sweet fold' (ll. 677–9). Initially, Lucrece hopes to find 'refuge' in her steadfast mind:

> Though my gross blood be stained with this abuse,
> Immaculate and spotless is my mind.
> That was not forced, that never was inclined
> To accessory yieldings, but still pure
> Doth in her poisoned closet yet endure. (ll. 1655–9)

Yet the material result of the assault is irreversible for Lucrece, as 'she that was Lucrece' is no more. 'How may this forcèd stain be wiped from me?' she asks rhetorically:

> What is the quality of my offense,
> Being constrained with dreadful circumstance?
> May my pure mind with the foul act dispense,
> My low-declinèd honour to advance?
> May any terms acquit me from this chance?
>   The poisoned fountain clears itself again,
>   And why not I from this compellèd stain? (ll. 1701–8)

Despite the insistence of the onlookers that 'Her body's stain her mind untainted clears', Lucrece insists that 'no dame hereafter living / By my excuse shall claim excuse's giving' (ll. 1710, 1715).

This is the path Lucrece must take to secure her legend as exemplar of female moral purity, but it is one that charts a difficult course along the material/immaterial divide. Though her 'spotless' mind was 'never forced', the 'closet' in which it was encased was nonetheless poisoned by Tarquin's touch. Her argument that Tarquin abandon the attack is mounted on both material and immaterial fronts. First, she appeals to his material body's 'scarlet lust' which 'came evidence to swear / That [her] poor beauty had purloined his eyes' (ll. 1650–1), pleading 'In Tarquin's likeness I did entertain thee / Hast thou put on this shape to do him shame?' (ll. 596–7). But then she turns to address his immaterial self:

> To thee, to thee, my heaved-up hands appeal,
> Not to seducing lust, thy rash relier.
> I sue for exiled majesty's repeal;
> Let him return, and flatt'ring thoughts retire.
> His true respect will prison false desire
>   And wipe the dim mist from thy doting eyne,
>   That thou shalt see thy state and pity mine. (ll.638–44)

Following the attack, Lucrece, 'wakes her heart by beating on her breast / And bids it leap from thence, where it may find / Some purer chest to close so pure a mind' (ll. 759–61). The weakened body is susceptible to infection, as her subsequent musings on the corruption of nature reveal (ll. 848–75). She laments this weakness, noting that 'Unruly blasts wait on the tender spring', drawing on the same natural image that Laertes will invoke in counselling Ophelia against Hamlet's advances: 'in the morn and liquid dew of youth, / Contagious blastments are most imminent' (1.3.39–40).[5] The release of the soul from the body – and, by extension, Lucrece from her undeserved moral taint – also marks a transition from mind to soul:

> Even here she sheathèd in her harmless breast
> A harmful knife, that thence her soul unsheathed.
> That blow did bail it from the deep unrest
> Of that polluted prison where it breathed.

> Her contrite sighs unto the clouds bequeathed
>> Her wingèd sprite, and through her wounds doth fly
>> Life's lasting date from cancelled destiny. (ll. 1723–9)

Shakespeare's Lucrece thus maintains that the mind can remain pure while the body is irrevocably 'polluted' through corrupting touch.

The poem seems to allow for a fairly complete isolation of mind/soul from body, as Lucrece can shed her irrevocably stained material body ('polluted prison') in order to preserve the purity of her 'wingèd sprite'. What is left out of the account is the nature of the interaction between soul and body. The key is the contact point, as is evident in an example from *The Comedy of Errors*. Union and separation are central to the thematics of the early comedy, as the primary action stems from the violent separation of Egeon and Emelia, resulting in a severing of family ties, husband from wife and twin from twin. A recurrent image in the play is the liquid self. Early on, Antipholus of Syracuse compares himself to a drop of water in the ocean:

> I to the world am like a drop of water
> That in the ocean seeks another drop.
> Who, falling there to find his fellow forth,
> Unseen, inquisitive, confounds himself.
> So I, to find a mother and a brother,
> In quest of them, unhappy, lose myself. (1.2.35–8)

In scolding Antipholus of Syracuse whom she believes to be her husband Antipholus of Ephesus, Adriana uses the same image, but here the concern is with contamination:

> How comes it now, my husband, O how comes it
> That thou art thus estrangèd from thyself? –
> Thy 'self' I call it, being strange to me
> That, undividable, incorporate,

Am better than thy dear self's better part.
Ah, do not tear away thyself from me;
For know, my love, as easy mayst thou fall
A drop of water in the breaking gulf,
And take unmingled that same drop again,
Without addition or diminishing,
As take from me thyself, and not me too. (2.2.119–29)

Adriana's image extends Antipholus's earlier image of the drop mingled and lost in the larger body of water. He loses his 'self' in the ocean in search of his mother and brother, as he becomes part of that body in which he searches, just as Adriana and Antipholus become corporally mingled in one fluid self through marriage. The conventional language of marriage as an incorporation of two bodies into one ensures that it is impossible for her to distinguish her substance from his. The notion of incorporation is tactile, as Adriana's subsequent concern over contamination makes clear:

How dearly would it touch thee to the quick,
Shouldst thou but hear I were licentious
And that this body, consecrate to thee,
By ruffian lust should be contaminate?
Wouldst thou not spit at me and spurn at me
And hurl the name of husband in my face
And tear the stain'd skin off my harlot-brow
And from my false hand cut the wedding-ring
And break it with a deep-divorcing vow?
I know thou canst; and therefore see thou do it.
I am possess'd with an adulterate blot;
My blood is mingled with the crime of lust:
For if we two be one and thou play false,
I do digest the poison of thy flesh,
Being strumpeted by thy contagion. (2.2.130–44)

As it turns out, unsurprisingly in the context of the comedy, neither Antipholus of Syracuse nor Adriana's actual husband

Antipholus of Ephesus is actually an adulterer, thus heightening the rhetorical effect of the hypothetical contamination at a distance that Adriana feels as a result of her presumption of Antipholus's guilt. Adriana's vivid description of Antipholus's hypothetical disavowal of their marriage is very like the scene at the altar in *Much Ado*. The later play includes a disturbingly similar excursus on the nature of self-division from Leonato, just before he describes Hero's fall into the pit of ink. Though wishing she was adopted to avoid his present despair, Leonato must admit that Hero is his own: 'mine, and mine I loved, and mine, I praised, / And mine that I was proud on, and mine so much / That I myself was to myself not mine / Valuing of her' (4.1.134–7). Leonato's tenderness at his worst moment in the play (the moment he loses faith in Hero) parallels the way Adriana frames her hypothetical with an earnest piece of advice for upholding marital virtue: 'Keep then fair league and truce with thy true bed, / I live dis-stain'd, thou undishonourèd' (2.2.145–6).[6] The sense here is that if Antipholus can be faithful, the irreversible stain on their incorporate flesh will be removed (she 'dis' stained, he 'un' dishonoured), a reversal that is paradoxically only achievable through prevention. For as we learned from Lucrece, once stained, the mortal flesh is irreversibly corrupted. It is this irreversibility that ostensibly leads the loving Leonato to command that Hero 'Do not live' (4.1.120).

Perhaps even more familiar is the prominent role contagion and moral staining play in *Hamlet*. Much has been written of the disease imagery in the play, which finds its emblem in Marcellus's ominous observation that 'Something is rotten in the state of Denmark' (1.4.90). The comment, to which no one responds, establishes corruption within the body of the state. Disease, leading to decay from within, is consonant with the Galenic conception of illness as a result of an internal imbalance of humours. Such imbalances were thought to expose one to external threats, usually borne by corrupt air. Importantly, Shakespeare always uses the term 'contagious' to indicate a dangerously corrupt atmosphere, usually in the form of corrupted air, fog or clouds, as when Titania describes the 'contagious fogs' that hover over the wasted landscape that has resulted from her feud with Oberon in *A Midsummer Night's Dream*. Yet, such seemingly literal references to the contagious nature of the corrupted atmosphere consistently turn on the contagiousness of mental states.[7] Even Titania's ostensibly literal reference to corrupted air alludes to the mental and emotional discord that plagues the fairy world. More overt examples include King Henry's threat at the gates of Harfleur that 'the filthy and contagious clouds / Of heady murder, spoil and villainy' may overcome his men should he lose command of them (3.4.31–2). Though the use of the term appears to suggest a proto-modern pathogenic understanding of contagion originating with Girolamo Fracastoro, the emphasis is actually on the soldiers to whom such behaviour is presumably endogenous. Or consider *Henry VIII* when Gardiner advocates harsh punishment for Cranmer in order to avoid the spread of heresy:

> If we suffer,
> Out of our easiness and childish pity
> To one man's honour, this contagious sickness,
> Farewell all physic: and what follows then?
> Commotions, uproars, with a general taint
> Of the whole state (5.3.31–6)

The connection between the contagious sickness of heresy and the 'general taint' of the state recalls the rotten state of Denmark and suggests that such corruption spreads in the minds of the infected. Both 'rotten state' and 'general taint' conjure the spectre of the plague, a disease still attributed to supernatural, immaterial powers in the seventeenth century.[8]

Throughout *Hamlet,* a material language of pathogenic contagion fails to account for the characters' desire to contain or control the greater threat of the immaterial, that which, according to Hamlet, 'passes show' (1.2.85). Hamlet resists the horrors of the night – the time of day most often associated with contagion in Shakespeare – opting instead for a verbal rather than physical assault on his mother:

> 'Tis now the very witching time of night,
> When churchyards yawn and hell itself breathes out
> Contagion to this world: now could I drink hot blood,
> And do such bitter business as the day
> Would quake to look on. Soft, now to my mother.
> O heart, lose not thy nature; let not ever
> The soul of Nero enter this firm bosom –
> Let me be cruel, not unnatural:
> I will speak daggers to her, but use none.
> My tongue and soul in this be hypocrites.
> How in my words soever she be shent
> To give them seals never, my soul, consent. (3.2.377–89)

But as Hamlet's words become 'daggers' to Gertrude's ears, the material or immaterial cause of the tainted mind or soul (confused here as in *Lucrece*) is the central concern. Hamlet's stated reason for choosing words over force is an attempt to avoid the 'unnatural' act of violence against his mother, but it is the Ghost's command to leave her judgement to God that prefigures this decision. The Ghost implores Hamlet to stay focused on the 'unnatural' Claudius: 'taint not thy mind nor let thy soul contrive / Against thy mother aught' (1.5.85–6).

   Warning against the 'tainted mind' raises some intriguing questions for the present consideration of material and immaterial interactivity. Johnathan Gil Harris notes that 'taint' was a 'hybrid word' in the Renaissance, with two distinct origins, the first deriving from 'attaint' (attain), to 'reach', 'touch' or 'strike', the second from the Latin *tinctus,* to 'tint' or 'colour'.⁹ The noun-form *tinctus* is subsequently derived from the verb *tingo*, which emphasises the tactile nature of staining through explicit reference to the act of 'wetting', 'soaking', or figuratively saturating, 'imbuing'. Foregrounding the relations among these terms, the exchange between Hamlet and Gertrude in the closet scene increases the ambiguity of the direction of the action. Hamlet's first spoken dagger, his admission that his murder of Polonius is 'almost as bad ... As kill a king and marry with his brother', is his first strike at Gertrude's soul. As his words become daggers, the language clearly moves from material to immaterial contamination. According to Hamlet, Gertrude has committed

> Such an act
> That blurs the grace and blush of modesty,
> Calls virtue hypocrite, takes off the rose
> From the fair forehead of an innocent love
> And sets a blister there, makes marriage-vows
> As false as dicers' oaths: O, such a deed
> As from the body of contraction plucks
> The very soul, and sweet religion makes
> A rhapsody of words: heaven's face doth glow:
> Yea, this solidity and compound mass,
> With tristful visage, as against the doom,
> Is thought-sick at the act. (3.4.38–49)¹⁰

'Thought sickness' is intriguing as an example of the 'tainted mind' that Hamlet has been urged to resist himself and now strives to reveal in his mother. But of course, the play is not forthcoming about the extent of Gertrude's guilt, the extent to which she has actually committed such an act. Her incredulity in the face of Hamlet's initial accusations ('to kill a king?' and 'What have I done that thou dar'st wag your tongue / In noise so rude against me?') suggests that what we are witnessing in this scene is the tainting of Gertrude's mind in response to Hamlet's verbal assault. Certainly, she has married Claudius, her husband's brother, to the horror of her mourning son, but it is not at all clear that she colluded in her husband's murder; the scene suggests that she needs an external stimulus to spread the contagion of Claudius's iniquity.

Only when Hamlet forces her to look on the pictures of the two kings, emphasising the disconnect between her rational and sensuous faculties, does he begin to reveal (or invent) her guilt: 'thou turn'st my very eyes into my soul / And there I see such black and grained spots / as will not leave their tinct' (3.4.87–9).[11] Yet Hamlet is arrested at this very moment by the Ghost's return and the suggestion that the source of the stain was not internal. The tainted soul revealed to Gertrude by Hamlet as in 'a glass / Where you may see the inmost part of you' (3.4.18–19) may have an external cause. Hamlet did set up a glass, but it does not reflect her inner soul (something we learned mirrors incapable of in *Richard II*). The Ghost's injunction to 'step between her and her fighting soul' rests on the idea that she is not yet lost, not yet stained in Lucrece's irrevocable sense. The aphorism that the Ghost provides – 'Conceit in weakest bodies strongest works' – is actually a repetition of Hamlet's own earlier recognition that in his mourning state he is weakened and vulnerable to the devil's illusions, for the devil 'is very potent with such spirits' (3.1.537). The solution, the Ghost suggests, is to 'speak to her': make contact, albeit through voice rather than touch.

For all that the closet scene reveals, then, it is what it leaves concealed that matters most. Like all of the play's tantalising ambiguities, Gertrude's tainted soul eludes the view. The language of contagion, so promising in its ability to make visible the invisible, debunk the immaterial, and explain the source of corruption in the play, fails in the end to reveal convincingly the mysteries that drive the action. Tellingly, it is the resolution of the action in the plot of poisoned cups and swords that brings the play's meditation on material corruption and the tainted mind together in a final, unambiguous, if not satisfying conclusion. Prompted to revenge by Claudius, Laertes reveals his plan to 'touch' Hamlet with his 'contagion':

> I bought an unction of a mountebank,
> So mortal that, but dip a knife in it,
> Where it draws blood no cataplasm so rare,
> Collected from all simples that have virtue
> Under the moon, can save the thing from death
> That is but scratch'd withal: I'll touch my point
> With this contagion, that, if I gall him slightly,
> It may be death. (4.7.139–46)

Laertes' poison, the 'contagion', though clearly material, is not borne on the air, and has no power to infect without explicitly visible contact – the tip of the foil touching the body, or the cup meeting the lips. Laertes must touch Hamlet with the 'unction' for it to work.[12] That the contest is a game of touches fittingly completes the rhetorical circle. The ensuing action is defined by a series of hits, or strikes, 'very palpable' according to Osric, whose role is to observe the sport and confirm contact. It is these hits from the 'envenomed' foil that lead to Hamlet's, Laertes' and Claudius's deaths, their poisoned bodies irrevocably contaminated such that 'No med'cine in the world can do thee good' (5.2.256, 293).

The Perceptual Body and the Body of the Mind

If The Rape of Lucrece and Hamlet depict the tragic consequences of the corrupting touch, in which material contamination is mirrored in the minds of the characters with an irreversible force such that can lead only to death, by shifting our attention to genre of comedy, we can find in Much Ado

About Nothing an apparently positive alternative. As Adriana's argument for the proactive avoidance of sin suggests, though comedy is equally concerned with the problem of contamination, its action focuses on the ideas we have about others rather than the things we do to them materially. *Much Ado About Nothing* stages the consequences of the corruption and purification of thought, while avoiding touch at almost every turn. Bodies are invoked both sexually and violently, as Hero is accused of fornication and Benedict challenges Claudio to physically defend his trespass against Hero's honour and avenge her death. But no fornication has occurred and no sword fight ensues. In other words, in the comedy, the material/immaterial script is flipped. Hamlet's interaction with the immaterial spirit leads to material corruption, murder and contamination of the blood, and despite maintaining a purity of mind, Lucrece suffers a material assault that contaminates her mortal body and leads to her death. The tragedies are tragedies with material consequences, felt in the bodies of the characters as they descend to their deaths. The comedic genre, concerned as it is with the affirmation of life rather than the contemplation of its corruption and decay, focuses squarely on the immaterial complement to the material, considering its susceptibility to corruption and change.

Much Ado About Nothing repeatedly dramatises the role of the ideal rather than material body in shaping both the characters' and the audience's judgements about the principal persons of the play. The very first exchange between Beatrice and the messenger sets up the thematic interest in one of the play's key terms – nothing. Ignoring the messenger's report of Benedict's 'good service', Beatrice comments on his character in the language of the body, calling him a 'very valiant trencher-man' with an 'excellent stomach' (1.1.40, 42). The messenger's attempt to return the conversation to Benedict's reputation, by generously interpreting her comment on his stomach as a compliment to his courage, reaches its peak in his declaration that Benedict is 'stuffed with all honourable virtues' (1.1.45–6). This honorific statement produces a curious restraint in Beatrice, who exclaims that 'It is so indeed, he is no less than a stuffed man; but for the stuffing – well, we are all mortal' (1.1.47–8).

Beatrice's comment can be read as an application of Falstaff's catechism on honour in *1 Henry IV*, as Benedict's honourable virtues are reduced to stuffing, or simply stuff (*OED* 'dust'), the corrupt materiality that defines our mortality (and humanity). The exchange is enough to prompt Leonato to intervene, proclaiming Beatrice's banter the result of a 'merry war', the product of which, Beatrice is quick to add, is 'nothing' (1.1.50, 52). Her subsequent quip, that in their last 'conflict, four of his five wits went halting off, and now is the whole man governed with one' (1.1.52–4), further adds to the play's thematic emphasis on the gap between the material and immaterial, corporeal and incorporeal. The insult relies on the distinction between the five wits and the five senses as internal and external human capacities (mental faculties and physical senses). Beatrice's 'five wits' are generally taken to be the mental faculties of 'memory, imagination, judgment, fantasy, and common sense'.[13] She concludes her jab with a conventional insult to Benedict's intelligence: 'so that if he hath wit enough to keep himself warm, let him bear it for a difference between himself and his horse, for it is all the wealth that he hath left to be known a reasonable creature' (1.1.54–7). If one considers mental activity to be material, Beatrice's jab can be seen to draw on not only the distinction between the internal faculties and the external senses but also the interrelations among them that depend on the medical spirits.[14] In other words, though Beatrice is referring to the mental faculties here, the mental realm was not so distinct from the sensuous as it appears to be in more modern, post-Cartesian accounts. Daniel Heller-Roazen has suggested that the Aristotelian account of the mental faculties, and common sense in particular, may have been aimed at sensation as much as cognition, or rather, that consciousness – that which we associate with mental activity – was more closely connected to the sensuous than the reflective. As opposed to reflection in the modern sense of inward contemplation, Heller-Roazen proposes an 'inner touch'.[15] The most developed synthesis of the Aristotelian system with the Galenic theory of bodily spirits was developed by Avicenna, whose 'complex hierrarchy' can be seen as the direct influence behind early modern theories of cognition.[16]

The French surgeon Paré, discussed in the last chapter, is a good example:

> Actions [of the body] are two-fold; for they are either Naturall, or Voluntary. They are termed Naturall, because they are performed not by our will, but by their owne accord and against our will: As are that continuall motion of the Heat, the beating of the Arteryes, the expulsion of the Excrements, and such other like which are done in us by the Law of Nature whether we will, or no.[17]

The mind only enters into the discussion when Paré turns to the issue of the 'voluntary actions', which he divides further into the three subsets 'sensitive, moving, and principle'. The first two categories are overtly bodily – the 'sensitive associated with the organs of sense', and the 'moving' resulting from the motion of muscles produced 'either by bending and contraction, or by extension'. He then goes on to describe what would seem to be the properly mental faculties:

> The Principall Action and prime amongst the Voluntary is absolutely divided in three, Imagination, Reasoning and Memory.
>
> Imagination is a certaine expressing, and apprehension which discernes and distinguisheth betweene the formes

and shapes of things sensible, or which are knowne by the senses.

Reasoning is a certaine judiciall æstimation of conceived or apprehended formes or figures, by a mutuall collating, or comparing them together.

Memory is the sure store of all things, and as it were the Treasurie which the minde often unfolds and opens, the other faculties of the minde being idle and not imployed . . .[18]

The reduction of the five faculties of the soul into the three here identified as imagination, reasoning and memory was conventional in the Middle Ages, as was the theory that these operated with the assistance of the spirits.[19] Paré notes that 'all the forementioned Actions whether they be Naturall, or Animall and voluntary, are done and performed by the help and assistance of the Spirits'.[20] Just as the more material spirits support involuntary bodily functions, the more ethereal spirits guide mental faculties.

Beatrice's insult, quite simply that Benedict is dim-witted and thus not a worthy mental sparring partner for her, carries with it the implication that his physiological–mental interface is corrupt. Bret Rothstein notes the implication of the connection between the material spirits and mental activity in late medieval medical discourse:

Mental function, though frequently considered in terms of its relationship with the soul, is bound up with the state of the body . . . Variegation of intelligence arises from the degree to which and ease with which spirits move about within the body.[21]

When the two future lovers exchange wits for the first time only lines later, their exchange follows a conversation between Leonato and Don Pedro concerning Hero, and specifically Hero's identity as Leonato's daughter. This fact, they all agree, is confirmed by her visual appearance: 'Truly the lady fathers herself' (1.1.90), which is intimately intertwined with her immaterial character: 'Be happy, lady, for you are like an *honourable* father' (1.1.91, my emphasis). The conversation offers a contrast to Beatrice's lowest insult to Benedict in the same scene. In response to Benedict's mocking relief that she will not seek the company of men, 'so some gentleman or other shall scape a predestinate scratched face', she disparages his appearance: 'Scratching could not make it worse, an 'twere such a face as yours were' (1.1.111–12).

All this banter – animated by language highlighting the connection between bodily appearance and internal character – introduces the initial catalyst for the comedy's action, Claudio's apprehension of Hero as 'a modest young lady': 'In mine eye she is the sweetest lady that ever I looked on' (1.1.135, 153–4). This most crucial act of perception happens before we learn of it in the dialogue, as Claudio only reveals his love after Hero exits. Once alone with his friend, Claudio asks if Benedict has 'noted' Hero, hoping, apparently, to confirm through her outward appearance that she is worthy of his love. Benedict's response, 'I noted her not, but I did look on her' (1.1.134), emphasises the difference between apprehension and comprehension – between Hero's body provided by the senses and her body as seen through the lens of cognitive judgement. In Paré's terms, Benedict admits only to the act of 'imagination' while Claudio's objection that Benedict 'speak in sober judgment' invokes the faculty of 'reasoning'.[22] Reasoning requires the third category of actions described by Paré: memory, 'the sure store of all things'. For in order to compare and estimate, one needs more than one term. Claudio's claim that Hero is 'the sweetest lady that ever I looked on' is comparative: as far as he can judge, based on the evidence of his senses ('in mine eye'), Hero is sweeter than any other lady. Claudio's positive judgement here provides the template for the play's subsequent action: by drawing on this process of comparing the 'mental bodies' or phantasms of memory and imagination (bodies perceived through the senses), the play realises its remarkable scenes of both recognition and misrecognition.

Recognition and Misrecognition

Claudio's ability to recognise Hero's inner 'modesty' in her outward appearance is only the first of the play's many examples of the successful exercise of judgement, the act of reasoning that allows one to compare the objects provided to the mind by the senses through phenomenal experience (phantasms, or what Paré calls 'apprehended formes or figures') to the objects of prior experience (those mental images retained in the rational soul for the purpose of comparison and reflection). For Avicenna, recognition is on a spectrum that includes an instinctive 'power that permits the lamb to judge that the wolf should be avoided', as well as what we might consider judgement proper.[23] It is suggestive that Claudio himself apparently frustrated the faculty of judgement in others, as he is described by the Messenger as one who has done 'in the figure of a lamb, the feats of a lion' (1.1.12–13). Claudio applauds Don Pedro for just such an ability in judgement when he notes that the Prince is able to 'know love's grief by his complexion' (1.1.269).[24] Such examples suggest that the mental actions of imagination and reasoning interpenetrate one another in the experience of material bodies. While the imagination enables one to recognise what it is that distinguishes one sensible shape from another (Claudio from Benedict, for example, or Hero from Margaret), judgement is supposed to allow one to determine what difference the difference makes. While the play sometimes suggests that the inner truth of a character is available in his or her outward appearance (written onto the body), internal character and external appearance are continually correlated ('collated' in Paré's term) through the exercise of imagination, reason and memory.

The intertwining of perceptual and mental bodies is evident when Don John's claim to Conrad, 'I cannot hide what I am' (1.3.11), is confirmed at the beginning of the masked ball. In response to Beatrice's comments about Don John's appearance, 'How tartly that gentleman looks!', Hero agrees that 'He is of a very melancholy disposition' (2.1.3, 5). Later in the ball scene Ursula recognises Antonio through his costume 'by the waggling of [his] head' and his 'dry hand', and Borachio recognises Claudio 'by his bearing' (2.1.100, 104, 141).[25] Beatrice and Benedict likewise recognise each other and use the opportunity to trade barbs under the pretence of anonymity.

In such cases, when everything is working correctly, recognition is a result of the human capacity for cognition: the act of comparing the impressions that material bodies make on the senses to the mental bodies retained by the memorial faculty, judging or estimating the extent of their similarities and differences. This process is fairly straightforward when the substance to be recognised in sensuous experience is the material form of the body in question. When extrapolating this process to the recognition of a person's 'disposition', things get a bit messy.[26] The crucial point here is that the material or immaterial status of thoughts, ideas and mental images was in question at the moment that the play was produced. Importantly, in early modern medical and philosophical accounts, material bodies are never directly compared in the act of cognition because they must first be converted into phantasms by the imaginative faculty. In the case of the more abstract kinds of knowledge about human character – the kinds of observations about temperament, loyalty, trustworthiness that Shakespeare explicitly explores in *Much Ado* – the language of the body used in the process of cognitive understanding is explicitly divorced from sense experience and corporeality but not necessarily the materiality of the person doing the thinking. E. Ruth Harvey cites Avicenna's

discussion of the weakened cognitive abilities of the drunk-
ard to illustrate this point. Avicenna argued that 'wine is too
damp for serious thought: drinkers concern themselves with
the pleasant rather than the profitable, the present and not
the future'.[27] 'The reason for this', explains Avicenna,

> is that the power of the soul performs its actions in the
> brain, and it needs spirit of moderate humidity, which will
> obey the motions of cogitation, and the operations of intel-
> lect. But [after drinking] the spirit is very moist and ...
> [t]herefore it obeys the intellect and the motions of cogni-
> tion only in very material and corporeal matters, not in
> anything very subtle or incorporeal; and, in its instability
> and agitation, it will not serve to form or present immate-
> rial things, but only to form the most corporeal ones.[28]

More complex understanding – the proper domain of the
rational soul – requires contemplation of immaterial things,
formed for contemplation by the cognitive faculties. The positive gain in divorcing cognition from the immediacy of sensual experience is to avoid the influence of strong sensation
to enflame the passions and thus cloud judgement. This was
Avicenna's motivation for 'disrobing' phantasms from materiality, thus giving intellect a pure object.[29] The disadvantage
of separating the objects of intellection from those of sensation, as I believe Shakespeare was well aware, was to give
authority to a realm of detached mental contemplation without any material reality against which to check the validity
of one's judgement. If, as Aristotle claimed, everything begins
with the senses, the movement away from sense experience
in mental experience has the potential to lead thought into a
world of confusion.

In the case of *Much Ado*, the confusion begins when the
characters are tricked into comparing multiple phantasmatic
versions of the other characters with whom they continue to
interact. As Rothstein argues, "Imagination is the crux of the

matter, for it is the faculty that provides judgment not only with things seen but also with items that result from mental fabrication.'[30] Philosophers since antiquity had noted the human ability to contemplate things that cannot have been derived from the senses. The examples proffered to make this philosophical point tend to be extreme: 'an emerald man or a flying mountain'.[31] But the observation also suggests that it is possible to contemplate mental fabrications that are false but possible in the world of sense experience. This idea is particularly important for the dramatist whose interest is in creating plausible illusions. The confusions that animate the action of *Much Ado* are precisely of this sort. Consider the gulling of Benedict. Prior to his manipulation in the garden, Benedict responds to Beatrice's appearance ('look here she comes') with disdain: 'here's a dish I love not' (2.1.232, 242). But after he hears the description of 'the effects of passion' that Hero has supposedly witnessed in Beatrice, his mind is altered. The fiction offered to Benedict's ear in the gulling scene reconstructs his memory of Beatrice's body – creating her mental body in his cognitive experience – by endowing it with the 'effects of passion' vividly described by the plotters:

> LEONATO Oh, she tore the letter into a thousand half-pence; railed at herself, that she should be so immodest to write to one that she knew would flout her. 'I measure him', says she, 'by my own spirit. For I should flout him if he writ to me, yea, though I love him, I should'.
>
> CLAUDIO Then down upon her knees she falls, weeps, sobs, beats her heart, tears her hair . . .
>
> (2.3.127–34)

The very next time he sees Beatrice approach, his judgement of her appearance is entirely different: 'Here comes Beatrice. By this day, she's a fair lady! I do spy some marks of love in her' (2.3.216–17).

At this point in the play, Benedict's belief that he sees 'some marks of love' in Beatrice is an example of misrecognition, or mis-estimation (the failure of properly judging the data of the senses). In fact, Benedict contemplates an imaginative fiction: the 'love-struck Beatrice' is plausible, but not actual, as no such material form exists in the play at this point. Having yet to be gulled by Hero and Ursula, Beatrice would not yet bear the signs Benedict sees; they are apparently the product of Benedict's comparison of the material body standing before him on stage and the immaterial, mental body lodged only moments before in his mind by Don Pedro, Claudio and Leontato. This harmless tutoring of Benedict's judgement sets up the much more sinister scene of misrecognition with which I began this chapter – the misrecognition of Margaret as Hero that leads to Hero's public shaming. According to Borachio, the misrecognition of Margaret for Hero on the balcony is the product of three things: Claudio and Don Pedro are fooled 'partly by [Don John's] oaths, which first possessed them, partly by the dark night, which did deceive them, but chiefly by my villainy, which did confirm any slander that Don John had made' (3.3.136–9). Considering that Borachio is bragging of his villainy to Conrad, his claim that he played the chief role is dubious at best. In fact, though each of the factors is important for the deception to come off, it is Don John's framing of the events to come that determines the perceptual experience for both Claudio and Don Pedro. The dark of the night and Borachio's theatrical performance (calling Margaret by Hero's name) ensure that neither Claudio nor Don Pedro rely on the evidence of their eyes in a simple comparison of Hero's bodily appearance to the one before them on the balcony. But they mis-recognise Margaret as Hero in large part because the object of comparison, Don John's planted story that 'you shall see her chamber window entered, even the night before her wedding day' (3.2.94–5), provides them something to compare to the scene they witness on the balcony. This something is in fact nothing, but the revelation simultaneously confirms how important nothing – here an immaterial idea – is in the process of human judgement. Don John's admonition, 'If you dare not trust that you see, confess not that you know' (3.2.100–1), places special emphasis on the evidence of the senses – and particularly vision – while at the same time deflecting scrutiny from his fabricated story of Hero's infidelity. Don John's comment to Claudio that 'it would better serve your honour to change your mind' (3.2.96–7) than marry Hero doubles as the catalyst for a literal change in Claudio's mind.

Rather than show us the scene in which Margaret's outward appearance is mistaken for Hero's, Shakespeare chooses to stage the much more jarring scene in which Claudio tragically mischaracterises Hero's inner character at the altar. In this scene, the playwright emphasises how Hero's outward appearance, and in particular her blush, can simultaneously signify the truth of her inner character and the misguided view of the deceived Claudio and Don Pedro. The blush is a particularly important marker of inward character in the period. According to Levinius Lemnius in his *Touchstone of Complexions* (1576):

> There is no surer way (sayeth Galene) certainly to knowe the humours and juyce in a Creature, then by the colour and outward complexion. If the body loke very white, it is a token that phlegme in that body, chiefly reigneth and most aboundeth. If it be pale or yellow, it argueth the humour to be greatly Melancholique and Cholerique, and the blood to be fresh and reddye: if it be blackish, it betokeneth blacke ... Choler ...[32]

According to this kind of humoral observation, one's disposition is available on one's face. However, Lemnius goes on to assert that both 'outwarde accidental occasion' and internal emotional states can alter the appearance of the complexion. The complexion is a good guide

> if no outwarde accidentall occasion happen, as great heat or chaffing, labor or wearinesse: or if the mynde bee not intoxicate, and perplexed with affects and passions, as Anger, Joye, Sorrow, Care, pensivenesse: for these make the humours sometime to resort unto the skin and utter parts, and sometime to hyde and conveyghe themselves farre inwardly: and for this cause we see men that are . . . testy to be in a marvelous heat, proceeding not from any sickness or disease, but of the motion and stirring of the humours: againe, them that be affrighted and in mynde amazed, to be pale.[33]

Thus, despite humoral theory's taxonomic potential for deciphering disposition, in actual practice identifying inward character from the face is a difficult matter. Claudio admits that Hero's blush can betray either modesty or guilt depending, he suggests, on the condition of her conscience. The more sinister revelation of the scene, however, is that the signifying power of the blush is actually reliant on the state of mind of the beholder. I have already commented on Claudio's response to the blush – proclaiming it to be evidence of her guilt. Perhaps more striking, though, is how Friar Francis draws on the same visual evidence to come to the opposite conclusion:

> I have marked
> A thousand blushing apparitions
> To start into her face, a thousand innocent shames
> In angel whiteness beat away those blushes,
> And in her eye there hath appeared a fire
> To burn the errors that these princes hold
> Against her maiden truth. (4.1.156–62)

The Friar attributes his ability to discern Hero's 'innocent shames' from guilty 'blushing apparitions' to his mental training: his 'reading' and his 'observations . . . which with experimental seal doth warrant the tenor of [his] book' (4.1.163–5). His is a more discerning eye, due to a training in recognising appearances confirmed through years of experience in comparing perceptual and phantasmatic bodies. His subsequent plan relies on this ability, as he proposes to reconstruct the phantasm of Hero's body lodged in Claudio's brain:

> When he shall hear she died upon his words,
> Th'idea of her life shall sweetly creep
> Into his study of imagination,
> And every lovely organ of her life
> Shall come apparelled in a more precious habit,
> More moving-delicate, and full of life,
> Into the eye and prospect of his soul,
> Than when she lived indeed. (4.1.223–30)

The phantasmatic, mental body that the Friar describes exceeds the one still present on the stage. Hero's material presence throughout the scene foregrounds the reality granted to both her sensuous body and her phantasmatic body. The innocence that Hero's material body is unable to confirm, her mental body will. It is the body in the mind, 'more moving-delicate, and full of life', that has the power to touch the 'prospect of his soul'. The 'thousand blushing apparitions' recall the animating, thin spirits that bring life to the human body. Despite the living Hero's presence on the stage during this scene, in hypothetically recuperating Hero's reputation for the absent Claudio the Friar uses the language of spirit intermediaries to bring her back to life.

This is all the more striking in the context of the theatre, where Hero's blush is most likely to be known to the audience through the dialogue rather than her ruddy face. As Michael

Neill has pointed out, most spectators would not have been close enough to the actors to read facial expressions, much less recognise an actor's blush. But the detail is crucial for the action, and Shakespeare clearly exploits the commonplace that the blush conveyed an ambiguous significance.[34] What Don John has done to Claudio and Don Pedro and what Claudio has in turn done to Leonato is precisely what Shakespeare does to the audience throughout the play: he creates a mental image or phantasm that replaces or supersedes the material sensorium before our eyes.

This intertwining of the material body ('every organ of her life') with the mental body and ultimately the soul is foregrounded in Benedict's response to the Friar's plan: 'I will deal in this / As secretly and justly as your soul / should with your body' (4.1.247–9). Benedict's reassurance that he will 'deal justly' is underwritten by his characterisation of the soul's relationship to the body – the soul *deals with* the body both 'justly' *and* 'secretly'. The inaccessibility of the soul, and its resulting secrecy, highlights the distinction as well as the interaction between body and soul, material and immaterial, that the play exploits. Later, when he is challenged by Beatrice to judge the truth of Claudio's accusation, Benedict blurs the line between body and soul, asking, 'Think you in your soul the Count Claudio hath wronged Hero?' (4.1.320–1). In asking this, Benedict ostensibly asks Beatrice to go beyond her material experience to confirm the truth of the events at hand. But Beatrice's response, 'Yea, as sure as I have a thought or a soul' (4.1.322), reinscribes the problem that is at the centre of the play: unlike sensuous bodies, others' thoughts and souls cannot be known materially, and as such they elude the kind of certainty Benedict seeks. In her response, Beatrice acknowledges the gap between the soul's absolute comprehension of truths and the embodied mortal's thinking mind, dependent on material substances for its subject matter.

Though successfully rescuing Hero's reputation from slander, the Friar's intervention in defence of proper judgement fails to resolve the more troubling implications of the mysterious cognitive interplay between the material body, corporeal spirit and immaterial soul that Shakespeare explores throughout the play. The various examples of recognition and misrecognition in *Much Ado* reveal both the fallibility of the senses and the fallibility of reason. If, following my epitaph from Crooke, 'The soule . . . is so diuine, that . . . it comprehendeth . . . all incorporeall things seuered and divided from all matter and substance', this is precisely what the embodied mind cannot do. Benedict notes the dependence of thought on the body: 'if their wisdoms be misled in this, / The practice of it lives in John the Bastard, / Whose spirits toil in frame of villainies' (4.1.185–7). The practice of misleading is intertwined with Don John's body – 'frame' – wherein his 'spirits toil'.[35] Similarly, in rejecting Antonio's advice to use reason against his grief for Hero's defamation, Leonato specifically points to the inability of the intellect to counsel one who is impassioned bodily:

> men
> Can counsel and speak comfort to that grief
> Which they themselves do not feel; but tasting it,
> Their counsel turns to passion, which before
> Would give preceptial medicine to rage,
> Fetter strong madness in a silken thread,
> Charm ache with air, and agony with words. (5.1.20–6)

Leonato's insistence that he be allowed to feel his grief – 'I will be flesh and blood' (5.1.34) – is set against things that border the immaterial: 'preceptial medicine', 'air' and 'words'. The 'silken thread' capable of fettering 'strong madness' is especially suggestive of spirits as the thinnest of substances.

The thoughts that slander and redeem in this play are embodied in the minds of Shakespeare's characters. These mental bodies, being dependent on rather than free from matter, are subject to its distortions, to the vagaries of sense experience, to suggestion, and to time. Leonato's entrance upon learning of the plot to defame Hero encapsulates the problem:

> Which is the villain? Let me see his eyes,
> That when I note another man like him,
> I may avoid him. Which of these is he? (5.1.244–6)

Though his desire to know villainy by its outward appearance is understandable, the play insists that such a desire is futile. Claudio's attempt at contrition muddles the question of what even counts as villainy: 'Impose me to what penance your invention / Can lay upon my sin; yet sinn'd I not / But in mistaking' (5.1.258–60). Claudio's hedged defence of his actions highlights the deeper problem haunting the play's portrayal of action based on misunderstanding. If the goal is to align one's actions with immaterial truths – another's virtue, love or ill will, for example – the path is through material experience that can never adequately represent those truths. Without unencumbered access to the soul's unfettered comprehension of things immaterial, cognition in the embodied mind is messy, unpredictable and ultimately bound to the flesh of material bodies. As it is represented here and elsewhere in Shakespeare, even the disciplined mind, perhaps especially the disciplined mind, offers no guarantee that we will recognise innocence or guilt by its outward appearance.

The play's final scene presents a recapitulation of these material/immaterial conflicts in four rapid movements. First, Benedict reveals his plan to marry, in the language of vision. Benedict begins by telling Leonato 'the truth': 'Your niece regards me with an eye of favour' (5.4.21–2). In return Leonato offers his own revelation:

> LEONATO   That eye my daughter lent her – 'tis most true.
> BENEDICT   And I do with an eye of love requite her.
> LEONATO   The sight whereof I think you had from me,
>   From Claudio, and the Prince. But what's your
>   will?
> BENEDICT   Your answer, sir, is enigmatical. (5.4.23–7)

Despite remaining in the dark about the gulling, even as Leonato spills the beans, Benedict sticks to his plan to marry, and by association, his belief in Beatrice's love for him.

The next moment Claudio and the Prince enter, and Claudio claims that nothing experience can offer will alter his will to keep his word to Leonato in marrying Hero's 'cousin': 'I'll hold my mind were she an Ethiope' (5.4.38). Setting aside the racist implications of the line, Claudio's focus is apparently on the betrothed's appearance – 'I'll marry her no matter how she appears' – rather than reputation – 'I'll marry her regardless of what she has done'.[36] What Claudio is saying, then, is that there is nothing he could *see* that would change his mind about how he is about to act. This, in turn, sets up the revelation of Hero, which only happens (at Leonato's command) after the two are married before the Friar. Leonato explicitly denies Claudio's request to see Hero's face (5.4.55–6). The ploy ensures that Claudio set aside his former habits of judgement: comparing phantasms in his mind's eye, his image of Hero with those of other women presumably borne of previous experience or suggestion, reduced to abstract universals such as modesty and wantonness. Instead, at this point he submits himself to her view of him: 'I am your husband, if you like of me' (5.4.59).

Hero's response foregrounds the problem of sensuous and ideational bodies:

> HERO   And when I lived I was your other wife,
>   And when you loved you were my other husband.
> CLAUDIO   Another Hero?
> HERO   Nothing certainer,
>   One Hero died defiled, but I do live,
>   And surely as I live, I am a maid. (5.4.60–4)

Hero's two bodies are here placed side by side, the one a material woman, living and dynamic, the other an idea, static and dead. According to Hero, the only thing that is certain is that the mind is powerful enough to understand the difference.

The scene's final movement repeats this conclusion. Just when we think Beatrice and Benedict will drop their defences, the opposite happens. Returning wit to its proper place – or, one could say, getting their wits about them – they each proclaim that their love for the other is within the bounds of reason. Benedict's question to Beatrice, 'Do you not love me?' is presumably meant to make public the love they have already proclaimed to one another in private. In 4.1, they had set aside another game of wit in a moment of vulnerability, as Benedict proclaims, 'I do love nothing in the world so well as you', and Beatrice confirms her love in return: 'I love you with so much of my heart that none is left to protest' (4.1.264–5, 283–4). Though this intimate moment is disrupted by the business with Claudio and Hero, and specifically Beatrice's demand that Benedict 'Kill Claudio', their expressions of love for one another are unambiguous. Their denials in the final scene are thus all the more surprising and can only be taken as public performance, a return to the way their characters have always appeared to others, as locked in a never-ending exchange of wit. Each indicates that they love the other 'No more than reason' (5.4.74, 77). As Walter N. King points out, the relationship between love and reason here is no simple matter: '. . . is reason an attribute of love; does it induce or qualify love; can love be measured by reason; can one love reasonably? And are love and reason as truly antithetical as traditional belief insisted?'[37] For King, these questions suggest that 'love, whatever it is, cannot be entirely "much ado about nothing"'.[38] The material evidence that ultimately settles the matter comes in the form of words – poems, to be precise – that are explicitly identified with the process of cognition, 'a halting sonnet of his own pure brain' and another 'Containing her affection unto Benedict'. Faced with such evidence, they can give up the game of wits, with Benedict admitting, 'Here's our own hands against our hearts' (5.4.91–2). The material representation of their affection, in the form of badly written verse, ultimately overrides the resistance of their hearts. The touch of hand to paper, giving thought a material presence, a precedence over the unseen, immaterial affection itself, nevertheless allows their hearts to remain internal and inaccessible.

This movement is profoundly phenomenological. *Much Ado* sets up two sets of parallel worlds – the visible and invisible – that are subsequently reversed. In the play's opening scenes, Claudio and Hero hold idealised versions of their beloved in their minds. It is important that they have only seen but not spoken to each other before the scene at the altar when their first words are exchanged. Beatrice and Benedict have equally idealised anti-beloveds in their minds as the play opens; both are impossible. Beatrice's ideal man must 'be made of some other metal than earth' (2.1.50), for 'He that have a beard is more than a youth, and he that have no beard is less than a man; and he that is more than a youth is not for me, and he that is less than a man, I am not for him' (2.1.29–32). Benedict's ideal woman has all the possible qualities of woman in perfection, save her hair 'shall be of what colour it please God' (2.3.30–1). As the action of the play ensues, Claudio's ideal version of Hero is replaced with that of a 'common stale' and Hero's 'dear Claudio' (3.1.93) becomes a shallow cad at the altar. Simultaneously,

Benedict replaces the impossible and thus inaccessible ideal of his mind with the real Beatrice, just as Beatrice abandons her logical contradiction for the real person in the form of Benedict. This perfect symmetry – as ideal but unreal, replaced with real but imperfect – places phenomenal experience at the heart of the play's development. When Claudio accepts Hero for a second time, she is not a phantasm but a living wife. When Beatrice and Benedict find that their hearts are betrayed by their hands, it is once again their own experience that informs against them.

Notes

1. Crooke, *Microcosmographia*, B2r–B2v.
2. Not surprisingly, this scene has attracted a great deal of critical attention. See, for example, Carol Thomas Neely, *Broken Nuptials in Shakespeare's Plays*, pp. 24–57; Carol Cook, '"The Sign and Semblance of Her Honour": Reading Gender Difference in *Much Ado About Nothing*'; Nova Myhill, 'Spectatorship in/of *Much Ado About Nothing*'; Andrew Fleck, 'The Ambivalent Blush: Figural and Structural Metonymy, Modesty, and *Much Ado About Nothing*'.
3. The emphasis on visual perception as the source of Claudio's misguided certainty can also be seen in Othello's misuse of 'ocular proof' and Leontes's unwillingness to properly understand the evidence of his eyes in *The Winter's Tale*. Such examples confirm Katharine Maus's conclusion that 'The period's social and religious upheavals arguably provoke a keen, apparently nearly universal suspicion of "appearances"' (*Inwardness*, p. 210). For recent studies of visual perception and knowledge in the period, see my *Image Ethics* and Clark, *Vanities of the Eye*.
4. This is by no means a foregone conclusion. The fact that we can judge Claudio's behaviour suggests that he crosses the line, even if he were justified. Yet, even Beatrice, Hero's most forceful defender, hangs her defence on Hero's innocence,

implying that it is the wrongful accusation rather than the misguided punishment that is at stake.

5. Interestingly, Lucrece directly contradicts Laertes' moral that 'best safety lies in fear' (l. 42), when she notes that 'Mine enemy was strong, my poor self weak, / And far the weaker with so strong a fear' (ll. 1646–7). Air, as Carla Mazzio has reminded us, is among the most contested sites of exchange between material and immaterial conceptions of infection in the early modern era. References to contagion in Shakespeare almost always refer to air – fogs, clouds and so on, ethereal substances that can have a corrupting effect on those exposed. See Mazzio, 'History of Air'.

6. Here there is the textual issue of the Folio's 'dis-stain'd' usually emended to 'unstained'. See my textual comment on this line in the digital edition of *The Norton Shakespeare*, 3rd edn.

7. Darryl Chalk has written eloquently on affective contagion. See, for example, '"Make Me Not Sighted Like the Basilisk": Vision and Contagion in *The Winter's Tale*'; '"To Creep in at Mine Eyes": Theatre and Secret Contagion in *Twelfth Night*'; and 'Contagious Emulation: Antitheatricality and Theatre as Plague in *Troilus and Cressida*'.

8. Jonathan Gil Harris has pointed out the odd resistance to the view that plague was contagious through touch, as older views including the explanation that it was a punishment from God persisted well into the Restoration. See *Sick Economies*, p. 111.

9. Harris, *Sick Economies*, p. 77.

10. F has 'Yea' where Q2 has 'O're'; the F reading makes 'is thought-sick' the subject, which is closer to my sense than Q2's subject 'Heaven's face'.

11. I quote F, but Q2 has 'And there I see such black and grieved spots / As will leave there their tinct'. While 'grieved' seems inferior, the idea that the spots are 'such' spots – e.g. like the kind of spots that bad deeds would leave on one's soul, resulting in a stain – is powerful for my reading here.

12. The spiritual association of 'unction' with the anointing of the sick and extreme unction is relevant here.

13. *Norton*, p. 530. In the Arden edition, A. R. Humphreys identifies them as 'wit, imagination, fantasy, judgment, and memory' (p. 153). Also see E. Ruth Harvey, *The Inward Wits*.

14. In *Twelfth Night*, Feste (impersonating Sir Topas) urges the afflicted Malvolio to 'Endeavor thyself to sleep, and leave thy vain bibble-babble' in order to aid the 'heavens' to restore his wits (4.3.95–7). Similarly, Kent's concern that Lear's 'wits begin t'unsettle' (3.4.160) as a result of his exposure to the storm demonstrates Shakespeare's emphasis on the connection between the inward wits and the external perceptual body.

15. Heller-Roazen, *Inner Touch*, pp. 40–1 and *passim*.

16. E. Ruth Harvey argues that 'The tendency to solve the question of the communication between soul and body by inserting another term between them becomes more marked in later writers. Spirit is universally accepted, and the faculties are more precisely sub-divided in an attempt to define the point of contact between material and immaterial, rational and irrational. The whole scheme reaches its greatest elaboration with Avicenna, where the two extremes are arranged in a complex hierarchy' (*Inward Wits*, p. 37).

17. Paré, *Workes*, C6v.

18. Ibid., D1r.

19. Agamben cites the twelfth-century French master, William of Conches, in identifying the three faculties with three chambers in the brain. See *Stanzas*, p. 79.

20. Paré, *Workes*, Dir. The natural spirit is at once the least substantial in terms of dignity (that which separates humans from animals) and the most grossly material (beastly as in basic bodily function). Paré notes that there is some debate as to the existence of the natural spirit, perhaps due to the incompatibility of its gross materiality and the intermediary character of the spirits as conduits between the material body and immaterial soul. The elegant division of labour among the animal, vital and natural spirits allows for the complex voluntary actions to function properly. Bono ('Medical Spirits', p. 92) points out that the natural spirit is not found in Galen's extant texts, but was attributed to him by his followers.

21. Rothstein, 'Description, Intelligence, and the Excitation of Sight', pp. 58–9.

22. As noted above, Paré distinguishes between 'imagination' as 'apprehension which discernes and distinguisheth betweene the formes and shapes of things sensible, or which are knowne by the senses', and 'reasoning', which is described by Paré as 'a certaine judiciall æstimation of conceived or apprehended formes or figures, by a mutuall collating, or comparing them together'.

23. See Agamben, *Stanzas*, p. 78.

24. Sibylle Baumbach, *Shakespeare and the Art of Physiognomy*, has traced the importance of this kind of reading of outward appearances in relation to the pseudo-science of physiognomy. She quotes Sir Thomas Browne's *Religio Medici*: 'there are mystically in our faces certain Characters which carry in them the motto of our Souls, in which he that cannot read ABC may read our natures' (Browne, quoted in Baumbach, p. 24). Also see the essays in my collection *Shakespeare and the Power of the Face*.

25. For a catalogue of the ways of reading physiognomic features and for a specific discussion of masking and physiognomy, see Baumbach, *Physiognomy*, ch. 4 and pp. 162–8.

26. *OED* indicates that the early modern senses of disposition referred to both 'mental constitution or temperament; turn of mind' and 'physical constitution' or 'physical aptitude, tendency, or inclination (to something or to do something)' ('disposition' s.v. 6., 9[a]. 9b.).

27. Harvey, *Inward Wits*, p. 26.

28. Avicenna, quoted in ibid., p. 26.

29. This also reveals the influence of Neoplatonism. See above, Chapter 8.

30. Rothstein, 'Excitation', p. 55.

31. The examples are from Avicenna via Rothstein, 'Excitation', p. 55.

32. Lemnius, *Touchstone of Complexions*, M2r.

33. Ibid.

34. See Fleck, 'Ambivalent Blush' and Schoenfeldt, *Bodies and Selves*, pp. 6–7.
35. 'Frame' is usually glossed as 'contriving' or 'plotting' but also carries the meaning of bodily makeup, as in *OED* 9a: 'Applied to the animal, esp. the human body, with reference to its make, build, or constitution.'
36. Of course, buried in the racist comparison is the idea that if she were an 'Ethiope' she would also be stereotyped as overly sexualised, precisely the reason he disavows Hero at the altar.
37. King, 'Much Ado About Something', p. 154.
38. Ibid.

CHAPTER 10

'NEITHER FISH NOR FLESH, NOR GOOD RED HERRING': PHENOMENALITY, REPRESENTATION AND EXPERIENCE IN *THE TEMPEST*

. . . one might think that I hold that man lives only in the realm of the real. But we also live in the imaginary, also in the world of ideality.

Maurice Merleau-Ponty, *The Primacy of Perception*[1]

Perhaps more than any other Shakespeare play, *The Tempest* seems to invite symbolic or allegorical interpretation.[2] We sense that what we *see* is not necessarily what we are supposed to *get*. The implication is that the play is a kind of thought exercise. We are asked to convert the overloaded sensorium on stage – replete with music and spectacle – into ideas. In this chapter, rather than try to argue for what those ideas are supposed to be, to determine the play's message, moral or lesson, I explore how Shakespeare puts a particular kind of theatrical pressure on the intertwining of perception and ideation in *The Tempest*. Shakespeare's Duke Theseus might call these two mental faculties 'apprehension' and 'comprehension', the former involved in seizing phenomena given to experience, and the latter focused

on the subsequent experience in which the first is translated into coherent conceptual terms.[3] Rather than seeking
to determine what various characters, events or references
might represent, I am interested in how the playwright's
manipulation and destabilisation of the representational
options becomes a central focus of the play. As audience
members, we are consistently invited to witness characters
adjusting or reversing their sense of what is given on the
island – what the environment offers, or affords, phenome-
nally speaking. In other words, I argue that the play repeatedly stages moments in which phenomenal experience is
inadequately represented in intelligible terms, foregrounding the difficulty of reconciling mental and embodied experience as long as they are considered to be distinguishable.
As we are invited to witness the adaptation of the characters to their environment, we are also invited to adjust our
own sense of what is given in the play. The play's repeated
thematic reversal of what appears to be the case produces a
perceptual dynamic that makes comfort in thought difficult
at best. Rather than allowing for a settling of our senses
through cognitive understanding, *The Tempest* continues
to unsettle. In its continuous movement between thought
and sense, I argue that we are presented with the potential of theatrical play to mirror the phenomenological play
that structures embodied experience. My guide in what follows will be the work of Maurice Merleau-Ponty, though
other phenomenologists haunt my approach here. Like
the play, Merleau-Ponty invites a rethinking of the world–
word interaction that begins with an interrogation of the
terms by which this interaction is represented. Seeking to
dismantle Descartes' dualism, Merleau-Ponty's target is the
philosophical system that was about to reshape the landscape of early modern theories of mind–body interaction,
ushering in a description of modern subjectivity that would
dominate thought on the subject into the twentieth century.

Beyond the Material–Immaterial Distinction

At the heart of Merleau-Ponty's phenomenology is a resistance to philosophical dichotomies.[4] In an important sense, his career-long engagement with Descartes can be understood as an effort to undo the Cartesian dualism that distinguishes mind from body, as *res cognitans* and *res extensa*, respectively. For Descartes, this distinction was enabling; for Merleau-Ponty, it is deceptive. In privileging 'clarity and distinctness' while seeking to establish his philosophy from first principles, Descartes relied on categories to distinguish among different substances.[5] Merleau-Ponty does not give up the categories, but he undermines their distinctiveness, their ability to usefully isolate the facts of the world for philosophical reflection, due to the temporal nature of phenomenality. Consider the following, rather early statement of his position arguing for the primacy of perception in human experience:

> Naturally, it is necessary to establish here a difference between ideal truth and perceived truth. I do not undertake this immense task just now. I am only trying to show the organic tie, so to speak, between perception and intellection. Now it is incontestable that I dominate the stream of my conscious states and even that I am unaware of their temporal succession. At the moment when I am thinking or considering an idea, I am not divided into the instants of my life. But it is also incontestable that this domination of time, which is the work of thought, is always somewhat deceiving. Can I seriously say that I will always hold the ideas I do at present – and mean it?[6]

Even a cursory reflection on the way thought functions in time prompts Merleau-Ponty to be wary of reaching hard conclusions about not only objective truth but what he calls 'perceived truth' as well. The problem is the separation of thought from perception, as if one can inhabit the activity of thinking without the perceptual body. For Merleau-Ponty, this separation of idea from perception is never absolute. A little further on, he elaborates on the temporal element:

> We must say, on the contrary, that our ideas, however limited they may be at a given moment – since they always express our contact with being and with culture – are capable of being true provided we keep them open to the field of nature and culture which they must express. And this possibility is always open to us, just because we are temporal. The idea of going straight to the essence of things is an inconsistent idea if one thinks about it. What is given is a route, an experience which gradually clarifies itself, which gradually rectifies itself and proceeds by dialogue with itself and with others. Thus what we tear away from the dispersion of instants is not an already-made reason; it is, as has always been said, a natural light, our openness to *something*. What saves us is the possibility of a new development, and our power of making even what is false, true – by thinking through our errors and replacing them within the domain of truth.[7]

One might recall here Hamlet's cynical jab 'there is nothing either good or bad but thinking makes it so' (2.2.231.10–11).[8] Hamlet is wrong for precisely the reasons Merleau-Ponty identifies: his neglect of his essential 'contact with being and with culture' and the fact that 'we are temporal'. Hamlet, like Merleau-Ponty, leaves the things themselves intact, while worrying about the way we interact with them (and they with us), but unlike the phenomenologist, at this point in the play Hamlet denies any productive interaction between ideation and perception, denying himself the openness which might enable positive change, a 'new development'. As we saw in Chapter 9, he eventually returns to the body and to touch, and even if it results in his death, this return is a crucial step in the purging of the Danish state and a return to generative possibility.

Merleau-Ponty's response to Descartes' dualism involves a similar returning of thought to the body, and specifically to touch and sensation, which in turn calls for a resistance to certitude (Descartes' 'clarity and distinctness') in one's ongoing experience with the world. He specifically takes on Descartes with the aim of redefining the essential insight of the *Meditations*. Where Descartes deploys the sceptic's orientation to confirm his existence as a thinking subject, Merleau-Ponty foregrounds the ongoing act of doubting as a potentially positive orientation towards perceptual experience:

> But here is a third meaning of the *cogito*, the only solid one: the act of doubting in which I put in question all possible objects of my experience. This act grasps itself in its own operation [*à l'oeuvre*] and thus cannot doubt itself. The very fact of doubting obturates doubt. The certitude I have of myself is here a veritable perception: I grasp myself, not as a constituting subject which is transparent to itself, and which constitutes the totality of every possible object of thought and experience, but as a particular thought, as a thought engaged with certain objects, as a thought in act; and it is in this sense that I am thinking this or that as well as being certain that I am simply thinking. Thus I can get outside the psychological cogito – without, however, taking myself to be a universal thinker .... I am a thought which recaptures itself as already possessing an ideal of truth (which it cannot at each moment wholly account for) and which is the horizon of its operations. This [is a] thought, which *feels* itself rather than *sees* itself, which searches after clarity rather than possesses it, and which creates truth rather than finds it ...[9]

This resistance to clarity and certitude which appears so early in Merleau-Ponty's work only becomes more important in his developed phenomenology. In an attempt to overcome not only dualism, but also those philosophical positions that prioritise one or the other pole of the dichotomy – let's call them materialism and idealism – Merleau-Ponty increasingly insists on the hybridity of perceptual experience, ultimately developing a phenomenology that has among its central terms the *chiasm* or 'intertwining'.[10] Intertwining, the folding back of thought and touch, vision and idea, upon themselves leads Merleau-Ponty to the concept of the 'flesh of the world'. In Merleau-Ponty's 'flesh' we have a truly novel philosophical term, which resists categorisation as much as it offers clarification:

> The flesh is not matter, in the sense of corpuscles of being which would add up or continue on one another to form beings. Nor is the visible (the things as well as my own body) some 'psychic' material that would be – God knows how – brought into being by the things factually existing and acting on my factual body. In general it is not a fact or a sum of facts 'material' or 'spiritual'. Nor is it a representation for a mind: a mind could not be captured by its own representations; it would rebel against this insertion into the visible which is essential to the seer. The flesh is not matter, is not mind, is not substance. To designate it, we should need the old term 'element', in the sense it was used to speak of water, air, earth, and fire, that is, in the sense of a general thing, midway between the spatio-temporal individual and the idea, a sort of incarnate principle that brings a style of being wherever there is a fragment of being. The flesh is in this sense an 'element' of Being.[11]

The liminal nature of Merleau-Ponty's flesh is what makes it suggestive for overcoming the difficulties of understanding material/immaterial interactivity that so fascinated early modern poets. In rejecting 'psychic matter' as well as 'a representation of a mind', Merleau-Ponty rules out two of the most problematic ways of understanding mental material as distinct from somatic experience. Flesh 'is not matter, is not mind, is not substance', but it is elemental in a way that combines the usual functions of each of these in temporal experience. Later in *The Visible and the Invisible*, he elaborates on the operation of the flesh in experience:

> Once again, the flesh we are speaking of is not matter. It is the coiling over of the visible upon the seeing body, of the tangible upon the touching body, which is attested in particular when the body sees itself, touches itself seeing and touching the things, such that, simultaneously, *as* tangible it descends among them, *as* touching it dominates them all and draws this relationship and even this double relationship from itself, by dehiscence or fission of its own mass.[12]

Merleau-Ponty developed this phenomenological perspective by continually returning to experience, and by rejecting previously held truths in favour of an evolving attention to phenomenality. Settled truths held up by philosophy and science congeal around concepts articulated in language. Language offers the illusion of arresting the temporality of experience and allowing for a rebuilding of the world out from the stasis of abstraction:

> When we ask what it is for the things and for the world to exist, one might think that it is only a matter of defining a word. After all, the questions take place in language. Even if it seems to us that an affirmative thought can detach itself from words and rest on its internal adequation, negation and especially interrogation, which do not express any property intrinsic to the things, can be sustained only by the apparatus of language.[13]

Though language is unavoidable in any attempt to make sense of phenomenal experience, to reflect on one's relationship to the material world, it must be interrogated with the same energy with which one would hope to undertake such reflection:

> One can reduce philosophy to a linguistic analysis only by supposing that language has its evidence within itself, that the signification of the word 'world' or 'thing' presents in principle no difficulty, that the rules for the legitimate use of the word can be clearly read in a univocal signification. But the linguists teach us that this is precisely not the case, that the univocal signification is but one part of the signification of the word, that beyond it there is always a halo of signification that manifests itself in new and unexpected modes of use, that there is an operation of language upon language which, even without other incitements, would launch language back into a new history, and makes of the word-meaning itself an enigma. Far from harboring the secret of the being of the world, language is itself a world, itself a being – a world and a being to the second power, since it does not speak in a vacuum, since it speaks *of* being and *of* the world and therefore redoubles their enigma instead of dissipating it.[14]

Always returning to the situatedness of perception, and its relation to utterance, ideality and cognition, Merleau-Ponty recognises the importance of interrogation and negation not as philosophical principles but as essential steps in an ongoing process. As we have seen in earlier chapters, negation is powerful because it adjusts understanding without entirely eliminating what has been negated; negation is thus both productive and destructive.[15] It enables recognition of the limitations of perception in the face of the reality of temporal, embodied experience of the world, its things, both living and inanimate.

Brutus's observation that 'the eye sees not itself, / But by reflection, by some other things' (*Julius Caesar*, 1.2.52–3) comes in response to Cassius's question 'can you see your face?' (1.2.51). Brutus's negative response opens up his truth. Accepting the truth of Brutus's observation, Cassius goes on to lament, also in the negative, that Brutus has 'no such mirrors as will turn / your hidden worthiness into your eye, / That you might see your shadow' (1.2.55–8). The metaphor of the mirrors is complex here, as Cassius's 'shadow', the ostensible reflection in the mirrors, would supposedly reveal a 'worthiness' that is only 'hidden' to Brutus. For Cassius goes on to say that others, 'many of the best respect in Rome', wish Brutus 'had his eyes', suggesting his worthiness is not hidden to them, that only Brutus is blind to it. The 'shadow' here, as elsewhere in the period, invokes a contrast to 'substance'; Cassius wishes, like Richard in the deposition scene, that Brutus might see his 'substance', his essential quality: 'yourself which yet you know not of' (1.2.70). Offering himself as the mirror Brutus lacks, Cassius serves as intermediary, the shadow of Brutus's substance, the image of which is reflected in his linguistic counsel.[16] Though Cassius here wants Brutus to see the way he is seen, this is impossible without mediation. Brutus is right – we can never see ourselves as we are seen, except 'by some other things'. This is also precisely the phenomenological problem that Merleau-Ponty identifies throughout his late work as the aspect of experience that we ought to emphasise. We can see him working through this point in the working notes to the *Visible and the Invisible*:

> what stands in the way of my seeing myself is at first a *de facto* invisible (my eyes invisible for me), but beyond this invisible (which lacuna is filled by the other and by my generality) a *de jure* invisible: I cannot see myself in movement, witness my movement.[17]

What he means here is that, in being situated in the body, the act of perceiving is always located: 'I am for myself a zero of movement even during movement, *I do not move away from myself.*'[18] This insight brings him to the heart of the problem that dualism introduces and that he seeks to overcome:

> The touching of oneself and the touching have to be understood as each the reverse of the other – the negativity that inhabits the touch (and which I must not minimize: it is because of it that the body is not an empirical fact, that it has an ontological signification), the untouchable of the touch, the invisible of vision, the unconscious of consciousness . . . is the *other side* or the *reverse* (or the other dimensionality) of sensible Being; one cannot say that it is *there*, although there would assuredly be points where it *is not* – It is there with a presence by investment in another dimensionality . . .'[19]

Merleau-Ponty is extending the phenomenological observation that in perception we can always only see certain facets of a three-dimensional object, though we know the others exist and we hold them in our minds as real. Rather than extend this in the service of a form of idealism, Merleau-Ponty seeks to return to the world of sensuous perception to confirm a relational perceptual ontology while maintaining a place for the invisible, the immaterial, in that ontology:

> Phenomenology is here the recognition that the theoretically complete, full world of the physical explanation is not so, and that therefore it is necessary to consider as ultimate, inexplicable, and *hence as a world by itself* the whole of our experience of sensible being and of men. A world by itself: i.e. it is necessary to translate into perceptual logic what science and positive psychology treat as fragments of the In Itself *absque praemissis* [without premises].[20]

Both/And

What attracted me to the expression in this chapter's title, 'neither fish nor flesh', is its positive operation from negation. 'Neither fish nor flesh' makes its only direct appearance in Shakespeare when Falstaff tells Hal that Mistress Quickly is 'neither fish nor flesh; a man knows not where to have her' (*1 Henry IV*, 3.3.115–16). This quip follows some idle banter in which Falstaff and the hostess quibble over her status as a 'thing':

> FALSTAFF Go, you thing, go!
>
> HOSTESS Say, what thing? What thing?
>
> FALSTAFF What thing! Why, a thing to thank God on.
>
> HOSTESS I am no thing to thank God on, I would thou shouldst know it; I am an honest man's wife: and, setting thy knighthood aside, thou art a knave to call me so.
>
> FALSTAFF Setting thy womanhood aside, thou art a beast to say otherwise.
>
> HOSTESS Say, what beast, thou knave, thou?
>
> FALSTAFF What beast! Why, an otter.
>
> PRINCE An otter, Sir John! Why an otter?
>
> FALSTAFF Why, she's neither fish nor flesh; a man knows not where to have her. (3.3.104–16)

According to Jean Howard's gloss in the *Norton Shakespeare*, 'The otter's unusual appearance led to debates about whether it was a fish or animal', a point confirmed by Isaac Walton's reference to the otter in *The Compleat Angler*.[21] Yet Edward Topsell includes the otter in his *History of Four Footed Beasts* (1607) derived from Conrad Gesner's mid-sixteenth-century bestiary. In an illustration included in both texts the aquatic mammal is depicted eating a fish, a detail that would seem to distinguish it from the fish rather than blur the boundary.

It is the linguistic movement from 'thing', to 'beast', to specific beast 'otter' that interests me here. Falstaff's reference to the hostess as a 'thing' – ostensibly too materially indistinct to categorise – only becomes meaningful through linguistic play. His jab calls on the connotation of 'thing' as

a euphemism for female genitalia, thus reducing her to a sexual object through reference to the hostess's gender-defining
anatomical feature. However, in the next line Falstaff 'sets
her womanhood aside' and removes any clarity in the connotation of 'thing' by shifting to the equally general 'beast',
a thing that is explicitly non-human. When prompted by
the Prince, he is able to supply a suitably ambiguous if specific beast, the otter, which is 'neither fish nor flesh'.[22] In this
movement towards clarification, the terms actually get less
and less distinct. Falstaff negates the positive denotations of
each of the clarifications he offers, arriving at his definition
of the hostess by negation, she is 'neither fish nor flesh', indicating she fits in no category – she is nothing. It is worth noting that this is common in Shakespeare: when categorisation
fails, the result is often 'nothing', as in the Duke's comment
to Mariana in *Measure for Measure*, 'why you are nothing
then: neither maid, widow, nor wife?' (5.1.182).[23]

Yet, the reduction to nothing is not troubling here.
'Nothing' is not pure nothingness, but rather *not those
things*. Put another way, what we experience in this scene
is a harmless (and necessary) process: Falstaff and Mistress
Quickly at play. The scene enacts multiple senses of play,
as it seems clear this is a regular form of recreation for the
two, while at the same time the pleasure of the exchange
comes in the movement between the terms that constitute
the banter. The expression, 'neither fish nor flesh', though,
adds another aspect of playfulness to the exchange. The
expression is recorded in the sixteenth century as short-
hand for something that defies categorisation, something
that can't be named or brought under the understanding,
and is thus useless (perhaps as a result of its resistance to
categorisation). Moreover, it is an expression that is closely
connected to the everyday lived experience of its users. The
opposition between flesh and fish arises from the consump-
tion of flesh and fish on designated days according to the

Christian calendar, as other references to eating fish and flesh in Shakespeare attest. In *Pericles*, for example, the first fisherman comforts Pericles by telling him they 'will have flesh for holidays and fish for fasting days' (2.1.80). The exchange follows the musing of the third fisherman about the nature of the porpoise as a predictor of sea storms: 'said not I as much when I saw the porpoise how he bounced and tumbled? They say they're half fish, half flesh: a plague on them, they ne'er come but I look to be washed' (2.1.23–6).

The third fisherman's question, 'I marvel how the fish live in the sea', reflects his fear of the sea's unpredictable nature, something the monstrous – half fish, half flesh – of which the porpoise seems to have a supernatural understanding.[24] Rather than see porpoise behaviour as useful equipment for his own relationship with the sea, the third fisherman blames them for his misfortune with the storm. His question about how fish live in the sea – something he clearly sees as untenable – is turned back on him by the first fisherman:

> Why, as men do a-land; the great ones eat up the little ones: I can compare our rich misers to nothing so fitly as to a whale; 'a plays and tumbles, driving the poor fry before him, and at last devours them all at a mouthful: such whales have I heard on o'th' land, who never leave gaping till they've swallowed the whole parish, church, steeple, bells, and all. (2.1.28–34)

The fisherman connects his subordinate's worry about the porpoise's action in the sea – how it 'bounced and tumbled' – to the action of the predatory whale who 'plays and tumbles, driving the poor fry before him', but he also conceptualises it, abstracting the ideas of predator and prey to construct a socio-economic moral. Along the way he blurs the fish/flesh distinction, as his whales take to the land to devour the parish. Overhearing the exchange, Pericles marvels at the fisherman's ability to extract social morals from the sea's unruly chaos:

> How from the finny subjects of the sea
> These fishers tell the infirmities of men
> And from their wat'ry empire recollect
> All that may men approve or men detect. (2.1.47–50)[25]

Pericles's social position has lifted him from the world of things to the extent that he cannot connect with the everyday experiences that inform the fishermen's knowledge. Perhaps more importantly, he cannot connect the rarified world that he comes from with the fishermen's material reality. For Pericles, the distinction between 'finny subjects' and 'the infirmities of men' is clear. Not so for the fishermen. In their exchange, the third fisherman connects folk wisdom about the porpoise as portent with his own embodied experience: when he sees the porpoise, he expects to get wet, 'washed' by the storm. Both the experience and the language used to express it make the scene possible, suggesting an intimate connection between the worlds of language and sense.

This brings me to the variant of the expression in my chapter title, recorded in John Heywood's *A dialogue conteinyng the nomber in effect of all the prouerbes in the Englishe tongue* (1546): 'neither fish nor flesh nor good red herring'.[26] The extended expression adds a socio-economic dimension to the religious differentiation by fast days and holidays, as flesh may have indicated wealth, and 'good red herring' a common staple easily accessible to the poor. In fact, Andrew Hadfield has recently reminded us how Thomas Nashe stressed the importance of herring in *Lenten Stuff*, which 'sees the herring, especially when preserved through smoking as red herring, as the staple food that has made England powerful, preserved its liberties and sustained its people'.[27] As important as the sustaining character of the ubiquitous herring was to England at the turn of the seventeenth century is the linguistic association of the red herring with a distraction, a figurative use perhaps initiated by Nashe himself.[28]

I want to stress how the material and conceptual, the natural and the intellectual overlap and intertwine in this delightful expression. When perception and language fail to fall into an accord, when the conceptual apparatus at hand to the perceiver cannot adequately account for the world before one's eyes, it is possible to fall back on the playfulness of such an expression, to hover in the indeterminate relation of embodied experience and cognitive control. Reason urges either flesh or fish or good red herring, but not all three at once, or even any combination of the two. Such distinctions provide order, name facts and make sense of the days, or the social degrees by which people are to be known. In such cases the assumption is that we know what we see and we can account for it in language. When something – or some 'thing' – frustrates that expectation, we are faced with an indistinct and, perhaps, troubling phenomenon. How we react to this indeterminacy shapes us as much as it shapes the world we seek to understand. And this brings me to *The Tempest*, the primary subject of the present chapter.

Phenomenality, and the Materials of Theatrical Play

I'll begin with a celebrated scene from the second act, when Trinculo discovers Caliban for the first time:

> What have we here, a man or a fish? Dead or alive? A fish: he smells like a fish; a very ancient and fish-like smell; a kind of not of the newest poor-john. A strange fish! Were I in England now, as once I was, and had but this fish painted, not a holiday fool there but would give a piece of silver. There would this monster make a man; any strange beast there makes a man. When they will not give a doit

to relieve a lame beggar, they will lay out ten to see a dead Indian. Legged like a man and his fins like arms! Warm o'my troth! I do now let loose my opinion, hold it no longer: this is no fish, but an islander, that hath lately suffered by a thunderbolt. (2.2.24–36)

As playgoers, we watch as Trinculo works through an experience for which he has no precedent. He begins with sight – 'what have we here' – though quickly turns to smell, 'he smells like a fish, a very ancient and fish-like smell', which brings to his mind the association with the poor-john, or salted hake, a poor man's fish like the red herring. But this is not that fish; it is 'strange'. And the strangeness leads to the memory of street wonders Trinculo has personally witnessed for sale in London, including the reference to a 'dead Indian'. This, of course, ties back to his initial question, 'dead or alive?' but it also extends the frame of reference to the audience – as the display of a 'dead Indian' in England could have been in the collective memory of audience members who had either witnessed or read about the display of Canadian Inuits brought back by Martin Frobisher in 1577.[29] But Trinculo returns to the present scene before him and begins to note recognition – the fish becomes man, as Trinculo recognises his legs, and sees that his fins are 'like arms'. This is inverted, of course, as it is Trinculo who had made them fins in the first place. Only when he touches Caliban does he come to his final conclusion – the warmth of the touch confirms both that Caliban is alive and that he is not cold-blooded like a fish. When he lets loose his opinion, he is able to come to a fully coherent account of what he had previously been unable to understand. Not only is Trinculo convinced that Caliban is a man (a native of this isle), but his appearance can be explained as the result of a trauma – he has been struck by lightning.

Of course, Trinculo's conceptual understanding is not actually more clear and distinct than his somatic impressions: is

Caliban a native struck by lightning or an odd-looking, smelly, indistinct creature, whose warmth is the only sign of life? Unlike the jester, the audience is not in the same position to assess Caliban, for we have already been introduced, though what we have learned from our earlier experience may complicate rather than clarify. Unlike Trinculo, who first perceives and then attempts to understand Caliban's appearance, the audience first hears Caliban described by Prospero as 'a freckled whelp, hag born', the son of a 'damned witch' (1.2.263), 'litter[ed]' on the island before Prospero and Miranda arrived. We also learn that he is Prospero's slave and that in Miranda's estimation he is 'a villain . . . I do not love to look on' (1.2.310–11); he 'serves in offices that profit' Prospero and Miranda, despite that he 'never Yields' them 'kind answer' (1.2.312–13, 8–9). Prospero directly addresses him as 'earth' before offering one last detail about his parentage prior to his appearance on stage: 'Thou poisonous slave, got by the devil himself / Upon thy wicked dam; come forth!' (1.2.19–20). While this last incantation could tell us more about Prospero than Caliban, calling into question as it does the nature of his magic, Prospero's details nevertheless prefigure our experience of Caliban before we ever see the actor's body.

These two extremes represent opposite poles on a spectrum of material and immaterial objectivity that make up what I will call the 'materials of theatrical play'. In the first example, Shakespeare stages an encounter with the embodied Caliban, in the form of an actor embodying the character Caliban, and, another actor, Trinculo's embodied experience with the material sensorium of the staged world, here specifically an unknown or unrecognisable body. The bodies in this first example are the primary theatrical materials, as Trinculo's reactions to his environment are a direct result of his sensuous experience with Caliban's prostrate body, 'flat' on the stage before him – his confusion at the shape, disgust at the smell, and recognition with the touch.

In the second example from earlier in the play, a complex language of description and categorisation precedes and thus prefigures Caliban's appearance as an embodied figure on the stage. The Caliban we eventually see has already been given form by the language used to introduce him. Here, I am particularly interested in the movement – the play, if you will – between these two Calibans: the embodied Caliban, 'a thing as strange as ere I looked on', as Alonso describes him in act 5, and the conceptual Caliban, the 'freckled whelp', the 'hagborn' son of a witch and devil who had attempted to rape the young Miranda, thus bringing on his 'deserved' enslavement.[30] I suggest that this kind of play between the Caliban of thought and the Caliban of body is repeated throughout the entirety of *The Tempest*'s movements. Moreover, it is important to note that a third Caliban, the speaking embodied character, occupies a space between these two extremes.

The oft-noted contrast between the opening scene of the sea storm and the extended verbal exposition of Prospero's history in the following scene relies on a similar kind of play. The important political message of the opening scene, with its inversion of social order brought on by the storm, as the mariners take precedence over aristocrats in the moment of crisis – 'What care these roarers for the name of king?' (1.1.15–16) – is a kind of invitation for the audience to indulge in a kind of play. We in the audience can see the inverted order, just as, and perhaps as a result of the fact that, we can see the phenomenal event: the storm, the ship, the impending threat of the wreck in the angry sea. This scene is not infected by the perspective of a particular character; rather it is presented to us as a natural spectacle, and we are to make sense of it from our position in the audience. But as soon as the storm appears, it disappears, and we are shifted to another perspective, this time Miranda's witnessing of the tempest from the shore in scene 2. From her perspective, outside of the storm rather than in it, the ship becomes an entirely inarticulate spectacle that affects Miranda emotionally, leading her to beg her father to 'allay' the 'wild waters . . . roar' (1.2.2). A spectator rather than a participant in the watery struggle, Miranda nevertheless responds to the spectacle as if she were herself in danger of some harm. Though she can have no experiential reference for the human disaster – it is like nothing she has seen before – she claims that she has felt the pain of those lost in the storm:

> The sky, it seems, would pour down stinking pitch
> But that the sea, mounting to th' welkin's cheek,
> Dashes the fire out. O, I have suffered
> With those that I saw suffer – a brave vessel
> (Who had no doubt some noble creature in her)
> Dashed all to pieces. O, the cry did knock
> Against my very heart! Poor souls, they perished. (1.2.3–9)

As Miranda tells it, she is immersed in the spectacle, moved by rather than master of what she sees. Prospero's efforts to reassure her come not from the somatic, but the linguistic, intellectual register. In this dimension, there is 'no harm', as Prospero tells her in the hopes of calming her agitated state:

> The direful spectacle of the wreck which touched
> The very virtue of compassion in thee,
> I have with such provision in mine art
> So safely ordered, that there is no soul –
> No, not so much perdition as an hair
> Betid to any creature in the vessel
> Which thou heard'st cry, which thou saw'st sink. (1.2.26–32)

Prospero essentially tells Miranda that she has not seen what she has seen. But the 'cry' (perhaps, Gonzalo's fatalistic repetition 'we split!') that knocked 'against her very heart', that 'touched / The very virtue of compassion' in her, has become a part of Miranda's felt existence, regardless of its claim to 'objective' reality. The phantasm of the shipwreck, embodied for us as audience in the opening spectacle, becomes for Miranda a real experience of a traumatic event. Her conclusion, 'they perished', is understandable but false; just as (in a very different register) Trinculo's initial conclusion that Caliban is a fish is false. Only time will enable correction.

Prospero's confidence in his ability to 'safely order' the events suggests that, at this point in the play, he is completely detached from sensuous experience, and particularly the sensuous as a path to truth. Despite losing his dukedom through practical neglect due to an obsession with ideas, he is still 'all dedicated / To closeness and the bettering of [his] mind' (1.2.89–90). But as Prospero explains how their history accounts for his current actions, Miranda's physical agitation shifts from the empathic suffering with the mariners to the impatience of an unsatisfied auditor: 'for still 'tis beating in my mind, your reason for / Raising this sea storm' (1.2.176–7). Prospero's explanation elaborated over the course of more than 150 lines, so much linguistic exposition, tells us (and Miranda) quite a lot, but it raises as many questions as it answers.[31] Is the whole of the plot the result of chance or fate? What is Prospero's relation to the 'auspicious star' whose 'influence' he must 'court' or his fortunes will 'ever droop'. If he 'omits' the influence of this star, will it change his fate, suggesting fate is subject to will? Because he must act in either case, deliberately omitting the influence of the star or 'courting' it, his silence on what precisely it is that he plans to do makes the explanation that much more enigmatic.

Perhaps more importantly, Miranda never gets to respond to Prospero's explanation. Instructing her to leave her questioning, Prospero arrests her 'beating mind' with sleep he knows she 'canst not choose' to resist. Despite the magic that brings on her sleep, the somatic character of her escape from thought is worth noting. Just as she succumbs to sleep, Ariel appears, ready to offer us another perspective on the sea storm. We might be surprised at Prospero's first question to Ariel, 'Hast thou, Spirit, / Performed to point the tempest that I bade thee?' (1.2.93–4). The question qualifies his earlier claim to Miranda that he 'safely ordered' the spectacle she witnessed; rather than orchestrating (ordering) the entire scene in which his control would ensure the safety of those aboard the ship, now it seems he has only commanded (ordered) that no harm be done in Ariel's performance of the tempest. Prospero's question suggests that unlike those of us in the audience, and even Miranda herself, he has not seen the spectacle he ordered. We thus get another perspective as Ariel reports his first-hand account:

> I boarded the King's ship; now on the beak,
> Now in the waist, the deck in every cabin
> I flamed amazement. Sometime I'd divide
> And burn in many places – on the topmast,
> The yards and bowsprit would I flame distinctly,
> Then meet and join. Jove's lightning, the precursors
> O'th' dreadful thunderclaps, more momentary
> And sight-outrunning were not; the fire and cracks
> Of sulpherous roaring, the most mighty Neptune
> Seem to besiege and make his bold waves tremble,
> Yea, his dread trident shake. (1.2.196–206)

Ariel's description emphasises his immersion in the scene of shipwreck – he is everywhere, 'on the beak', 'in the waist, the deck in every cabin'. Delighted with Ariel's work, Prospero still must ask 'but are they . . . safe?' (217). His knowledge of the events is distinguished here from the kind of first-hand experience that Ariel describes. This is true throughout most of the play: he does not witness the events to which he responds. Examples include his knowledge of the plot against Alonso, Caliban's plot against him, and the pivotal spectacle of the weeping Gonzalo, all of which he either 'foresees' 'through his art' (2.1.290) or has reported to him by Ariel. Important exceptions include his oversight of Ariel's visitation on the usurpers in the form of a harpy and his involvement in the courtship of Ferdinand and Miranda. Unlike the majority of the play's scenes in which Prospero gains control through language, in the case of such exceptions he is very much immersed – to the point of creepiness – intertwined in the action as direct witness and participant. In the banquet scene the needs of the body are offered and denied, while the latter denies the needs of the body only to offer their fulfilment in the exorbitant pageantry of the wedding masque. Both are witnessed by Prospero, who remains removed, either in the wings or 'on the top, invisible' (3.3.17SD), but engaged. The reversals of the banquet and the masque involve fantastic spectacles produced by spirits that are explicitly conceptual (the Harpy represents torment by starvation, while the generative goddesses of the masque represent plenty). These shows vanish abruptly, leaving the characters with an altered sensorium and an inexplicable encounter with the immaterial, both equally real experiences, though seemingly impossible to reconcile. Throughout the play, Prospero's detachment of reflective thought from sensuous experience – chief among the faults he himself identifies with his usurpation – is set in relief by the immersion of other characters in their environment.

Returning to the scene of Trinculo's discovery of Caliban, recall that his initial encounter with the incomprehensible object is interrupted by his sensuous acknowledgement of the approaching storm, heralded by thunder. Though many editors add the stage direction '[Thunder]' just after Trinculo reaches his conclusion about what he is looking at, the text clearly indicates that Trinculo *feels* the storm – both Trinculo's exclamation at the storm's arrival, and the Folio's capitalised 'Thunderbolt', serve as an effective stage direction:

> this is no fish, but an islander that hath been lately suf-
> fered by a Thunderbolt. Alas, the storm is come again! My
> best way is to creep under his gaberdine; there is no other
> shelter hereabouts: misery acquaints a man with strange
> bed-fellows. I will here shroud till the dregs of the storm be
> past. (2.2.33–8)[32]

This is quite an evolution from his initial reaction upon seeing – and smelling – what he could only imagine was a dead
fish. One could read the moment allegorically, as Trinculo
takes on the flesh of the world (in the conventional sense)
and becomes associated with the 'earth' (as Caliban is called)
rather than the air. But the scene does not end here; the next
movements invite a continual reappraisal of its conceptual
offerings.

Now that Trinculo has climbed under Caliban's gaber-
dine, Stefano enters and the phenomenological scene repeats,
this time with the added feature of sound. Stefano responds to
both the unexpected visual spectacle of Caliban's body now
intertwined with Trinculo's as well as Caliban's exclamation:
'Do not torment me! O!' (2.2.53). 'What's the matter?' asks
Stefano, 'Have we devils here? Do you put tricks upon's with
savages and men of Ind? Ha! I have not 'scaped drowning to
be afeared now of your four legs . . .' (2.2.55–60). After Caliban complains 'the spirit torments me! O!' (2.2.60), Stefano
tries again to work out the scene before him:

> This is some monster of the isle with four legs, who hath
> got, as I take it, an ague. Where the devil should he learn
> our language? I will give him some relief, if it be but for
> that. If I can recover him and keep him tame and get to
> Naples with him, he's a present for any emperor that ever
> trod on neat's leather. (2.2.64–9)

Stefano's response to Caliban is an echo of Trinculo's, including the idea that Caliban's exotic form will be worth a reward in Europe. His description of Caliban as 'some monster of the isle with four legs' also plays on Trinculo's earlier impression that Caliban is a fish, with arms like fins.[33] More entrepreneurial than Trinculo, Stefano's instinct is to nurse the monster to health in order to receive his financial reward. The 'monster of the isle' must have an 'ague', he reasons, for which the obvious cure is drink. Stephano's surprise at the monster's ability to speak his language highlights the play's interest in precisely the dichotomy between thought and sense that Merleau-Ponty hopes to collapse.

As many critics have commented, language acquisition looms large in this play. Ferdinand is struck with wonder at Miranda's ability to speak his language, a result of parentage and training under Prospero, her 'schoolmaster', and she and her father are together responsible for Caliban's knowledge of Italian. Though Miranda rebukes Caliban for his ingratitude, he makes a trenchant point when recounting that learning their language added nothing to his command of the material resources of the island, 'The fresh springs, brine-pits, barren place and fertile' (1.2.338). Importantly, the play never questions Ariel's ability to speak the language of the Italians. In this way, the play aligns language with the intellect, and with spirit, the connection to the mind beyond the brain, seemingly a world apart.[34] Stefano's interaction with the four legged, two-voiced monster draws out but also complicates this association of language with spirit:

STEFANO   Come on your ways; open your mouth; here
is that which will give language to you, cat:
open your mouth; this will shake your shaking,
I can tell you, and that soundly: you cannot tell
who's your friend: open your chaps again.

TRINCULO   I should know that voice: it should be – but he
is drowned; and these are devils: O defend me!

STEFANO   Four legs and two voices: a most delicate monster! His forward voice now is to speak well of
his friend; his backward voice is to utter foul
speeches and to detract. If all the wine in my
bottle will recover him, I will help his ague.
(2.2.76–86)

It is wine, the very material spirit in Stefano's bottle,
that will 'give language' to the beast ('cat') Caliban. This
detail – the European giving the gift of language and thus
'civilisation', like the exchange over Prospero and Miranda's gift of language to Caliban earlier – has taken a central
place in post-colonial readings of the play. But in terms of
the scene's phenomenological exploration of experience,
we see here something of the intertwining of perception and
language to which Merleau-Ponty directs our attention. To
be sure, the champion of language is equally the villain in
the phenomenological account as he is in the reading that
foregrounds the violence of colonial expansion. But viewed
through the phenomenological lens, we see another layer
of the play's playfulness on the question of understanding. Rather than simply valorise the natural Caliban as the
passive victim of the oppressive colonial master – in which
the oppressor defines himself by dehumanising the other –
a phenomenological reading emphasises that Caliban is
part of the master and the master is part of Caliban. In
identifying the only gift to come from learning Italian as the
ability to curse, Caliban gestures towards what Merleau-
Ponty would call the 'pre-reflective' perception of the
world. Though he has been taught to 'name the bigger
light and the less that burn by day and night' (1.2.336–7),
this in no way obviates his reliance on previous experience
with the sun and moon in his daily routine. Cursing and
naming are moments in the temporal experience of the
phenomenal world.

If we follow Merleau-Ponty, however, this ought not lead to a simple opposition between an uncorrupted pre-reflective natural position – represented by the pre-colonial, pre-enslaved Caliban. This would amount to the search for a pre-linguistic primordial being, a fool's errand that Jacques Lacan specifically, and mistakenly, accused Merleau-Ponty of championing.[35] It is possible to see a parallel here to Michel Serres's materialist goal of overcoming philosophical language by returning to the sensuous body.[36] But for Merleau-Ponty, we must recognise that language is our only means to discuss this pre-reflective perceptual position – a position, moreover, that is always obscured from our view. Shakespeare seems to have recognised this as well, for Caliban himself offers the pre-reflective version – the childlike 'bigger and the lesser light' – in language. As the post-colonial readings of the play have stressed, Caliban's language acquisition doesn't transform him from silence to speech, but from one form of speech to another.[37] Nevertheless, the play provides us with a view of the degrees by which language and abstraction effect a distancing of perception from itself. Caliban knows the materials of the island, where to drink, eat and shelter, while Prospero controls their representation.

Caliban is, in Prospero's description, 'savage' (or 'salvage'); in his first extended speech he stresses his basic material needs: he 'must eat [his] dinner' (1.2.330). As Dan Brayton reminds us, 'salvage' is derived from the Latin for 'wood' or 'forest' and could be used to describe a landscape, animal or human outside of society.[38] The term is etymologically linked to the 'wild' and thus the 'weald' or 'wood'.[39] In *The Tempest*, this wildness is the product of European reflection on the pre-reflective state; what would one's existence feel like before the triumph of reason over desire? 'Wild' is also the term that Merleau-Ponty settles on in his search for a non-dualist ontology based in perception and experience: 'wild being'. The wild being for Merleau-Ponty is variously associated with the 'brute' and 'primordial'. While this may sound like a search for essences, it is quite the opposite: 'What I want to do is restore the world as a meaning of Being absolutely different from the "represented", that is, as the vertical Being which none of the "representations" exhaust and which all "reach", the wild Being.'[40] On the other hand, Prospero's rarified search for the betterment of his mind that takes him from the world and his dukedom is likely a search for essences (as work on Prospero's magic, as magus and alchemist, have shown).[41] The embrace of the wild, not its transcendence, is what will set him free. This is not the embrace of pure materiality, or fallen human nature, however. It is, in my reading, the intertwining of the representational and the embodied. Merleau-Ponty writes that 'The in itself–for itself integration' – in other words, the temporal supersession of the dualist opposition – 'takes place not in the absolute consciousness, but in the Being in promiscuity. The perception of the world is formed in the world, the test for truth takes place in Being.'[42]

Being represented in the play, through its materials, 'reaches' this 'wild Being', without exhausting or accounting for it. The play of being and the play of theatre is open to that something yet to come. The play begins on a ship, a 'bark' if you will, containing the representatives of civilisation and reason, the sinking of which introduces the story of Prospero's misfortunes that are intimately tied to his 'books', the ostensible containers of his knowledge and magic; these books in turn become the singular and representative 'book' he will drown in the final act, as he returns to the world. We witness a burlesque of this play between world and word in Stefano's command that Trinculo 'kiss the book', a blasphemous parody of monotheistic allegiance, especially considering that the book is, in fact, a bottle made of bark, a detail that cannot help but remind us of the 'bark' or boat that got Prospero and Miranda to the island with their books. Moreover, the contents of Stefano's book made of bark is spirits (liquor), just as the contents of the cloven pine (with reference to the devil and Sycorax's consort) is a spirit (Ariel). The contents of Prospero's book is his power over spirits. We might even extend our play to Trinculo's suspicion of Caliban, who 'when his God's asleep, he'll rob his bottle', by which he means that Caliban will rob Stefano (his God's) bark-bottle of its spirits, with the double meaning that when Prospero (his true God) sleeps he will rob him of his power, both the contents of his books, and the spirit that animates his life. All of this intertwining of material and ideal is dizzying in precisely the way that Merleau-Ponty imagines wild Being (the flesh of the world) to be disruptive to the stasis of both materialism and idealism.

This brings me to the final scene, and in particular the presentation of another spectacle, here the *tableau vivant* of Ferdinand and Miranda at play. There is much to say about the only appearance of a game of chess in Shakespeare. As William Poole has noted, the game represents the full spectrum of society and 'was invented . . . to civilize tyrants, to allow them to engage in combat on the chessboard rather than the battlefield'.[43] In other words, to play chess is to play in a way that will cause 'no harm', to borrow Prospero's phrase. The chess game can thus be interpreted as a metaphor for the entire play, a game that, despite its serious themes, has caused no harm. But there is also a phenomenological angle here, in that we are presented with a particular spectacle of Ferdinand and Miranda playing chess, followed by the somewhat surprising accusation that the game is not played fair: 'Sweet lord, you play me false' (5.1.171). Rather than accept Ferdinand's insistence that he would not cheat 'for the world', Miranda turns his false play into 'fair play': '. . . for a score of kingdoms you should wrangle, / And I would call it fair play' (5.1.173–4).[44] I would recall here Merleau-Ponty's affirmation of negation as the promise of the temporal: 'What saves us is the possibility of a new development and our power of making even what is false, true – by thinking through our errors and replacing them within the domain of truth.'[45]

Prospero's self-acknowledged 'error' in his explanation to Miranda, his withdrawal into thought above all else, is the error that must be corrected at the end of the play. But I am not suggesting that we identify this error with a misguided privileging of intellect over the sensuous body, somehow denying him the essence of his humanity, which should be properly balanced between reason and emotion. Nor do I want to read this return as a disavowal of idealism in favour of pragmatism, choosing to rule in the imperfect system he has inherited in Milan rather than withdraw to imagine purified or perfected ideal societies (such as that glimpsed, and also undercut, in Gonzalo's Montaigne-influenced Golden Age speeches). Another way to see the ending is to see that the search is for that 'something' Merleau-Ponty ultimately identifies with the other side or dimension of vision. The invisible is always implicated in the visible, but as I have suggested above, it is not only unseen, but unseeable. There is a lot to see in this play, and the collection of characters on stage in the finale provides reference to most of it. Despite giving up his magic and freeing Ariel, Prospero is still in complete control, directly responsible for placing everyone on stage in their proper conceptual place: the usurping brother is forced to acknowledge his past crime; the complicit king is made to pause in his mourning before being granted forgiveness; the clownish conspirators are forced to admit their plot against Prospero; the good Gonzalo is rewarded for his initial act of kindness; and the future-oriented couple, Ferdinand and Miranda, offer the generative, comedic resolution. The final act of recognition, though, must come in Prospero's acknowledgement of Caliban, 'This thing of darkness'. The dark, unseen dimension of his own being is not, here, simply body, flesh in the conventional sense, that which might serve as counterweight to his mind or spirit. Ariel has flown, and Prospero is left by himself, his 'charms . . . o'erthrown', and his strength 'most faint' (epilogue, 1, 3). But of course, this isn't quite right either. He is not alone, but standing before a great crowd, asking them to see him. And in the fiction, though he has abandoned his desire for revenge, given away his daughter's hand in marriage, and freed his powerful spirit, he has only just begun to acknowledge something far less distinct and yet clearly inescapable.

Notes

1. Merleau-Ponty, *The Primacy of Perception*, p. 42.
2. See Richard Henze, '*The Tempest*: Rejection of a Vanity'. Henze notes that the primary allegorical readings have centred on the three primary characters of Prospero, Ariel and Caliban, reading them as representations of the parts of the soul (vegetative, sensitive and rational) or of the hierarchies of nature (p. 420). Later readings would focus on the play as an allegory of colonial expansion and oppression. See, for example, Paul Brown, '"This thing of darkness I acknowledge mine": *The Tempest* and the Discourse of Colonialism'; Deborah Willis, 'Shakespeare's Tempest and the Discourse of Colonialism'; Stephen Greenblatt, 'Learning to Curse: Aspects of Linguistic Colonialism in the Sixteenth Century'.
3. These are the terms Theseus uses in the remarkable speech at the beginning of act 5 in *A Midsummer Night's Dream*. 'Apprehension' derives from the Latin *apprehendĕre*, to 'lay hold of' or 'seize' (*OED* vI.1). See my 'Phenomenology and Images: Static and Transformative Images in Shakespeare's Dramatic Art'.
4. Françoise Dastur, 'World, Flesh, Vision'. Dastur notes that 'the philosophical problem that oriented Merleau-Ponty's entire approach is . . . the classical problem of the relations of the soul and the body' (p. 23).
5. See René Descartes, *The Discourse on Method and Meditations on First Philosophy*.

6. Merleau-Ponty, *Primacy*, p. 20.
7. Ibid., p. 21.
8. Or consider Satan's 'The mind is its own place, and in itself / Can make a heaven of hell, a hell of heaven' (Milton, *Paradise Lost*, ll. 54–5).
9. Merleau-Ponty, *Primacy*, p. 22.
10. This fertile term is drawn from the rhetorical trope chiasmus and optics. For a discussion of Merleau-Ponty's chiasm and Shakespeare, see my *Image Ethics*, ch. 4.
11. Merleau-Ponty, *Visible and Invisible*, p. 139.
12. Ibid., p. 146, emphasis original. The terms 'dehiscence' and 'fission', both indicating 'separation' or 'splitting', derive from science (biology/anatomy and physics, respectively).
13. Ibid., p. 96.
14. Ibid.
15. The negated term, Richard as 'un-kinged', is itself a term. Compare with the way *sous rature* or 'under erasure' is deployed in deconstruction.
16. On the contrast of 'shadow' and 'substance', see Chapters 2 and 3, above. The *OED* includes the following sense for 'shadow': 'An unreal appearance; a delusive semblance or image; a vain and unsubstantial object of pursuit. Often contrasted with *substance*' (*n. fig.* 6.a).
17. Merleau-Ponty, *Visible and Invisible*, p. 254.
18. Ibid., p. 255, emphasis original.
19. Ibid., emphasis original.
20. Ibid., p. 256, emphasis original.
21. See the Arden edition, ed. Kastan: 'The otter, an aquatic mammal with webbed feet and fin-like legs, seems generically ambiguous; its nature, as Walton says in *The Complete Angler*, "hath been debated among many great clerks, and they seem to differ about it; yet most agree his tail is fish" [Walton, D5r]' (pp. 275n124–6).
22. See Nathalie Vienne-Guerrin, *Shakespeare's Insults: A Pragmatic Dictionary*: 'The Hostess' reaction shows that she wants this "loose" word to have a specific and precise meaning' (p. 401).

23. Or compare Richard's complaint upon his deposition, discussed above, 'for I must nothing be' (4.1.194), and later when he muses: 'Then am I king'd again: and by and by / Think that I am unking'd by Bolingbroke, / And straight am nothing' (5.4.36–8).

24. On the porpoise see Steve Mentz, '"Half Fish/Half Flesh": Dolphins, the Ocean, and Early Modern Humans'. Dan Brayton also writes helpfully about this scene in *Shakespeare's Ocean*, pp. 120–6.

25. In the *Comedy of Errors*, Antipholus of Ephesus tells Balthazar that 'either at flesh or fish, / A table full of welcome makes scarce a dainty dish' (3.1.22–3). Interestingly, here too there is a quibble over the material in question and its linguistic counterpart, as Balthazar retorts, 'Good meat is common that every churl affords' and is met with Antipholus's 'And welcome more common, for that's nothing but words' (3.1.24–5).

26. Heywood, *Dialogue*, C3v.

27. Hadfield, 'A Red Herring? [with Illustrations]', p. 250.

28. Ibid., p. 248.

29. See *The Tempest: A New Variorum Edition*, pp. 128–9. On Frobisher and the 'marvels' of the New World, see Greenblatt, *Marvelous Possessions*, pp. 109–21.

30. The attempted rape is the explicit pretence for Caliban's enslavement according to both Prospero and Miranda. Caliban's unwillingness to repent ('Oh ho, oh ho! Would't had been done! Thou didst prevent me. I had peopled else this isle with Calibans' [1.2.48–50]) adds to the sense that the punishment is supposed to appear to be earned.

31. Douglas Bruster argues that Prospero's various admonitions to Miranda about paying attention is a sign that the playwright worried the exposition would be sleep inducing (*Quoting Shakespeare*, p. 131).

32. I've added the Folio's capitalisation of 'Thunderbolt' here.

33. Monster: *OED n.* A1a: 'Originally: a mythical creature which is part animal and part human, or combines elements of two or more animal forms, and is frequently of great size

and ferocious appearance. Later, more generally: any imaginary creature that is large, ugly, and frightening.'

34. The uncoupling of language from sense is a loss, representing a decline like that identified by Donne in the *Anatomy* discussed above. See Michel Serres, *The Five Senses*. Serres describes the condition of language removed from its connection to embodiment as 'asceticism', a current condition with disastrous human and environmental implications: 'language produces an abstract dominant class, drunk on codes: legislative, computerized, rigorous, thrice efficient, and in this manner producing a whole world' (p. 234).

35. Lacan's accusation is that Merleau-Ponty abandons the body for the 'flesh' (see Lacan, *The Four Fundamental Concepts of Psychoanalysis*, p. 81).

36. Serres, *Five Senses*, pp. 234–5 and *passim*.

37. See Greenblatt, *Marvelous Possessions*, ch. 4.

38. Brayton, *Shakespeare's Ocean*, p. 57.

39. Ibid.

40. Merleau-Ponty, *Visible and Invisible*, p. 253.

41. As I have noted in earlier chapters, the goal of the alchemist was to distil compound matter into its pure elements. Magic was similarly directed towards the activation of elemental sympathies within the enchanted world. On the relationship of Prospero to the magus, see Barbara Mowat, 'Prospero, Agrippa, and Hocus Pocus'.

42. Merleau-Ponty, *Visible and Invisible*, p. 253.

43. Poole, 'False Play: Shakespeare and Chess', p. 54.

44. Poole notes that in this exchange, 'a claim of falsity is followed by an admission that such falsity is in some sense fair' (p. 59).

45. Merleau-Ponty, *Primacy*, p. 21.

CODA

In *The Five Senses*, Michel Serres describes writing as the human activity poised on the precipice between the material and immaterial:

> The female embroiderer, sewer, spinner or even surgeon operating under a microscope, still stitch together seams with loose links, compared with the fine knots and intricate paths of writing. They have their hands in hard things while she who writes immerses her hands in the soft sign. A link so subtle that it is attached to nothing, a knot so tenuous that it is already passing into another order.[1]

Such a passage could have been found in the pages of the early modern works I have considered in this study. Offering advice for the cultivation of Christian virtue at the turn of the seventeenth century, for example, the Calvinist future Archbishop of Canterbury George Abbot urged attention to the interaction of the physical body and immaterial soul:

> In this, because [God] hath made all, he doth require all, our selues and all ours, the bodie and the soule, the inward and the outward, the sensible and inuisible; although especially the heart and immateriall soule, yet ioyntly the hand, and action from without, yea and the wealth also, that euery part may recommend a dutie to the authour. And

for these externall matters, he hath giuen vnto man not onely members, as in prayer his hands to be lifted vp, his breast to be beaten on, his knees to be bowed, his eyes to be bedewed, that so compunction in the mind may the more be stirred vp . . .[2]

In the previous pages, I have explored this abiding early modern interest in immateriality as the necessary correlate to material experience. My focus has been on what Elizabeth Grosz has termed 'extramateriality', 'the inherence of ideality, conceptuality, meaning, or orientation that persists in relation to and within materiality as its immaterial or incorporeal conditions'.[3] Grosz argues that the material and immaterial need to be 'thought together', an enterprise undertaken by the English writers working in the decades around the turn of the seventeenth century that I have considered here. Crucial to thinking materiality and immateriality together is to acknowledge, without overstating, the rise of materialism in the period's philosophy and science, and, perhaps more importantly, the dualism that would later isolate the material and immaterial as distinct and separable objects of enquiry. The current critical focus on materiality and material culture, especially when concerned with the ways that cultural forms shift and change over time, is enriched by an exploration of the intertwining of the visible and invisible that phenomenology enables. The critique of idealism need not excise ideas from the discussion of material culture and even materiality itself, nor should it suggest that material conditions are somehow more important for rigorous scholarly study than the ideas entangled with their development.

What the works considered here demonstrate is that there was a productive tension between the material and immaterial that was not resolved in the period. The immaterial realm provided solace from material suffering at the same time that it produced a fear of indeterminacy that only concrete experience could offset. Shakespeare, Donne and Herbert are only the most well known of the period's writers to draw on this tension. At a moment marked by important shifts in ontology, theology and epistemology, they gave expression to the ways in which the two poles of the dichotomy structured the understanding of concepts central to the human experiences I have explored in the chapters of this study – of 'self', 'honour', 'incomprehensibleness', 'life', 'love' and 'spirit'. The second half of the seventeenth century would be witness to an explosion of writing about the issues addressed here. The materialism of Hobbes and Cavendish would vie for currency with the substance dualism of Descartes and other views, including those of the Cambridge Platonists, such as Henry More, who defined his 'spirit of nature' as a properly immaterial substance. Poems by Thomas Traherne and John Milton offer perhaps the most complex treatment of the subject in the later seventeenth century, though these are by no means the only poets for whom this is a concern. By including Herbert here, I hoped to point forward to these deep wells of later poetry, in the hope that by drawing attention to immateriality as an animating cultural force I might encourage more work that seeks to approach the period through the entanglements of thought and sense. As we better understand how the visible was thought to reveal the invisible in the period, we gain a better understanding of how the invisible shaped what is visible in the material culture that is by default the object of our study.

Notes

1. Serres, *Five Senses*, pp. 83–4.
2. George Abbot, *An Exposition Upon the Prophet Ionah*, V2v–V3r.
3. Elizabeth Grosz, *The Incorporeal: Ontology, Ethics, and the Limits of Materialism*, p. 5.

BIBLIOGRAPHY

Primary Sources

Abbot, George, *An Exposition Upon the Prophet Ionah* (London, 1600).

Anderton, Lawrence, *The Non-Entity of Protestancy* (Permissu Superiorum, 1633).

Anon., 'Ordinance for removing superstitious Pictures, Images, & etc', *Journal of the House of Lords: Volume 6, 1643* (London: His Majesty's Stationery Office, 1767–1830), pp. 200–1.

Anon., *Physiology, or a Treatise of Naturall Philosophy* (BL MS Sloane 2521).

Anon., *A Short Catechism for Householders* (London, 1582).

Aquinas, Thomas, *A Commentary on Aristotle's De anima [Sentencia libri De Anima]*, trans. Robert Pasnau (New Haven, CT and London: Yale University Press, 1999).

Aquinas, Thomas, *On the Truth of the Catholic Faith (Summa Contra Gentiles)*, trans. Anton C. Pegis, James F. Anderson, Vernon J. Bourke and Charles J. O'Neil, 5 vols (New York: Doubleday, 1955–7, rpt. as *Summa contra gentiles*. Notre Dame: University of Notre Dame Press, 1975).

Aquinas, Thomas, *Summa Theologica*, trans. Fathers of the English Dominican Province (New York: Benzinger Brothers, 1947).

Aristotle, *The Complete Works of Aristotle: The Revised Oxford Translation*, 2 vols, ed. Jonathan Barnes, Bollingen Series LXXI: 2 (Princeton: Princeton University Press, 1984).

Aristotle, *De Anima (On the Soul)*, trans. Hugh Lawson-Tancred (New York: Penguin, 1986).

Aristotle, *The Metaphysics*, trans. Hugh Lawson-Tancred (London: Penguin, 1998).

Aristotle, *On the Generation of Animals*, trans. A. L. Peck, Loeb Classical Library 366 (Cambridge, MA: Harvard University Press, 1942).

Aristotle, *On the Soul, Parva Naturalia, On the Breath*, trans. H. S. Hett, 1937 rev. edn (Cambridge, MA: Harvard University Press, 1957).

Ashmole, Elias, *Theatrum Chemicum Britanicum* (London, 1652).

Augustine, *The confessions of the incomparable doctour S. Augustine*, trans. Toby Matthew (Saint Omer: English College Press, 1620).

Avicenna (Ibn Sīnā), *Avicenna's Psychology. An English Translation of Kitab al-Najat, Book II, Chapter VI with Historico-Philosophical Notes and Textual Improvements on the Cairo Edition*, trans. F. Rahman (London: Oxford University Press, 1952).

Avicenna (Ibn Sīnā), 'On the Rational Soul', in *Avicenna and the Aristotelian Tradition: An Introduction to Reading Avicenna's Philosophical Works*, by Dimitri Gutas, Islamic Philosophy and Theology: Texts and Studies, ed. Hans Daiber, vol. 5 (Leiden: Brill, 1988).

Bacon, Francis, *The Philosophical Works of Francis Bacon Reprinted from the Texts and Translations, with the Notes and Prefaces of Ellis and Spedding*, ed. John M. Robertson ([1905] rpt. Freeport, NY: Books for Libraries Press, 1970).

Bartholomaeus, Anglicus, *Batman vppon Bartholome his booke De proprietatibus rerum* (London, 1582).

Billingsley, Nicholas, 'Ἀνθρωποποιΐα: *Theological reflections on God's Admirable master-peece; or profitable instructions from the creation of man, relating to his visible/invisible nature, his body/soul* (MS BL Sloane 1161).

Bonaventure, *The Mind's Road to God*, trans. George Boas (New York: Library of the Liberal Arts, 1953).

Cicero. *Marcus Tullius Cicero, his three books of duties, turned out of Latine into English, by Nicholas Grimald* (London, 1600).

Cooper, Thomas, *Thesaurus linguæ Romanæ & Britannicæ* (London, 1578).

Cornwallis, William, *Essayes of Certaine Paradoxes* (London, 1616).

Crooke, Helkiah, *Microcosmographia* (London, 1615).

Daneau, Lambert, *The wonderfull vvoorkmanship of the world* (London, 1578).

Darrell, John, *A Suruey of Certaine Dialogical Discourses* (London, 1602).

Davies, John (of Hereford), *Microcosmos: The Discovery of the Little World, with the government thereof* (Oxford, 1603).

Davies, Sir John, *Nosce Teipsum* (London, 1599).

Deacon, John, and John Walker, *Dialogical Discourses of Devils and Spirits* (London, 1601).

Dee, John, *A Letter, containing a most briefe discourse apologeticall* (London, 1599).

Descartes, René, *The Discourse on Method and Meditations on First Philosophy*, trans. Donald A. Cress ([1637, 1641] Indianapolis: Hackett, 1980).

Dod, John, *Seven Godly Sermons . . . to which is added A brief discourse touching the extinguishing of Spirit* (London, 1614).

Donne, John, *Complete English Poems*, ed. A. J. Smith. ([1971] rpt. New York: Penguin, 1996).

Donne, John, *Devotions on Emergent Occasions*, ed. Anthony Raspa (Oxford: Oxford University Press, 1987).

Donne, John, *Fifty sermons. The second volume preached by that learned and reverend divine, John Donne . . .* (London: Printed by Ja. Flesher for M.F., J. Marriot, and R. Royston, MDCXLIX [1649]).

Donne, John, *The Letters to Several Persons of Honour (1651): A Facsimile Reproduction with an Introduction by M. Thomas Hester* (Delmar, NY: Scholars' Facsimiles & Reprints, 1977).

Donne, John, *The Poems of John Donne*, ed. Herbert Grierson (Oxford: Clarendon Press, 1912).

Donne, John, *Selected Prose*, ed. Neil Rhodes (New York: Penguin, 1987).

Donne, John, *The Variorum Edition of the Poetry of John Donne, Vol. 6: The Anniversaries and the Epicedes and Obsequies*, ed. Gary A. Stringer et al. (Bloomington: Indiana University Press, 1995).

Donne, John, *The Works of John Donne, D.D., with a Memoir of His Life*, ed. Henry Alford (London: John W. Parker, 1939).

E.D., *The Prayse of Nothing* (London, 1585).

Euclid, *The elements of geometrie . . . With a very fruitfull præface made by M. I. Dee.* (London, 1570).

Eusebius, *The auncient ecclesiasticall histories of the first six hundred yeares after Christ*, trans. Meredith Hanmer (London, 1577).

Fernal, Jean, *The Physiologia of Jean Fernal (1567)*, trans. John M. Forrester (Philadelphia: American Philosophical Society, 2003).

Ficino, Marsilio, *Platonic Theology*, vol. I, trans. Michael J. B. Allen with John Warden, Latin text ed. James Hankins with William Bowen (Cambridge, MA: I Tatti Renaissance Library Harvard University Press, 2001).

Fielding, Henry, *Miscellanies, by Henry Fielding Esq; In three volumes* (London, 1743).

Florio, John, *A vvorlde of wordes, or Most copious, and exact dictionarie in Italian and English* (London, 1598).

Foxe, John, *Actes and Monuments* (London, 1583).

Gifford, George, *A Short Treatise against the Donatists of England Whom We Call Brownists* (London, 1590).

Harsnett, Samuel, *A declaration of egregious popish impostures* (London, 1603).

Herbert, George, *The Complete English Poems*, ed. John Tobin ([1991] rpt. New York: Penguin, 2004).

Herbert, George, *The English Poems of George Herbert*, ed. Helen Wilcox (Cambridge: Cambridge University Press, 2007).

Herbert, George, *The Latin Poetry of George Herbert: A Bilingual Edition*, trans. Mark McCloskey and Paul R. Murphy (Athens: Ohio University Press, 1965).

Herbert, George, *Latin Poetry*, trans. Greg Miller, *The George Herbert Journal*, 39 (2015/16), pp. 99–117.

Heywood, John, *A Dialogue Conteinyng the Nomber in Effect of all the Prouerbes in the Englishe Tongue* (London, 1546).

Hobbes, Thomas, *Part I of De Corpore*, trans. A. P. Martinich (New York: Abaris Books, 1981).

Holinshed, Raphael, *Chronicles of England, Scotland, and Ireland*, 2nd edn ([1587]; rpt. 6 vols. London: Longman et al., 1807–8).

Hutchinson, Roger, *The Image of God* (London, 1580).

James I (King of England), *Daemonologie* (Edinburgh, 1597).

Jenney, George, *A Catholic Conference between a Protestant and a Papist* (London, 1637).

Jewel, John, *The Homily Against Peril of Idolatry, and Superfluous Decking of Churches* (London: Society for Promoting Christian Knowledge, 1837).

Jewel, John, *The Second Tome of Homilies* (London, 1570).

Jonson, Ben, *The Alchemist*, ed. Elizabeth Cook, New Mermaids (London: A&C Black; New York: Norton, 1991).

Jonson, Ben, 'Ben Jonson's Conversations with William Drummond of Hawthornden', in *Ben Jonson*, ed. C. H. Herford and Percy Simpson (Oxford: Clarendon Press, 1925), vol. I, pp. 128–78.

Lemnius, Levinius, *Touchstone of Complexions*, trans. Thomas Newton (London, 1576).

Lombard, Peter, *The Sentences: Book 1, The Mystery of the Trinity*, trans. Guilio Silano (Toronto: Pontifical Institute of Medieval Studies, 2007).

Loyer, Pierre Le, *A Treatise of Specters* (London, 1605).

Michaelis, Sebastian, *Pneumalogia*, trans. as *A Discourse of Spirits* (London, 1613).

Milton, John, *Paradise Lost*, ed. and intro. Stephen Orgel and Jonathan Goldberg (Oxford: Oxford University Press, 2004).

Mornay, Phillipe de, seigneur du Plessis-Marly, *A vvoorke concerning the trewnesse of the Christian religion*, trans. Sir Philip Sidney and Arthur Golding (London, 1587).

Morton, Thomas (of Berwick), *A Treatise of the Nature of God* (London, 1599).

Newton, Sir Isaac, *Newton's Principia: The Mathematical Principles of Natural Philosophy*, trans. Andrew Motte ([1729] New York: Daniel Adee, 1847).

Paré, Ambroise, *The workes of that famous chirurgion Ambrose Parey* (London, 1634).

Parsons (Persons), Robert, *The seconde parte of the booke of Christian exercise* (London, 1590).

Perkins, William, *Two Treatises: I. Of the nature and practice of repentance II. Of the combat of the flesh and spirit* (Cambridge, 1595).

Plato, *Philebus*, trans. J. B. C. Gosling (Oxford: Clarendon Press, 1975).

Plotinus, *Enneads*, trans. Stephen MacKenna, abridged and intro. John Dillon ([1917–30] rpt. New York: Penguin, 1991).

Plutarch, *The philosophie, commonlie called, the morals*, trans. Philemon Holland (London, 1603).

Rogers, Thomas, *The English Creede* (London, 1585).

Scot, Reginald, *Discoverie of Witchcraft* (London, 1584).

A Select Library of Nicene and Post-Nicene Fathers of the Church, 14 vols, ed. Philip Schaff and Henry Wace (New York: The Christian Literature Company, 1898).

Shakespeare, William, *Henry IV, Part I*, ed. A. R. Humphreys, Arden Shakespeare 2nd series (London: Methuen, 1960).

Shakespeare, William, *King Henry IV, part 1*, ed. David Scott Kastan, Arden Shakespeare 3rd series (London: Thompson Learning, 2002).

Shakespeare, William, *Much Ado About Nothing*, ed. A. R. Humphreys, Arden Shakespeare 2nd series ([1981] rpt. London: Thompson Learning 2004).

Shakespeare, William, *The Norton Shakespeare*, 3rd edn, ed. Stephen Greenblatt, Walter Cohen, Suzanne Gossett, Jean E. Howard, Katharine Eisaman Maus and Gordon McMullan (New York: Norton, 2016).

Shakespeare, William, *The Tempest: A New Variorum Edition*, ed. Horace Howard Furness ([1892] rpt. New York: Dover, 1964).

Shakespeare, William, *The Tragical History of Hamlet, Prince of Denmark* (London, 1603).

Sibbes, Richard, *A Miracle of Miracles, or Christ in our nature* (London, 1638).

Sidney, Sir Philip, *The Defence of Poesy* (London, 1595).

Spenser, Edmund, *The Faerie Queene*, ed. Thomas P. Roche (New York: Penguin, 1979).

Thomas, Thomas, *Dictionarium linguae Latinae et Anglicanae* (Cambridge, 1587).

Tyndale, William, *Answer to Sir Thomas More's Dialogue, The supper of the Lord, after the true meaning of John VI. and 1 Cor. XI., and Wm. Tracy's Testament expounded*, ed. Henry Walter, Parker Society (Cambridge: Cambridge University Press, 1850).

Ursinus, Zacharias, *A Catechism, or short kind of instruction* (Heidelberg Catechism), trans. John Seddon (London, 1588).

Vergil, Polydore, *An abridgeme[n]t of the notable worke of Polidore Vergile . . . Compe[n]diously gathered by Thomas Langley* (London, 1546).

Walton, Isaac, *Life of George Herbert*, in *George Herbert: The Complete English Poems*, ed. Tobin, pp. 265–314.

Watts, William, *Augustines confessions translated* (London, 1631).

Wilson, Thomas, *A Christian dictionarie* (London, 1612).

Secondary Sources

Adamson, Peter, *The Arabic Plotinus: A Philosophical Study of 'The Theology of Aristotle'* (Piscataway, NJ: Gorgias Press, 2017).

Agamben, Giorgio, *Stanzas: Word and Phantasm in Western Culture,* trans. Ronald L. Martinez (Minneapolis: University of Minnesota Press, 1992).

Althusser, Louis, 'Ideology and Ideological State Apparatuses: Notes Toward an Investigation', in *Lenin and Philosophy, and Other Essays*, trans. Ben Brewster (London: New Left Books, 1971), pp. 85–126.

Altick, Richard, 'Symphonic Imagery in *Richard II*', in *Twentieth Century Interpretations of* Richard II, ed. Paul M. Cubeta (Englewood Cliffs, NJ: Prentice Hall, 1971), pp. 66–81.

Anderson, Judith H., *Light and Death: Figuration in Spenser, Kepler, Donne, and Milton* (New York: Fordham University Press, 2017).

Anderson, Judith H., 'Matter and Spirit, Body and Soul, Time and Eternity in Donne's Anniversaries', *Connotations*, 25.1 (2015/16), pp. 59–73.

Aston, Margaret, *England's Iconoclasts, Vol. 1: Laws Against Images* (Oxford: Clarendon Press, 1988).

Badiou, Alain, *Ethics: An Essay on the Understanding of Evil*, ed. Peter Hallward (London: Verso, 2013).

Bamborough, J. B., *The Little World of Man* (London, New York and Toronto: Longmans, Green, and Co., 1952).

Banchetti-Robino, Marina Paola, 'Ibn Sīnā and Husserl on Intention and Intentionality', *Philosophy East and West*, 54 (2004), pp.71–82.

Barker, Roberta, 'Tragical-Comical-Historical Hotspur', *Shakespeare Quarterly*, 54.3 (2003), pp. 288–307.

Barr, Steven M., *Modern Physics and Ancient Faith* (Notre Dame: University of Notre Dame Press, 2003).

Barroll, Leeds, 'A New History for Shakespeare and His Time', *Shakespeare Quarterly*, 39.4 (1988), pp. 441–64. Rpt. in Farrell (ed.), *Critical Essays*.

Bate, Jonathan, *How the Classics Made Shakespeare* (Princeton: Princeton University Press, 2019).

Baumbach, Sibylle, *Shakespeare and the Art of Physiognomy* (Tirril, Penrith: Humanities Ebooks, 2008).

Bayer, Thora Ilin, and Donald Phillip Verene (eds), *Giambattista Vico: Keys to the New Science* (Ithaca: Cornell University Press, 2008).

Beckwith, Sarah, *Christ's Body: Identity, Culture, and Society in Late Medieval Writings* (New York: Routledge, 1996).

Bloom, Harold, *Shakespeare and the Invention of the Human* (New York: Riverhead Books, 1998).

Bloom, Harold (ed.), *William Shakespeare's Richard II: Modern Critical Interpretations* (New York: Chelsea House, 1988).

Bonnell, William, 'Anamnesis: The Power of Memory in Herbert's Sacramental Vision', *George Herbert Journal*, 15.1 (1991), pp. 33–48.

Bono, James J., 'Medical Spirits and the Medieval Language of Life', *Traditio*, 40 (1984), pp. 91–130.

Brayton, Dan, *Shakespeare's Ocean: An Ecocritical Exploration* (Charlottesville: University of Virginia Press, 2012).

Brown, Bill, 'Thing Theory', *Critical Inquiry*, 28 (2001), pp. 1–22.

Brown, Paul, '"This thing of darkness I acknowledge mine": *The Tempest* and the Discourse of Colonialism', in *Political Shakespeare: New Essays in Cultural Materialism*, ed. Jonathan Dollimore and Alan Sinfield (Ithaca and London: Cornell University Press, 1985), pp. 48–71.

Brownlow, F. W., *Shakespeare, Harsnett, and the Devils of Denham* (Newark: Delaware University Press, 1993).

Bruster, Douglas, *Quoting Shakespeare: Form and Culture in Early Modern Drama* (Lincoln: University of Nebraska Press, 2000).

Caldwell, Ellen M., '"Banish all the wor(l)d": Falstaff's Iconoclastic Threat to Kingship in *1 Henry IV*', *Renascence*, 59.4 (2007), pp. 219–45.

Cavell, Stanley, *Disowning Knowledge in Seven Plays of Shakespeare* (Cambridge: Cambridge University Press, 1987).

Cefalu, Paul, *The Johannine Renaissance in Early Modern English Literature and Theology* (Oxford: Oxford University Press, 2018).

Chalk, Darryl, 'Contagious Emulation: Antitheatricality and Theatre as Plague in *Troilus and Cressida*', in *'This Earthly Stage': World and Stage in Late Medieval and Early Modern England*, ed. Brett D. Hirsch and Christopher Wortham (Turnhout, Belgium: Brepols, 2010), pp. 75–101.

Chalk, Darryl, '"Make Me Not Sighted Like the Basilisk": Vision and Contagion in *The Winter's Tale*', in *Embodied Cognition and Shakespeare's Theater: The Early Modern Body-Mind*, ed. Laurie Johnson, John Sutton and Evelyn Tribble (New York: Routledge, 2014), pp. 111–32.

Chalk, Darryl, '"To Creep in at Mine Eyes": Theatre and Secret Contagion in *Twelfth Night*', in *'Rapt in Secret Studies': Emerging Shakespeares*, ed. Darryl Chalk and Laurie Johnson (Newcastle upon Tyne: Cambridge Scholars, 2010), pp. 171–93.

Charles, Amy M., *A Life of George Herbert* (Ithaca: Cornell University Press, 1977).

Clark, Stuart, *Thinking with Demons: The Idea of Witchcraft in Early Modern Europe* (Oxford: Oxford University Press, 1999).

Clark, Stuart, *Vanities of the Eye: Vision and Early Modern European Culture* (Oxford: Oxford University Press, 2007).

Close, Frank, *Nothing: A Very Short History* (Oxford: Oxford University Press, 2009).

Colie, Rosalie, *Paradoxia Epidemica: The Renaissance Tradition of Paradox* (Princeton: Princeton University Press, 1966).

Cook, Amy, 'Staging Nothing: Hamlet and Cognitive Science', *SubStance*, 110, 35.2 (2006), pp. 83–99.

Cook, Carol, '"The Sign and Semblance of Her Honour": Reading Gender Difference in *Much Ado About Nothing*', PMLA, 101 (1986), pp. 186–202.

Crosbie, Christopher, *Revenge Tragedy and Classical Philosophy on the Early Modern Stage* (Edinburgh: Edinburgh University Press, 2019).

Crowell, Steven, 'Transcendental Phenomenology and the Seductions of Naturalism: Subjectivity, Consciousness, and Meaning', in Zahavi (ed.), *The Oxford Handbook of Contemporary Phenomenology*, pp. 25–47.

Cummings, Brian, *The Literary Culture of the Reformation: Grammar and Grace* (Oxford: Oxford University Press, 2002).

Curran, Kevin, and James Kearney (eds), 'Shakespeare and Phenomenology', Special issue of *Criticism*, 54.3 (2012).

Damasio, Antonio, *Descartes' Error: Emotion, Reason, and the Human Brain* ([1994] rpt. New York: Penguin 2005).

Danesi, Marcel, *Vico, Metaphor, and the Origin of Language* (Bloomington: Indiana University Press, 1993).

Dastur, Françoise, 'World, Flesh, Vision', in *Chiasms: Merleau-Ponty's Notion of Flesh*, ed. Fred Evans and Leonard Lawlor (Albany: SUNY Press, 2000), pp. 23–49.

Davidson, Clifford, 'George Herbert and Stained Glass Windows', *George Herbert Journal*, 12.1 (1988), pp. 29–39.

Davidson, Scott, 'Translator's Preface', in Michel Henry, *Material Phenomenology* (New York: Fordham University Press, 2008), pp. xi–xvi.

Dickson, Donald R., 'Between Transubstantiation and Memorialism: Herbert's Eucharistic Celebration', *George Herbert Journal*, 11.1 (1987), pp. 1–14.

Dyck, Paul, 'Altar, Heart, Title Page: The Image of Holy Reading', *ELR*, (2013), pp. 541–71.

Eagleson, Hannah, 'Inhabiting Time: Donne, Herbert, and the Individual Body', unpublished dissertation, University of Delaware, 2011.

Eggert, Katherine, *Disknowledge: Literature, Alchemy, and the End of Humanism in Renaissance England* (Philadelphia: University of Pennsylvania Press, 2015).

Elsky, Martin, 'George Herbert's Pattern Poems and the Materiality of Language: A New Approach to Renaissance Hieroglyphics', *English Literary History*, 50.2 (1983), pp. 245–60.

Empson, William, *Seven Types of Ambiguity*, 2nd rev. edn (London: Chatto & Windus, 1949).

Farrell, Kirby (ed.), *Critical Essays on Shakespeare's Richard II* (New York: G. K. Hall, 1999).

Farrell, Kirby, 'Introduction: Play, Death, and History', in Farrell, *Critical Essays*, pp. 1–22.

Fernie, Ewan, *Shakespeare for Freedom: Why the Plays Matter* (Cambridge: Cambridge University Press, 2017).

Fish, Stanley, *The Living Temple: George Herbert and Catechizing* (Berkeley: University of California Press, 1978).

Fleck, Andrew, 'The Ambivalent Blush: Figural and Structural Metonymy, Modesty, and *Much Ado About Nothing*', ANQ, 19.1 (2006), pp. 16–23.

Floyd-Wilson, Mary, *Occult Knowledge, Science, and Gender on the Shakespearean Stage* (Cambridge: Cambridge University Press, 2013).

Forker, Charles (ed.), *Richard II: Shakespeare The Critical Tradition* (Cambridge: Cambridge University Press, 1998).

Freeman, Margaret, 'The Aesthetics of Human Experience: Minding, Metaphor, and Icon in Poetic Expression', *Poetics Today*, 32.4 (2011), pp. 717–52.

Gordis, Lisa, 'The Experience of Covenant Theology in George Herbert's "The Temple"', *The Journal of Religion*, 76.3 (1996), pp. 383–401.

Grady, Hugh, and Terence Hawkes (eds), *Presentist Shakespeares* (New York: Routledge, 2006).

Grady, Hugh, *Shakespeare's Universal Wolf* (Oxford: Clarendon Press, 1996).

Grafton, Anthony, *Cardano's Cosmos: The Worlds and Works of a Renaissance Astrologer* (Cambridge, MA: Harvard University Press, 2001).

Greenblatt, Stephen, 'Learning to Curse: Aspects of Linguistic Colonialism in the Sixteenth Century', in Greenblatt, *Learning to Curse: Essays in Early Modern Culture* (New York: Routledge, 1990), pp. 22–51.

Greenblatt, Stephen, *Marvelous Possessions: The Wonder of the New World* (Chicago: University of Chicago Press, 1992).

Greenblatt, Stephen, 'Shakespeare among the Exorcists', in *Shakespeare and the Question of Theory*, ed. Patricia Parker and Geoffrey Hartman (New York: Methuen, 1985), pp. 163–87.

Greenblatt, Stephen, *Shakespearean Negotiations* (Berkeley and Los Angeles: University of California Press, 1988).

Greenblatt, Stephen, *The Swerve: How the World Became Modern* (New York: Norton, 2012).

Grossman, Marshall, *The Story of All Things: Writing the Self in English Renaissance Narrative Poetry* (Durham, NC: Duke University Press, 1998).

Grosz, Elizabeth, *The Incorporeal: Ontology, Ethics, and the Limits of Materialism* (New York: Columbia University Press, 2017).

Guibbory, Achsah, 'John Donne and Memory as "the Art of Salvation"', *Huntington Library Quarterly*, 43.4 (1980), pp. 261–74.

Hadfield, Andrew, 'A Red Herring? [with Illustrations]', *ELR*, 45.2 (2015), pp. 231–54.

Halverson, John, 'The Lamentable Comedy of *Richard II*', in Farrell, *Critical Essays*.

Harris, Jonathan Gil, *Sick Economies: Drama, Mercantilism, and Disease in Shakespeare's England* (Philadelphia: University of Pennsylvania Press, 2004).

Harrison, Peter, *The Territories of Science and Religion* (Chicago: University of Chicago Press, 2015).

Harvey, E. Ruth, *The Inward Wits: Psychological Theory in the Middle Ages and the Renaissance* (London: Warburg Institute, 1975).

Harvey, Elizabeth D., 'Passionate Spirits: Animism and Embodiment in *Cymbeline* and *The Tempest*', in *The Oxford Handbook of Shakespeare and Embodiment: Gender, Sexuality, and Race*, ed. Valerie Traub (Oxford: Oxford University Press, 2016), pp. 369–84.

Harvey, Elizabeth D. (ed.), *Sensible Flesh* (Philadelphia: University of Pennsylvania Press, 2002).

Harvey, Elizabeth D., and Timothy M. Harrison, 'Embodied Resonances: Early Modern Science and Tropologies of Connection in Donne's *Anniversaries*', *ELH*, 80 (2013), pp. 981–1008.

Hawkes, David, 'Against Materialism in Early Modern Studies', in *The Return to Theory in Early Modern English Studies: Tarrying with the Subjunctive*, ed. Paul Cefalu and Bryan Reynolds (New York: Palgrave Macmillan, 2011), pp. 237–57.

Hawkes, Terence, *Shakespeare in the Present* (New York: Routledge, 2002).

Heidegger, Martin, *The Essence of Truth: On Plato's Cave Allegory and Theaeteus*, trans. Ted Sadler (New York and London: Continuum, 2002).

Heidegger, Martin, 'The Thing', in *Poetry, Language, Thought* (New York: Harper & Row, 1971), pp. 161–84.

Heilbron, John L., 'Was There a Scientific Revolution?', in *The Oxford Handbook to the History of Physics*, ed. Jed Z. Buchwald and Robert Fox (Oxford: Oxford University Press, 2013), pp. 7–24.

Heller-Roazen, Daniel, *The Inner Touch: Archaeology of a Sensation* (New York: Zone, 2009).

Henry, Michel, *Material Phenomenology*, trans. Scott Davidson (New York: Fordham Oxford University Press, 2008).

Henze, Richard, '*The Tempest*: Rejection of a Vanity', *Shakespeare Quarterly*, 23.4 (1972), pp. 420–34.

Hesselink, I. John, *Calvin's First Catechism: Featuring Ford Lewis Battles's Translation of the 1538 Catechism* (Louisville, KY: Westminster John Knox Press, 1997).

Hintikka, Jaakko, 'The Notion of Intuition in Husserl', *Revue Internationale de Philosophie*, 224 (2003), pp. 169–91.

Hunt, Maurice, 'Time and Timelessness in *1 Henry IV*', *ERIC*, 10 (1984), pp. 56–66.

Hunter, Jeanne Clayton, '"With Winges of Faith": Herbert's Communion Poems', *The Journal of Religion*, 62 (1982), pp. 57–71.

Husserl, Edmund, *Ideas: General Introduction to Pure Phenomenology* [known as *Ideas I*], trans. W. R. Boyce Gibson ([1931] rpt. New York: Collier, 1962).

Hutson, Lorna, 'Fortunate Travellers: Reading for the Plot in Sixteenth-Century England', *Representations*, 41 (1993), pp. 83–103.

Johnson, Kimberly, *Made Flesh: Sacrament and Poetics in Post-Reformation England* (Philadelphia: University of Pennsylvania Press, 2014).

Jorgensen, Paul, *Redeeming Shakespeare's Words* (Berkeley: University of California Press, 1962).

Kantorowicz, Ernst H., *The King's Two Bodies: A Study in Medieval Political Theology* ([1957] rpt. Princeton: Princeton University Press, 1997).

Kastan, David Scott, '"The King Hath Many Marching in His Coats," Or What Did You Do in the War Daddy?', in *Shakespeare Left and Right*, ed. Ivo Kamps (New York: Routledge, 1991), pp. 241–58.

Kehler, Dorothea, 'King of Tears: Mortality in *Richard II*', *Rocky Mountain Review of Language and Literature*, 39.1 (1985), pp. 7–18.

King, Walter N., 'Much Ado About Something', *Shakespeare Quarterly*, 15.3 (1964), pp. 143–55.

Knapp, James A., 'Beyond Materialism in Shakespeare Studies', *Literature Compass*, 11/10 (2014), pp. 677–90.

Knapp, James A., *Image Ethics in Shakespeare and Spenser* (New York: Palgrave Macmillan, 2011).

Knapp, James A., 'Phenomenology and Images: Static and Transformative Images in Shakespeare's Dramatic Art', *Criticism*, 54.3 (2012), pp. 377–89.

Knapp, James A. (ed.), *Shakespeare and the Power of the Face* (Burlington, VT: Ashgate, 2015).

Kristeller, Paul Oskar, *Medieval Aspects of Renaissance Learning* (New York: Columbia University Press, 1992).

Kuchar, Gary, 'Distraction and the Ethics of Poetic Form in *The Temple*', *Christianity and Literature*, 66.1 (2016), pp. 4–23.

Kuchar, Gary, *George Herbert and the Mystery of the Word: Poetry and Scripture in Seventeenth-Century England* (Cham, Switzerland: Palgrave Macmillan, 2017).

Kuchar, Gary, 'Poetry and the Eucharist in the English Renaissance', *The George Herbert Journal*, 36 (2012–13), pp. 128–49.

Kuchar, Gary, *The Poetry of Religious Sorrow in Early Modern England* (Cambridge: Cambridge University Press, 2008).

Lacan, Jacques, *The Four Fundamental Concepts of Psychoanalysis*, ed. Jacques-Alain Miller, trans. Alan Sheridan (New York: Norton, 1981).

Levinas, Emmanuel, *The Theory of Intuition in Husserl's Phenomenology*, trans. André Orianne (Evanston: Northwestern University Press, 1973).

Lewis, C. S., *Miracles: A Preliminary Study* (New York: Macmillan, 1948).

Lewis, Michael, and Tanja Staehler, *Phenomenology: An Introduction* (London: Blackwell, 2001).

Lindberg, David C., *Theories of Vision from Al Kindhi to Kepler* (Chicago: Chicago University Press, 1976).

Lorenz, Philip, 'Christall Mirrors: Analogy and Onto-Theology in Shakespeare and Francisco Suarez', *Religion and Literature*, 38 (2006), pp. 101–19.

Lupton, Julia, 'Macbeth's Martlets: Shakespearean Phenomenology of Hospitality', *Criticism*, 54.3 (2012), pp. 365–76.

Mahony, Patrick J., 'The Anniversaries: Donne's Rhetorical Approach to Evil', *JEGP*, 60 (1969), pp. 407–13.

Malloch, A. E., 'The Techniques and Functions of the Renaissance Paradox', *Studies in Philology*, 53.2 (1956), pp. 191–203.

Manley, Frank, *John Donne: The Anniversaries* (Baltimore: Johns Hopkins University Press, 1963).

Marion, Jean-Luc, *Being Given: Toward a Phenomenology of Givenness*, trans. Jeffrey L. Kosky (Stanford: Stanford University Press, 2002).

Marion, Jean-Luc, *In Excess: Studies of Saturated Phenomena*, trans. Robyn Horner and Vincent Berraud (New York: Fordham University Press, 2004).

Marotti, Arthur, and Ken Jackson, 'The Turn to Religion in Early Modern Studies', *Criticism*, 46.1 (2004), pp. 167–90.

Maus, Katharine Eisaman, *Inwardness and Theater in the English Renaissance* (Chicago: University of Chicago Press, 1995).

Mazzio, Carla, 'The History of Air: *Hamlet* and the Trouble with Instruments', *South Central Review*, 126.1&2 (2009), pp. 153–96.

McGiffort, Michael, 'Grace and Works: The Rise and Division of Covenant Divinity in Elizabethan Puritanism', *Harvard Theological Review*, 75.4 (1982), pp. 463–502.

McGinnis, Jon, *Avicenna* (Oxford: Oxford University Press, 2010).

McMillin, Scott, *Henry IV, Part One*. Shakespeare in Performance Series (Manchester: Manchester University Press, 1991).

McMillin, Scott, 'Shakespeare's *Richard II*: Eyes of Sorrow, Eyes of Desire', *Shakespeare Quarterly*, 35 (1984), pp. 40–52.

Mebane, John S., *Renaissance Magic and the Return of the Golden Age: The Occult Tradition and Marlowe, Jonson, and Shakespeare* (Lincoln: University of Nebraska Press, 1989).

Mentz, Steve, '"Half Fish/ Half Flesh": Dolphins, the Ocean, and Early Modern Humans', in *The Indistinct Human in Renaissance Literature*, ed. Jean E. Feerick and Vin Nardizzi (New York: Palgrave, 2012), pp. 29–46.

Merleau-Ponty, Maurice, 'Indirect Language and the Voices of Silence', in *Signs*, trans. Richard McCleary (Evanston: Northwestern University Press, 1964), pp. 39–83.

Merleau-Ponty, Maurice, *The Primacy of Perception* (Evanston: Northwestern University Press, 1964).

Merleau-Ponty, Maurice, *The Visible and the Invisible*, ed. Claude Lefort, trans. Alphonso Lingis (Evanston: Northwestern University Press, 1968).

Miller, Edmund, 'Herbert's Baroque: The *Passio Discerpta*', *Renaissance and Reformation / Renaissance et Reforme*, n.s. 3.2 (1979), pp. 201–8.

Miller, Greg, with Catherine Freis, 'Introduction', *George Herbert Journal*, 39 (2015/16), pp. vii–xxxi.

Miller, Henry Knight, 'The Paradoxical Encomium with Special Reference to Its Vogue in England 1600–1800', *Modern Philology*, 53.3 (1956), pp. 145–78.

Miller, Perry, 'The Marrow of Puritan Divinity', in *Errand into the Wilderness* ([1956] rpt. New York: Harper and Row, 1964), pp. 48–98.

Minor, Earl, *The Metaphysical Mode from Donne to Cowley* (Princeton: Princeton University Press, 1969).

Morrissey, Mary, 'Scripture, Style, and Persuasion in Seventeenth-Century English Theories of Preaching', *The Journal of Ecclesiastical History*, 53.4 (2002), pp. 686–706.

Moser, Robbie, 'Thomas Aquinas, Esse Intentionale, and the Cognitive as Such', *The Review of Metaphysics*, 64 (June 2011), pp. 763–88.

Mowat, Barbara, 'Prospero, Agrippa, and Hocus Pocus', *ELR*, 11.3 (1981), pp. 281–303.

Mueller, Janel, 'Donne's Epic Venture in the "Metempsychosis"', *Modern Philology*, 70.2 (1972), pp. 109–37.

Myhill, Nova, 'Spectatorship in/of *Much Ado About Nothing*', *SEL*, 39 (1999), pp. 291–311.

Neely, Carol Thomas, *Broken Nuptials in Shakespeare's Plays* (New Haven, CT: Yale University Press, 1985).

Netzley, Ryan, *Reading, Desire, and the Eucharist in Early Modern Religious Poetry* (Toronto: University of Toronto Press, 2011).

Nevo, Ruth, 'The Genre of *Richard II*', in *William Shakespeare's Richard II: Modern Critical Interpretations*, ed. Harold Bloom (New York: Chelsea House, 1988), pp. 7–35.

Nietzsche, Friedrich, *The Birth of Tragedy and The Case of Wagner*, trans. Walter Kaufmann (New York: Vintage, 1967).

Nietzsche, Friedrich, *The Birth of Tragedy and the Genealogy of Morals*, trans. Francis Golffing (New York: Anchor Books, 1956).

Palfrey, Simon, *Poor Tom: Living 'King Lear'* (Chicago: University of Chicago Press, 2014).

Palmer, Ada, *Reading Lucretius in the Renaissance* (Cambridge, MA: Harvard University Press, 2014).

Parker, Patricia, 'Othello and Hamlet: Dilation, Spying, and the "Secret Place" of Woman', *Representations*, 44 (1993), pp. 60–95.

Parry, Glyn, *The Arch Conjurer of England: John Dee* (New Haven, CT: Yale University Press, 2011).

Passannante, Gerard, *The Lucretian Renaissance: Philology and the Afterlife of Tradition* (Chicago: University of Chicago Press, 2011).

Paster, Gail Kern, *Humoring the Body: Emotions and the Shakespearean Stage* (Chicago: University of Chicago Press, 2004).

Paster, Gail Kern, Katherine Rowe, and Mary Floyd Wilson (eds), *Reading the Early Modern Passions: Essays in the Cultural History of Emotion* (Philadelphia: University of Pennsylvania Press, 2004).

Patterson, Annabel, *Reading Holinshed's Chronicles* (Chicago: University of Chicago Press, 1994).

Pinker, Steven, *Enlightenment Now: The Case for Reason, Science, Humanism, and Progress* (New York: Viking, 2018).

Platt, Peter G., *Shakespeare and the Culture of Paradox* (Burlington, VT: Ashgate, 2009).

Poole, William, 'False Play: Shakespeare and Chess', *Shakespeare Quarterly*, 55.1 (2004), pp. 50–70.

Priest, Stephen, 'Duns Scotus on the Immaterial', *The Philosophical Quarterly*, 48.192 (1998), pp. 370–2.

Purcell, Sebastian L., 'After Hermeneutics?', *Symposium: Canadian Journal of Continental Philosophy*, 14.2 (2010), pp. 160–79.

Pye, Christopher, *The Regal Phantasm: Shakespeare and the Politics of Spectacle* (London: Routledge, 1990).

Rackin, Phyllis, *Stages of History: Shakespeare's English Chronicles* (Ithaca: Cornell University Press, 1990).

Read, Sophie, *Eucharist and the Poetic Imagination in Early Modern England* (New York: Cambridge University Press, 2013).

Ricoeur, Paul, 'Explanation and Understanding: On Some Remarkable Connections Among the Theory of the Text, Theory of

Action, and Theory of History', in *The Philosophy of Paul Ricoeur: An Anthology of His Work*, ed. Charles E. Regan and David Stewart (Boston, MA: Beacon Press, 1978), pp. 149–68.

Ricoeur, Paul, 'The Human Experience of Time and Narrative', in *A Ricoeur Reader: Reflection and Imagination*, ed. Mario J. Valdés (Toronto: University of Toronto Press, 1991), pp. 99–116.

Ricoeur, Paul, 'Narrative Time', *Critical Inquiry*, 7.1 (1980), pp. 169–90.

Ricoeur, Paul, *Oneself as Another*, trans. Kathleen Blamey (Chicago: University of Chicago Press, 1992).

Ricoeur, Paul, *Time and Narrative*, 3 vols (Chicago: University of Chicago Press, 1984–90).

Robertson, Kellie, *Nature Speaks: Medieval Literature and Aristotelian Philosophy* (Philadelphia: University of Pennsylvania Press, 2017).

Romdenh-Romluc, Komarine, 'Thought in Action', in Zahavi, *The Oxford Handbook of Contemporary Phenomenology*, pp. 198–215.

Rothstein, Bret, 'Description, Intelligence, and the Excitation of Sight', in *Spirits Unseen: The Representation of Subtle Bodies in Early Modern European Culture*, ed. Christine Göttler and Wolfgang Neuber (Leiden and Boston, MA: Brill: 2008), pp. 47–70.

Rowe, Katherine, 'Humoral Knowledge and Liberal Cognition in Davenant's Macbeth', in *Reading the Early Modern Passions: Essays in the Cultural History of Emotion*, ed. Gail Kern Paster, Katherine Rowe and Mary Floyd-Wilson (Philadelphia: University of Pennsylvania Press, 2004), pp. 169–91.

Roychoudhury, Suparna, *Phantasmatic Shakespeare: Imagination in the Age of Early Modern Science* (Ithaca: Cornell University Press, 2018).

Rust, Jennifer, *The Body in Mystery: The Political Theology of the Corpus Mysticum in the Literature of the English Reformation* (Evanston: Northwestern University Press, 2013).

Ryan, John K., *The Reputation of St. Thomas Aquinas Among English Protestant Thinkers of the Seventeenth Century* (Washington, DC: Catholic University of America Press, 1948).

Sands, Kathleen, *Demon Possession in Elizabethan England* (Westport, CT: Praeger, 2004).

Schmitt, Charles B., *Aristotle and the Renaissance* (Cambridge, MA: Harvard University Press, 1983).

Schmitt, Charles B., *John Case and Aristotelianism in Renaissance England* (Montreal: McGill-Queens University Press, 1983).

Schoenfeldt, Michael, *Bodies and Selves in Early Modern England: Physiology and Inwardness in Spenser, Shakespeare, Herbert, and Milton* (Cambridge: Cambridge University Press, 1999).

Schoenfeldt, Michael, 'Herbert and Pleasure', *The George Herbert Journal*, 38 (2014–15), pp. 145–57.

Schoenfeldt, Michael, *Prayer and Power: George Herbert and Renaissance Courtship* (Chicago: University of Chicago Press, 1991).

Schwartz, Regina, *Sacramental Poetics at the Dawn of Secularism: When God Left the World* (Stanford: Stanford University Press, 2008).

Serres, Michel, *The Five Senses: A Philosophy of Mingled Bodies (I)*, trans. Margaret Sankey and Peter Cowley (New York and London: Continuum, 2008).

Simpson, Christopher Ben, *Merleau-Ponty and Theology* (London: T&T Clark, 2014).

Smith, Barbara Herrnstein, *Poetic Closure: A Study of How Poems End* (Chicago: University of Chicago Press, 1968).

Smith, Bruce R., *The Acoustic World of Early Modern England: Attending to the O Factor* (Chicago: University of Chicago Press, 1999).

Smith, Bruce R., *The Key of Green: Passion and Perception in Renaissance Culture* (Chicago: University of Chicago Press, 2009).

Smith, Bruce R., *Phenomenal Shakespeare* (Chichester: Blackwell, 2010).

Smith, Bruce R., 'Phenomophobia, or Who's Afraid of Merleau-Ponty?', *Criticism*, 54.3 (2012), pp. 479–83.

Smith, Justin E. H., 'Spirit as Intermediary', in *Spirits Unseen: The Representation of Subtle Bodies in Early Modern European*

Culture, ed. Christine Göttler and Wolfgang Neuber (Leiden and Boston, MA: Brill: 2008), pp. 269–91.

Smith, Matthew, 'Describing the Sense of Confession in *Hamlet*', in *The Return to Theory*, *Vol. II*, ed. Paul Cefalu, Gary Kuchar and Bryan Reynolds (New York: Palgrave Macmillan, 2014), pp. 165–84.

Soergel, Philip M., *Miracles and the Protestant Imagination: The Evangelical Wonder Book in Reformation Germany* (Oxford: Oxford University Press, 2012).

Sofer, Andrew, *Dark Matter: Invisibility in Drama, Theater, and Performance* (Ann Arbor: University of Michigan Press, 2013).

Sokolowski, Robert, *Introduction to Phenomenology* (Cambridge: Cambridge University Press, 2000).

Spiegelberg, Herbert, *The Context of the Phenomenological Movement* (The Hague: Martinus Nijhoff, 1981).

Spiegelberg, Herbert, *The Phenomenological Movement: A Historical Introduction*, 2nd edn, vol. 1 (The Hague: Martinus Nijhoff, 1971).

Stanwood, P. G., 'Time and Liturgy in Herbert's Poetry', *George Herbert Journal*, 5.1&2 (1981–2), pp. 19–30.

Stein, Arnold, *George Herbert's Lyrics* (Baltimore: Johns Hopkins University Press, 1968).

Stewart, Stanley, 'Author Esquire: The Writer and "Immaterial Culture" in Caroline and Jacobean England', *Ben Jonson Journal*, 20.2 (2013), pp. 241–59.

Stewart, Stanley, 'Time and *The Temple*', *SEL*, 6.1 (1966), pp. 97–110.

Strier, Richard, 'Ironic Ekphrasis', *Classical Philology*, 102 (2007), pp. 96–109.

Strier, Richard, *Love Known: Theology and Experience in George Herbert's Poetry* (Chicago: University of Chicago Press, 1983).

Strier, Richard, *Resistant Structures: Particularity, Radicalism, and Renaissance Texts* (Berkeley and Los Angeles: University of California Press, 1995).

Stull, William L., '"Why Are Not 'Sonnets' Made of Thee?" A New Context for the "Holy Sonnets" of Donne, Herbert, and Milton', *Modern Philology*, 80.2 (1982), pp. 129–35.

Sullivan, Ceri, 'Cement, Summers, Pulleys, Plummets, Pipes, Timber, and Screws: George Herbert's Building Works', *Essays in Criticism*, 66.2 (2016), pp. 168–97.

Summers, Joseph H., *George Herbert: His Religion and Art* (Cambridge, MA: Harvard University Press, 1968).

Sypher, Wylie, *The Ethic of Time: Structures of Experience in Shakespeare* (New York: Seabury Press, 1974).

Targoff, Ramie, *John Donne: Body and Soul* (Chicago: University of Chicago Press, 2008).

Taylor, Mark, *The Soul in Paraphrase: George Herbert's Poetics* (The Hague: Moulton, 1974).

Tillich, Paul, 'Relation of Metaphysics and Theology', *The Review of Metaphysics*, 10.1 (1958), pp. 57–63.

Trudell, Scott, *Unwritten Poetry: Song, Performance and Media in Early Modern England* (Oxford: Oxford University Press, 2019).

Turner, Frederick, *Shakespeare and the Nature of Time* (Oxford: Clarendon Press, 1971).

Tuve, Rosemond, *A Reading of George Herbert* (Chicago: University of Chicago Press, 1952).

Vico, Giambattista, *The New Science of Giambattista Vico: Unabridged Translation of the Third Edition (1744) with the Addition of 'Practic of the New Science'*, trans. Thomas Goddard Bergen and Max Harold Fisch (Ithaca: Cornell University Press, 1984).

Vienne-Guerrin, Nathalie, *Shakespeare's Insults: A Pragmatic Dictionary* (London and New York: Bloomsbury, 2016).

von Rohr, John, *The Covenant of Grace in Puritan Thought*, American Academy Religion Studies in Religion no. 45 (Atlanta: Scholars Press, 1986).

Waldron, Jennifer, *Reformations of the Body: Idolatry, Sacrifice, and Early Modern Theater* (New York: Palgrave Macmillan, 2013).

Wall-Randell, Sarah, *The Immaterial Book: Reading and Romance in Early Modern England* (Ann Arbor: University of Michigan Press, 2013).

Waller, Gary F., 'John Donne's Changing Attitudes to Time', *SEL*, 14 (1974), pp. 79–89.

Waller, Gary F., *The Strong Necessity of Time: The Philosophy of Time in Shakespeare* (The Hague: Mouton De Gruyter, 1976).

West, Will, 'What's the Matter with Shakespeare: Physics, Identity, Playing', *South Central Review*, 26 (2009), pp. 103–26.

Westphal, Merold, 'Transfiguration as Saturated Phenomenon', *Journal of Philosophy and Scripture*, 1.1 (2003), pp. 26–35.

Whalen, Robert, *Poetry of Immanence: Sacrament in Donne and Herbert* (Toronto: University of Toronto Press, 2002).

White, Hayden, *Figural Realism: Studies in the Mimesis Effect* (Baltimore: Johns Hopkins University Press, 1999).

White, Hayden, *The Content of the Form: Narrative Discourse and Historical Representation* (Baltimore: Johns Hopkins University Press, 1987).

Williams, Pieter D., 'Music, Time and Tears in *Richard II*', *The American Benedictine Review*, 22.4 (1971), pp. 472–85.

Willis, Deborah, 'Shakespeare's Tempest and the Discourse of Colonialism', *SEL*, 29.2 (1989), pp. 277–89.

Wolfe, Judith, *Heidegger and Theology* (London: T&T Clark, 2014).

Young, R. V., 'Herbert and the Real Presence', *Renascence: Essays on Values in Literature*, 45.3 (1993), pp. 179–96.

Zahavi, Dan, 'Michel Henry and the Phenomenology of the Invisible', *Continental Philosophy Review*, 32.3 (1999), pp. 223–40.

Zahavi, Dan (ed.), *The Oxford Handbook of Contemporary Phenomenology* (Oxford: Oxford University Press, 2012).

INDEX

CPSIA information can be obtained
at www.ICGtesting.com
Printed in the USA
JSHW030146240222
23300JS00004B/29